"Those who believe in Allah and hold firmly to Him, Allah will admit them into His mercy and grace from His presence, and guide them to a straight path leading to Him."

(Nisâ: 175)

HAKIKAT PUBLISHER

For Information:
Ankara Cad. Cagaloglu Yokusu Sadet Han
No: 28/1 Cagaloglu / ISTANBUL / TURKEY
Tel : (90-212) 511 84 98 - 511 08 95
511 21 41 - 513 72 00
Fax : (90-212) 513 72 45

www.Hakikat.com
Email: Hakikat@.com

PRESENTATION

Sufism is a school of knowledge and wisdom. It is a school established to fathom the divine secrets within the chamber of mysteries and to comprehend the Truth. Through this education, one delves into the essence of all sciences. The true meaning, however, is refined essence.

Just as the Exalted the Allah did not deprive the earth of scholars to teach the outward sciences, He also did not leave it devoid of the people of Sufism to impart the inward sciences.

As it has been in all times, Sufism exists today just the same. It has not lost any of its originality. And this path will remain until the Day of Judgment. Especially in the Naqshbandi order, there will never be a shortage of spiritual guides until the end of time. That sacred chamber has passed from room to room, from circle to circle, and has never been corrupted. The Exalted the Allah closes the era of whom He wills and opens the era of whom He wills.

"Among Our creations, there is a community who guide by the Allah the Almighty and judge by it." (Araf: 181)

To reach Allah the Almighty one must find those who lead to Allah the Almighty. If you find the one who leads to Allah the Almighty then you will come to understand the reality.

When you reach Allah the Almighty when you learn the reality, you will both see and know that only "He" exists. For it is always Him...

Allah the Almighty reveals as much as He wills to those endowed with gnosis. The knowledge found in the depths of the hearts of those close to Allah the Almighty which is not present between the lines of books, is the knowledge of gnosis.

In the Noble Verse, it is decreed:

"The Qur'an is composed of clear signs which reside in the hearts of those endowed with knowledge." (Ankabut: 49)

Through the knowledge bestowed by the Noble Qur'an, with the clear, radiant light glowing in their hearts, Allah the Most High reveals and shows to them as much of the divine secrets as He wills. Hence, they possess a knowledge beyond the grasp of others. The apparent scholars neither know nor understand this, for it is a transcendent knowledge.

Allah the Most High manifests Himself to these select and beloved servants in any manner He desires and appoints them to their duties. Each is sent with different responsibilities. These described souls are the true Sufis.

The true guide is Allah the Most High. Genuine Sufis and true adherents of The Unity of Being both see and recognize that Existence is He, and the existent is He. They understand that everything comes into being by His command **"Be,"** and that a form is given to everything, knowing that the divine secrets reside in every particle, revealed from the manifestations of the light of existence in the universe.

Those who are permitted to practice spiritual connection are only these individuals. For they have extinguished their own being within the being of Allah the Most High, realizing that the true guide is Allah the Most High.

They know Truth, see Truth, and describe Truth.

Because they are students of Allah the Most High, only they truly know Allah the Most High. They learn and see whatever Allah the Most High teaches and shows them, comprehending and deciphering those divine secrets. They guide others to Allah the Most High.

As for those who claim, "I am a scholar, I know," they have merely understood their own ego and followed its desires. They do not genuinely know Allah the Most High in the truest sense, for the lock on their heart has not been opened.

Those who falsely present themselves as Sufis and adherents of The Unity of Being without being truly qualified should read the declarations in this work with contemplation.

Some of the topics here had previously appeared in other works by the esteemed author. However, knowing that many have not had the opportunity to read those books, we felt the necessity to publish this work in a distilled form, proclaiming and declaring that the true guide is none other than Allah.

In this book, true Sufis and genuine believers in the concept of The Unity of Being are presented along with their signs, supported by Noble Verse and Noble Saying. Simultaneously, counterfeit Sufis and false adherents of The Unity of Being are also meticulously explained.

“Peace be upon His chosen servants.”

(Naml: 59)

“Peace be upon those who follow guidance.”

(Taha: 47)

Prepared for Publication by the Editors

Allah

For some people to hear,

Some people to know,

Some people to find;

It is necessary to read “Gerçek Mürşid Hazreti Allah’tır.”

("The True Guide is His the Exalted the Allah").

My essence is Allah, my words are again Allah.

To convey this, we reflect the feeling within us in this book.

•

We also honor our Master, the Seyyid of the Universe, and the Cause of creation

-Peace be upon him-.

For some people to hear,

For some people to know,

And for some people to find;

It is necessary to read the "Nuri Muhammedî" (Light of Muhammad) book.

Our Master, the Honorable Prophet -peace be upon him-,

Is the light of Allah, the pride and joy of the worlds?

This is how we know him...

•

"Say: 'Who provides for you from the heavens and the earth? Who owns hearing and sight? Who brings the living out of the dead and the dead out of the living? Who regulates every affair?' They will say, 'Allah.'

Say: 'Will you not then be mindful of your duty to Him?'

Such is Allah, your true Lord. What remains beyond the truth but error? How are you then turned away?'"

(Yunus: 31-32)

TO HEAR, TO KNOW, TO FIND

To convey how essential it is to elucidate certain topics in the books, we delve into three words:

To Hear,

To Know,

To Find.

The knowledge of those who hear of Allah the Exalted is Knowledge of Certainty. That is, it remains in the external. Zâhir means that which is outward.

These people have gained from the lines. They've learned something, yet they've not learned about themselves.

Because they do not know themselves, they do not know their Creator either. "Is Allah there? Yes, He is," they say. "Where?" they ponder. In the throne, in the sky, on the earth. They have heard that He exists. Some even say, "Allah is above." If a mufti (Islamic scholar) says this, judge his outward state from here. He does not realize how far he is from Allah and how heedless he is with this statement.

In the Noble Verse, it is stated:

"Indeed, man is most unjust and ignorant." (Al-Ahzab: 72)

Both oppressing his own self and misguiding humanity through his ignorance, he deviates people from Allah the Almighty and drives them into seventy-two different paths. This is a form of spiritual massacre. For this reason, he is both a tyrant and an ignorant. He oppresses himself and, at the same time, oppresses humanity.

In the Noble Verse, Allah the Almighty says:

"They did not estimate Allah as He deserves to be estimated." (Hajj: 74)

Why? Because they are deprived of beneficial knowledge. Yet, they consider themselves to be scholars. They are entirely unaware of the self and its various levels. Writing and drawing on the blackboard, they imagine themselves to be erudite. They do not realize their hearts are hardened, their spirits are like walking dead, and they think they possess all knowledge. But all they have is merely conjecture.

"Most of them follow nothing but assumptions. Certainly, assumptions can never replace the Truth. Indeed, Allah is knowledgeable of what they do." (Yunus: 36)

Even though he was known as "Hujjat al Islam" (proof of Islam), Imam al Ghazali -may his secret be sanctified- turned towards Sufism. After experiencing the journey of spiritual purification, he expressed his state as follows:

"...Then I examined my state. What did I see! I was submerged and entangled in worldly engagements. These engagements had surrounded me from all sides. I reviewed my actions; the best of them was teaching and instruction. However, I realized that I was occupied with insignificant sciences devoid of benefit for the afterlife. I scrutinized my intention in teaching, and I was convinced that it was not for the sake of Allah but for gaining position and fame. In this state, I concluded that I was standing at the edge of a cliff, and if I did not make a move to rectify my condition, I would surely fall into the fire." (Al Munqidh min al Dalal)

•

Those who possess gnosis of Allah the Almighty have Vision of Certainty. They have penetrated the inner dimensions. They have gained their share from both the outer and the inner aspects. They have believed in the Exalted the Allah. As much as possible, they wander within the boundaries, striving to fulfill His commands, and wish to live in piety.

They strive to remain within the boundaries set by Allah the Almighty and do not transgress divine decrees. However, because they cannot completely empty their hearts and detach from their ego, they are preoccupied with created beings, rotating in this atmosphere. They love the creations of the Exalted the Allah, and spend their time with them. They try to fulfill the commandments of the Allah the Almighty, yet remain engaged with the love for created beings. Their involvement with their family, children, and possessions is driven by that love, not a connection with the Allah the Almighty.

•

Those who find Him are those who possess Reality of Certainty. The Exalted the Allah created these individuals for Himself. Allah the Almighty has loved, chosen, and brought them into His presence. They love and prefer Allah above all else, and Allah loves them in return. They have reached Allah, losing themselves in His Presence. They have attained the esoteric knowledge. In other words, they have reached the Exalted the Allah, becoming annihilated in the Allah the Almighty. They love Allah the Almighty and turn away from all else. They yearn to always be with the Exalted the Allah and never desire to be absorbed with creations. They are not preoccupied with created beings. They do not love them.

They see the Creator, knowing the creations. The Exalted the Allah created them solely for Himself. Therefore, He does not wish for them to be engaged with anything else.

"All praise is due to Allah, the Lord of all the worlds." (Al-Fâtiha: 1)

He sees the Creator of the worlds and even refuses to see the worlds because He already created the worlds from the light of His beloved; this light was created from Himself, naming it **"âlem" (world). "Rabbil Âlemin" (Lord of all the worlds);** what a magnificent Creator. Seeing the Creator, they place no value on the created. They do not regard them. They see the Creator and are occupied with the Creator, in the presence of the Creator.

They love the Allah the Almighty, they convey people to Allah the Almighty and they judge by Allah the Almighty.

The Noble Verse says:

"Among those we have created is a community that guides by the Truth and establishes justice therewith." (Araf: 181)

"Say: ' Allah the Almighty has come, and falsehood has vanished. (Isra: 81)

Only these have been illuminated by the manifestations of this Noble Verse. They occupy themselves with Allah the Almighty, not with falsehood. This is their unique task.

The Messenger of Allah -peace be upon him- stated in a Noble Saying, **"Indeed, there is a paradise in this world. Whoever finds it, no longer desires the paradise of the Hereafter. That paradise is gnosis."**

We describe this as the paradise of the heart. This life transcends everything.

"Ma arafnâke Hakka ma'rifetike ya ma'rûf = We have not truly known you as you deserve to be known, O the Known One!"

Allah the Almighty declares in His Noble Verse:

"Among the believers are men who have been true to their covenant with Allah. Some of them have fulfilled their vow by sacrificing their lives, and some are still waiting to do so." (Al-Ahzab: 23)

These are the ones who are deeply devoted to Allah, who have pledged their word and await His command.

When The Messenger of Allah -peace be upon him- asked Harisa -may Allah be pleased with him- , **"What is the reality of your faith?"** he replied, **"I have spent my nights without sleep, my days without fulfilling my thirst, and have detached myself from the world."** The Messenger of Allah -peace be upon him- then said to him, **"You have become a one who knows, you have understood, continue on your path."**

The scholar is greatly in need of the saint, but the saint has no need for the scholar.

The scholar disciplines the ignorant, while the saint disciplines the scholars.

The one who disciplines the saint is none other than the Exalted the Allah and The Messenger of Allah, -peace be upon him-.

As mentioned in the Noble Verse:

"If you fear Allah and possess piety, Allah will be your teacher." (Al-Baqarah: 282)

These individuals harbor no worldly desires, not even the desire for paradise. At their core is Allah, and their words are again Allah.

•

"Creation,

Particles of the Light of Existence

It is a place of manifestation.

Everything is not Him,

Yet nothing is without Him."

•

"No one can grasp anything from His knowledge except what He wills."

(Throne Verse)

THE TRUE SPIRITUAL GUIDE ALLAH THE MOST HIGH

CHAPTER 1

- I boast in existence! Yet I am ashamed of my own being...
- Surah Al-Fatiha
- Surah Al-Ikhlas
- The Throne Verse
- He is such an Allah that...

THE TRUE SPIRITUAL GUIDE

ALLAH THE MOST HIGH

I confess His greatness. I admit my helplessness, my insignificance, and worthlessness. You are such an Allah that only you can know and praise yourself. I am incapable of comprehending even a speck of the boundless blessings and grace you bestow.

You created Light from Your Light, and adorned the universe with that Light. I am also incapable of comprehending that Light.

•

The true Sufis, true adherents of The Unity of Being, and their signs will be presented to you through Verse of Quraniyya and Noble Saying. The artificial, fake Sufis and false proponents of The Unity of Being will also be explained one by one.

•

The true guide is the Exalted the Allah. The genuine Sufis and true adherents of The Unity of Being are the chosen and special servants of Allah the Almighty. They are the ones He created, loved, and selected for Himself.

"They will be in a seat of Truth, near the Omnipotent King." (Qamar: 55)

As declared in this Noble Verse, they are those accepted into the divine presence.

Then, no veil remains between that servant and Him. He draws that servant to His presence with an irresistible pull, and after drawing them, He fills their ranks with His grace. By pouring light into their hearts, knowledge of gnosis, which is not found in the lines of books, arises in the depths of their hearts.

"Allah guides to His light whom He wills." (Nur: 35)

In accordance with this Noble Verse, that servant has reached the light and grace of Allah the Almighty. These are the ones who are truly beloved by the Exalted the Allah. He has gazed upon them and elevated them to the station of veracity.

For these are the ones who lead people out of darkness and into the Light. All their actions and deeds are commanded by the Truth. For this reason, they are the true guides.

In summary, those whom Allah the Exalted has loved and chosen, to whom He has entrusted His mantle, and upon whom He has bestowed the light of The Messenger of Allah -peace be upon him-, they are the inheritors of the Prophets.

Our Master, the Messenger of Allah -peace be upon him- stated in his Noble Saying:

"The scholars are the inheritors of the Prophets." (Bukhari)

Since no rank can surpass prophet hood, there can be no greater honor than to inherit this rank.

Master Es'ad Sir -may his secret be sanctified- spoke regarding this Noble Saying:

"It is permissible to say, **'The scholars are the inheritors of the Prophets.'** just as it is permissible to interpret it as**, ''Whoever is the heir of the Prophet is also a scholar.''**

In this respect, it is fitting to prefer the second interpretation of the Noble Saying. For it is not appropriate to call someone a scholar who neither knows nor recognizes the Exalted the Allah, nor fears Him and engages in sin.

A true scholar, fearing Allah, invites people for His sake to the commandments of the pure Islamic law without seeking any worldly reward. For such individuals, there is a great announcement:

"You are the best community ever raised for humanity: you encourage good, forbid evil, and believe in Allah." (Al' Imran: 110)

No prophet's community has attained the rank of inheritors of the prophets. In other words, no prophet's community was given the duty of **"Emri bilma'ruf ve nehyi anil-münker" (enjoining good and forbidding wrong);** however, this duty was bestowed and honored upon the community of Muhammad.

By the most virtuous of the community tasked with this duty, the external scholars are not meant. For, the scholars known as the external scholars cannot be called the inheritors of prophets. Because the term "inheritance" refers to something that transfers from a father to a child without earning it. The knowledge of the external scholars, however, is not inherited but acquired. It is taught in madrasahs (Islamic schools), and is not gifted knowledge. A knowledge that is not gifted but acquired cannot be accurately termed as inheritance. It would be utterly incorrect to claim the external scholars are the inheritors of the prophets.

In the Noble Verse:

"Among His servants, only those who possess knowledge truly fear Allah." (Fatir: 28)

For the one who knows Allah the most, fears Him the most.

As for the artificial Sufis, they are truly in the lap of Satan.

•

I confess His greatness. I admit my helplessness, my insignificance, and worthlessness. You are such an Allah that only you can know and praise yourself. I am incapable of comprehending even a speck of the boundless blessings and grace you bestow.

You created Light from Your Light, and adorned the universe with that Light. I am also incapable of comprehending that Light.

The true Sufis, true adherents of The Unity of Being, and their signs will be presented to you through Noble Verse and Noble Saying. The artificial, fake Sufis and false proponents of The Unity of Being will also be explained one by one.

•

The true guide is the Exalted the Allah. The genuine Sufis and true adherents of The Unity of Being are the chosen and special servants of Allah the Almighty. They are the ones He created, loved, and selected for Himself.

"They will be in a seat of Truth, near the Omnipotent King." (Qamar: 55)

As declared in this Noble Verse, they are those accepted into the divine presence.

Then, no veil remains between that servant and Him. He draws that servant to His presence with an irresistible pull, and after drawing them, He fills their ranks with His grace. By pouring light into their hearts, knowledge of gnosis, which is not found in the lines of books, arises in the depths of their hearts.

"Allah guides to His light whom He wills." (Nur: 35)

In accordance with this Noble Verse, that servant has reached the light and grace of Allah the Almighty. These are the ones who are truly beloved by the Exalted the Allah. He has gazed upon them and elevated them to the station of veracity.

For these are the ones who lead people out of darkness and into the Light. All their actions and deeds are commanded by the Truth. For this reason, they are the true guides.

In summary, those whom Allah the Exalted has loved and chosen, to whom He has entrusted His mantle, and upon whom He has bestowed the light of The Messenger of Allah -peace be upon him-, they are the inheritors of the Prophets.

Our Master, the Messenger of Allah -peace be upon him- stated in his Noble Saying:

"The scholars are the inheritors of the Prophets." (Bukhari)

Since no rank can surpass prophet hood, there can be no greater honor than to inherit this rank.

Master Es'ad Sir -may his secret be sanctified- spoke regarding this Noble Saying:

"It is permissible to say, 'The scholars are the inheritors of the Prophets,' just as it is permissible to interpret it as, 'Whoever is the heir of the Prophet is also a scholar."

In this respect, it is fitting to prefer the second interpretation of the Noble Saying. For it is not appropriate to call someone a scholar who neither knows nor recognizes the Exalted the Allah, nor fears Him and engages in sin.

A true scholar, fearing Allah, invites people for His sake to the commandments of the pure Islamic law without seeking any worldly reward. For such individuals, there is a great announcement:

"You are the best community ever raised for humanity: you encourage good, forbid evil, and believe in Allah." (Al' Imran: 110)

No prophet's community has attained the rank of inheritors of the prophets. In other words, no prophet's community was given the duty of "Emri bilma'ruf ve nehyi anilmünker" (enjoining good and forbidding wrong); however, this duty was bestowed and honored upon the community of Muhammad.

By the most virtuous of the community tasked with this duty, the external scholars are not meant. For, the scholars known as the external scholars cannot be called the inheritors of prophets. Because the term "inheritance" refers to something that transfers from a father to a child without earning it. The knowledge of the external scholars, however, is not inherited but acquired. It is taught in madrasahs (Islamic schools), and is not gifted knowledge. A knowledge that is not gifted but acquired cannot be accurately termed as inheritance. It would be utterly incorrect to claim the external scholars are the inheritors of the prophets.

In the Noble Verse:

"Among His servants, only those who possess knowledge truly fear Allah." (Fatir: 28)

For the one who knows Allah the most, fears Him the most.

As for the artificial Sufis, they are truly in the lap of Satan.

•

I BOAST WITH THE EXISTENT!

I AM ASHAMED OF MY EXISTENCE!

I boast with the exists. I am ashamed of my existence. For it is always Him...

Allah the Exalted and Glorified is and is one. He is Ahad (The One and only). There is no other existence besides Him.

In a Noble Saying it is stated:

"Allah existed, and there was nothing except Allah." (Bukhari)

Everyone searches for Him within this world, within places. Yet, all places are within Him. He has no place.

"Wherever you turn, there is the face of Allah." (Al-Baqarah: 115)

The Exalted the Allah is closer to everything than anything. Because this is not known, everything is known, but He is unknown. Everything is seen, but He is unseen. Yet He is closer to everything than anything.

For those who see, He is the only reality, and nothing else exists. When He says **"Be"** they appear; when He says **"Be not,"** there is nothing. Again, there is nothing besides Him.

In a Noble Verse it is stated:

“Everything on earth will perish. But the face of your Lord, full of majesty and honor, will remain.” (Rahman: 26-27)

The one who truly exists is the Exalted the Allah.

I take pride in the Existence; the secrets of these lie hidden in the mystery of a single atom. If that mystery is unraveled, the secrets of everything will be revealed. He is the Al-Awwal, the Al-Akhir, the Az-Zahir, and the Al-Batin. All is He. His unity is manifest and hidden. That is, He both reveals and conceals Himself. His existence is hidden in His unity. Yet shapeless, without quality.

“There is nothing like unto Him.” (Shura: 11)

He is the essence of the first of letters. He is the essence of the last of letters. Apparent and Hidden are the same. All that is described by names and the named ones is Him...

I boast with the existence of the Exalted the Allah.

The purpose is to know the Creator.

From a single atom, He creates a noble human being. How magnificent a creator He is! That's why I take pride in Him. But there is nothing praiseworthy in the vile water. It is always Allah who directs and manages it.

My wrongful deeds stem from myself. I am ashamed of them. I take pride in my Allah who bestows these blessings and countless good deeds.

Within, He; outside, He... Divinity's secrets are present in every particle... As for the manifest; the manifest too says, "I." But humanity does not see Him, instead, they see the veil.

In short, the true guide is Him. Because it is always Him.

Allah, who created the drop of fluid.

"We created man from a drop of mixed fluid from male and female." (Insan: 2)

And when I look at that drop, that fluid, I am ashamed. I only take pride in the existence of the Exalted the Allah.

How could I not be ashamed of my existence when my origin is a despicable drop of water?

"Let man consider from what he was created! He was created from a fluid ejected, emerging from between the backbone of the male and the breastbones of the female." (Tariq: 5-6-7)

While all humans originate from Adam -peace be upon him-, each has their places of permanence and trust. From the loins of the father to the womb of the mother, from the womb to the world, from the world to the grave, sometimes settling and sometimes deposited temporarily. Some still remain in their starting place, the loins, others have been placed in the womb, waiting to be born.

"He is in a new state of creativity every moment." (Rahman: 29)

As expressed in the divine Verse, all of these are manifestations of Allah the Almighty who is in a state of constant creation.

"O deniers! We created you. Will you still not acknowledge? Have you observed the semen you emit? Is it you who create it into a perfect human, or are we the Creator?" (Waqi'ah: 57-58-59)

The entities within cells, which we call genes, are barely visible even under a microscope, yet they bear all the characteristics and capacities, every particularity of the future human being.

Whether it will be male or female, its beauty or ugliness, its height, its mental and spiritual structure, emotions and aspirations, abilities and anomalies... All of these are hidden within this tiny particle.

The unique traits that have never made any two people on Earth exactly alike reside in this feeble particle. Where is the particle, and where is the human?

He has embedded all its destiny within that particle. Then, He shaped the despised fluid as He willed and transformed it from one form into another.

The divine Verse states:

"Do you deny your Lord who created you from dust, then from a drop of fluid, and finally shaped you into a human?" (Al-Kahf: 37)

One must contemplate that a drop of fluid is such a worthless substance, so weak and fragile. Creating such a valuable human from this insignificant substance is indeed a great power!

He is The One who brings everything into existence from nothing with perfect order and harmony. The prototype of every beauty and every maturation belongs to Him.

Allah the Almighty declares in the Verses 7, 8, and 9. Of Surah Al-Sajda that He created man's progeny from a despised drop of fluid, then fashioned and perfected him, breathed into him of His spirit, and subsequently endowed him with hearing, sight, and hearts.

Allah the Almighty mentions the ears, eyes, and heart in an orderly manner so that one first hears the Truth, then sees what they have heard with their eyes, and finally contemplates those seen things with their heart.

"He granted you hearing, sight, and hearts. Little are you grateful!" (Sajda: 9)

Ultimately, when the 280 days are completed, an extraordinary baby is born into the world.

"Then we bring you forth as a baby." (Hajj: 5)

From this stage onward, having previously been lifeless, he becomes a living being; having been speechless, he speaks; having been deaf, he hears; and having been blind, he sees.

Allah the Almighty mixed the essence of man, a drop of despised fluid, with the soil of His divine decree. He sowed the seed of judgment, launched it with the water of life, said **"Be,"** and it was. All the rest is mere detail. We merely say, a child was born, and move on. Everyone sees the shell; very few see the essence.

When a person does not know the Creator, he forgets the created. What were you, and what have you become?

One must always keep this in mind. The self says "I" and thus leads to one's ruin. How did you come to be? You originated from a drop of vile water. I look at that vile water and feel ashamed of my own existence.

Therefore, the truly real is Him. Your essence is a drop of vile water. Look at how He transformed that drop, how He created you from it and adorned you with countless blessings.

It is with this existence that I take pride.

In summary,

I take pride in existence,

Yet I am ashamed of my own being.

Why do I feel shame for my existence?

He created the seminal fluid.

He created me from that seminal fluid; my being is nothing more than that seminal fluid.

I feel ashamed when I look at the seminal fluid,

But I feel proud when I think of the Creator,

How magnificent a creator is the Exalted the Allah!

"Glory be to Allah, the best of those who fashion." (Mu'minun: 14)

•

O Allah, without you, there is no strength.

O Allah, without you, there is no existence.

O Allah, without you, nothing exists.

There is no existence except Allah.

You are the Glorious,

You are the Sovereign,

You are the Creator,

You are the Sustainer.

You are my Allah, possessing boundless grace!

SURAH AL-FATIHA

This sacred surah, being the first of the Qur'an al-Karim, is called "Fatiha," meaning "The Opener," or "Opening."

It is also known as "Umm al-kitab," meaning "Mother of the Book," and "Sab' almathani," meaning "The Seven of Repeated Verses."

Allah the Almighty states in His Noble Verse:

"O Messenger! Indeed, we have given you the seven of repeated Verses and the great Qur'an." (Hijr: 87)

Ebu Sa'id bin Mualla -may Allah be pleased with him- recounts:

"I was offering my prayer in the mosque. The Prophet -peace be upon him- called for me. I did not break my prayer to go. Later, I approached him and said**, 'I was delayed because I was in prayer, O the Messenger of Allah!'**

Upon this, The Messenger of Allah -peace be upon him- reminded me:

'Did Allah not say in the Qur'an:

"O you who believe! Respond to Allah and the Messenger when he calls you to that which gives you life!" (Anfal: 24)

Then he told me, 'O Sa'id! Before I leave the mosque, **I will teach you a surah that is the greatest in the Qur'an.'** He then took my hand. As he was about to leave the mosque, **I said, 'O the Messenger of Allah! Did you not promise to teach me a great surah?'**

He said:

"That surah is 'Alhamdulillahi Rabbil Alamin' (All praise is to Allah, Lord of all worlds). It is the Seven of repeated Verses and the magnificent Qur'an given to me." (Bukhari. Tecridi Sarih: 1672)

In another Noble Saying, he stated:

"By Allah, in whose hand my soul is, Allah has not revealed the like of Fatiha in the Torah, the Gospels, the Psalms, or the Furqan (another name for the Qur'an). It is the seven of repeated Verses and the magnificent Qur'an granted to me." (Tirmidhi)

Abdullah ibn Abbas -May Allah be pleased with him- said:

While Gabriel -peace be upon him- was with The Messenger of Allah -peace be upon him- he heard a sound like that of a door opening above. He lifted his head towards the sky and said, **"A door has been opened in the heaven today which has never been opened before."** Then an angel descended from it. Gabriel continued, **"This is an angel who has come down to the earth for the first time."**

The angel greeted and said to The Messenger of Allah -peace be upon him-, **"I bring you good news of two lights given to you, which no prophet before you was given: one is the Fatiha, and the other is the last Verses of Surah Al-Baqarah. You will be rewarded for each letter you recite from them."** (Muslim)

In another Noble Saying, The Messenger of Allah -peace be upon him- said:

"There is no prayer without the recitation of Fatiha." (Bukhari, Tecridi Sarih: 422)

It is recited in every unit of prayer.

The Surah al-Fatiha is considered the preface of the Holy Qur'an and is valued as equivalent to the Qur'an in its essence.

Surah al-Fatiha encapsulates the purpose and core principles of the Noble Qur'an, which was sent to lead people to world happiness and eternal salvation by guiding them to the path of righteousness.

It is declared that Allah the Almighty is worthy of all praises and glory, that He is unparalleled in His oneness and greatness, that there is no true deity except Him, that all support and assistance come solely from Him, and that both guidance and misguidance are within His divine power.

•

According to a narration by Abu Huraira -may Allah be pleased with him-, The Messenger of Allah -peace be upon him- conveyed this Sacred saying from Allah the Majestic and Exalted:

“I have divided the Fatiha between Myself and My servant into two halves. One half is for me, and the other half is for My servant. My servant shall be granted what he asks for.”

Our Master, The Messenger of Allah -peace be upon him- explains it thus:

“When a servant says, ‘Alhamdulillahi Rabbil Aalamin’ (All praise is due to Allah, the Lord of all the worlds), Allah the Almighty says, ‘My servant has praised Me.’”

When the servant recites ‘Errahmânirrahim’ (the Most Gracious, the Most Merciful), Allah the Almighty proclaims, ‘My servant has mentioned me with both general and specific mercy, praised and glorified me.’

When the servant recites ‘Mâliki yevmiddin’ (Master of the Day of Judgment), Allah the Almighty declares, ‘My servant has reverenced me, shown respect, and recognized my greatness.’

When the servant recites 'Iyyake na'büdü ve iyyâke nestaîn' (You alone we worship, and you alone we ask for help), Allah the Almighty says, 'This is between me and my servant. Worship belongs to my servant, and assistance belongs to me. My servant's request will be granted.'

When the servant recites 'İhdinassıratal müstakîm sıratallezine en amte alayhim, ğayrilmağdubi alayhim veleddâlliyn' (Guide us to the Straight Path, the path of those who have received Your grace; not the path of those who have brought down wrath upon themselves, nor of those who have gone astray), Allah the Almighty declares, 'This supplication belongs to My servant, and it will be granted to them." (Ahmad ibn Hanbal)

•

• **"Praise be to Allah, the Lord of all worlds."**

Though the Verse states that praise is due to Allah the Almighty it implies in its meaning: "Offer praise to Allah, the Lord of all worlds." Praise is commanded by Allah and is a duty of mankind.

In another Verse, it is said:

"Say: All praise is for Allah!" (Naml: 59)

He created all worlds, bestowed abundant blessings without expecting anything in return. The soul belongs to Him, the body belongs to Him, the dominion belongs to Him, the blessings belong to Him, the grace belongs to Him... He is the source of every blessing.

Praise is to laud Him in response to His blessings. This is only possible by recognizing the blessing itself. Enumerating His blessings, however, is an impossible task. Once this Truth is acknowledged and confessed, it becomes evident that every extolment and praise is uniquely reserved for Allah the Almighty.

When a person says **"Alhamdulillah,"** they verbally acknowledge and confess the sovereignty of praise to Allah. Simultaneously, with their heart, they must affirm the oneness, grandeur, and unmatched worthiness of Allah the Almighty for worship; recognizing that He alone creates, sustains, and brings life and death. Furthermore, while seeking His pleasure, they should continually fulfill their servitude duties by wholeheartedly submitting to His commands and prohibitions.

It is a clear Truth that no matter how much a person endeavors to offer praise and commendation, they simply cannot truly extol Him as He deserves.

The Noble Prophet -peace be upon him- expressed in one of his prayers:

"I cannot extol you as you deserve. You are as you have extolled yourself." (Muslim)

Lord means the one who nurtures, reforms, and cultivates, but it also means owner.

This term is used exclusively for Allah the Almighty as it signifies the Creator who brought the universe into being out of nothing, perfected His creation in an orderly manner, sustained and nurtured it, provided for every need, and possesses the power and will to do whatever He desires.

He is the sole educator of humanity. He nurtures their external needs with blessings and their inner needs with mercy. Humanity, among all creation, has received the greatest share of this nurturing.

• "He is the Ar-Rahman, the Ar-Rahîm."

Ar-Rahman derives from the word "mercy" and means exceedingly merciful. Allah the Almighty's mercy is infinite from eternity to eternity. His creation of all universes, all living and nonliving beings, His provision of sustenance to the living, and His perfect order of all things are the Results of His infinite mercy. This mercy is so universal and all-encompassing that it extends to believers and nonbelievers, the obedient and the rebellious, the knowledgeable and the ignorant, the diligent and the lazy, the just and the unjust, without distinction.

Ar-Rahîm, on the other hand, refers to rewarding those who believe and perform righteous deeds, who make good use of His blessings, with greater and eternal rewards in the hereafter.

In this world, He bestows countless blessings on all His creatures, whether they believe or not, whether they strive or not, showing mercy to them. In the hereafter, however, He will distinguish between the believers and the diligent, rewarding them accordingly this is the outcome of His **Ar-Rahîm** attribute.

• "Master of the Day of Judgment."

The Day of Judgment refers to the day of reckoning in the hereafter. That promised day will certainly come, and people will be called to account before Allah the Almighty facing the consequences of their actions.

"To whom belongs the dominion today? To Allah, The One, the Subduer." (Mü'min: 16)

On that day, the believers will be separated from the nonbelievers, the obedient from the rebellious, the thankful from the ungrateful, and the oppressors from the oppressed. The righteous will be rewarded, the wrongdoers will be punished, and He will forgive whom He wills.

"On that day, the true sovereignty will belong to the Ar-Rahman Allah." (Al-Furqan: 26)

In this world, those who temporarily hold dominion and authority will lose their power upon death, leaving them accountable for their deeds, whether good or bad. On that day, no one will possess sovereignty other than Him; they will have no ownership as they did in the world.

• "You alone we worship, and from you alone we seek help."

Worship means to display humility, obedience, submission, full adherence, and to hold onto something steadfastly without letting go. Worship is a servant binding himself to his Lord, being with Him through remembrance and contemplation, living in His presence, and performing all duties required by servitude. In its broadest sense, servitude is to show acceptance and submission to every decree of Allah the Almighty.

Worship is a lofty station. A servant attains the bliss of being in the presence of this station.

The ultimate aim of worship is Allah the Almighty and His Glorious Presence. Seeking help is to approach Him. Allah the Almighty commands us to worship Him with sincerity and to seek help from Him alone in all matters.

By saying **"You alone we worship,"** a servant distances himself from polytheism, and by saying **"from you alone we seek help,"** he detaches from all other sources of power and strength, relying solely on Allah the Almighty for all his affairs. For without His help, a person can neither fulfill his duties of servitude nor accomplish any other tasks... Every matter concludes only with His assistance.

This Verse is between the servant and the Creator. The servant directly supplicates to his Creator.

• "Guide us on the Straight Path."

Straight Path is the path of Allah. It means to find and reach a path of struggle that culminates in witnessing Allah the Almighty in order to attain nearness to Him.

"This is my straight path, so follow it. Do not follow other ways, or they will lead you away from His path." (An'am: 153)

A servant cannot reach the **"Straight Path"** without turning away from everything other than Allah.

One who attains the Straight Path succeeds in following the path of the prophets, the truthful ones, the martyrs, and the righteous, upon whom Allah has bestowed His blessings.

A servant is in constant need, day and night, in every moment and condition, for Allah to keep them steadfast on the Straight Path. This need continuously increases and persists. Hence, in every prayer and at other times, this need is presented to Allah: **"Guide us to the Straight Path."**

• "The path of those upon whom you have bestowed your favor, not of those who have evoked your anger or of those who are astray."

This path is the way of those whom Allah has blessed with His favors and has granted happiness in this world and salvation in the hereafter.

Allah has graced them with the blessings of faith and certainty, knowledge and understanding, obedience and submission, and has illuminated them with the light of Truth.

The greatest aid a servant can request from Allah the Almighty is to reach the path walked by His beloved servants to whom He has given blessings. People are in need of these friends of Allah, who will guide them to the Truth, direct them to reality, and enhance their effort and resolve.

Those who have incurred Allah's wrath and those who are cursed are the Jews, and those who have gone astray are the Christians. They attributed unworthy qualities to Allah the Almighty, persisted in their disbelief and deviation, forgot the countless blessings granted to them, befriended Satan, made their desires their Allah's, forgot the hereafter and indulged in the world. Deliberately, they strayed from Allah the Almighty's true religion. They forgot Allah, and Allah also forgot them and was enraged with them.

• Then, for the acceptance of these blessed prayers, one says, **"Amin."**

•

THE NOBLE SURAH AL-IKHLAS

The belief in Allah in Islam, the existence, and oneness of Allah the Almighty are most beautifully and perfectly expressed in the Noble Surah **Al-Ikhlas:**

"Say: He is Allah, The One. Allah, the Eternal Refuge. He neither begets nor is born, nor is there to Him any equivalent."

The term **"Ehad,"** meaning **"The One,"** is a unique attribute exclusive to the Divine Essence, not used for anyone else. This is because Allah the Almighty's one and singular in His essence.

In His attributes, He is one; none of His attributes have any equal. In creation, particularly in humans, there are signs, not likenesses, of His attributes. These signs help perceive and believe in the divine attributes of Allah the Almighty. In His actions, He is one; He needs no helper in creating and managing His creation. In His names, He is one; in His beautiful names (Asma'al-Husna), each one has no real equivalent.

Allah the Almighty's the Most Noble Sharif, the greatest Al-Azim, the most perfect Al-Halim, and the most knowledgeable Al-Alim. He embodies perfection in every kind of nobility and grandeur. These attributes are not used for anyone else.

• In the Verse **"Say: He is Allah, The One (Kul Hu Allahu Ehad),"** three classes of people and their ranks are indicated.

"Hu," meaning "It is He!" denotes something known both to the speaker and the addressee. This is the rank of the **"purest of the purest".** Because the Gnostics do not need evidence for the gnosis, a mere indication suffices for them.

Later, the name **"Allah"** is mentioned to signify the rank of the "elect" individuals. For they strive to prove Allah the Almighty through evidence. They deduce the existence of the Great Creator from the delicate artistry in the creation of beings.

Regarding the rank of the "common people," the term **"Ehad"** is used. Because their capacity for understanding is not like that of the elect, to prevent them from fall into associating partners with Allah, the term **"Ehad**," expressing the unity and oneness of Allah, is mentioned.

In His judgments, He is one; sovereignty is His dominion.

"Allah is Samed." Allah (The Eternal Refuge), characterized by the attribute of unicity, is the sole authority to whom all creation turns for their needs and desires.

He is such a Allah that;

He created mankind from nothing, bestowed upon them countless blessings, sustains them in His dominion, attends to every affair of theirs, and fulfills their every need.

All wants and needs are given by Him. Needs are sought from Him alone. Requests are only fulfilled by Him.

As requests increase, so does His grace and generosity. As needs multiply, His benevolence and favor also increase. His goodness and beauty are inexhaustible.

In His Noble Verse:

"He has granted you everything you could ask of Him." Thus it is spoken. (Ibrahim: 34)

In days of distress and hardship, the door to turn to is His door. He is The One who needs nothing from anyone, while everything and everyone is in need of Him. He is the divine being whose generosity and grace have reached their utmost extent; without His permission and command, no deed is decreed.

He is the kind of Allah who **"Begets not, nor is He begotten**." He is free from having children, a father, or a spouse.

The Jews declared, **"Uzair is the son of Allah."** The Christians said, **"Jesus is the son of Allah."** The Arab polytheists, claiming, **"The angels are the**

daughters of Allah," disregarded the belief in His Oneness **(Ehadiyet)** and pursued a path contrary to the **faith in Divine Unity.**

Due to these slanders, they have been subject to Allah's divine wrath:

"They say that the Ar-Rahman has begotten a son. Indeed, you have uttered a gross blasphemy. The heavens almost rupture therefrom and the earth splits open, and the mountains collapse in devastation, that they attribute to the Most Compassionate a son. But it is not appropriate for the Most Compassionate to take a son." (Maryam: 90-91-92)

The Muslims, on the other hand, have completely freed themselves from these corrupt beliefs through the creed of **"Lem yelid velem yûled" (He neither begets nor is born).**

Allah Almighty, in the conclusion of the noble surah, declares, **"There is nothing comparable to Him,"** affirming the outcome of all His divine attributes.

Allah the Almighty is preexistent and eternal. Just as His essence has neither beginning nor end, nor equal or counterpart, so do His attributes have no previous or subsequent counterpart.

His being One and As-Samed (Self-Sufficient) signifies that He neither begets nor is begotten, and there is none comparable to Him.

Therefore, the Surah Ikhlas contains the essence of the **"faith in Divine Unity."** Due to its special importance in Islam, The Messenger of Allah -peace be upon him- said in a Noble Saying:

"By Him in whose hand my soul is, Surah Ikhlas is equivalent to one third of the Qur'an." (Bukhari)

This Surah has many names.

It is called **Surah al-Ikhlas** because it signifies that one who embraces and believes in its Truths becomes sincere in his religion, and it saves The One who dies with this faith from the fire of Hell.

Surah Tawhid: It declares the existence, oneness, and incomparability of Allah the Almighty, with no partners.

Surah Tajrid: It attributes to Allah the Almighty all perfect qualities, separating Him from any imperfect attributes.

Surah Ma'rifat: The gnosis of Allah is defined by fully grasping the meaning of this noble surah.

Surah Wilayah: Whoever reads this noble surah with utmost reverence and penetrates its meanings is elevated to the rank of sainthood.

Surah Nur: It enlightens the hearts of people.

Surah Muzammil: When this noble Surah is recited, the angels, with utmost respect, gather to listen attentively.

Surah Asas: The meaning of this sacred Surah constitutes the essence of the faith. The heavens and the earth are established upon its foundation.

Surah Najat: It provides salvation from polytheism and disbelief in this world, and from Hellfire in the hereafter.

Surah Samed: This holy Surah proclaims that Allah the Almighty is self-sufficient and absolutely independent; everything and everyone is in need of Him, while He needs no one.

Surah Bara'a: The Messenger of Allah -peace be upon him-, has said about the one who recites this sacred Surah, **"Truly, this man is free from polytheism."**

•

THE THRONE VERSE

The 255th Verse of the Surah Al-Baqarah: It eloquently and beautifully describes the divine attributes of Allah the Almighty, His sovereign authority, and His grandeur and majesty.

According to the narration of Abu Huraira -may Allah be pleased with him- , The Messenger of Allah -peace be upon him- said in his Noble Saying:

"Everything has a pinnacle, and the pinnacle of the Quran is Surah Al-Baqarah. In this Surah, there is a Noble Verse that is the master of all Quranic Verses. It is The Throne Verse." (Tirmidhi: 2881)

Ubayy ibn Ka'b -may Allah be pleased with him- relates:

"The Messenger of Allah -peace be upon him- asked me:

'O Abu Mundhir! Do you know which Noble Verse from the Book of Allah that you have memorized is the greatest?'

I replied, **'Allah and His Messenger know best.'**

He asked again:

'O Abu Mundhir! Do you know which Noble Verse from the Book of Allah that you have memorized is the greatest?'

In response, I said:

I replied, "'Allahu lâ ilâhe illâ hüvel-Al-Hayyül-kayyum' is the Verse."

Upon hearing this, The Messenger of Allah -peace be upon him-placed his hand on my chest and said:

"By Allah, may knowledge be blessed for you, O Abu Munzir!" (Muslim: 810)

In the Verse known as The Throne Verse, which consists entirely of ten sentences, Allah Ta'ala's oneness is proclaimed: that He is the Al-Hayy and the Al-Qayyum; that He is untouched by drowsiness and heedlessness, which are human attributes, and that He holds the universe under His governance; that no one can intercede without His permission; that His knowledge encompasses the past and the future; that His power envelops the heavens and the earth; and that His essence is exalted. This Verse articulates the foundations of the belief in Divine Unity with clarity.

It is stated thus:

"Allah is He, than whom there is no other Allah."

Divinity and servitude belong solely to Him. He is unique in every respect. His existence has no beginning. His existence is perpetual, without end.

His existence testifies to itself. Every being is a manifestation of His power. Whatever exists, exists through Him.

"He is the Al-Hayy, the Al-Qayyum."

Al-Hayy: He who is eternally and perpetually alive. From pre eternity to post eternity, all life and immortality exist through His essence.

Al-Qayyum: He who is self-sustaining and sustains all things through His perfect attributes, with all existence standing by His will.

Allah the Almighty is alive through His own essence, while His creations live by His granting of life and His power. To everything, He bestows reasons to stand for a determined time. Everything stands by the Allah the Almighty. Only He is the Al-Hayy and the Al-Qayyum.

Such is the Al-Hayy and Al-Qayyum that:

“Neither slumber nor sleep overtakes Him.”

No deficiency or heedlessness reaches His exalted essence, and He never neglects His creations. He is always aware of every state of the cosmos.

“To Him belongs whatever is in the heavens and whatever is on the earth.”

He is the owner of all that is in the heavens, on the earth, and in between. He is both the proprietor and sovereign of His dominion, wielding authority as He wills. No one shares His sovereignty or dominion.

“Who is it that can intercede with Him except by His permission?”

Who dares to approach this? Those granted intercession do so solely by His will and permission.

"He knows what His servants have done and what they will do."

With His eternal and infinite knowledge, He knows everything that has happened and everything that will happen. Nothing is hidden from His boundless and limitless wisdom.

"Humans can grasp nothing of His knowledge except what He wills."

Human knowledge is limited. They can only comprehend as much as Allah the Almighty wills. He is the one who teaches humans what they do not know.

"His throne encompasses the heavens and the earth."

All beings in the heavens and the earth are surrounded inside and out by this throne. There is not a single particle that escapes the realm where the authority of Allah the Almighty's throne manifests.

Nothing can exist outside His power and dominion.

"Guarding and keeping the heavens and the earth does not burden Him."

Guarding the heavens and the earth, preserving all within them and everything between them, is effortless for Him. His unique essence remains unsullied by any hardship. He oversees everything; nothing is concealed from Him, no knowledge is hidden from His sight.

He is the true Protector, everything exists under His safeguarding and preservation.

"He is so exalted, so majestic." (Al-Baqarah: 255)

True exaltation and grandeur belong to Him. His majesty is boundless in every respect. The universe bears witness to His grandeur.

Human minds cannot fathom His magnificence, they fall short in comprehending His grandeur. He is as great as His greatness dictates. Everything testifies to His magnificence.

•

HE IS SUCH AN ALLAH THAT...

Allah the Almighty describes His divinity and oneness, His knowledge and mercy, His grandeur and exaltation through some of His names and attributes in the Noble Verse:

"He is such an Allah that, there is no deity but Him." (Hashr: 22)

The True Being is He; there is no deity deserving of worship other than Him. He alone is the object of His servants' devotions; there is none other.

"He knows what is unseen, and what is seen." (Hashr: 22)

The knowledge of the universe belongs to Him. Nothing on earth or in the heavens, whether large or small, is hidden from Him. He knows down to the smallest detail what happened in the past, what is happening now, and what will happen in the future. Not a single particle is beyond His eternal and infinite knowledge.

Ghayb (the unseen): It is used in two senses, absolute and relative. The absolute ghayb is what no created being can access. Relative ghayb is that which is unknown to some creatures but may be known to others.

"He is the Ar-Rahman, the Ar-Rahim." (Hashr: 22)

Ar-Rahman: In this world, He bestows countless blessings upon all His creatures, without distinguishing between those who believe in Him and those who do not, between those who obey Him and those who do not.

Ar-Rahim: He is exceedingly merciful, rewarding those who believe and perform righteous deeds, those who use the blessings He bestows in good ways, with even greater and eternal blessings in the hereafter.

He is the Ar-Rahman and Ar-Rahim of both this world and the Hereafter; these two names are fitting only for Him.

"He is Allah; there is no deity other than Him." (Hashr: 23)

As this is a very important Truth, it has been reiterated.

"He is the Al-Malik, the Al-Quddus, the As-Salam, the Al-Mu'min, the Al-Muhaymin, the Al-Aziz, the Al-Jabbar, and the Al-Mutakabbir." (Hashr: 23)

Al-Malik: Independent in His essence and attributes from all means. He is the sole owner of both worldly and spiritual realms, the true governor, the absolute sovereign.

No matter how powerful a servant may be as a ruler, he remains in need of the true Owner of the realm; his dominion and power are ephemeral.

Everything is under His control and power, subject to Him. There is nothing that can limit His sovereignty.

Al-Quddus: Free from all deficiencies and imperfections, perfect in every attribute, pure and immaculate.

He is exalted and pure beyond all qualities that any sense or thought could conceive. His perfection is boundless. He is endowed with attributes of perfection far beyond human comprehension.

As-Salam: Free from oppressing His creations, He delivers them from dangers, greets His blissful servants with peace.

A believer who is devout and perfects his faith is blessed with the manifestation of the attribute of peace. Muslims remain safe from his tongue and hands, and such a person attains the blessing of meeting the Truth with a sound heart.

Believers find themselves in safety and tranquility under their Lord's protection and care.

Just as He is the source of all peace, He is also The One who leads those who seek peace to it.

Al-Mu'min: He bestows faith, grants security, takes under His special protection those who seek refuge in Him, and brings them to serenity.

He is The One who provides safety and security from all dangers and calamities. Everything, at every moment, is in need of turning towards and seeking refuge in Him.

He confirms the faith of His believing servants.

In this name, a person is characterized by one of the sublime attributes of Allah the Almighty. With this attribute of faith, one ascends to the highest rank, the Melei Ala (the highest celestial assembly).

Al-Muhaymin: He observes, oversees, directs, and protects all beings He has created. He is the absolute ruler.

Al-Aziz: The only sovereign who cannot be defeated, invaluable and honorable beyond compare, powerful and eternally supreme is He.

To prevail and not be defeated is only possible through Him.

Al-Jabbar: He mends every kind of plight and hardship, and has the power to enforce His will as He pleases; His presence is profoundly exalted.

No force or might can oppose Him; He executes His decrees as He wills.

Al-Mutakabbir: He is unparalleled in majesty and grandeur, manifesting His greatness in all things and events.

He alone possesses the attributes of greatness, exaltation, and magnificence.

"Allah is free from what the polytheists ascribe to Him." (Hashr: 23)

The idols and entities associated with Him are far removed from the Truth. Allah the Almighty is free from partners and similitudes, and is sanctified.

"He is Allah, Al-Khaliq, Al-Bari, Al-Musawwir." (Hashr: 24)

Al-Khaliq: He brings everything into existence with perfect order and regulation, creating and arranging their needs from nothing.

Al-Bari: He creates each being in harmony with one another, innovating uniquely from the void without any precedent.

Al-Musawwir: He bestows form and distinctiveness to everything with meticulous care, arranging and organizing in the most beautiful manner, revealing the perfection of His beauty.

The attributes and names of Allah the Almighty are not limited to these:

"The most beautiful names belong to Him." (Hashr: 24)

The most beautiful names, indicating the highest meanings, are all His. Each of these names points to exceedingly beautiful meanings and lofty attributes. The effects of these names manifest in creation. Beauty is inherent in them.

"Everything in the heavens and on earth glorifies and praises Him." (Hashr: 24)

Glorification: To exalt Allah the Almighty above any deficiencies not befitting His supreme majesty, whether through belief, speech, or heart, and to keep Him pure and exalted. He deserves the finest praise and perfect attributes both in this world and the hereafter.

Everything in the heavens and on earth, whether seemingly insignificant or visibly present, living or nonliving, performs glorification of Allah the Almighty. Every created thing testifies to the existence of the Creator adorned with sublime attributes.

"He is Al-Aziz, Al-Hakim." (Hashr: 24)

He is the absolute victor.

All His commands and deeds are full of wisdom. He possesses profound wisdom in His judgments, and everything He does is perfectly and beautifully orchestrated. The beauty of His wisdom is clearly evident in all existence.

•

"Whoever purifies their soul will indeed be saved."
(Ash-Shams: 9)

THE SELF

AND ITS LEVELS

CHAPTER 2

- What Does the Self Mean?
- "Whoever Purifies Their Self Will Indeed Be Saved."
- People of Truth
- People of Action
- The Self and Its Levels:
    - *1."The commanding* self"
    - *2."The reproaching* self"
    - *3."The inspired* self"
    - *4."The* tranquil self"
    - *5."The content* self"
    - *6."The pleasing* self"
    - *7."The pure* self"
- An Analogy to Better Understand the Levels of the self

WHAT DOES THE SELF MEAN?

The self is that which wishes to obstruct all good, opens the doors to all evil, yet blends into your being as your companion. It is your companion in this world, in the grave, on the Day of Judgment, in paradise, or in hell.

Prophet Muhammad -peace be upon him-, who commanded seeking a skilled physician for diagnosing and treating bodily diseases, also indicated the necessity of consulting a spiritual doctor, a divine scholar for deliverance from spiritual maladies.

These spiritual diseases are of utmost importance.

"In their hearts is a disease." (Al-Baqarah: 10)

This Verse points to such dreadful diseases that, if left untreated, can destroy eternal life, making them immensely dangerous.

Just as a physically sick person cannot savor the taste of delicious foods, the spiritual pleasure returns only with the treatment of the ailment. Similarly, someone subdued by the "The commanding self" has a sick heart, and thus cannot derive delight from worship and obedience.

Resentment, pride, wrath, lust, envy, hypocrisy, greed, self-admiration... such negative attributes are ailments of the heart. To become a perfect believer, these qualities must be eliminated from the heart one by one.

Exalted The Exalted Truth states in the Noble Verse:

"Avoid both open and secret sins." (An'am: 151)

It is obligatory to forsake sins, both apparent and hidden. Just as it is not permissible to commit any evil openly, harboring feelings like envy, hypocrisy, pride... and acting upon them in secret is also forbidden.

In another Noble Verse, it is stated:

"Abandon open and secret sins. Surely, those who commit sins will be requited for what they have earned." (An'am: 120)

"Successful indeed is the one who purifies their soul."

It is conveyed in the Noble Verse:

"O Messenger! Tell them: If you love Allah, follow me, so that Allah may love you." (Al' Imran: 31)

According to this Noble Verse, establishing a chain of love with Allah the Almighty can only be achieved by strictly adhering to the Sunnahi seniyye (the customs and practices of Prophet Muhammad). Consequently, it is essential to seek a spiritual path.

In other words, to adorn our outward appearance, one must follow the Islamic law of The Messenger of Allah, -peace be upon him-, and to beautify our inner self and illuminate our soul, one must adhere to his path. Through Islamic law, external order is established; through path, internal order is maintained.

The enlightened path originally came to us from the Prophet, -peace be upon him-, in a state of great purity and sincerity, playing a significant role in embodying Islamic ethics. Through its profound secret, the divine laws will remain until the end of time.

Just as Allah does not leave the earth devoid of scholars to teach exoteric sciences, He also ensures that there are always followers of path to transmit esoteric knowledge. At all times, He provides a perfect guide.

In another Noble Verse, it is stated:

"Among those we created, there is a community who guide by Truth and establish justice thereby." (A'raf: 181)

And in a sacred Noble Saying, it is revealed:

"None knows my saints under my domes except me."

Though they may be known outwardly, their inner spiritual states and divine illumination remain hidden.

It can be seen from here that these are advisors sent by Truth. Only the Exalted the Allah knows them, people do not. They also know the Exalted the Allah and see that the true guide is the Exalted the Allah. That is, people do not know them; Truth knows them, and they know Truth.

“O you who have believed, fear Allah and be with the Truthful Ones.” (At-Tawba: 119)

The intended Truthful ones in this Noble Verse are guides who have attained Annihilation in Allah. They are those who know Truth and see that everything is from Truth.

Allah the Almighty commands all the faithful to be with them and to benefit from their companionship. Why?

“Allah chooses unto Himself whom He wills.” (Shura: 13)

Indeed, He commands us to be with these chosen and drawn truthful servants. For they lead to Truth and rule with Truth. Allah the Almighty Himself describes them.

In the Noble Verse, it is stated:

"He has succeeded who purifies it." (Ash-Shams: 9)

We combine this Noble Verse so that you may clearly grasp the command of Allah the Almighty.

A purified heart leads one to acts of worship and devotion. Just as a sick person cannot discern the taste of delicious food, a heart mired in worldly distractions cannot appreciate the sweetness of worship and devotion. Hence, an ailing heart needs cleansing.

For this reason, the Master of the Universe, the Reason for Existence, -peace be upon him- has stated in a Noble Saying.

"Remembrance of Allah is the cure for hearts." (Munawi)

As long as base attributes like envy, hypocrisy, rancor, arrogance, lust, anger, and deceit remain in a person, that heart is sick. Its nature is akin to that of animals. The sole remedy for such a heart is the entrance of the light, remembrance, and contemplation of Allah. Gradually, the base attributes fade away, and one day, the heart becomes luminous and an abode for divine manifestations.

Sufism has been a significant agent in the realm of knowledge and Truth for perfecting faith. It is not just a science of words, but rather a practice and a state. It cannot be truly comprehended or imparted through mere theoretical knowledge unless it is lived, tasted, and felt. It is akin to seeing or licking a jar of honey from the outside. One must know that they will never truly reach its essence in such a manner.

The purpose of entering the exalted path, the noble path, is to attain certainty and sincerity in what must be believed according to Islamic law. This is true faith. It means that claiming to be a Muslim is one thing, living Islam is another, and living Islam with knowledge is yet another.

•

The path is twofold: The path of worship, and the path of spiritual ascent.

The path of worship is the Islamic law, involving worship and devotion, remembrance, and contemplation.

The Path to Ascension is the path of the path. With Islamic law, closeness and love are achieved. Through path, the states of **Annihilation in the Master, Annihilation in the Messenger, and Annihilation in Allah** are attained. Those who pass through these stages dissolve their egos.

Sufism is a school of knowledge and wisdom. In this school of knowledge and wisdom, for a person to know their nothingness, they must be purified, pass through the stages, burn in the fire of love, and be reduced to ashes, to become nothing.

I entered as a great man, but realized my utter insignificance. This is the ultimate aim of Sufism, and we have declared it.

Sufism relies on the knowledge of the heart; it is an inner world affair. Just as it is not known from the outside, it cannot be unraveled. How can someone who is not admitted through the gate of Truth, who has only bookish knowledge, understand Sufism, speak of Truth and Truth?

Truth Most High says in His Noble Verse:

"Allah guides to His light whom He wills." (Nur: 35)

For this reason, Allah the Most High says in another Noble Verse:

“Be with the Truthful Ones.” (At-Tawba: 119)

Because the Lord, in His Majesty, has annihilated that person's own existence, placed his own merciful presence in them, and commands us to be with them.

Who Are the True Devotees?

They are indeed the Perfect guide. They are those who attain the “a spiritual share in the saintly inheritance” or both the “a spiritual share in the saintly inheritance” and the “a spiritual share in the prophetic inheritance”. These are the inheritors of the Prophet -peace be upon him-. That is, they are his direct heirs. This divine knowledge is granted by grace and cannot be learned through study alone.

Unless one attains this, they are not, in the true sense, the representative of The Messenger of Allah -peace be upon him-, nor do they possess the bestowed knowledge; they remain in the apparent realm.

Allah the Almighty states in the Noble Verse:

“Whomsoever Allah guides, he is the one rightly guided.” (A’raf: 178)

No one can know the Truth unless Allah the Almighty reveals it. This knowledge of Truth belongs to those who possess gnosis those in the apparent realm cannot comprehend this knowledge. They may say, “So-and-so said this,” or refer to what they read in a certain book, but they do not grasp the essence. They only understand and repeat what they can, yet they are blind in the realm of Truth. They speak as though they know, but it is as if the knowledge hasn’t been conveyed to them.

Those who possess gnosis know, see, and speak with the guidance of Allah the Almighty. Their teacher is none other than the Exalted the Allah Himself.

In the Noble Verse, it states:

"If you fear Allah and attain piety, Allah will be your teacher." (Al-Baqarah: 282)

One who is bereft of this knowledge has only heard of Sufism or read about it in books. He resembles an artificial flower lacking fragrance and any sign of life. Artificial Sufis are like artificial flowers. They try to convey the Truth as if they truly understand it.

This, however, is a gift from Allah, given to whom He wills.

As stated in the Noble Verse:

"This is Allah's grace and favor; He bestows it upon whom He wills." (Al-Jumu'ah: 4)

•

The Messenger of Allah, peace and blessings be upon him, said in his Noble Saying:

"The knowledge of the inner self is one of Allah the Almighty's secrets, a wisdom among His wisdoms. He bestows it only upon the heart of the servant He chooses." (Jami' alSaghir)

Those who practice apparent Sufism and are artificial do not understand the knowledge of gnosis. They are truly deprived of reality, and they remain unaware of their ignorance. Indeed, they do not even know themselves because they are not privileged with the secret of **'Men Arafah...' (Who knows himself...?)** Knowledge and understanding are never attained by mere reading or hearing. It is only possible when Allah the Almighty pours His light into the heart.

In a Sacred saying, Allah the Almighty, states:

"Then I turn my face towards them. Do you think anyone can know what I wish to bestow upon those whom I turn my face towards?"

Allah the Almighty continued:

"The first thing I will give them is the light that penetrates their hearts. Only then, as I inform them about myself, they in turn inform about me." (Hâkim)

This grace is reserved exclusively for the servants whom exalted the Allah loves and chooses; it encompasses no others.

It is understood from the Sacred saying that Allah only bestows this light and knowledge upon the heart of His chosen servant. These are the secret chambers of Allah's mysteries. Only these individuals are truly aware of the realities. They know whatever Truth reveals to them; though they might disclose some, they do not reveal all. Thus, they are the confidants of Exalted the Allah. This state is limited to Allah the Almighty's special servants and does not extend to anyone else. He has loved them, drawn them close, and imparted His secrets to them. Such a person becomes the friend and confidant of Allah.

"None but I know my saints beneath my domes."

The manifestation of this Noble Saying emerges here. No one else can attain this knowledge, nor can the public recognize these possessors of wisdom.

Those who truly know Allah are only these individuals, and those who speak of Allah are only these individuals, as are the true sufis.

Examine the lives of those who speak of Sufism! Are they living according to Islam? Do they pay heed to all the commands and prohibitions of Islamic law? Do they possess awareness of path, the ultimate Truth, and gnosis? Or are they merely living corpses, spiritually dead?

In a Noble Verse, All-powerful Allah Himself declares:

"But they cast it behind their backs and sold it for a small price. What a bad bargain they made!" (Al' Imran: 187)

For sincerity is essential on this path. It is indeed a gift from Allah.

•

Allah Almighty, in a sacred saying, declares:

"Sincerity is one of my secrets. I place it in the hearts of my beloved servants. Neither angel can record it nor can devil spoil it."

How will an artificial sufis comprehend a secret that even an angel is unaware of? Never! They cannot comprehend it.

The difference between the people of Truth and the people of action is like the difference between the living and the dead. For the people of Truth have killed their ego, and their spirit remains alive.

"Die before you die." (K. Hafâ)

They embody the secret of the Prophet's Noble Saying.

However, the practitioners of mere action have a soul deadened, with the self-ruling over them, and they merely pay lip service to Sufism.

Those of Truth are close to Allah, and all their actions and deeds are performed for the sake of Allah. That is, in every matter, they expect no payment or reward from anyone.

As stated in the Noble Verse:

"Follow those who do not ask you for any reward, for they are rightly guided." (Yasin: 21)

They have no goal or purpose other than Allah.

The practitioners of mere action are close to the people, their deeds are superficial, and they seek and receive their rewards and compensation from the people.

THE SELF AND ITS DEGREES

The ethereal soul, once united with this dark body, becomes veiled by seven curtains from its original state. Each of these curtains is referred to as a stage or degree of the self.

The fully veiled state is termed "“The commanding self” ". With one curtain lifted, it is called “The reproaching self ", with two curtains lifted, “The inspired self ", and with three curtains lifted, “The Tranquil Self ".

With every curtain that lifts, spiritual light from the heavenly realms seeps into the soul. In the fully veiled state, no light penetrates. As the number of curtains decreases, the self purifies. When all the curtains are lifted, the soul becomes completely suffused with divine light. This stage is the station of The Messenger of Allah -peace be upon him-.

Though six degrees are explicitly mentioned in the Holy Qur'an, the "The Purified Self" is implied through various Noble Verse.

1. “The commanding self”:

This stage is characterized by a soul that compels a person towards evil.

When the human soul submits to and obeys the carnal desires of the lower self, succumbing to its every inclination, this state is called "“The commanding self”.

In the “The commanding self” state, the heart indulges in corporeal pleasures, altering its state and distancing itself from the Divine. Once a commander, it falls to a subordinate rank. If the heart remains in this condition for an extended period, it loses its ability to turn towards the unseen realms. The unseen is like a mirror: the clearer and more polished it is from dust and rust, the more distinct and pure the images it reflects. If left unpolished for long, rust covers its essence completely, and no amount of polishing can restore its clarity. Thus, it loses its reflective nature.

Our Master, the Pride of the Universe -peace be upon him-, has said in a Noble Saying:

“Undoubtedly, there is a tool to polish everything, and the polish for the heart is the remembrance of Allah.” (Jami' alSaghir)

If the heart turns towards the realm of the unseen, avoids sins, and strives to unveil the veils through remembrance and contemplation, the rust and obscurities are completely cleared away. It becomes capable of perceiving the Truths of beings, subtle meanings, and divine manifestations. It ascends back to the states it had descended from.

As the Exalted the Allah said in a sacred saying:

“I did not fit into the heavens and the earth, but I fit into the heart of my faithful servant.”

The meaning of fitting into a believer's heart is, “He manifests Himself in their heart,” not that Allah physically enters the hearts of His servants.

At the first station, the human soul, having succumbed to the carnal self and being commanding of evil, was called The commanding self.

In the Noble Verse:

“The self indeed instigates great evil, except for those upon whom my Lord has mercy.” (Yusuf: 53)

The journey of this soul is **“towards Allah,”** that is, directed to Allah. Its realm is this visible world of testimony. Its locus is the chest. Its state is inclination. Its path is the outer measures of the Islamic law.

Attributes: Ignorance, stinginess, greed, resentment, arrogance, wrath, lust, covetousness, envy, ill temper, preoccupation with idle and useless things, sarcasm, foolishness, forgetfulness, enmity, quickness to rebellion, gluttony, excessive drinking, verbosity, over exuberance, idleness, insolence, and denial of the conditions of the faithful... and so forth.

The “The commanding self” is also a delicate creation of the Lord. However, it has become tainted due to its inclination towards evil and preoccupation with carnal desires. By succumbing to its lustful, animalistic nature, it has taken the path of beasts and has become the greatest enemy to humankind.

As stated in the Noble Saying:

"Your most severe enemy is yourself between your sides."

(Bayhaqi)

For while an apparent enemy may become a friend and show loyalty in response to kindness and generosity, the self, failing to comprehend grace and benevolence, only increases its harm.

People who remain at the level of “The commanding self” fall into three categories:

1. Those who strive to fulfill the commands of the Exalted the Allah but do not avoid His prohibitions.

"Do as you wish, you will taste death,

Live as you like, you will be separated in the end."

2. He does not obey the Exalted the Allah's commands, nor does he refrain from what is forbidden. However, he loves those who obey.

"The love of the world, the bliss of the hereafter,

Whichever you choose, you sell yours*elf *to it."

3. His name is Islam. Yet, not only does he not follow any command of Islam, but he also does not love Islam and Muslims.

"He who rejects the Sunnah and the Book,

For him, silence means not speaking at all."

2. *The reproaching self*:

When the human soul, after committing sins and evils as the "The commanding self" h, begins to feel remorse and starts to reproach itself, this state is called "The reproaching self."

The seeker who rises to the second station has now removed one of the seven veils over his heart. He performs his devotions, avoids prohibitions, and strives to fulfill divine commands. Despite this, he still commits sins, but immediately afterward, he feels remorse and repents.

There are good promises for those like these:

"They are those who refrain from great sins and shameful deeds, except for minor faults. Indeed, your Lord's forgiveness is vast." (Najm: 32)

The journey of this station is "Towards Allah." Its place is in the heart. Its state is love.

Its attributes: Blame, envy, wrong thoughts, conceit, indulgence, conflict with people, oppression, desire, hidden hypocrisy, love for status, and lust.

Though some attributes of the "The commanding self" still exist, it sees and knows the Truth as Truth and falsehood as falsehood. The practice of Islamic law and love does not diminish. It becomes distressed due to its bad states. However, escaping these bad attributes is beyond its strength.

In The reproaching self, there is a hidden hypocrisy and a disease of self-admiration. It desires that people know about its good deeds. It is pleased by being praised. Even though it dislikes this bad trait, it cannot uproot it from its heart.

A person in the state of the reproaching self is considered among the people of piety. The highest degree of this station is sincerity. However, even with sincerity in actions, the seeker is still not free from danger.

Despite this, it is a station that signifies sanctity in the sight of Allah.

As stated in the Noble Verse:

"I swear by the self that constantly reproaches itself..." (Qiyamah: 2)

3. The inspired self:

When worship, remembrance, and spiritual exercises intensify, and a fierce struggle with, a veil from the heart may be lifted. Reaching this third station of the self is termed "The inspired self."

This degree is called "The inspired self" because the Exalted the Allah directly inspires the human soul with both rebellion and obedience.

As the soul ascends and gains strength, it strives to dominate the self. After numerous struggles and endeavors, the self at this stage becomes reformed. The soul now holds sovereignty over the body.

A person may reach this level through their sincerity and effort, but advancing further requires the guidance of a perfect mentor, a Perfect guide.

Those who remain in this station are often half mad, half saintly. They are known as "attracted ones."

Just as a military officer needs special training to become a staff officer, the progression beyond the inspired self-necessitates the spiritual training of a perfected guide who has attained Annihilation in Allah. The guides the seeker out of the darkness of doubt into the light of divine manifestation.

The journey of the inspired self is towards Allah. At this station, Truths radiance dawns in the seeker's heart, dissolving all else within. The universe, to them, becomes the realm of souls. Their habitat is the soul. Their state is love. The meaning revealed to them is gnosis.

Attributes: Knowledge, generosity, contentment, humility, patience, tolerance of hardships, accepting apologies, good opinion, tolerance...

In this station, the seeker witnesses that all beings are under the power of Allah, the Lord of all worlds, and therefore, has no objections to any creature. The seeker observes the acts of the Absolute Actor.

The other features of the inspired self are as follows: falling into bewilderment, reaching spiritual stations, the coming of contraction and expansion, the departure of fear and hope, loving the remembrance of Allah, a cheerful demeanor, speaking with wisdom, observation, and mindfulness...

In this station, the disciple is weak and cannot journey to the Truth. They cannot distinguish between the Majestic and the Beautiful. Since the human attributes have not completely disappeared, at a heedless moment, the self instantly descends to the lowest of the low and resumes former bad habits. Their belief gets corrupted, and they abandon worship. They mistake satanic imaginations for divine manifestations, leading themselves to ruin.

For the seeker in this station, the most critical and necessary thing is to obey the complete guidance of their Perfect guide with their free will and meticulousness, surrendering to every command. Additionally, they must strongly oppose the desires and wishes of the self. Because although advancement is possible in this station, there is also a perpetual danger of falling.

The inspired self is mentioned in the Qur'an al-karim in these terms:

"By the_self and He who proportioned it and inspired it with discernment of its wickedness and its righteousness, he who purifies it succeeds." (Ash-Shams: 7-8-9)

Here, purification refers to cleansing from the vile traits known as "Desire, anger, hatred, arrogance, hypocrisy, envy..." This divine statement signifies that **"the one who purifies is successful."** It should not be taken to imply superficial cleanliness or simplistic meanings such as "I fasted, so I am purified."

4. *The Tranquil Self:*

It refers to a self-cleansed of idolatry, doubt, rebellion, and error, liberated from sufferings by the call of Lord and attaining tranquility. With the lifting of the fourth veil over the heart, the soul ascends to the station of the Tranquil Self.

Indeed, the Exalted the Allah addresses a self-elevated to this level with the words:

"O tranquil self!" (Fecr: 27)

In The Tranquil Self, the traveler's journey is "Journey with Allah". Its realm is the reality of Muhammad. Its place is a secret. Its state is one of sincere contentment. The meanings that come to it are among the secrets of Islamic law.

Its attributes include: Generosity, reliance on Allah, patience, gratitude, forbearance, submission, acceptance, Truthfulness, worship, gentleness, cheerfulness, complete observation, constant tranquility, and reverence for elders, heart's joy, sweet speech, covering faults, and forgiving errors.

In this station, the wayfarer fully adheres to the Quran and Sunnah. Those who see a person in this state feel delight, as do those who listen to them. Their words do not bring weariness but convey Truthfulness and purity. Their tongues interpret the wisdom of Islamic law, the secrets of reality, and the subtleties of meaning. These individuals have neither studied books nor sought knowledge from others because **they are favored with divine inspirations**. Therefore, they are immersed in the ocean of modesty and decency. They have been granted an awe-inspiring state and clothed in the garment of dignity.

Occasionally, they conVerse with people, sharing the wisdom born from their inner realm. They guide their friends according to their capacities.

They spend most of their time in worship, so as not to be deprived of reaching higher stages.

In this station, with continued prayers and litanies, the love for The Messenger of Allah -peace be upon him- takes on a completely distinct state.

5. The content self:

The state of the self that has shown steadfastness through all of Allah the Almighty's tests and trials, has been content with all that has come and will come, and whose sole effort and desire is to earn the pleasure of the Lord is called "The content self."

In this station, the seeker has become like a leaf fallen into the ocean. Just as the ocean waves carry the leaf wherever they wish, the seeker surrenders completely to the divine decree. He has bound his will to the Will of Truth and has given his decisions to Him.

The journey of this soul is "in Allah". Its realm is the divine world. Its place is the secret within secrets. Its state is reaching annihilation in Allah.

Its attributes include: renunciation, sincerity, love, and friendship with the Lord, divine presence, miracles, and abandonment of anything other than Allah, submission, contentment, patience in the face of hardships, guiding people, and the most delicate manners. His prayers are never rejected. He is held in high regard by everyone.

The selves in the stations of content and the subsequent pleasing are honored in the Qur'an al karim with this divine address:

"Return to your Lord, well pleased and pleasing [to Him]..." (Fajr: 28)

6. The pleasing self:

The self that reaches this station is called "The pleasing self" because Exalted the Allah is pleased with it. It means the self that has been approved.

Its journey is "Toward Allah". The realm is this visible world of testimony. Its abode is the hidden. Its state is amazement. Its path is Islamic law.

Attributes: Adorning oneself with the morals of Allah and His Messenger, forgiving faults, covering up defects, harboring good intentions, showing kindness and compassion to all, and harboring love and affection for saving people from darkness...

However, this love and affection is solely for Allah, embodying only mercy and compassion. Outwardly, one is not distinguished from people, but inwardly, one is with Truth. The heart is freed from everything other than Allah.

The necessary knowledge is conveyed from the spiritual realm to the material world by Allah's permission so that people may benefit.

One avoids excess and deficiency, adhering to the middle path.

7 The Purified self:

In this station, the self has been purified, refined, transformed from the worst part of the body to the best, like a stone becoming a diamond.

In this station, the seeker is in the hands of Truth. He knows Truth and attributes everything to Truth. He neither considers himself nor his sustenance. He says, "What is it to me, it belongs to my Master." For he knows and sees well that Allah the Exalted, is the owner of the house, while he is merely a guest. As the saying goes, "Hû, neighbor!" the "Hû..!" here directly addresses the owner of the house.

He recognizes none other than Him and seeks everything solely from Him. He is already content with the Divine decree that will come to pass.

Their attributes are briefly as follows:

1. They are slaves of the Truth. They know well that if the Lord wills, He holds, and if He wills, He casts aside. If He wills, He protects, and if He wills, He does not.

2. They are aware of their need for a drop of divine mercy.

3. They understand that nothing can be known unless it is revealed.

4. If the Lord wills, He takes them into the circle of happiness, and only they are admitted into this circle.

These are measures of Truth. Actions are understood from this standpoint.

•

A REPRESENTATION TO HELP YOU BETTER UNDERSTAND THE LEVELS OF THE SELF

We present the image of a walnut so that you may better understand the stages of the self. Let each person measure themselves.

"Setefteriku ümmetî..." In accordance with the Noble Saying, our Master, The Messenger of Allah -peace be upon him- said, **"My community will split into seventy-three sects, seventy-two of which are doomed to Hell."** This is a definitive declaration of the Prophet. How terrifying this is!

Since seventy-two out of seventy-three sects are condemned to Hell, it is understood that seventy-two out of seventy-three walnuts are rotten.

All of these are from his community, yet seventy-two are hell bound, and only one will be saved.

Our subject now concerns that one sound walnut. If you carefully observe how this sound walnut is processed, you will learn.

"The commanding self":

The green outer husk of the walnut represents the "The commanding self". This green husk is also a subtlety created by Allah the Almighty. However, because it tends toward evil deeds and commits them, like the husk of the walnut, the "The commanding self" is bitter. This is the thickest veil.

The reproaching self:

The hard shell beneath the green husk represents the reproaching self. Since it does not penetrate inside, it is always caught up in the claim of ego. Unless one breaks the desires of the self like breaking the shell of the walnut, it is truly impossible to penetrate inside.

Here, all selves gather together. A crucial point. This is the place and station of those who cry out, "I!.. I!.. I!.."

I now compare this self to a walnut:

Whoever you hear saying "I, I!..", they all remain in the shell, unable to penetrate their inner self, unable to make use of what lies within. The self-inside says, "I, I!..", "You cannot enter here!..". Further on, a significant allegory on this matter will arise.

The inspired self:

It has shattered the shell of self-assertion and penetrated inward. Yet, the desires and yearnings stand as a curtain within. It must cleanse itself from the pests inside.

The Tranquil Self:

It has cleansed itself of pests, leaving only the membrane. It has drawn considerably closer to Truth. To remove this membrane, one must ascend the ladder of Content so that the "Core" the essence of the walnut, comes to fruition.

When we spoke of stages earlier and mentioned Content, we used the term ladder. For as one grows, they diminish; and as they diminish, they grow. At that point, one always descends the ladder and diminishes, beginning to perceive the divine grandeur.

The pleasing self:

The vermin have been cleansed. After reaching Tranquil, one attains Content and the veil is lifted. In the state of the pleasing self, only the "core" remains, like the essence of the innermost part of a walnut.

Those who ascend the ladder of Pleasing can take what they desire and discard what they wish.

Allah the Almighty states in the Noble Verse:

"Allah forgives whom He wills and punishes whom He wills." (Baqarah: 284)

It is essential to understand this. The creature has no authority; the decree and value belong solely to Allah, the Lord of Majesty and Perfection.

The Purified self:

Here, the walnut has been emptied. At this stage, one sees only the existence of Allah the Almighty within.

I express this very clearly: One realizes that both one and the universe are but mere shells. Indeed, both self and universe are nothing but shells.

Those who can truly proclaim the Word of Divine Unity are these individuals.

•

Now, we proceed to the second parable.

Allah, exalted and sublime is He, states in His Noble Verse:

"Allah has not made for any man two hearts in his breast." (Al-Ahzâb: 4)

So that one heart may be dedicated to the love of the Creator, and the other to the love of worldly things. Two loves cannot coexist in one heart.

This Noble Verse has been mentioned many times, yet it was never truly explained. Even if it was addressed, its deeper meaning wasn't explored.

Whosoever has only Allah in their heart, they are with the Ultimate Truth. Whosoever has worldly things in their heart, they are with the people.

Now, I bring forth an analogy of The Word of Divine Unity using a walnut. A person says "There is no Allah but Allah", but the green husk covers the heart with seven veils; they utter it, yet it remains upon the lips, not descending into the throat.

In the state of the reproaching self, one says "There is no Allah but Allah" but inside the self-cries, "I, I!", the hard shell has not been pierced.

Pay close attention to this matter.

In the state of the inspired self, saying "There is no Allah but Allah" pierces the shell, meaning it penetrates the heart; yet, there remains much affection for things other than Truth. Because of this much affection, one must strive diligently to cleanse away base morals.

In the state of The Tranquil Self, saying "There is no Allah but Allah" descent more easily. Here, it descends in such a manner that the heart frees itself from doubt and polytheism. One achieves true awareness and becomes a real believer.

In the state of the content self, a person reaches a point where they are content with the Exalted the Allah. They say, "He created me, He sustains me, He feeds me, He gives me to drink." They are content with every condition. Whether bitter or sweet, they are satisfied with His every decree. Why? Because faith has begun to take root. The seed of the Word of Divine Unity has fallen into the heart and is slowly germinating. This sprout spreads throughout the entire body, imbuing every limb with faith. Knowing their Creator, they are free from doubt and shirk. They are pleased with the Creator and accept everything.

This state persists for a long time. Then, because the person performs their worship and devotion sincerely, Allah the Most High becomes pleased with them.

However, upon reaching the state of The Purified self, nothing remains. The shell, insects, and even the membrane around the walnut are gone; the "Core" is emptied.

When they say "There is no Allah but Allah", they see the Exalted the Allah, and within themselves, they perceive that nothing exists except Him. Only these individuals can truly declare the creed in its true meaning.

This divine secret has been unveiled for you. The secret of the Word of Divine Unity has been revealed.

For Allah Most High says, **"I have not given you two hearts... Whoever harbors only my love within them is with me, and I am with them."**

There's no room for Lord in a heart filled with worldly distractions. Two loves cannot coexist in one heart.

Nothing exists but Him. The one who perceives and knows the Creator understands that both their essence and the universe are but a corpus. For Exalted the Allah is spirit, yet He also created that body. What remains of you? Nothing!

The entire universe is made of mere bodies.

•

The Exalted Truth declares:

“We are closer to him than you are, though you do not see us.” (Waqi’ah : 85)

In this Noble Verse, Allah the Almighty reveals that He is near to everything in every way, and that the secrets of divinity exist in every particle. He created the atom, He created you, and He created the universe. Apart from Him, there is nothing in existence.

For He is the Being, He is the Existence… The enlightened ones who possess **perfect faith and gnosis** understand that the manifestations of existence are mere reflections of His light, and nothing else truly exists but Him. This knowledge is exclusive to them.

Let everyone look into this mirror and see themselves! Are they of the people of Truth? Do they possess perfect faith? Or do they not?

If one is aware of all these Truths, they are of the people of Truth. If not, let them learn what they truly are. For Sufism is exclusive to its own people.

The Perfect guide, the Exalted the Allah and His Messenger invite us. For he has believed in the Exalted the Allah, the true guide, and His Messenger. He knows and sees his own nothingness. He also knows that the Exalted the Allah is the true guide. But only he knows this.

As for those who claim, "I am also a guide," they are appointed by Satan. They use the Exalted the Allah and His Messenger to bind people to themselves.

Therefore, you can discern the genuine guide from the false one and understand true faith from this.

•

"Peace be upon those who follow guidance."
(Taha: 47)

SAINTLY FIGURES

-May Allah sanctify their secrets-

REVELATIONS FROM

IMPORTANT DISCLOSURE

CHAPTER 3

- **Imam Rabbani (-may his secret be sanctified-)**
- **AbdulQadir Gilani (-may his secret be sanctified-)**
- **Muhyiddin Ibn Arabi (-may his secret be sanctified-)**
- **Ali al-Hawwas (-may his secret be sanctified-)**
- **Bediuzzaman Said Nursi (-may his secret be sanctified-)**
- **Master Es'ad Effendi (-may his secret be sanctified-)**
- **On the Revelations of Bediuzzaman**
- **The Greatest Verse of the Quran**

Allah the Almighty says in His Noble Verse:

"We have sent you as a mercy to the worlds." (Anbiya: 107)

Allah the Most High, the possessor of the blessed name Ar-Rahim, has granted the Source of Existence, our Master -peace be upon him- who is **"Mercy to the worlds,"** a source of spiritual life. This source of spiritual life comes exclusively from him.

Thus, whatever is bestowed spiritually upon a believer is granted through our Master, The Messenger of Allah may blessings and -peace be upon him-. Without that life-giving water from him, no one would have faith and no one would possess spiritual life. Just as Allah the Most High dispenses existence and life to all people from The Throne of the Most Merciful with His name Ar-Rahman, spiritual life too comes solely from Allah the Most High's Beloved, the Noble Muhammad -peace be upon him- the Master of the Universe and the Cause of Existence. Divine grace also comes exclusively to believers, who are honored with the gift of faith, from The Messenger of Allah -peace be upon him-, who is Allah the Most High's Beloved, His Friend, and His Light.

The divine mercy and grace from the ocean of Allah the Most High's favor flow into the ocean of His Beloved may blessings and -peace be upon him-, from where it then flows into the ocean of the Perfect guide of the time, and from there it is dispersed to the universe.

The Messenger of Allah may blessings and -peace be upon him- was sent to the entire world, whereas his deputies are sent to specific people.

Regarding those sent to specific people, the Noble Saying states:

"The heart of a believing servant is the throne of the Most Compassionate Allah." (K. Hafa: 2/130)

Just as The Messenger of Allah -peace be upon him- provides spiritual life to the universe, the heart of his deputy becomes the Throne of the Most Compassionate, from which he bestows upon those who are destined, from that throne.

Whether they realize it or not, those who receive the spiritual water of life receive it from him.

Imam Rabbani -may his secret be sanctified-

Indeed, Imam Rabbani -may his secret be sanctified- states in his 260th letter, while discussing the Perfect guide of his time:

"The Pole of Guidance is a highly esteemed individual, who encompasses complete personal perfection. Such a gem descends upon the world only after countless ages and epochs. The darkened world is illuminated

by his radiance. His light of guidance and spiritual instruction spreads across the entire universe.

From the bounds of the Throne to the depths of the earth, anyone who attains guidance, faith, and gnosis does so through his path, derives benefit from him, and is spiritually nourished by him. Without his intermediation, no one can achieve this blessing; such a fortune is not granted to anyone without him. His guidance permeates the universe like an encompassing ocean; he is a sea, frozen like an icy ocean, never tumultuous.

A seeker who knows this saintly personage and is sincere towards him, if they focus their thoughts on him, or if the saintly personage loves a seeker, focuses on them, and desires their spiritual advancement, a window opens in the seeker's heart. To the extent of their love, focus, and sincerity, they gain spiritual nourishment from this boundless ocean.

If someone turns their attention towards the remembrance of Allah the Almighty but does not focus on this saintly person due to ignorance rather than denial, they still receive some benefit. However, the benefit of the first scenario is greater than that of the second.

If a person denies or disdains this saintly person, or if this saintly person is displeased with them, even if the person engages in the remembrance of Allah the Almighty, they are deprived of true guidance and spiritual instruction. Their disbelief or offense becomes a barrier, closing the path to spiritual nourishment. The exalted pole, even if not focusing on denying them benefit nor wishing them harm, will still be of no avail to them. They will possess only the outward form of instruction and guidance, which is of minimal benefit.

However, those who believe in and love this saintly person, even without directly focusing on them or being constantly engaged in the remembrance of Allah the Almighty, reach the light of guidance and spiritual instruction solely through their love."

....

To advance in this exalted Path, it is essential to harbor a bond of love and connection with the Master who is followed. This person has traversed this path as the beloved and, drawn by great strength, has attained these virtues.

His gaze is a remedy for diseases of the heart, and his spiritual attention dispels maladies of the soul.

A person of such perfection is the religious leader of his time, the caliph of his era.

The Spiritual Poles and the substitutes are willing to sacrifice their lives to merely glimpse his rank. The Pillars and the Nobles are satisfied with a single drop from the ocean of his virtues.

The light of his guidance and instruction reaches everyone, just like the rays of the sun, whether he wills it or not. However, he sends more to those he desires. His will is not within his own control. Often, he wants to exercise his will, but it is not granted to him.

Those who are guided and elevated through his light do not need to be aware of their earnings. A person who achieves guidance and the light of Truth through him cannot fully grasp his state. Even then, they may not understand their own enlightenment and guidance as it truly is. For knowing one's state is not a gift given to everyone, and the knowledge of advancing through each station is not bestowed upon all.

Indeed, this person, who has been entrusted with the leadership of a path, is surely knowledgeable. He understands the subtleties of the journey. Because he knows, it was not deemed necessary for the travelers to know. They also assist, and through annihilation and permanence in Allah, they are honored.

A poem:

What challenge is there for Allah?

"He fills the universe into a single person."

Our beloved Prophet, the Messenger of Allah -peace be upon him-, **as "Mercy to the worlds",** is the spiritual life source for all believers. However, his successor, the Perfect guide of the time, grants life to his spiritual followers.

"This is a perfection, a superiority that emerged a thousand years after The Messenger of Allah -peace be upon him-. It is an end so reminiscent of the beginning.

Surely, The Messenger of Allah -peace be upon him- said regarding this:

'My Community is like rain. It is uncertain if the first or the last of it is better.' (Tirmidhi)

He did not say, 'Is the beginning better, or the middle?' It implies that those who come later resemble the first ones more, creating a moment of hesitation.

In another Noble Saying, he stated:

'The most virtuous members of my Community are those at the beginning and at the end; the middle part is turbulent.'

Indeed... Among the latter of this Community, there will be those who greatly resemble the pioneers. However, their number is small, even exceedingly so. While those in the middle may not resemble the earliest as much, their numbers are vast. Yet, the scarcity of the latter has only amplified their value, drawing them closer to the virtues of the first ones."

The Messenger of Allah -peace be upon him- blessed them with this Noble Saying:

"Islam began as something strange and it will return to being strange just as it started.

So blessed are the strangers!" (Muslim)

The end of this Community commenced a thousand years after the passing of The Messenger of Allah -peace be upon him-, marking the beginning of the second millennium. For, with the passage of a thousand years, significant changes in people and impactful influences on things have emerged.

Since Allah the Almighty decreed that this religion shall remain unchanged until the Day of Judgment, the freshness observed in those who came first is also seen in the latter ones, thereby fortifying this religion at the dawn of the second millennium.

To substantiate this claim, we can present two strong witnesses: the existence of Jesus -peace be upon him- and Exalted the Mehdi within this millennium.

A poem:

"If one had sought aid from the Holy spirit,

Anyone other than Jesus could have done what he did."

O brother! Today, these words seem heavy to many and far from their understanding. However, if they measure knowledge and gnosis with fairness and compare it to Islam, they will see and accept which one shows more reverence and respect towards Islam." (Letter 261)

Abd al-Qadir al-Gilani -may his secret be sanctified-

Abd al-Qadir al-Gilani also described that revered person in the 5th assembly of his work, Fath al-Rabbani, as follows:

"Healing is found on this path. Nearness begins here. Dominion is here, fame, sovereignty on this horizon. Leadership is also on this path. For the one who establishes their palace here, a speck becomes a mighty mountain, a drop turns into an ocean. Their star shines as brightly as the moon. They

surpass the moon and the year. Their little becomes much, their emptiness becomes abundance. The exhausted is embraced by eternity. Their motion seems as if it can move the universe. Like the branches of a cypress, they ascend to the heights, embraced by the Throne. Its roots are hidden in the depths of the earth. Its branches provide cool relief to both the world and the hereafter. These branches are knowledge and wisdom. Those who possess them desire nothing else. The world shrinks before them to the size of a ring's stone. The world cannot bind them. The hereafter cannot set limits for them. Kings cannot command them. Dominion cannot console them. Concealers cannot hide anything from them. No hand can reach them. Sorrow stays away from them. This is where the path leads, the journey ends. The servant finds righteousness in this way and returns to the people, holding their hands as a savior, pulling them from the sea of the world, of course, those who are destined, those who adhere to the Truth.

This great soul, who attains the goodness of Allah's will, becomes merciful. He is the guide, protector, educator, and leader of people. He loosens the tongues hidden in hearts. His light illuminates on his right and left. Indeed, those whom Allah has willed goodness for find this person. Those not willed for goodness do not see him; they remain blind. They do not find him, they become lost. These are unique.

When they enter among the people, their protector is the Truth. The harm of the people does not touch them. They are safe in every respect. They achieve whatever benefit is for the people. With the help of the Truth, even the most difficult tasks become easy for them. With Allah's help, they call the servants to the right path."

They indicated that those whom Allah wills goodness for must find this person, and those whom He does not will goodness for cannot find him. That is to say, the Perfect guide, being his deputy, grants spiritual life from that Throne to those destined.

Muhyiddin Ibn 'Arabi -may his secret be sanctified-

The Greatest Master, Muhyiddin Ibn 'Arabi -may his secret be sanctified-, also speaks of this person in his work, Fusus al-Hikam, as follows:

"This knowledge is the highest form of knowledge of Allah. It has been given only to the last of the prophets and saints. Those who perceive this wisdom from among the Prophets and Messengers see it only through the niche of Khatam al-Anbiya (Seal of the Prophets), Muhammad -peace be upon him-. Similarly, those who perceive it from among the saints see it only through the niche of the Khatam al-Awliya (Seal of the Saints), the heir of Muhammad. Indeed, even the Prophets, whenever they witness this knowledge, see it through the light of the lamp of Khatam al-Awliya (Seal of the Saints). For the role of being a Messenger and Prophet has ended, but

sainthood never concludes. The Prophets sent with the Book were also saints, and they received this knowledge from the lamp of Khatam al-Awliya (Seal of the Saints). Therefore, how can it be that saints of lower ranks do not obtain this knowledge from the same source? Although Khatam al-Awliya (Seal of the Saints) is subordinate to Khatam al-Messenger (Seal of the Prophet) in the law brought by them, this does not diminish his rank. Neither does it contradict our path. Hence, in one aspect, the Khatam al-Awliya (Seal of the Saints) is lower, but in another aspect, he is higher." (Fusûsu'l-Hikem. Translated by N. Gençosman. pp: 4344)

•

A. Avni Konuk's explanation on this subject in his commentary on Fusûsu'lHikem is as follows:

"For the Khatam al-Awliya (Seal of the Saints) is the blessed person predestined internally by the Khatam al-Anbiya (Seal of the Prophet). Outwardly, he follows the law brought by Khatam al-Anbiya (Seal of the Prophet). He himself does not bring a new law. Although this illustrious person's body and form differ from Muhammad -peace be upon him-, his inner essence is entirely Muhammad Mustafa -peace be upon him-. Even the Khatam al-Anbiya Muhammad -peace be upon him-, who is outwardly manifested in the world of testimony, acquired the laws and commandments of the Islamic law from his inner reality, the Khatam al-Awliya (Seal of the Saints). To put it differently: The body and form of the Khatam al-Awliya (Seal of the Saints) may change through different times, but the essence remains unchanged; it is always the same. Therefore, irrespective of the time or form, while Khatam al-Awliya (Seal of the Saints) adheres to the Islamic law of Khatam al-Anbiya (Seal of the Prophets), he is the fountainhead of wisdom for all saints.

As Exalted the Mawlana Jalaluddin may Allah have mercy upon him informs us from their blessed selves:

Verse:

"They have unlocked the treasury of graces, and you are clad in the robe of sanctity

Mustafa has come again; all of you, believe in him."

(Fusûsu'l-Hikem. Dr. Mustafa Tahralı Dr. Selçuk Eraydın. pp: 214215)"

•

"One time, the Prophet -peace be upon him- was shown a vision of prophet hood as a wall made of bricks. There was a single missing brick in that wall. The Prophet, -peace be upon him-, became that last brick. However, as The Messenger of Allah said, he only saw the missing brick, without any other in its place. As for the Khatam al-Awliya (Seal of the Saints), this vision is also true for him. Accordingly, he too sees what was shown to the Prophet, -

peace be upon him-. In fact, he sees two brick places in that wall, one of gold and the other of silver. He sees the missing brick that completes the wall as partly gold and partly silver. Thus, he needs to see himself reflected in the place where these bricks were placed. Consequently, the Khatam al-Awliya (Seal of the Saints) becomes the symbol of these two bricks, completing the wall. The reason why the Khatam al-Awliya (Seal of the Saints) sees these as two bricks is his outward adherence to the Islamic law of the Khatam al-Anbiya (Seal of the Prophets). The symbol of his adherence is the silver brick, which represents the outward aspect and necessitates his following it in rulings. Just as he outwardly follows the rulings, inwardly he receives from Allah. For he sees the command in its true state, and such a vision is necessary for him. This vision represents the place of the hidden brick. He takes from a source so profound that the same source from which the angel who brought revelation to the Prophet, -peace be upon him-, also takes. If you understand this subtle point I have indicated, you have achieved beneficial knowledge." (Fusûsu'lHikem, translated by N. Gençosman, p. 45)

•

This esteemed person piqued the curiosity of the Great Master (Shaykh al-Akbar), who wondered who it could be. Meanwhile, he reported hearing a faint voice saying:

"O Muhyiddin! This matter is not as you think. It is a gift meant for a saint to come in the End Times."

So much so that:

"I immediately turned all my vision and insight to the unseen world. I wished to learn the name, rank, and origin of this person, but Allah did not grant me knowledge of any of these."

"Allah the Exalted has not granted this seal of sainthood to us, nor to those before us, and has kept this rank hidden from us," he said.

•

In the questions and answers section of his work 'Futuhat al-Makkiyya,' he states:

"The station of prophetic law thus concluded, yet the station of sainthood still persists. Consequently, it has also earned the right to be brought to an end one befitting its rank and resembling its own conclusion.

The one who will bring this end and whom we await is not the Mahdi. This individual will be from his own household." (Translated by S. Alpay. Page: 216)

•

"From the era of Adam to the last Prophet, every prophet, despite differing in nature, derived his knowledge from the light of the final Prophet, Muhammad -peace be upon him-. For he exists in Truth, as affirmed by the Prophet's words, 'I was a Prophet while Adam was still between water and clay.' Other prophets became messengers only when sent to their communities. Similarly, the last of the saints, Khatam al-Awliya (Seal of the Saints), was a saint while Adam was still between water and clay. Other saints achieved sainthood only after attaining the divine attributes and receiving the grace of Allah's names, Al-Wáli and Al-Hamid.

Therefore, the relationship between the last Prophet's sainthood and the last saint is akin to the relationship between Prophets and the final Prophet. Hence, the last of the Messengers is both a saint, a prophet, and a messenger. The Khatam al-Awliya (Seal of the Saints) is the inheritor who receives his knowledge directly from the Divine. He witnesses the ranks and is a benefaction from Muhammad -peace be upon him- for the opening of the door of intercession, being the master of the sons of Adam and the leader of the congregation." (Fusus alHikam. Translated by N. Gençosman. Page: 46)

•

A. Avni Konuk's commentary on this topic in his exposition on Fusus alHikam is as follows:

"As for the Khatam al-Awliya (Seal of the Saints), he is a saint in the pre-eternal form of his immutable essence. Following the Islamic law of the Khatam al-Anbiya (Seal of the Prophets), he inherits all his sciences and tastes, obtaining knowledge directly from the origin, the Truth. Since he is situated in the maqam of 'the Reality of Realities' of the Muhammadan Reality, he observes the degrees of 'prophet hood,' 'messenger ship,' 'sainthood,' and 'caliphate,' as well as other divine and cosmic ranks. In this way, the Khatam al-Awliya (Seal of the Saints) is a grace from Muhammad -peace be upon him- for opening the door of intercession, being the master of humanity and leader of the community of prophets and saints. Because he perfectly follows the rulings of the Khatam al-Anbiya (Seal of the Prophets), in the outward, he is outwardly a grace. And as he is determined in the Muhammadan Reality, encompassing all Truths, and assists from this inner station, he is also inwardly a grace. As the Khatam al- Rasul exists before all manifestations, he is naturally the leader of all prophets and saints." (Fusus alHikam. Dr. Mustafa Tahralı Dr. Selçuk Eraydın. Page: 223)

"The Khatam al-Awliya (Seal of the Saints), though he may not comprehend this from the perspective of elemental composition, knows it entirely in terms of Truth and station. Thus, the Khatam al-Awliya (Seal of the Saints) is knowledgeable in Truth and rank, yet ignorant in physical and elemental being. This implies that just as true existence accepts attributes that seem dissimilar, the Khatam al-Awliya (Seal of the Saints) also embraces opposing traits. Like the Majestic and the Beautiful, the Manifest and the

Hidden, the First and the Last. However, he is the reflection of his own essence, and none other. For he both knows and does not know, perceives and does not perceive, sees and does not see." (Fusūs alHikam, translated by N. Gençosman, pp. 4950)

Ali Havvas -may his secret be sanctified-

Imam al-Sha'rani -may his secret be sanctified-, the guide of Ali Havvas -may his secret be sanctified-, an unlettered saint, also said regarding this matter:

"In this community, there are two seals who encompass all ranks and positions, inheriting all stations. They are completely immersed in the unity of Ahadiyyah (The Oneness of Allah in His essence) and Wahidiyyah (The Oneness of Allah in the multiplicity of creation). Their support and assistance, whether ahadi or wahidi, reach both absolute and contingent realms. Indeed, all saints that have come and will come receive their grace and help from these two individuals. One is the Khatam al-Anbiya (Seal of the Prophets), and the other is the Khatam al-Awliya (Seal of the Saints)."

Bediüzzaman Said Nursî -may his secret be sanctified-

Though many saints have expressed their views on this subject, Bediüzzaman Said Nursî in his work Emirdağ Lahikası, on page 259, speaks about the mission of the Mahdi -peace be upon him- and mentions this individual who will come before the Mahdi:

"With the dominance of naturalism and materialism spreading among humanity through the influence of science and philosophy, the foremost task is to provide a comprehensive way to silences these ideas and save faith.

Protecting the people of faith from misguidance requires significant dedication and long-term study, which leaves no time for the Mahdi to undertake this mission himself. For his role as the successor of Muhammad -peace be upon him- in the caliphate leaves him occupied. Therefore, a group will perform this task prior to him in one way or another. That person will prepare a groundwork with what that group has labored on for a long time, thus effectively fulfilling the primary duty.

The strength and spiritual army supporting this mission consist of a select group of disciples who fully embody sincerity, loyalty, and solidarity. Although they may be few, they are considered as powerful and valuable as an entire army in spiritual terms."

Master Es'ad Effendi -may his secret be sanctified-

Our esteemed Muhammed Es'ad Erbili -may his secret be sanctified- has declared in his work titled Mektubat:

"Perhaps my faults may be pardoned by one of the Venerable ones from my ancestors or my descendants." (Letter 73)

The one who is the Khatam al-Awliya (Seal of the Saints) grants spiritual life uniquely to those spiritually affiliated with him. This is because he is the deputy of The Messenger of Allah -peace be upon him- and the bearer of his divine light, distributing the spiritual life bestowed from the divine loftiness.

All saints allude to this same being. Just as all the Prophets -peace be upon them- announced a Prophet to come after them, who is the Khatam al-Anbiya (Seal of the Prophets), The Noble Messenger

Many saints have foretold the coming of a highly esteemed being, the Khatam al-Awliya (Seal of the Saints) who would arrive many years later.

"Peace be upon those who follow guidance."

(Taha: 47)

***Note by the Editors:**

We would like to take this opportunity to present some disclosures by Master Şerafeddin -may his secret be sanctified- one of the revered Masters of the Naqshbandi Order. This distinguished individual was born in Dagestan in 1876 (Gregorian calendar) and migrated to Turkey with a large group of people due to the Russian oppression. He settled in Güney village, Yalova, and passed away in 1936, where he was also laid to rest.

According to a very elderly woman residing in Pamukova, known as Hacı Fatma Nine (Grandmother Hacı Fatma), Master Şerafeddin -may his secret be sanctified- gathered with his close ones on a blessed night around the year 1927. He said, ***"Tonight, a very exalted person has come into the world. We will not see him, but my daughter Fatma will."*** That morning, he sacrificed several animals and mentioned that all the great trees wept tears of joy and fell into prostration.

Finally, fifty-five years later, in June 1982, Master Şerafeddin -may his secret be sanctified- conveyed to Hacı Fatma Nine in a spiritual vision, ***"My daughter, the person I mentioned to you will visit you in three days."*** Indeed, three days later, he came, and they met.

The voice recordings of some highly significant disclosures by Hacı Fatma Nine, who passed away in March 1986 at over a hundred years old, are preserved in our archives.

Upon the Revelations of Our Master Bediüzzaman:

Körpe said: *"There was a mufti named* Abraham *in our area. In the early years when 'Words and Notes' first emerged, he had a dream. In this dream, Exalted the Bediüzzaman was sitting on a pulpit. He had placed the book before him and was reading from it, explaining the mysteries within to the people."*

The dream seen then has now come to fruition and manifestation.

The All-powerful Allah has informed and shown this honorable individual many events that would occur in the future. We have now become aware of this today.

Let's elaborate a bit on the statements of Exalted the Bediüzzaman:

"With the influence of science and philosophy..."

The corruption and philosophy of the infidel will dominate Islam to such an extent that, due to this dominance, the admiration of Muslims towards them will increase, leading them to distance themselves from Islam.

According to the narration of Abu Huraira -may Allah be pleased with him- , The Messenger of Allah -peace be upon him- said in a Noble Saying:

"Indeed, you will follow the ways of those who came before you, step by step, inch by inch, and span by span, so much so that if they entered into a lizard's hole, you would follow them in."

The Companions asked, **"O the Messenger of Allah! Do you mean the Jews and Christians?"**

The Messenger of Allah -peace be upon him- said, "If not these, then who else?" (Ibn Majah: 3994)

At that time, both the rulers and the scholars will side with the disbelievers; some will become Freemasons, some leftists, and some adherents of their own desires.

You saw how King Hussein of Jordan wept for the death of the greatest Jew. Imagine the state of the leaders of the Islamic countries now.

As a matter of fact, The Messenger of Allah -peace be upon him- said in a Noble Saying thus:

"The Hour will not come until hypocrites become the leaders of every nation." (Majma' alZawa'id)

"The plague of materialism and naturalism..."

By "materialism" here is meant that such a veneration for the world will prevail that religion will be forgotten.

The Messenger of Allah -peace be upon him- foretells their condition in another Noble Saying:

"Their religion will be their dirhams and dinars." (Daylami)

They will prefer the deceptive, transient pleasures of the world to the eternal blessings of the hereafter.

The term "Tabiiyyun" literally means naturalists, but it also implies those who follow. That is to say, it carries both meanings.

Such faithless leaders will emerge that the misguided and deceitful followers who adhere to them will stray from the religion.

Allah the Almighty describes them as **"deviants"** in the 54th Verse of Surah Al-Mu'minun. The Messenger of Allah -peace be upon him- refers to them as **"offspring."**

In one of his Noble Saying, he states:

"Undoubtedly, a group from my Community will come after me. They will recite the Qur'an, but its (blessing) will not go beyond their throats. (It will remain only on their tongues.) Just as an arrow passes through its target, they will depart from the religion and never return to it. Indeed, they are the worst of people and animals." (Muslim: 1067)

"With their spread among humanity..."

These departures from religion will become so numerous that they will occupy every corner.

"The foremost task is to save faith in a manner that completely silences philosophy and materialist thought."

With these words, he describes and declares that person as the "Redeemer of Faith."

Indeed, that person will be sent with this mission. During a time when those who deviate into numerous sects are confusing and misleading the people, when they are determined to mix Truth with falsehood, he will be tasked with refuting all erroneous ideas, unveiling the Truth, and rescuing faith from the hands of those pervasive thieves of religion and belief. The goal is to save faith. He will confront all forms of mischief and corruption aimed at obliterating Islam without fear from anyone, will speak the Truths, and will prove his cause with Noble Verse and Noble Saying. He will manifest the Truth with the commands and decrees of Allah and His Messenger.

And all these have been spiritually determined. In terms of words, they have been silenced.

"To protect the believers from deviation, and because this duty requires abandoning both the world and everything else, and necessitates long hours of study, exalted the Mahdi cannot personally perform this task."

These books have been written for nearly twenty years. The caliphate of Exalted the Mahdi is said to last about seven years.

"Because his sovereignty related to the Caliphate of Muhammad -peace be upon him- does not leave him time to engage in it."

Exalted the Mahdi will directly carry out the mission of The Messenger of Allah -peace be upon him-. His duty will be with the sword, not the pen. His life will be solely devoted to Holy Struggle. He will not write anything because he will not have time to do so.

"Surely, a group will perform that duty before him, and he will make use of the extensive works written by this group as his ready program."

It is now understood that these books are being prepared both to save faith and to serve as a ready program for Exalted the Mahdi.

Exalted the Bediüzzaman, twenty years after his passing, it turns out that the books that began to be published were introduced to us by him; first and foremost, he elucidated them.

We have prayed thus:

"O Allah! Send a gift to this Community of Muhammad! Let this man unveil these secrets and collect these pearls." But he will not reveal even a crumb to you. Because this is the morsel of an elephant, an ant cannot swallow it.

And when you read these, you will say: "What revelations, how he has scattered these divine secrets! Would one sell mirrors in a market of the blind?" I know in my heart that you will feel this way. From these clear expressions, it becomes apparent that these books were prepared for Exalted the Mahdi.

"With that, he will fulfill the first task completely."

Indeed, we had said this on the matter as well:

"The Exalted the Allah has sent us to strive with the pen, to cut down divisive enemies of religion with the pen. As for him, He will send him to struggle with the sword."

"The force and spiritual army that this task rests upon are merely a group of disciples who fully possess the qualities of sincerity, loyalty, and solidarity. Even if they are few in number, they are considered as powerful and valuable as a whole army spiritually."

The meaning of this saying is:

The Messenger of Allah -peace be upon him- stated in his Noble Saying:

"Islam began as something strange and will return to being strange as it started. Blessed are the strangers!" (Muslim)

Today, Islam finds itself in a profound state of estrangement.

The reason for this estrangement:

The Messenger of Allah -peace be upon him- stated in another Noble Saying:

"A time will come upon people when nothing will remain of Islam except its name, and nothing will remain of the Qur'an except its script. Their mosques will be splendidly built but devoid of guidance.

Their scholars will be the worst under the heaven; strife will emerge from them and will return to them." (Bayhaqi)

Truly, Islam today is in a state of estrangement. The Messenger of Allah -peace be upon him- defines this spiritual group with his words, **"Blessed are the strangers!"** and signifies that this spiritual group will remain until the Day of Judgment. Additionally, this era is of great significance, with struggles that are profoundly serious. This spiritual group, though small in number, will be immensely strong with the support of Allah Almighty.

The honorable Mahdi Messenger has a distinct mission. He will directly bear the representation of The Messenger of Allah -peace be upon him-, fulfilling his caliphate and his duties. He will strive to rescue Islam from its state of estrangement, for this is the mission for which he will be sent.

The Messenger of Allah -peace be upon him- Our Master began alone and endured many hardships while spreading Islam. Then, at Badr, Allah the Almighty aided him, and Islam emerged victorious. However, the awaited Messenger mission, he will start the struggle with around 305 individuals, the same number as the companions at Badr.

With the companionship of Gabriel and Michael -peace be upon him-, and directly supported by Allah the Almighty he will undertake a significant reform. He will create a profound transformation much like The Messenger of Allah -peace be upon him-, following in his footsteps and revitalizing the religion of Islam.

Through these declarations, Exalted the Bediüzzaman indicated that these books were prepared for Exalted Mahdî Messenger, and also pointed out that these books would serve as a readymade program for him. Additionally, he implied that many people would save their faith by reading these works.

As a matter of fact;

We understand from his revelations that he will confront false scientists and philosophers, fake proponents of The Unity of Being, pseudo sufis, groups that create discord within Islam and go against its teachings, those who seek to extinguish the light of the Islamic faith, and heretical offshoots that have strayed from the religion. He will refute their false and baseless ideas using Noble Verse and Noble Saying, thereby unveiling the Truth.

Even the head of the Directorate of Religious Affairs, who spoke against divine rulings, was confronted by him, and it was directly shown that he had fallen into disbelief, to which he could not respond.

This blessed individual, exalted the Bediüzzaman, through Allah the Almighty's enlightenment, foresaw, knew, and declared everything. Now, we strive to understand his words from that time. Evidently, the ultimate aim was to rescue faith from these opposing groups.

What is the evidence that he was sent by Allah the Almighty?

Firstly, Allah the Almighty has granted the poor what He has never given to anyone else before. Despite having no formal education, these books are sealed with Noble Verse and Sacred saying and Noble Saying.

And for now, these books span approximately seven thousand pages. If destiny allows, with the grace of the Almighty, there will be more.

Within these pages, detailed discussions and explanations are provided on the exoteric knowledge, the knowledge of the path, the knowledge of Truth, and the knowledge of Gnosis.

How should this **"Bestowal"** be understood?

Allah the Most Exalted states in the 7th and 8th Verses of Surah Ad-Duha, **"I have given."** This is how the bestowal happens; it is not personal. An individual cannot comprehend this, nor is it possible for them to do so.

•

The second proof is found in a Noble Saying narrated by Nuaym bin Hammad from Ka'b -may Allah be pleased with him- . This Noble Saying reveals the bearers of the flags and hints at how they will struggle.

"One of the signs of the emergence of the Mahdi is the appearance of flagbearers from the west, led by a lame man from the kinda tribe." (Imam Suyuti, Kitab alArf'il Verdi Fi Akhbar'il Mahdi, p. 99, 13th Noble Saying of the 7th chapter.)

•

The third evidence comes from the awliya of Allah and His Messenger, who have elucidated this matter. We present their explanations before you regarding this knowledge.

This knowledge is so profound that it is called **"Ilmullah" (the Knowledge of Allah).**

These books are composed of secrets. There are many subjects that neither the people of the outer world nor even the people of the inner world can decipher.

For example;

The **"The Greatest Name"** was hidden, but now it has been revealed and can be found in the books.

The **"The Noble Surah Yasin"** was concealed, but now it has been unveiled and is included in the book "Nuri Muhammadi" (the Light of Muhammad).

The hidden meaning in the **Verse "Allahu nurussamawati walard" (Allah is the Light of the heavens and the earth)** has been uncovered.

Some of the declarations of the Saints of Allah we now explain to you, while others we keep concealed.

A brother inquired earlier.

"Could it be that you are the one whom the Great Master Muhyiddin Ibn alArabi -may his secret be sanctified- hinted at?" they asked.

At that time, we responded, "No."

They say again, "Everything that these friends of Allah describe fits you. Are you the Pole?"

Throughout my life, I have strived not to be a Pole, but to be a servant. And always, in my supplications, I earnestly prayed**, "O Allah, make me a servant to you and a follower of Your Beloved!"** Allah the Exalted, grants to whom He wills whatever He wills.

We take pride in our poverty.

As The Messenger of Allah -peace be upon him- said:

"I take pride in my poverty." (Munawi)

The creature has no authority; it is without power. Authority belongs solely to Allah the Exalted.

As I have previously mentioned, the Perfect guide knows himself to be merely a picture. The Perfect guide sees and knows himself to be merely a mask. The Perfect guide sees and knows himself to be merely a rag. He sees and knows how that rag is to be used. Therefore, we say, **"I am a creature without authority, without value. Authority and value belong solely and exclusively to Allah, the Possessor of Majesty and Perfection."**

Understanding this Truth, and to convey it, I felt it necessary to write the book titled "The True Guide is Exalted Allah." For it is always He, always from Him... There is nothing existing except Allah. Because existence is He, and what exists is He... There is no other independent existence or entity...

•

THE GREATEST VERSE OF THE QUR'AN

What is the greatest Verse in Exalted the Qur'an?

The Messenger of Allah, -peace be upon him-, informed us in his Noble Saying that the greatest Verse is in Surah Al-Baqarah.

According to the narration of Abu Hurairah, -may Allah be pleased with him- , The Messenger of Allah, -peace be upon him-, said:

"Everything has its pinnacle, and the pinnacle of the Qur'an is Surah Al-Baqarah. In this Surah, there is a Verse that is the master of all Verses in the Qur'an. That is The Throne Verse." (Tirmidhi: 2881)

Ubey bin Ka'b, -may Allah be pleased with him- , says:

The Messenger of Allah -peace be upon him-, said to me:

"O Abu Mundhir! Do you know which Verse from the Book of Allah you hold in your memory is the greatest?" he asked.

I replied, "Allah and His Prophet know best."

He asked again, **"O Abu Mundhir! Do you know which Verse from the Book of Allah you have memorized is the greatest?"**

In response, I said, **"Allah! There is no deity but Him, Al-Hayy, Al-Qayyum.' (The Throne Verse)"**

Upon this, The Messenger of Allah -peace be upon him- struck my chest and said, **"By Allah, may knowledge be blessed for you, O Abu Mundhir!"** (Muslim: 810)

The Throne Verse, comprising ten sentences, clearly articulates the principles of Divine Unity. It declares Allah's unique unity, His being Al-Hayy and Al-Qayyum, His transcendence above human attributes like slumber and forgetfulness, His maintenance of the universe, that no one can intercede without His permission, His knowledge encompassing the past and future, His power encompassing the heavens and the earth, and His majestic essence. These are the core tenets of the belief in Allah's oneness thoroughly expressed.

We are now unveiling and explaining the secret of the greatest Verse of Exalted the Qur'an.

Allah the Almighty declares:

"Allah is He beside whom there is no deity, the" Al-Hayy", the "Al-Qayyum"." (Al-Baqarah: 255 Al' Imran: 2)

Divinity and servitude belong solely to Him. He is singular in every aspect. His existence has no beginning. His existence is perpetual, it never ends.

His existence testifies to itself. Every being is a manifestation of His power. Everything that exists, exists through Him.

He is the Al-Hayy (Living): He is endowed with life from eternity to eternity. All life and perpetuity from past eternity to future eternity depend on His essence.

He is the Al-Qayyum (Eternal Sustainer): With His essence and perfect attributes, He rules over all and every being exists through Him.

Allah the Almighty is alive with His essence, while His creations live by the life He grants, by His power. He has bestowed means for everything to stand firm until a designated time. Everything exists through the Truth. This Verse explains that the Exalted the Allah sustains all existence with life and that everything stands through Him.

A human attempts to measure everything yet cannot measure himself, for he perceives from the outside.

It was previously stated that no created thing is Allah. Everything is a veil to the Exalted the Allah; He is within all. He is closer to everything than everything is to itself. Everything is not Him, yet nothing is separate from Him.

In other words, He created everything. All that exists subsists through His presence. And you too are there, you too subsist through the Exalted the Allah, a mere particle subsists through the Exalted the Allah, as does an entire universe.

Yet, everyone sees themselves, sees the particle, and sees the universe. They read the Noble Verse separately but do not understand what they are reading.

In summary, everything subsists through Him, you subsist through Him, the particle does, the cosmos does, everything...

A person reads the Noble Verse but does not know that they and the universe subsist through Him.

This is why this is the greatest Verse.

The Grand Commentators have said, *"Everything subsists through Him,"* but they did not say, *"You also subsist through Him,"* because they remained on the exterior point of the spiritual, inner knowledge.

The people of gnosis know what Allah the Almighty has taught. Because He teaches and manifests distinctly to each person, this knowledge is unique to each.

Since He does not give what He gives to one to anyone else, no one can know that knowledge.

Exalted the Muhyiddin Ibn al-Arabi -may his secret be sanctified-:

"Allah the Almighty neither granted this seal of sainthood to us nor to those before us, but He has hidden this station from us," he declared.

In other words, what He granted to him, He did not grant to those before us, nor will He grant to those after us. He will grant it only to him. Just as in the Surah Al-Duha, when Allah addressed the Prophet Muhammad -peace be upon him- saying, **"I have given,"** this knowledge is also a **"Granting"** and nothing else. This knowledge is purely a gift from Allah the Almighty. It does not depend on the person or on learning. It is the benevolence of Allah the Almighty.

•

There is no end to The Word of Divine Unity. However, reciting The Word of Divine Unity is very arduous.

There is no Allah but Allah, Muhammad the Messenger of Allah; as we say this, we know, see, and declare that everything is from Him and through Him, whether it pertains to ourselves or the entire universe, that it is merely a mask. Since the universe is a mask, it is not Allah. That constitutes **"No"**. The truly existent is Allah. "O Lord! I am not among those who worship the mask. I know and declare that these are masks and say **"No"** to them. Only **"There is no Allah but Allah "You** exist, and when I say **"Muhammad the Messenger of Allah,"** I acknowledge that the universe was created from him (Prophet Muhammad). I know that the entire universe is a mask and that only He exists. From His own light, He created His beloved, confirming in the second phrase that His beloved is His light. This is how we declare The Word of Divine Unity. And we both know, see, and declare Allah the Almighty. The core of The Word of Divine Unity is this. For I declare The Word of Divine Unity knowing that I am a mask in the universe. Only He exists. From His light, He created light, and from that light, He adorned the universe. Wherever you look, you will see Exalted the Muhammad.

In a Sacred saying:

"If it were not for you, I would not have created the spheres," He declares. (K. Hafâ. vol. 2, p. 164)

The reason for the existence of creation lies here.

"The universe's name is Muhammad -peace be upon him-."

•

Our esteemed Prophet, The Messenger of Allah -peace be upon him-has pointed in a Noble Saying:

"Allah's Greatest Name through which prayers are accepted, is found in these three surah:

Al-Baqarah, Al' Imran, and Taha." (Abu Dawood)

In these surah, the Verse **"Allahu la ilaha illa Huwal Al-Hayyul Al-Qayyum" (Allah! There is no deity except Him, the EverLiving, the Sustainer of existence)** is mentioned.

This Verse is the Greatest Name. However, it is concealed. Why is the Greatest Name hidden, and who should know it? Let's first unveil this mystery. The Greatest Name is revealed only to one who seeks Allah the Almighty through Allah the Almighty Himself. Those who know this secret ask for nothing but Allah the Almighty. Those who know the Greatest Name choose only Allah the Almighty.

If you throw money in the trash, it's waste; if you turn it into gold, it's a gain. Because if you ask for something else with the Greatest Name, He grants it, but this granting leads to one's destruction. The Greatest Name is surely accepted, but it is only given to those who seek refuge in Allah the Almighty and ask for nothing but Him. It is not given to anyone else. Internal, never external. This is the distinction between the external and the internal. It is bestowed only to those whom He wills. Not all saints seek internally; they one who knows this secret does not ask for anything except Allah the Almighty. Such a person asks with a loving plea. Allah the Almighty loves them, and they love Allah the Almighty seeking no one else. Through the Greatest Name, they seek only Allah's love, His consent, His grace, His mercy. They ask for nothing else. They supplicate to Him alone with Greatest Name. This is the unopened secret of the Greatest Name. Whatever one asks for with Ismi Azam, Allah the Almighty bestows, but it may lead to their ruin. Hence, it remains undisclosed. Yet, the one to whom the Greatest Name is revealed desires only Allah the Almighty. They are in direct communion. They do not seek Allah the Almighty outside but inside themselves. Their entire purpose, their trade, is internal. They ask with loving pleadings. They do not seek Allah the Almighty outside; they search inside. When they stand in prayer, they stand with Him. Their supplication, worship, and remembrance are all with Him but always search externally. For some, it manifests internally as much as He desires. This individual has dealings with Allah the Almighty alone. However, this is disclosed only to those He intends.

In the Sufi narrative book "Keys of the Hearts: Words and Notes" Volume 2, page 244, this topic was previously explained as follows. We include it here for blessings:

"True gratitude is gratitude directed to Allah with Allah. Genuine prayer and true remembrance are of this nature. Praise is similarly so.

When worship is performed with Him, the essence of worship is attained. If a person boasts with the Exalted the Allah, they make the most beautiful boast.

Being grateful to Allah with Allah, remembering Allah with Allah, worshipping with the Exalted the Allah, and boasting with the Exalted the Allah... These are not achieved by leafing through books, nor by empty words. If the Exalted the Allah, from eternity, grants a servant favor and grace, and connects them to a beloved; through this intermediary, He places the essence of these in the heart. Through this, the book of the heart is perused, and these are realized. Do not think they occur otherwise. In other words, supplications are made to Him with the capacity He has inscribed.

The blessings, favors, and grace of the Exalted the Allah are infinite. In The Noble Qur'an, it is stated:

'And whatever blessings you have, it is from Allah.' (Nahl: 53)

Everything belongs to Him, and everything is from Him."

In other words, the essence is Allah, and my words are Allah, as Allah Most High had made known to me in my youth.

I, the humble one, express this in three words: Upon entering, they said to me Allah; upon leaving, they said to me Allah.

•

Allah the Almighty created The Messenger of Allah, -peace be upon him- from His own light. He adorned the universe with that light. Wherever you look, you find that light. Because He bestowed upon him, the entire cosmos is in need of him.

The humble one says, "You are the light of Allah the Almighty the pride and joy of all worlds." I take pride in him, I find joy in him. Because he is the Mercy to all worlds, I find my existence through him.

In the Verse of the Qur'an:

"We sent you as a mercy to all worlds." (Anbiya: 107)

Since he is the A mercy to all worlds, you have also received your share of that mercy, and your existence is through him. The entire universe receives from there. The moon, the sun, the earth, the sky, everything receives from there.

The saint of the time also finds his existence through him. As it manifests in the Khatam al-Awliya (Seal of the Saints), the entire world receives from him. But not from him personally, rather from what is within him.

However, a person does not see what is within that origin and believes they find their existence through the individual. Lift the veil, Allah. Thus is the universe.

•

When it comes to Khatam al-Awliya (Seal of the Saints), he too received what he desired. How did he wish for it? It is not difficult for Allah the Almighty to encompass all worlds within a single being.

Imam Rabbani "-may his secret be sanctified-" states:

"What difficulty is there for Allah?

To fill the universe within one person."

When Allah the Almighty reveals Himself to a heart, not a single particle other than Allah remains in that heart. In the place where His manifestation occurs, everything exists. All the worlds are encompassed within it.

"I boast of my poverty." (K. Hafâ)

The secret of this Noble Saying has manifested within him.

He knows he owns nothing. He boasts of his poverty. He attains the same secret. Lift the veil, He is there.

Is there any difficulty for Allah to encompass all worlds within him?

In a Sacred saying:

"I cannot be contained by the heavens or the earth, but I am contained in the heart of my believing servant."

When He resides there, there is no one else but Him. Within that heart, neither garments nor masks hold sway. He has encompassed all worlds within it. When He manifests, there is no individual, no garment, no mask only Him. Indeed, all the worlds are in Him. He is in it.

He, who cannot be contained anywhere, is present in whichever heart can contain Him.

The entire universe draws from Him, drawing from that heart. However, the heart itself holds no authority; only His authority prevails. Yet, He manifests in that heart. All the world's reception from that heart is essentially a reception from Him, from the Exalted the Allah. Hence, the past and the future receive in this manner.

"The heart of a believing servant is The Throne of the Most Merciful Allah." (K. Hafa: 2/130)

How can The Throne of the Most Merciful be? Lift the veil, and He is there. But He is beneath that veil.

It means:

Encapsulating all creation within one person is not beyond His power. So, how does He fit the entire universe into one person? When the Exalted the Allah manifests in that heart, not a speck of the person remains only He exists. He folds all worlds into him. The condition is that no particle of the person remains in it.

Ali Havvas "-may his secret be sanctified-" said:

"Indeed, all the saints who have come and will come, receive their spiritual grace and aid from these two blessed entities."

In reality, it is always Allah. He gives to one through another, and so forth.

Allah the Almighty the Most High, has conveyed this secret to these great individuals. He has informed them of what He has bestowed upon each one.

From the Khatam al-Anbiya (Seal of the Prophets), the entire universe receives.

From the Khatam al-Awliya (Seal of the Saints), all of humanity receives.

In Truth, there is nothing but Allah the Almighty. They are merely veils. However He manifests, so it is.

The entire universe doesn't receive, rather it is given to the universe from there. That is to say, Allah the Most High, gives beneath that veil. It is directly Allah the Most High, who gives; there is no question of receiving. It is given from there. The individual is a veil, and within that veil is Him.

When He occupies it, there is nothing else besides Him. At that point, the clothes or masks hold no significance.

•

Journey from Truth to Truth; Journey to Allah with Allah: These are the people of Allah. It signifies Allah the Almighty drawing and bringing a servant closer to Himself. These are the individuals predestined from eternity by the grace of Allah the Almighty. They are born in that state, even before birth, they're predestined. Hence, the paths of progress are open to them as much as the portion given to them from eternity. They came from Truth, and they go to Truth with Truth. They reach Truth. If Allah does not draw a servant to Himself, no one can approach Truth on their own.

The path from Truth to the servant is filled with happiness. The path from the servant to Truth is full of calamities. The journey from Truth does not mean heading to Truth. These are the chosen ones of Allah.

Journey to Truth; Journey to Allah with the self: These are the people of the devil. They are promoted and supported by the devil and chosen by their mothers, fathers, and siblings. They try to walk on the path of Truth with their desires, supported by the devil. They have taken their own desires as Allah, holding the idol of self and claiming to guide others. They may appear to move towards Truth, but it is a movement towards perversion, not guidance. They strive for three things: profit, fame, and rank.

They follow in the way and footsteps of the devil. These are called the masters of the devil. They are bandits, obstructing those who wish to reach Truth.

Hence, life and Truth lie in the journey bestowed by the grace of Allah the Almighty. All misguidance and deviation are on the path supported by the devil.

•

The summary of the word;

Manifested in one is the Khatam al-Anbiya (Seal of the Prophets), and in the other is the Khatam al-Awliya (Seal of the Saints) and those who receive, receive from these two sources.

The essence and secret of all knowledge is this. If The Glorious Truth had not taught or informed me of this knowledge, how would I ever know it? It is not found in any book that I might read.

In His Noble Verse, Allah the Almighty states:

"Allah grants wisdom to whom He wills. To whom wisdom is granted, they indeed receive an abundant good. But only those of sound intellect understand and ponder this." (Al-Baqarah: 269)

The knowledge hidden deep within the hearts and the chests of those close to Allah the Almighty is the knowledge of gnosis. It is not found in the lines of books.

Thus, the reason why these Noble Ones have described today and this knowledge is explained. Allah the Most High has truly revealed and informed them of this Truth. We hear this mystery through their communication. By listening to these subtleties, we become acquainted with the Truth.

•

"For each of you, we have appointed a law and a way."
(Al-Maeda: 48)

SUFISM

A SCHOOL OF KNOWLEDGE AND WISDOM

CHAPTER 4

- What Is Sufism? Who Are Its People?
- Sufism: A School of Knowledge and Wisdom
- The Exalted Path Is an Army
- The Exalted Path Is a Hospital
- The Exalted Path Is a Marketplace
- The People of Sufism Are Divided into Three Categories
- The Ranks of Saints
- Its Evidences of Existence
- The Harmony in the Universe

WHAT IS SUFISM?

WHO ARE ITS PEOPLE?

• Sufism is a school of knowledge and wisdom. It is a school established to comprehend the divine secrets within the chamber of mysteries and understand the Truth. Through this education, one delves into the essence of all knowledge. It is about distillation of meaning, like butter being purified, passing through stages. I entered as a significant person, only to realize I was a humble particle. This is the purpose of Sufism. To achieve this state, Sufism is essential. It is an indispensable path for every Muslim.

The necessity has been proven by Noble Verse. Allah the Almighty states in His Noble Verse:

"For each of you we have appointed a way and a path." (Al-Maeda: 48)

Fakruddin Razi and some other expositors have interpreted this Noble Verse as, **"O my servants! I have made two things obligatory for each of you. First, the Islamic law, and then the path."** This is because **"Minhaj"** linguistically means **"an enlightened path."**

And there are many similar Noble Verse.

Allah the Almighty:

"Establish prayer for my remembrance!" (Taha: 14)

With this Noble Verse, just as He commanded the prayer;

"O you who believe! Remember Allah abundantly!" (Al-Ahzab: 41)

In this Noble Verse, He commands remembering Him. Thus, prayer is a divine order, and so is remembrance of Allah.

Since people's temperaments differ by nature, when the Prophet -peace be upon him- received the command for remembrance of Allah, he directed Exalted the Abu Bakr -may Allah be pleased with him- to practice silent remembrance and Exalted the Ali -may Allah be pleased with him- to teach vocal remembrance and to guide others in this practice.

From that day to the present, this tradition has been passed down the hands and hearts of great spiritual masters, reaching our time in an unbroken chain. This eminent lineage is confirmed by consistent transmission and has been acknowledged as true by a vast community in every era.

Imam Rabbani -may his secret be sanctified- stated:

"Denying what is established in religion through consistent transmission is disbelief."

A Verse from the Holy Qur'an also states:

"When you have completed the prayer, remember Allah standing, sitting, and lying on your sides." (An-Nisâ: 103)

Those who follow and execute this command earn the love of the Divine.

Those who remain on the surface interpret the remembrance mentioned in the Qur'anic Verses and Noble Sayings merely as prayer. Due to their ignorance, they overlook the deeper Truths. However, when they transition to the inner dimensions and turn within themselves, they will witness its reality.

Allah the Exalted says:

"Do not be like those who forgot Allah and so He made them forget themselves. They are the defiantly disobedient." (Hashr: 19)

According to this divine Verse, believers who are heedless of remembrance and reflection are described as "Fâsık" (Transgressor).

Allah the Exalted's love for a servant undoubtedly hinges on the servant's love for and engagement in remembrance of Allah.

To adorn our outward selves, we must follow the Islamic law of our Master, -peace be upon him-. To illuminate our inner world, we must adhere to his path. The outward order is established through Islamic law, and the inward order is established through path.

The inner realm is attained through obligatory and supererogatory acts. Just as the body is obligated to perform obligatory acts, the spirit is tasked with supererogatory acts.

It is clear that one cannot benefit from the path if they do not guide their words and actions within the boundaries of the Islamic law. They are like a patient who takes medicine but does not follow the prescribed diet.

It must be well understood that all paths have been pursued by the divine command of Allah the Exalted. The foundation and value of all paths, without exception, rest on the pure Islamic law. A path that contradicts Islam is not a true path at all.

Sufism is not merely a science of words but a science of states and practices. It cannot be comprehended or conveyed through theoretical knowledge alone, without being lived, tasted, and felt.

The purpose of entering the exalted path is to attain conviction in the beliefs required by Islamic law. This is the essence of true faith.

For instance, a person who first believes in the existence of Allah by hearing about Him begins to believe by discovering and understanding, thus, their faith reaches perfection.

On the other hand, the difficulties posed by the "The commanding self" in performing acts of worship are removed, allowing them to be carried out easily and with love.

In the realms of knowledge and Truth, Sufism serves as a great agent in perfecting faith. However, under certain corrupt perceptions, it was tarnished by suspicions, fame, and selfish gains, causing a loss of its purity and essence.

A few fake spiritual guides, deluding some ignorant people into believing they are wise, have claimed Sufism, creating instability in thoughts.

The illuminated path of Sufism consists of the words and actions of The Messenger of Allah -peace be upon him-. Its source is the Qur'an and Noble Saying. It has come to us with great purity and sincerity, without losing any of its originality. Throughout centuries, it has been the greatest agent in embodying Islamic morality, eradicating discord and corruption, establishing genuine brotherhood, ensuring unity and solidarity, curing the spiritual diseases of humanity, and perfecting faith. By the secret blessing of this tradition, the divine decrees will remain until the Day of Judgment.

As in every age, today too, Sufism exists in its entirety. Especially in the Naqshbandi Order, there will be no shortage of spiritual guides until the end of time. That sacred chamber; from room to room, from circle to circle, has been carried forward and has never been corrupted.

Regarding the Noble Saying: "Close all the doors leading to the mosque except for the door of Abu Bakr." (Bukhari),

Our esteemed **Master Es'ad Sir** -may his secret be sanctified- interpreted it as:

"O Allah! When all the paths of paths come to an end, may the path of Abu Bakr remain until the Day of Judgment?"

Allah the Almighty has ensured that scholars are always present on Earth to teach external sciences, just as He has supplied people of the path to impart esoteric knowledge.

Even though he was known as the "Proof of Islam," Imâmı Gazâli -may his secret be sanctified- turned towards Sufism. After tasting the pleasures of the path of spiritual journey, he described his condition as follows:

"...Then I reflected upon my condition. Oh, what did I see! I was deeply entangled in worldly ties. These connections enveloped me from every direction. I scrutinized my actions and found that the best of them were teaching and instructing. Yet, even in this domain, I was preoccupied with sciences that were insignificant and useless for the path to the Hereafter. I

examined my intention regarding teaching and realized that it was not for the sake of Allah's approval but to gain position and fame. I deduced that in my current state, I was standing at the edge of a cliff, and if I did not take action to correct my situation, I would fall into the fire."

"I realized with certainty that the Sufis are indeed the ones who have found the way to Allah. Their manner of proceeding is the most beautiful, their path the most correct, and their morals the purest of all.

Even if the intelligence of all the wise people in the world, the wisdom of the philosophers, and the knowledge of the scholars of external sciences who know all the details of Islamic law were combined, they could not change or improve upon the conduct and morals of the Sufis.

All their outward and inward movements and feelings are taken from the light of the Prophetic lamp. Indeed, on Earth, there is no guide or source of light other than the light of Prophet Hood." (Al Munqidh min al Dalal)

•

• **The Noble Path is like an army**. It has a magnificent organization. Firstly, it involves struggling with the self, at times fighting against the misguided, and providing material help in times of need... However, let me reveal to you that the greatest struggle is through the pen. This is called the greater Holy Struggle.

Struggling with the self is extremely important. Because without reforming the self, the struggle is futile. In this regard, we have said, "O ascetic! I see you equipped to conquer, but you do not realize you are conquered. First, turn inward, learn the enemy within, and liberate your home and rooms from occupation."

First, a person must conquer their ego and, after this conquest, perform their deeds in the way of divine pleasure. Otherwise, the idol within cannot be conquered. Break your inner idol first, then embark on the conquest.

You may battle an enemy, whether five or ten people; but with the pen, you battle millions. That is why we have called the struggle with the pen greater struggle.

By saying this, I am also encouraging you to join this Holy Struggle. And when you do this in the name of Allah, undoubtedly He will assist you, He will be your support, your protector. Even if the entire universe stands against you, if He wills, not a single hair of yours will be harmed.

Therefore, one who joins such an army must know very well the tasks they are to perform. It is essential to struggle with their self, their body, their wealth, and their pen.

The Most Noble Messenger -peace be upon him- said in a Noble Saying:

" Holy Struggle is ordained upon you." (Abu Dawood)

This path is so orderly and disciplined that it is managed by spiritual commanders. The Commander in Chief holds the proxy of The Messenger of Allah -peace be upon him-.

To the leaders of this path, the Exalted the Allah bestows such blessings and favors that their goal is not to reach but to make others reach. The spiritual commander thinks of the safety of the army, not of himself.

•

•The Noble path is akin to a hospital. Such a hospital where the chief physician is none other than the Master of the Universe, Prophet Muhammad -peace be upon him-. His representatives, the Perfect guides, serve as the doctors in this hospital.

The Messenger of Allah -peace be upon him- has instructed us to consult a skilled physician for the diagnosis and treatment of physical illnesses. Similarly, he commanded seeking out a spiritual healer for deliverance from spiritual maladies.

These spiritual diseases are of utmost importance.

"In their hearts is a disease." (Al-Baqarah: 10)

Pointed out by this Verse are the dreadful diseases that, if left untreated, destroy eternal life and are therefore exceedingly perilous.

A person who is ill cannot appreciate the taste of exquisite food. The return of one's sense of taste is contingent upon treating the illness. Similarly, a heart conquered by the commanding self is sick and cannot savor acts of worship and devotion.

Envy, arrogance, wrath, lust, envy, hypocrisy, greed, self-admiration... these vices are heart diseases.

We came with a beautiful heart. To preserve that beauty, one must shed these base, animalistic traits.

To attain healing:

"Healing for hearts is in the remembrance of Allah." (Munawi)

As per the Noble Saying, it is imperative for us to frequently remember the Exalted the Allah.

With remembrance of Allah, the chambers of the heart, self, secret, hidden, and most hidden, are liberated from the occupation of the soul. If the final chamber of the whole self is also freed, sovereignty then shifts to the soul. The lamps of the subtleties light up, a person repents from all evil, shedding even the thought of wrongdoing.

Such a person becomes purified from ignoble morals and liberated from bestial attributes. They discover the paths of perfection. All their limbs begin to act according to divine laws.

Moreover, even those preordained by Allah the Almighty from eternity require surgery. This surgery can only be performed by the Perfect guides, who are deputies of The Messenger of Allah -peace be upon him-. The doctor designated as the surgeon performs this essential operation for those with eternal fortune: to deliver their destiny, eradicate the roots of worldly attachments, expel the devil, expand the chest, and plant the saplings of gnosis.

•

• The Noble Path is a marketplace. It is such a marketplace that one who steps into this field must be ready to sacrifice life and possessions to engage in trade with the Exalted the Allah. What bliss it is to attain the honor of trading with the Creator!

Allah the Almighty has decreed:

"Indeed, Allah has purchased the lives and properties of the believers in exchange for Paradise. They fight in the cause of Allah, kill and are killed." (At-Tawba: 111)

Anyone who enters this marketplace must seek refuge in Allah, saying, "O Allah! I accept this transaction, accept it from me and make it easy for me." Once on the field, they should not turn back. Since you have made a covenant with Allah and accepted the transaction, your task is over.

In another Noble Verse, it is said:

"O you who believe! Shall I guide you to a commerce that will save you from a painful torment?" (As-Saff: 10)

This question is posed to encourage you. Following this, Allah the Almighty clarifies this commerce by saying:

"That you may believe in Allah and His Messenger and strive in the way of Allah with your wealth and your lives. That is best for you, if you but knew." (As-Saff: 11)

Commerce; is the act of putting forth one's wealth, labor, and all capabilities to gain profit. In this context, faith and Struggle in the path of Allah are likened to commerce. The believer, who strives with their wealth and life for Allah's cause, has not merely spoken of doing so but has taken action to gain the great reward promised by Allah. By spending their material wealth in Allah's way, they have transformed it into spiritual wealth. The real profit of this commerce will be seen in the hereafter:

“Then Allah will forgive you your sins and admit you into gardens beneath which rivers flow and pleasant dwellings in the Gardens of Eternity. That is the supreme success.” (As-Saff: 12)

This commerce cannot even be compared to worldly trade.

•

Those on the Path of Sufism are divided into Three Categories:

1. Perfect

2. Complete

3. Imitator

The Perfect are divided into three categories:

1. Those who a spiritual share in the prophetic inheritance of our Master, The Most Noble Messenger -peace be upon him-.

Qur'anic Verse states:

“And of those we have created, there is a group that guides with the Truth and establishes justice thereby.” (A’râf: 181)

The officers of guidance, referred to here, are the honored Perfect guide, the Perfect guides among the great saints of Allah.

2. Those who inherit the portion of sainthood.

It is stated in the Noble Verse:

“If ye know not, ask of those who possess the Remembrance.” (Nahl: 43)

By "those who possess the Remembrance," it means the revered saints of Allah.

3. Those who have received a share from prophecy and a share from sainthood.

It is stated in the Noble Verse:

“If ye fear Allah, He will teach you.” (Al-Baqarah: 282)

Here, three Noble Verse have been presented to you. Exalted the Allah commands and announces that these people are the true experts in this matter.

The true spiritual guide is none other than the Exalted the Allah. A Perfect guide resembles a scarecrow, preventing crows from gathering grains... A Perfect guide is also a barrier, ensuring that Truth and falsehood do not intermingle...

A Perfect guide, remaining within his bounds, does not encroach upon others. He provides direction but does not possess the authority to lead the disciple to the ultimate destination. Those granted the authority to lead, by the permission of Allah the Almighty were recently elaborated upon through three Verses from the Qur'an Verses.

As for the imitators, these have indeed taken over the field today. They act on assumptions, and none of their deeds or actions align with divine commands.

Consider a metaphor: the honeybee produces honey, while the wasp merely buzzes. From a distance, they may appear identical, but those with true insight can distinguish between them.

For this reason, the path is one of practice, not merely theoretical knowledge. Its delight cannot be known until it is tasted and lived.

•

THE STATIONS OF THE SAINTS

We shall speak of some of the blessings, positions, and ranks that Allah the Almighty bestows upon His beloved and chosen servants.

These saints, who are assigned specific duties, hold meetings at appointed times. While most of these gatherings take place in the sacred city of Mecca and the Prophet's Mosque, they are also convened in various other places, even in locations one would never imagine.

They attend these gatherings by command and await the decree, the order that will be given.

This decree comes from the Exalted the Allah to The Most Noble Beloved -peace be upon him-, and from The Most Noble Beloved -peace be upon him- to the pole of the time, the deputy.

When The Messenger of Allah -peace be upon him- is present at these gatherings, the authority of the pole ceases, and the verdict of The Messenger of Allah -peace be upon him- prevails; he gives the orders. Subsequently, the deputy conveys the message and the execution of the command begins. They act according to the decree; no one can act independently without a command.

They are servants, attentive to the given orders. And they are only vested with the authority to execute what is commanded. However, without general authority, specific authority holds no power. That being said, they may discuss within the scope of their granted authority. They deliberate amongst themselves on their subjects. Yet, a given command is not to be deliberated.

Since that command carries the decree of Allah the Almighty these decrees cannot be contested. They have no right to the slightest intervention. Even the faintest desire to alter it in their hearts would be imperfect.

Why? Because they are servants. They are servants of the Exalted the Allah and His Messenger -peace be upon him-. They merely look at the command and execute what is commanded.

Whatever Allah the Almighty wills, that manifests. Not even a prophet, let alone a servant, can interfere with the divine decree. The dominion is His; He grants it to whomever He wishes. The creature holds no decree; He manifests as He wills.

Let us present to you the state of those who attend these gatherings:

If Allah the Almighty wills, He may have the person physically present in that assembly, or He may have their spirituality present, depending on what is commanded... That is to say, while the person is seated, their spirituality may attend the meeting, or while the person is physically present, their spirituality is here as a representative. Allah the Almighty commands whomever He wills as He wills; the creature has no decree.

Every era boasts one hundred and twenty-four thousand saints mirroring the one hundred and twenty-four thousand prophets.

These saints are divided into four categories:

1 Those who know they are saints, and the people know as well.

2 Those who know, but the people do not.

3 Those who are unknown to themselves, yet known to the people.

4 Those who neither know themselves, nor are known by the people.

Why do they not know themselves? Because they do not deem themselves worthy. Allah the Almighty has veiled and concealed them.

Not all of these saints are given tasks, only a few are chosen.

The most righteous among them number five hundred. From these five hundred, three hundred are selected. From these three hundred, forty are chosen. From these forty, seven are distinguished. From these seven, five are chosen. From these five, three are elevated. And from these three, one is singled out.

When one transitions to the hereafter, one of three successors is chosen, filling each vacancy from the next rank. Ultimately, an ordinary person is elevated to the rank of the recently deceased saint, ensuring that these 124,000 saints are always present. Their numbers do not diminish.

They are designated according to their duties: spiritual pole, nobles, substitutes, supports, two leaders, succor, trustees, deputies, attracted ones... and similar titles.

Their lives are a secret known to Allah, and they are safeguarded everywhere.

Allah the Almighty says in a sacred saying, **"None knows my saints under my domes but me."**

Their names and forms are known, but their spirituality and luminosity remain concealed.

The Messenger of Allah -peace be upon him- stated in a Noble Saying, **"Indeed, there is a paradise on earth. One who finds it will have no desire for the heavenly paradise. That paradise is the gnosis."**

We refer to this as the paradise of the heart, a life that surpasses everything.

"Ma arafnâke Hakka ma'rifatike ya Ma'ruf = we could not know you as you deserve to be known, O Known One!"

Allah the Exalted proclaims in His Noble Verse:

"Among the believers are men who have been true to their covenant with Allah. Some of them have fulfilled their pledge with their lives, and others are waiting to do so." (Al-Ahzab: 23)

These are the ones who are deeply devoted to Allah, keeping their promise and awaiting His judgment.

As The Messenger of Allah -peace be upon him- asked Haritha -may Allah be pleased with him- , **"What is the reality of your faith?" to which he replied, "I passed my nights in sleepless vigilance and my days in thirst, withdrawing myself from the world."** The Messenger of Allah -peace be upon him- then said to him, **"You have become a one who knows, you have understood. Continue on your path."**

The scholar often needs the saint, but the saint does not need the scholar.

A scholar disciplines the ignorant, while a saint disciplines the scholars.

And the one who disciplines the saint is none other than Allah and The Messenger of Allah -peace be upon him-.

As indicated in the Noble Verse:

"Fear Allah; and Allah will teach you." (Al-Baqarah: 282)

•

The Saints of Allah are known by various names and professions. Some scholars have described them according to their ranks:

Among Allah's creation, there is one person whose heart is aligned with the heart of Israfil (Angel of the Trumpet).

Among His creation, there are three individuals whose hearts are aligned with the heart of Mikail (Angel of Sustenance).

Among His creation, there are five individuals whose hearts are aligned with the heart of Gabriel.

Among His creation, there are seven individuals whose hearts are aligned with the heart of Abraham.

Among Allah's creation, there are forty individuals whose hearts are aligned with the heart of Moses.

Among the creation of Allah, there are three hundred individuals whose hearts are aligned with the heart of Adam.

Ultimately, there are five hundred saintly servants of Allah.

When he passes away, he ascends from three to one higher.

When he passes from three, he rises to five.

When he passes from five, he ascends to seven.

When he passes from seven, he rises to forty.

When he passes from forty, he ascends to three hundred.

When he passes from three hundred, he rises to five hundred.

When he passes from five hundred, Allah the Almighty places whomever He wills.

In every age, there are one hundred twenty-four thousand present.

Because of them, Allah the Almighty deflects all kinds of calamities.

The substitutes are distinguished by four traits: speaking little, eating little, sleeping little, and remaining separate from people.

They are called substitutes because when they disappear, a spiritual form is left in their place as a substitute.

•

The characteristics of each class of saints:

Spiritual pole: A singular being who embodies all perfection, known as the spiritual helper. There is only one in every era.

Nobles: Those who do not look towards anything but the Truth, carrying the burdens of creatures and striving to alleviate their hardships. They are devout in worship and obedience, generous, patient, modest, and find joy in giving everything to the Truth.

Substitutes: These are individuals free from delusion and fantasy, consistent and righteous, who sleep little and rise early for worship; they are people of virtue and excellence.

Supports: Found in the four corners of the world east, west, north, and south these individuals strictly adhere to divine commands, spending their nights awake in worship.

Two leaders: Positioned to the right and left of the Pole. They are exceedingly cautious of even the smallest sin; embodying asceticism, Allah consciousness, sincerity, and modesty.

Succor: Chief spiritual axis is a blessed individual. His prayers are not rejected but accepted; he is a majestic figure who resolves important and enigmatic matters.

Trustees: These are individuals who do not reveal their benevolence nor hide their malevolence, and they do not love the world or worldly possessions.

Deputies: Possessors of profound secrets who unveil the depths of their own self yet refrain from disclosing those secrets.

Attracted ones: Those whose place in the sight of Allah is like that of a nursing infant; they have no control over their will, being entirely under the divine power of Allah the Almighty. They are in the station of divine friendship.

•

In His Noble Verse, The Exalted Truth declares:

"Allah strengthens with His aid whom He pleases." (Al' Imran: 13)

These are the servants whom Allah the Almighty supports and assists with His grace.

"This is a mercy from my Lord." (Kahf: 98)

The Messenger of Allah -peace be upon him- Our Master, describes the friends of Allah the Exalted, in his Noble Saying:

"The friends of Allah are those who, when seen, remind one of Allah. (Provided the one who sees them has no other desire than worldly desires.)" (Jami' alSaghir)

"Not cursing any creature is a sign of the 'Substitutes' who are in the station of sainthood." (Munawi)

"The term 'Evvâb' is used for those who, reflecting on their past sins between themselves and Allah, repent and seek forgiveness." (Munawi)

•

These individuals provide spiritual guidance to societies, holding them under their spiritual supervision. Just as they take care of individuals, they also assist and manage the general issues of Muslims. This occurs with the permission and command of Allah the Exalted.

In the Noble Verse, it is stated:

"All praise is due to Allah, and peace be upon His chosen servants." (Naml: 59)

Just as Allah the Exalted, granted miracles to His chosen Prophets, peace be upon them, He also granted some of His friends, the saints, and miraculous gifts.

The extraordinary states manifested in the hands of our revered Prophets, known as miracles, are called "mucize" in Islam. Similarly, when such states occur through the permission and will of Allah the Almighty in His devoted servants, they are called "saintly miracles."

In a Noble Saying.

"Beware of the foresight of a true believer, for he sees with the light of Allah, the Mighty and the Majestic." (Munawî)

Both miracles and miraculous gifts fundamentally reflect the eternal and infinite power of Allah the Almighty manifesting at that moment.

A miraculous gifts is also considered a miracle for the Prophet whom the saint follows, as it is bestowed upon him as a reward for his adherence to the Prophet.

Miraculous gifts is not a prerequisite for sainthood. Just as it is obligatory for the Prophets to demonstrate miracles, it is obligatory for the Saints of Allah to hide their miraculous gifts.

It is not proper to evaluate these friends of Allah solely based on their unveiling and miraculous gifts. A *Saint* may exhibit no miraculous gifts at all.

Although he was the most esteemed among the companions of the Prophet, there is no record of any miraculous gifts from Siddiq al-Akbar -may Allah be pleased with him- .

The Messenger of Allah -peace be upon him- states in a Noble Saying:

"Except for the Prophet, Abu Bakr is the best among all people." (Jami' alSaghir)

When someone remarked to our Master, Shahı Naqshband -may his secret be sanctified-, "Sir, no miraculous gifts occur from you," he responded, **"Is being able to stand under the weight of our many sins not a miracle in itself?"**

Throughout their lives, only a few miracles were manifest from them.

Once, while traveling to a distant location with a disciple, night approached. They traveled and traveled, yet night did not fall. When they reached their destination, the sun suddenly set. Turning to his disciple, he remarked**, "My son, these are merely games of the Path. The goal is Allah."**

The people of Truth never valued miracles, for Exalted the Allah sufficed them. Yes, miracles are indeed divine blessings. However, let's explain why some seek to become known for miracles.

Some saints have their faces turned towards Exalted the Allah. They desire only His decree and presence. Imagine how purified they are by Him, such that they desire nothing but Him.

Others, however, turn their faces towards people, wishing to display the gifts given by Allah the Almighty. Many saints have been stripped of their station here. They show Allah's blessings yet lose His favor for preferring the people's approval. Unless held by divine grace, one is on the brink of destruction; the moment they are left alone, they are ruined.

Desiring to be known for performing miracles stems from self-admiration, and their efforts align with this desire. Allah the Exalted, tests His servant between Himself and the miracles to see if they'll acknowledge everything is from Him or boast as if it is their own.

Consider someone who has opened a shop for you, providing capital, and said, "Work, and the profit is yours." If you work honestly, you gather capital; if you betray, you go bankrupt. Knowledge is His, wisdom is His, etiquette is His, and guidance is His everything, in summary, is His. The moment you claim ownership, you betray the trust, becoming both a hypocrite and a liar.

Miracles can be like this; if embraced, they may lead to one's downfall. This is a vulnerability point for saints. Many have been stripped of their grace on this path of miracles.

•

Allow me to present an allegory:

The venerable Master Esad Sir -may his secret be sanctified- had a distinguished son, Master Ali Sir -may his secret be sanctified- as well. He narrated:

"We were in the front row of the exalted Kaaba, preparing to perform the Morning Prayer. As we waited, I wondered to myself, **"Is there a saint in this row?"** The person next to me leaned in and whispered in my ear, **"Including you, there are seven."**

Despite the crowd, there was an empty spot in the first row. No one sat there. I was curious about who the owner of this spot was, as no one dared to sit there. Soon enough, I saw a dark-complexioned, tall man approaching. Everyone made way for him, and he took the empty spot. I realized then that the place belonged to him.

Meanwhile, a pilgrim had become ritually impure and needed to leave to purify himself. However, the crowd was thick, and the prayer time was drawing close. In his bewilderment, the tall man motioned for him to come over. As he approached, the man opened the sleeve of his robe and within it was everything needed for purification. The pilgrim went inside, cleansed himself, and came out. After the prayer, we dispersed. That tall man never returned; I looked for him for several days but didn't see him again. One day, I met the person who had said **"Including you, there are seven"** in the market. I said, **"Sir, the man who showed that extraordinary miracle never appeared again."** He replied, **"Yes"**, he died, and he died without faith. On that day, while standing at the front of the row, he looked down upon the people and thought, "Is there anyone here greater than me?" Allah did not like his state and stripped him of his faith.'

May Allah protect us.

Say, 'Everything belongs to my Lord,' and escape these pitfalls. I know of no greater honor than being His humble servant.

•

When Solomon -peace be upon him- inquired who among his company could bring the throne of Bilqis, an ifrit from the jinn responded, *"Before you rise from your place, I will bring it to you."* Yet, it was Khidr -peace be upon him-, possessing the knowledge of the Book, who said, *and* ***"I can bring it to you before you blink an eye."***

Upon witnessing the throne placed beside him, Solomon -peace be upon him- proclaimed:

"This is by the grace of my Lord, to test whether I will be grateful or ungrateful. Whoever is grateful, it is for their own good; and whoever is ungrateful, let them know that my Lord is Self-Sufficient, Most gracious." (Naml: 40)

He did not say, *"So-and-so brought it."* Instead, he remarked, **"My Lord is testing me."** Being chosen as a prophet and endowed with divine grace, he immediately understood.

For nothing can occur without His permission and will. Whatever He grants becomes reality.

Above all is His pleasure. All manifestations, revelations, and miracles are insignificant next to His approval.

In the exalted path of Sufism, many states and conditions manifest. The spiritual insight of a sincere person may become enlightened. Yet, these are attributes of the heart. One must completely disregard and remain unattached to such states. Our attention should be directed towards humility and righteousness. These are distractions on the path. Our master, Yusuf Hemedâni -may his secret be sanctified- said, **"Such things are used to train the children of the path."**

One who knows, sees, and acts understands who is truly acting and thus never resorts to such a path. They act as if they have not seen, known, or done anything.

What Allah the Almighty ordains will come to pass. No one can summon what He has not decreed. No one can block what He has graced and bestowed. Therefore, there is no need for panic or anxiety.

Those whom Allah the Exalted supports have avoided seeking miracles, their only aim being to say "Allah."

If a person realizes that they are a worthless creature and that everything belongs to Allah, they rely on Allah.

Those whom Exalted the Allah does not support believe that there is something inherent in themselves. The favors bestowed by Exalted the Allah as a trust, they attribute to themselves. When they present their existence as their own, Exalted the Allah can destroy them at that moment if He wills.

Everything is His and from Him.

There is no such thing as "It happened, I made it happen." In reality, it is Allah who creates; what He created and what He bestowed, that exists. And He is the one seen.

People do not see or recognize the Creator and the Bestowed. Due to their ignorance, they attribute it to their own selves or seek it in others, thus attributing it to them.

However, it is He who creates, He who sustains, He who takes life, and He who gives life. Yet, you do not see Him and instead cling to the idol of your ego, or you idolize the other person.

In the Holy Qur'an, it is stated:

"It is He who gives life and causes death." (Mu'minun: 80)

The Almighty decrees, and you and I come into existence.

When He withdraws His decree, you die, becoming nothingness.

Those lying in these graves once said, "I know, I act."

Yet, when the Creator withdrew His decree, He scattered them all to the ground.

•

Allah the Almighty states in a sacred saying:

"Whoever frightens one of my saint servants, it is as if they have challenged me to war. My believing servant cannot draw closer to me with anything more beloved to me than what I have made obligatory upon them. My believing servant continues to draw near to me with nafile (supererogatory) acts until I love them. When I love them, I become their hearing with which they hear, their sight with which they see, and the strength behind them. If they ask something of Me, I undoubtedly grant it, and if they call upon Me, I respond. In all my actions, I have never been as hesitant as I am in taking the soul of my believing servant, for they dislike death, and I dislike causing them distress, yet it is inevitable.

Among My believing servants, some become deeply engaged in certain acts of worship, but I withhold them from this to prevent arrogance from seeping into their hearts and corrupting them.

There are also servants of mine for whom wealth is fitting. If I impoverish them, poverty would lead them astray."

There are servants of mine for whom only poverty is fitting. Should I grant them abundant provision, it would lead them astray.

There are servants of mine for whom only health is fitting. If I were to cause them illness, it would lead them astray.

There are servants of mine for whom only illness is fitting. Should I restore their health, it would ruin them.

Undoubtedly, I manage my servants knowing what lies within their hearts. Certainly, I am the All-knowing, the All Aware." (Kenzü'lummâl, a collection of Noble Sayings)

•

SIGNS OF HIS EXISTENCE

Allah the Almighty declares in His Noble Verse that the Qur'an is neither a human word nor could it ever be, but it is revealed by Allah, the Mighty and the Wise; directing His servants to reflect upon the clear signs in the universe and within themselves, inviting them to take heed:

“HaMim. The revelation of the Book is from Allah, the Mighty, and the Wise.” (Jathiyah: 12)

Allah the Almighty possesses perfect majesty and perfect wisdom. Therefore, His Majestic Book is also mighty and wise. Since it is impossible for any directive from the Wise Allah the Almighty to be incorrect, it is essential to abide by all His commands.

One manifestation of His wisdom is that He has created this universe in the most perfect form.

"Indeed, in the heavens and the earth are signs for the believers." (Jathiyah: 3)

Those with faith contemplate the heavens and the earth, discerning the most subtle secrets of their creation, understanding the divine wisdom they signify. They strive to perform beautiful deeds accordingly, thus strengthening their faith.

But the unbelievers are blind to the signs of Allah the Almighty. They cannot perceive these clear signs or comprehend the evident Truths, like the brightness of day. Consequently, these signs and portents hold no meaning for them. They neither learn lessons nor reflect upon them.

Then, Allah the Almighty declares:

"In your own creation and that of all the creatures He has spread about on the earth, there are signs (lessons) for people of certitude." (Jathiyah: 4)

At every stage of human creation, from earth and semen to a clot of blood, a morsel of flesh, and finally into human form, there are marvelous subtleties that signify the grandeur of Allah the Almighty’s power.

Just as the creation of humans, the creation and reproduction of animals also signify Allah the Almighty’s might and magnificence.

In another Noble Verse, He says:

"We will show them our signs on the horizons (in the outer world) and within themselves." (Fussilat: 53)

The proof of a Truth is either **"Exterior"** or **"Interior."** That is, it either comes from the eyes or from the heart. Allah the Almighty promises to show both types of signs.

"So that it becomes clear that He is the Truth." (Fussilat: 53)

This divine promise of Allah the Almighty is manifesting, showing both **"Exterior"** and **"Interior"** proofs moment by moment.

"Is it not sufficient that your Lord is Witness over all things?" (Fussilat: 53)

He is aware of everything, nothing is hidden from Him.

•

HARMONY IN THE UNİVERSE

Allah the Almighty has created everything in perfect balance and harmony, within an unparalleled order and system. Nothing is empty or unnecessary.

In His divine Verses, He states:

"We did not create the heavens and the earth and everything in between merely for play." (Anbiya: 16)

All that is created stands as clear evidence of the supreme power and unity of the Mudabbir's (Divine Planner's) high authority. Therefore, it cannot be claimed that humans were created in vain.

Those who stray into false paths may desire to play and amuse themselves, but creation is not a mere plaything, and the Creator is certainly not a player.

"If we had intended to take amusement, we could have taken it from within our presence, if we were to do that." (Anbiya: 17)

Allah the Almighty is far above taking amusement and play; His status is extraordinarily exalted. Such a notion is utterly unthinkable. Everything He has created, He has created with wisdom.

"Woe to you for the attributes you ascribe to Allah!" (Anbiya: 18)

Those who attribute unworthy qualities to the Supreme Creator have fallen into polytheism and have become polytheists.

"To Him belongs whoever is in the heavens and on the earth." (Anbiya: 19)

The existence of these beings serves as evidence of His existence and unity. How could anything He created be associated as a partner to Him?

"Those in His presence do not exhibit arrogance in serving Him, nor do they tire." (Anbiya: 19)

With great zeal, tirelessly and persistently, they continue their worship day and night, keeping Allah the Almighty free from attributes unbefitting of Him.

"They glorify Him without ceasing, night and day, without growing weary." (Anbiya: 20)

In their continuous glorification and sanctification of Allah the Almighty they experience a sublime joy and peace.

Allah the Almighty possesses certain eternal attributes that are unique to Him. His characteristics of creation and resurrection are among these. He alone has the power to bring the nonexistent into being and to raise the dead.

"Or have they taken Allahs from the earth who raise the dead?" (Anbiya: 21)

Those who associate partners with Allah demonstrate their clear misguidance by continuing in their polytheism despite knowing that none but Allah can give life to the lifeless. If they were to contemplate deeply, they would not turn away from the Truth, but would embrace it, attaining worldly happiness and eternal salvation.

"Had there been Allah's in the heavens and the earth besides Allah, they both would have been corrupted." (Anbiya: 22)

As understood from this Verse, whether the creations are in the heavens like stars or on the earth like animals and plants, the unchanging and unwavering order and wisdom prevailing for thousands of years definitively indicate that there is no deity besides Exalted the Allah.

Allah the Almighty governs as He wills. He is neither under anyone's command nor in need of any assistant. He creates everything without models, exemplars, or parallels. For there is no power that precedes Him to emulate.

"Allah, the Lord of the Throne, is exalted above what they describe." (Anbiya: 22)

Faith, knowledge, and sound reason all bear witness to this, establishing it without need for further proof.

"He is not questioned about what He does, but they will be questioned." (Anbiya: 23)

The Sovereign does as He wishes with His dominion. At the same time, He is wise in His decrees; everything He does is rooted in wisdom. The essence of His wisdom is known only unto Himself. If He chooses to disclose it, He does; if not, only He knows.

Allah the Almighty declares in the Noble Verse:

"It is He who shows you His signs and sends down provision for you from the sky. But none remember except those who turn to Him." (Mumin: 13)

Only those who are devoted to Him understand and take heed.

Just as Allah the Almighty manifests His divinity and oneness through His Noble Verses, evidence of His power and greatness, alongside signs and symbols of His boundless might, shine brightly before our eyes through the created beings.

As He sends down rain from the heavens, providing physical sustenance for people and distributing means of livelihood on earth, so too does He bestow spiritual sustenance and apportion His divine grace.

In another Noble Verse, He declares:

"Do they distribute the mercy of your Lord? It is we who divide among them their livelihood in the life of this world." (Zukhruf: 32)

Allah the Almighty who does not neglect the transitory and mundane provisions, surely does not neglect the enduring and noble rewards.

•

“ALLAH IS THE LIGHT OF THE HEAVENS AND THE EARTH.”

(AN-NUR: 35)

CHAPTER 5

- Explanation of the Verse: "Allah is the Light of the Heavens and the Earth." (Surah An-Nur: 35)
- Light Upon Light (*Nurun Ala Nur*)

“ALLAH IS THE LIGHT OF THE HEAVENS AND THE EARTH.”

(AN-NUR: 35)

EXPLANATION OF THE NOBLE VERSE

•

Allah the Almighty states in Noble Verse:

"Say: He is Allah, The One." (Ikhlas: 1)

Existence belongs to Him, He is the existent... All of creation is a manifestation of the particles of His light of existence. There is no independent existence apart from Him.

Allah the Almighty declares in His Noble Verse:

"He is theAl-Awwal,

And the Al-Akhir,

And the Az-Zahir,

And the Al-Batin.

And He has knowledge of all things." (Hadid: 3)

One who can recite this Noble Verse will come to understand, even if only through Knowledge of Certainty, that both they themselves and everything else stem from **"Him."**

Allah the Almighty is **"Al-Awwal,"** the First and Preeternal. Before Him, nothing existed. His Holy Essence is beyond any conceptualization of a beginning. His existence is a necessity by His Holy Essence. Everything that exists does so because of Him.

He is **"Al-Akhir,"** the Last, everlasting and untouched by any end. Just as His existence has no beginning, it has no end.

He is **"Az-Zahir,"** the Manifest; everything from the smallest particle to the largest sphere has become evident through His blessed name, Az-Zahir. All living and nonliving entities exist by His will. When He says **“Be!”** They become, and when He says **“Perish!”** they cease to exist.

He is **"Al-Batin,"** the Hidden; the mysteries of divinity are concealed in every particle of the universe, and He is aware of all things.

In another Noble Verse, Allah the Almighty says:

“And within yourselves... Do you not see?” (Adh-Dhariyat: 21)

There is naught but Him. Everything else is mere shell.

Consider a tree, covered with bark. Do they call it bark, or do they call it a tree? Of course, they call it a tree. The bark too is of the tree. The traces and marks upon it are all part of the tree.

You are but a shell, the universe is also a shell. Within it resides Him. However, mankind sees that shell but not what it contains. In other words, they see the veil but not The One who holds it. Yet, in His Noble Verse, He declares, **"I am within!"** He is within you and within the universe. But you do not see because neither your knowledge nor your intellect is at that level. Undoubtedly, there are those who see and know He is within.

One of the blessed names of Allah the Almighty is **"Al-Musavvir,"** the Fashioner. He bestows form and particularity to everything with great care, arranging them in the most beautiful manner.

This entire world you see is no more than a tray or a platter. Yet, the platter you recognize might be of tin or crystal. The platter of Allah the Almighty is, however, of light.

In His Noble Verse:

"Allah is the Light of the heavens and the earth." (Nur: 35)

From His Light, He created Light, and from that Light, He adorned the universe.

In the Sacred saying:

"If it were not for you, I would not have created the universe." (K. Hafa)

He is the Reason for creation.

And again, in the Noble Verse:

"Praise be to Allah, the Lord of all worlds." (Al-Fatiha: 1)

It is Allah who creates, nurtures, and shapes everything. He forms from the earth, lets us walk upon it, and sustains us with its bounty. He showcases His blessings and adornments on a grand tray.

One of His noble names is **"Al-Wahhab"**. He continually bestows innumerable blessings from the unseen treasures without expecting anything in return.

The night, the day, the moon, the sun, humans, animals, the inanimate, the plants, all of creation… All exist on that grand tray.

We are being tested on this stage.

"He who created death and life to test you, as to which of you is best in deed." (Mulk: 2)

As stated in the Noble Verse, He sent us to be tested. Yet you remained on the tray, lost in the blessings. You did not strive to know and find the Creator.

Therefore, Allah the Exalted says in a sacred saying:

"I have an important matter with jinn and humans! I create, yet worship is given to others. I provide sustenance, yet thanks are offered to someone else." (Taberânî)

The 'other' referred to here is Satan.

The ungrateful human forgot they were on the stage. They truly could not know and did not find their Creator. They seek the Exalted the Allah within the domain created by the Exalted the Allah. Is this not ignorance?

Some say, "He is in the heavens." Others say, "He is on the Throne of Mercy." Meaning, they seek the Creator within the platter He created.

How can you know Him? To know Him, you must find someone who knows Him. Without finding one who knows Him, how can you recognize the Truth, how can you reach the Truth?

"To reach the Allah the Almighty one must find those who have reached the Allah the Almighty,"

Indeed, Allah the Almighty commands in the Noble Verse:

"Be with the Truthful Ones." (At-Tawba: 119)

This is the reason for your coming into the world. If it is destined, you will find the Truth. If not, know that you are lost in your own assumptions.

In a Verse of the Holy Qur'an, Allah the Almighty says:

"I have only created Jinn and humans so that they may know me and worship me." (Adh-Dhariyat: 56)

To know Him, to find Him; it is sustained through worship with sincerity by knowing Him.

Therefore, pay attention! You say **"Alhamdulillahi Rabbil'Alamin**" (All praise is due to Allah, Lord of the worlds), acknowledging that He created all worlds; yet, you do not truly grasp the meaning of what you say. Because you do not know Him, you seek the Creator within His creation.

One of His noble names is **"Al-Qayyum"**. He is the sovereign over everything, keeps all things standing, and bestows reasons for everything to exist until a certain time. Everything subsists through the Truth.

He is **"Ar-Rahman"**. Enveloping all worlds with His mercy.

To grasp this, you must see that you are nothing and merely a facade. Only then does it become manifest.

For in another of the Noble Verse:

"Allah encompasses all things." (An-Nisâ: 126)

Yet, you neither perceive nor see.

"Whoever is blind in this world will also be blind in the Hereafter, and even more astray from the path." (Isrâ: 72)

One who is blind to the signs (âyât) and clear proofs (beyyinât) of Allah the Exalted in this world and unable to see the truth will remain blind in the Hereafter as well.

To attain the secret and mysteries of the Verse:

"Allah is the Light of the heavens and the earth" (Allahu Nurussemâvâti vel-ard), you must seek the guide who leads creation to the Truth. This guide has been appointed by Allah the Exalted.

As expressed in the Verse:

"Among those we created is a community who guide by the Truth and judge thereby." (A'râf: 181)

When you reach the Truth and realize the reality, you will both see and know that it is only **"Him."**

You will understand that it was always He, and that the world was but a tray.

Indeed, one of the sacred names of Allah the Almighty is **"Latif".** This signifies His handling of the finest matters and His knowledge of all subtleties.

His kindness is endless as **"Latif."** Just as He transforms the oyster into a pearl, the bee into honey, and the caterpillar into a silkworm treasure, He has made the human heart into a repository of divine knowledge through His grace.

Allah the Almighty imparts knowledge of gnosis to those He wishes. This knowledge, not found in the lines of books, is hidden in the bosoms and the depths of the hearts of those close to Allah the Almighty.

Allah the Almighty can teach knowledge without an intermediary, as He taught the **special knowledge** to Khidr -peace be upon him-.

Similarly, Allah the Almighty disclosed to Khidr -peace be upon him- the knowledge He did not disclose to Moses -peace be upon him-.

The Messenger of Allah, peace and blessings be upon him, revealed in a Noble Saying that Khidr -peace be upon him- said to Moses -peace be upon him-:

"I follow knowledge that Allah has given me of His own wisdom, which you do not know. And you have knowledge that Allah has taught you, which I do not know." (Bukhari. AlTajrid alSarih: 102)

In other words, would you know what Moses -peace be upon him- did not? This knowledge is a special gift from Allah the Almighty given to whom He pleases.

During the journey of Moses -peace be upon him- narrated in the noble Surah al-Kahf, a sparrow alighted on the edge of their boat and drank a couple of drops from the sea.

Khidr -peace be upon him- said:

"O Moses! My knowledge and yours, compared to Allah's knowledge, is like what this sparrow takes from the ocean." (Bukhari. AlTajrid alSarih: 102)

Yet, this knowledge also belongs to Allah the Most High. Khidr -peace be upon him- was informing Moses -peace be upon him- of this Truth.

Unless Allah the Most High discloses and communicates these Truths, no one can know them.

Indeed, regarding Jacob -peace be upon him-, who was given the secret knowledge of destiny, Allah the Most High says in a Noble Verse:

"Indeed, he possessed knowledge because we had taught him." (Yusuf: 68)

In other words, their teacher is the Almighty Allah. It can only be known through His teaching; otherwise, it is impossible.

In another Noble Verse, Allah the Most High says:

"If you fear Allah and have piety, your teacher will be Allah." (Al-Baqarah: 282)

As I wish to inform you of this knowledge, I also unveil many divine mysteries along the way.

There is an apparent teacher who begins instructing with "Alif." A person learns day by day. There is a deeper teacher who teaches from knowledge, explaining Noble Verse and Noble Saying as best as he can, striving to teach the sublime. However, what he teaches comes from the lines of texts. He relays what he has taken from the written words.

Then, there are those whom Allah the Almighty teaches. These students of Allah the Almighty receive knowledge directly from the heart. Allah the Almighty continuously manifests new revelations. By pouring and engraving His light into the heart, one becomes privy to hidden secrets. When the secrets of the heart are transcribed into books, everyone is astonished because the common folk know the knowledge of the lines, but this knowledge emerges from the heart. The instructor of the lines is human, while the instructor of the heart is Allah the Almighty.

It is to be noted that the knowledge bestowed belongs to whomever it is given. Whatever amount of essence is placed into a treasure, that much essence it contains. Yet, the essence does not belong to the treasure; it belongs to the one who placed it.

Water flows from the fountain, but the water does not belong to the fountain. When the water is cut off, nothing flows from the fountain.

Here, we continually strive to describe the Exalted the Allah and The Messenger of Allah -peace be upon him-. That is what we have been taught. When I first entered, they said "Allah!" and at the end, they still said "Allah!" I was not taught anything else.

This knowledge, "divine knowledge," is known through the revelation of Allah the Almighty. It is not possible for a human to know it unless it is revealed to them.

You might ask, "Then why do you present these explanations?"

Firstly, as Exalted the Bediüzzaman has declared, these books are being prepared for Exalted the Mehdi Messenger.

The second is to help you find the knower of these Truths. They are not absent.

In the continuation of the Noble Verse, it is stated:

"But most people do not know." (Yusuf: 68)

The reason for this ignorance is due to one's inability to find and achieve spiritual maturity. Just as a plant grows and develops from a seed moment by moment, Allah the Almighty manifests in a servant as they achieve spiritual maturity. The degree of manifestation is as much as the degree of maturity gained.

Unless Allah the Almighty informs, makes it known, and shows it, no one can know or see this knowledge.

This is because your intellect is the "**The intellect of livelihood** ". These matters pertain to the fifth level of intellect, "People of deep understanding". Your self is the "“The commanding self” ", whereas this knowledge pertains to those who have ascended to the seventh level of the self, "The purified self ".

You will only grasp this mystery when you see that you are nothing and that all identity is but a veil.

Everything that Allah the Almighty grants and makes known is conveyed to you. Indeed, Allah the Almighty reveals these Truths to whom He wills.

"This is the bounty and grace of Allah, He gives it to whom He wills." (Al- Jumu'ah: 4)

Nothing created is Allah. Remaining with these creations leads to not finding the Creator. If a person sees the created but not the Creator, they remain in "No".

What prevents you from grasping this concept is yourself. For it says "I am". This "I am" is polytheism, and the one who does this is a polytheist.

If you cast aside yourself, you would feel the presence of Allah the Almighty within you, you would not oppose these matters, and you would not fall into this shirk.

•

LIGHT UPON LIGHT

Nur (Light) is the manifestation of Allah the Almighty's noble Name **Az-Zâhir**. Beings come into existence through the manifestation of that Light. He is the one who brings forth all realms, shows the universe, and reveals the Truth.

It is stated in the 35th Noble Verse of Surah Nur in the Holy Qur'an:"Allah is the Light of the heavens and the earth." (Nur: 35)

The phrase **"the heavens and the earth"** in the Qur'an is specifically used for the **"universe"**. Therefore, the meaning of the Noble Verse is **"Allah is the Light of the entire universe."**

It is He who illuminates the heavens with angels and radiant stars and the earth with His friends, the prophets, and saints.

As a matter of fact, Allah the Almighty the Most Exalted describes His Messenger in another Verse as **"Sirâjen münîrâ = A Lamp Spreading Light."** (Al-Ahzab: 46)

Allah the Most Exalted has bestowed the name **Nur (Light)** upon His Sacred Self, made His holy scripture and His Messenger a light, and has placed this light as a veil between Himself and His creation.

In one of his supplications, The Messenger of Allah, peace and blessings be upon him, said:

"All praise belongs to you. You are the Light of the heavens, the earth, and all within them." (Bukhari)

Ibn Mas'ud, -may Allah be pleased with him- , states:

"In the presence of your Lord, there is neither night nor day. The light of the heavens and the earth is the light of His essence."

An illustration of the astonishing qualities of the light that illuminates the heavens and the earth is as follows:

"The example of His light is like a niche within which is a lamp." (Nur: 35)

Here, the light of Allah the Exalted, is likened to a lamp within a lantern.

•

The heart of a true believer is illuminated by the guidance of Allah the Exalted:

“That lamp is within a glass.” (Nur: 35)

The glass is the sacred soul.

The Spirituality accompanies the individual in this world, in the grave, and on the Day of Judgment.

Our Master, The Messenger of Allah, peace and blessings be upon him, said in his Noble Saying:

“Understand well that there is a piece of flesh in the body; if it is good, the whole body is good. If it is corrupted, the whole body is corrupted. That piece of flesh is the heart.” (Bukhari)

The light of the heart, the light of the sacred soul, is the light which Allah the Exalted, bestows from His grace, the light of the gnosis.

Therefore, the body, due to the successive layers of light, became a luminous dwelling. In the manifestation of divine the ophanies, all beings other than the Truth perish, descending to the level of Immutable Archetypes.

The soul and the sacred soul remain. The Immutable Archetypes remains. Allah the Exalted encompasses the entire universe.

"Allah is All-encompassing of everything." (An-Nisâ: 126)

The essence of man is the Immutable Archetypes. When a person descends to that state, only they can perceive that the Exalted the Allah is all-encompassing.

That person worships the Truth with that particle and sees that there is no deity other than Him, realizing that all things are but **"No"**.

•

This transparent glass enhances its brilliance even further while protecting it from the blowing wind.

Allah the Exalted has illuminated the heart of the perfect believer with it, freeing it from doubt and suspicion, bringing it to true certainty. Through this light, He shows people the reality.

"And that glass is as if it were a pearly white star." (Nur: 35)

It is of such beauty and brightness that it has been likened to a pearl to represent this beauty. For here, it has become “light upon light”, becoming the stars of the earth.

This glass, in terms of clarity and beauty, resembles a brightly shining star; and the star, in its luminosity, clarity, and beauty, is likened to a pearl. The small glass transforms into a grand star.

"It is lit from a blessed olive tree, neither of the East nor of the West." (Nur: 35)

That tree signifies the chosen servants whom Allah the Almighty loves and draws close to Himself. It burns with the love of Allah, and its oil is the divine grace. Even if it utters no words, that light, due to divine grace, becomes a model and example for humanity through its state.

The lamp gives light, fueled by the oil of a blessed olive tree. This tree is not one of the olive trees known and seen in the worldly realm. It is neither in the East to miss the morning sun nor in the West to miss the evening sun. Its location is beyond place.

Such a blessed tree it is, so pure and immaculate, that it is said:

"Whose oil would almost glow even if untouched by fire?" (Nur: 35)

That oil is a gift from Allah the Almighty. This servant always turns towards Allah the Exalted. Even if it does not receive any illumination from Allah, it is already a light by itself. Such a one is the **"Sirâjen münîrâ = Radiant Lamp."** Allah the Almighty has purified it to such an extent that even if no illumination occurs, it is already light. It is a light, an exemplar for humanity.

This exemplar could be in word, in state, or in action.

There is no distance such as far or near with the Exalted the Allah.

So illuminating that it can light up the surroundings even without burning the oil itself.

The heart of a perfected believer illuminated by this light is like this. Allah the Almighty has gifted him this light. In that light, there is no far or near.

•

Regarding these servants of Allah the Almighty there are many declarations in the Noble Verse and Noble Saying.

Indeed, in one Noble Verse, it is stated:

“If Allah expands anyone’s heart for Islam, he will be upon a light from his Lord.” (Zumar: 22)

Our Master, The Messenger of Allah -peace be upon him-, explains this light in a Noble Saying:

“Fear the discernment of the perfected believer. Indeed, he gazes with the light of Allah, the Mighty and Majestic.” (Munawî)

The greatest favor and grace Allah the Almighty can bestow upon a being is to draw that being close to Himself and be pleased with them.

The Noble Verse states:

"They will be in the presence of a Sovereign Mighty in Power, at the seat of true honor." (Qamar: 55)

These are the ones blessed with the secret of this Noble Verse.

Then, no veil remains between Him and that servant, and He welcomes the servant into His presence.

This aligns perfectly with:

"One divine attraction from the Most Merciful Allah equals the deeds of humans and jinn." (K. Hafa)

This Noble Saying manifests through this divine attraction. By it, He draws the servant close. After drawing them, He fills them with His grace at whatever station He wills.

When Allah the Almighty lets His light flow into the heart, an understanding and knowledge of gnosis unattainable through mere words, deep within their chest and heart, becomes evident in these servants.

Their being The Book of Allah is for this reason. Allah the Exalted poured that knowledge into them, thereby making them Allah the Exalted's book. From that book, He may reveal secrets into a written form if He wishes, or He may hold them back.

In another Noble Verse it is stated:

"The Qur'an is a collection of clear signs within the hearts of those who have been granted knowledge." (Ankabut: 49)

One who has reached this state knows only Him. The created is a mere mask. It is a speaker; it knows only what has been taught, and sees only what has been shown. This is called divine knowledge.

It is in this way that Allah the Exalted describes this light. He explains how He bestows this light and whom it resides within.

As indicated in another Noble Verse:

"Then we made the inheritors of the Book those of our servants whom we chose." (Fatir: 32)

•

Guidance is the success created by Allah the Exalted through His grace and favor, enabling one to know His essence. The servant to whom He bestows the light of faith and pours into their heart, He supports with the light of gnosis and the Holy Spirit.

They are the inheritors of the prophets, and thus they have been blessed with the manifestations of Noble Verse and Noble Saying. They know as much as they are informed, and see as much as they are shown. When annihilated in Truth, these realities come to fruition.

They see the glory of Truth yet do not perceive themselves, for they praise Truth with Immutable Archetypes and worship Him through it.

In the presence of Divine Majesty, they worship, obey, and prostrate to Allah the Almighty as a mere speck.

When they recite **"Kulhüvallahü Ehad" (Say: He is Allah, The One)**, they perceive the Divine Majesty.

Reciting **"Allahüssamed" (Allah, the Eternal Refuge)**, they acknowledge that all beings are in need of Him.

When does this divine mystery manifest, allowing them to see how all Immutable Archetypes are in dire need of the Exalted the Allah? And when they recognize that everything subsists through Truth, they are blessed with the secret of Throne Verse.

Proclaiming **"Elhamdülillahi, rabbil alamin" (All praise is due to Allah, the Lord of the worlds)** in the Noble Surah Fatiha, they embrace this secret. This can only occur when they are imbued with the hue of the Exalted the Allah.

"Be colored with the color of Allah! And who is better in coloring than Allah?" (Al-Baqarah: 138)

As a mere speck, they extol Truth with Truth. The soul is illuminated by the grace manifestations of The Glorious Truth, and the self-submits to the soul. Thus, it too becomes enlightened, and, consequently, the entire being radiates.

When all these unfold, they become **“Sirajen munira” (illuminating lamp).** With every divine manifestation, they become **“Nurun ala nur” (light upon light)**. They eternally dwell with Truth. Their utmost delight is in the decrees of the Exalted the Allah. No personal desires remain. There is no difference between life and death to them. They have preemptively submitted to the Divine decree. These are the bestowed graces upon them. They have surrendered to the Exalted the Allah and have submitted all their will to Him

•

Allah the Almighty described The Most Noble Messenger -peace be upon him- as a **"Lamp spreading light"** in the Noble Verse. (Al-Ahzab: 46)

The first creation of The Exalted Truth was the light of The Messenger of Allah -peace be upon him-. From the light of Jamal (beauty), His very first creation was this light. Then, from this light, He created the worlds and infused the entire universe with this light.

In the Noble Verse, it is stated:

"A light has come to you from Allah." (Al-Maeda: 15)

In the realm of spirits, during the **"Elest"** gathering (when the divine covenant and oath were initially taken with the question) he was the first to respond affirmatively to this majestic call. Though his **“Am I not your Lord?” (**A'raf: 172) prophet hood followed other prophets in the temporal world, in Truth, he preceded them. He is the last prophet in the realm of witness and the foremost prophet in the symbolic realm.

This Truth is clarified in his Noble Saying:

"While Adam was between spirit and body, I was a prophet." (Ahmed bin Hanbel)

It is declared that he was the first being created from the divine light of Allah the Almighty. This narration affirms The Messenger of Allah -peace be upon him- as a prophet and highlights that he was created as such at that primordial time.

“I was the first of the prophets in creation, yet I was sent after all of them.”

Allah the Exalted manifested His grace upon His beloved chosen prophet servants in unique ways. That grace was the light of Muhammad -peace be upon him-. When they came, they came with the trust of Muhammad -peace be upon him-, with the Light of Muhammad. Every virtue, excellence, and honor in our cprophets -peace be upon them- was due to the trust they bore, for they carried the light of Muhammad -peace be upon him-.

“It is light upon light.” (Nur: 35)

Indeed, Allah the Exalted created the light of His Most Beloved from His own light. All the great prophets -peace be upon them- were created from the light of His Most Beloved. The light within them was the light of The Messenger of Allah -peace be upon him-.

Since Adam -peace be upon him-, that light has revolved upon them. It shone on each of their foreheads. Finally, it arrived at its possessor. It was his light, and the light met the light.

After the door of prophet hood was closed, that light:

"Scholars are the inheritors of the prophets." (Bukhari)

As mentioned in the Noble Saying, it began to spread to his inheritors. Those who are his inheritors till the end of times carry that light.

Since the Holy Qur'an speaks to every era:

"Know that The Messenger of Allah is among you." (Hucurat: 7)

"How can you turn to disbelief when Allah's signs are recited to you and His Messenger is among you?" (Al' Imran: 101)

From these Noble Verses, it becomes clear that this light will remain until the end of time.

Therefore, the one who acts is his light; he is that light. This is what it pertains to.

Since they are the inheritants of that Light, the light comes to them from that Light. Hence, the light within them is that Light.

As mentioned in a Noble Saying:

"Whatever the Almighty poured into my heart, I have poured into the heart of Abu Bakr."

The only source of light is The Messenger of Allah.

Since he bestowed the light upon his successor, he too carries that light, and he too becomes a "Shining Lamp of Light." (Al-Ahzab: 46) The light belongs to Allah the Exalted. When it resides in a heart, it becomes a "Shining Lamp of Light."

"This is the grace and bounty of Allah; He grants it to whom He wills. Allah is the possessor of great bounty." (Al-Jumu'ah: 4)

•

In summary, the light of Allah the Exalted:

"Light upon light." (Nur: 35)

This light is one that cannot be confined. The lamp's light, the beauty of its glass, and the purity of the olive oil come together, completing each other.

How Is Light Upon Light?

Firstly, Allah the Exalted, has granted guidance, honored with the grace of faith, and adorned with obedience and piety. This is one light.

"If Allah opens someone's heart to Islam, they are upon a light from their Lord." (Zumar: 22)

Secondly, Allah the Exalted, has supported him with the Holy Spirit, protected him from everything, and endowed him with every grace. This too is a light.

"They are those whom Allah has inscribed faith onto their hearts and supported them with a spirit from Himself." (Mujadilah: 22)

The third group are those servants who, through His grace, have been granted His light, showered with His divine illumination, and filled with the knowledge of gnosis. They are honored with this pure knowledge, which completes a person's soul with a third light.

While humankind strives to comprehend this light, not everyone can attain it.

For:

"Allah guides to His light whom He wills." (Nur: 35)

That light is the divine light of the Word of Allah, the light of gnosis poured into the heart. This light surrounds the soul, protecting it from all harm with a Holy Spirit.

When these attributes converge in a person, it becomes Light upon Light. This state is reserved exclusively for those whom the Exalted the Allah has chosen, those upon whom He has bestowed the light of His Messenger, The Messenger of Allah -peace be upon him-. It is found solely in these servants, extending to no others.

"Allah is the Light of the heavens and the earth." (Nur: 35)

The heart of someone endowed with these qualities becomes The Throne of the Most Merciful.

"The heart of a believer is the throne of Allah, the Most Merciful." (K. Hafa: 2/130)

•

A believing servant is graced by the divine emanations from the Exalted the Allah.

Allah the Almighty lifts the veils, allowing His fortunate servants whom He wills to reach that light.

He draws His beloved and chosen servant close, manifesting His face upon theirs, bestowing whatever He wishes.

In a Sacred saying, it is said:

"Then, I turn towards them with my face. Do you think anyone can know what I wish to give to the one I turn towards with my face?"

(Allah the Almighty continued to say):

"The first thing I will bestow upon them is the light that I pour into their hearts. At that moment, just as I inform them, they will inform others about me." (Hakim)

Here, it is seen that what is given is given in this manner.

In another Sacred saying, it is stated:

"If a servant occupies himself with me to the utmost extent, I make his desire and pleasure consist in my remembrance. If I make his desire and pleasure consist in my remembrance, he will fall in love with me, and I with him. When he and I are in love, I will lift the veil between us. This state becomes his general condition. When people err, he does not. Their words are like the words of prophets. They are the true heroes.

They are such individuals that when I intend to impose a punishment and torment upon the inhabitants of the earth, I remember them and forego the punishment." (Abu Nuaym, Hilya)

Likewise, The Messenger of Allah -peace be upon him- says in a Noble Saying:

"The scholars of my Community are like the prophets of the Children of Israel." (K. Hafa)

These are the ones sent on missions every hundred years. From this Noble Saying, it is also understood that they are the special servants of Allah the Exalted, His beloved and chosen ones.

As for The Messenger of Allah -peace be upon him-;

He is the light of Truth and the source of knowledge and wisdom.

His essence is Truth, his words come from Truth.

Understanding this may be beyond your grasp, hence I do not delve into it further. For we have previously mentioned:

"I sought Exalted the Allah, and found Him in nothingness.

I sought The Messenger of Allah, and found him within the light of Allah the Almighty."

Indeed, it is impossible to describe this light to you. For wisdom is not attained by mere explanation or reading. It comes into being through the manifestation and will of Allah the Almighty.

•

Knowing that His servants would struggle to comprehend, Allah the Almighty explains many divine mysteries through examples.

"Allah uses such examples for mankind." (Nur: 35)

So that they may take advice and learn from the hidden secrets and wisdom within, He illustrates and represents direct Truths through analogies, as they might otherwise struggle to comprehend them directly.

"And Allah knows all things well." (Nur: 35)

His eternal and infinite knowledge encompasses everything. He knows what is hidden and what is revealed, the symbolic and the evident.

He is the one who best knows who deserves guidance and who deserves to be led astray.

•

Where can the lamp and the light, which symbolize the light of Allah, be found and kindled?

The Noble Verse states:

"This lamp is found in some houses, for which Allah has permitted that they be exalted and His name be remembered therein. In them, glorify Him, morning and evening." (Nur: 36)

Allah the Almighty command for "the exaltation of those houses and the remembrance of His name therein" is clear. These houses have been elevated and purified. Divine will has wished for these houses to be sources of goodness. The primary reason for their elevation and exaltation is the remembrance, glorification, and sanctification of Allah the Almighty within them.

Allah the Almighty's command to **"Exalt Him"** is both material and spiritual. Just as construction and elevation are commanded, so too is the demonstration of necessary reverence.

These places, where people's hearts are distinguished by Allah the Almighty in this manner, are where the lights of guidance shine forth. That lamp, that light, that crystal, that blessed tree, that oil, that light upon light, that guidance are all shaped and represented within them.

To declare who those who praise are, Allah the Almighty states in His Noble Verse:

"Men who are not distracted by trade or sale from the remembrance of Allah, from establishing prayer, and from giving alms." (Nur: 37)

Here, their elevated resolve, intention, and determination are indicated.

Even though they engage in trade to provide for their livelihood, this trade does not prevent them from fulfilling the rights due to Allah the Almighty.

"Those who humble themselves before their Lord." (Hud: 23)

All these virtues are exclusive to those who truly humble themselves before their Lord.

•

Allah the Almighty then describes the attributes of these men as follows:

"They fear a Day when hearts and eyes will be transformed." (Nur: 37)

Their hearts, trembling with awe of Allah, direct them towards the Creator, never becoming heedless of Him. They always prioritize adherence to His commands above all else.

"In order that Allah may reward them according to the best of their deeds and increase them from His bounty." (Nur: 38)

In addition to the promised rewards and blessings, they are bestowed with divine favors -unspecified and beyond imagination- granted abundantly by His generosity.

"And Allah provides sustenance to whom He wills without measure." (Nur: 38)

These are the people whom Allah the Almighty sustains without account. Divine manifestations reveal themselves to them moment by moment. Each manifestation becomes a means to understand, know, and perceive the Truth. For their teacher is none other than Allah the Almighty Himself.

Such is the state of the believers who have been graced with Allah the Almighty's light.

Every Noble Verse possesses both an apparent and a hidden meaning.

However, unraveling this meaning is reserved for the chosen servants to whom Allah the Almighty grants knowledge directly from His Presence. It is a matter between the Glorious One and His servant, determined by the knowledge each has been given.

These lamps, you see, are the lanterns radiating the light given by Allah the Almighty. For the light within them is His light. When He pours this light into their hearts, it becomes the book of Allah. For He transferred that book into their hearts, and they then transcribed the book in their hearts onto lines.

The knowledge they receive is the sacred gnosis of Allah the Almighty thus they are His chosen servants.

The Messenger of Allah, peace and blessings be upon him, stated in the Noble Saying:

"There is such knowledge that it is like hidden jewels. Only the gnostics (Ârif billâh those who know Allah) comprehend it. When they speak of this knowledge, those who are heedless of Allah do not understand.

Therefore, do not despise or belittle the scholars to whom Allah the Almighty has bestowed knowledge from His grace. For when the Almighty granted them this knowledge, He did not belittle them." (From Erbain, narrated by Abu Hurairah -may Allah be pleased with him-)

These hidden jewels are given by Allah the Almighty. By turning towards Him, His light flows into their hearts, and from His Knowledge of Allah, He grants them as much as He wills. This is a sacred knowledge that none knows except those to whom He reveals it.

For it is said:

"Above every possessor of knowledge, there is one more Knowing." (Yusuf: 76)

Indeed, in another Noble Verse, it is stated:

"Ask one who knows!" (Al-Furqan: 59)

This is a divine command. For He bestows upon whom He wills as much as He wills.

This Noble Saying confirms that the knowledge granted to them is beyond human comprehension. When they speak of this knowledge, humanity does not understand it, for their intellect and learning are insufficient. Since their teacher is the Exalted the Allah, the knowledge given to them is from Allah the Almighty. Thus, even a scholar cannot fathom this knowledge because his teacher is human. No matter how advanced he is in outward knowledge, he cannot understand this.

Those who object do so unknowingly, for they are deprived of the manifestations of these Noble Verse and Noble Saying.

Not being Versed in the way of knowledge, not having attained proficiency or sufficiency in wisdom and intellect, they remain at the first step. Yet they perceive themselves as erudite.

In a Noble Saying, our Master, The Messenger of Allah -peace be upon him-, said:

"Knowledge is of two kinds. One is the knowledge that is on the tongue (this is the outward knowledge) and it is a proof against Allah the Almighty's servants. The other is the knowledge that is in the heart (the knowledge of gnosis). It is this that is truly beneficial for reaching the ultimate goal." (Tirmidhi)

They object because they are deprived of this beneficial knowledge.

In another Noble Saying, he states:

"My Lord asked me a question. I could not answer Him. Without any tangible means, He placed His hand between my shoulders; I felt the coolness of that hand in my heart. Thus, He made me the heir of the knowledge of the past and the future. Furthermore, He taught me various sciences. My Lord took an oath from me to keep some of the knowledge secret, knowing that no one but me could bear it. With another type of knowledge, He gave me the choice, saying, 'You are free; if you wish, you may tell others, and if you wish, you may not.' He taught me the Qur'an. Exalted the Gabriel kept reminding me of the Qur'an. And there is another science that He appointed me to share with everyone." (AlMawahib alLadunniyyah)

In this Noble Saying, the knowledge commanded to be kept hidden pertains to the prophet hood. The knowledge ordered to be declared to the public is the science of Islamic law. The knowledge for which one is given a choice whether to disclose or not is esoteric knowledge.

Our Master, the Glory of the Universe, Muhammad -peace and blessings be upon him- disclosed the names of the hypocrites solely to Huzaifa -may Allah be pleased with him- as he unveiled these secrets to his closest friends.

•

"O you who believe! If you fear Allah and are mindful of Him, He will grant you a criterion (to distinguish between right and wrong), and a light and knowledge."

(Al-Anfal: 29)

THE SCIENCE OF GNOSİS

AND THE PEOPLE OF GNOSİS

CHAPTER 6

- The Strange State of the World
- Who Are the "Truthful Ones"?
- "A Believer Is the Mirror of Another Believer."
- The Value of Allah's Devoted Servants in His Presence
- The Perfect guide
- If Trees Were Pens and Seas Were Ink

THE SCIENCE OF GNOSİS

AND THE PEOPLE OF GNOSİS

Allah the Almighty says in His Noble Verse:

"No one can inform you like the All Aware Allah." (Fatir: 14)

The one who will reveal the Truth to you, who is perfectly aware of everything, is the Almighty, not other informers.

Allah the Almighty describes His beloved servants to us and declares in a sacred saying:

"If a servant's engagement with me becomes their most important affair, I make their desire and joy reside in my remembrance. When I place their desire and joy in my remembrance, they fall in love with me, and I fall in love with them. When a servant and I are mutually in love, I remove the veil between us. I make this their perpetual state. While others err, they do not. The words of such people are akin to the words of prophets. They are the true heroes.

These are the ones whom, when I intend to inflict punishment and wrath upon the inhabitants of the earth, I remember, and I relent." (Abu Nuaym, Hilye)

To follow this subject properly, we shall combine three Noble Saying.

The Messenger of Allah -peace be upon him- stated:

"The scholars of my Community are like the prophets of the Israelites." (K. Hafâ)

"Allah the Almighty will send a renewer for this community at the head of every hundred years to rejuvenate the religion." (Abu Dawood)

These are the ones sent every hundred years with a specific duty.

The Messenger of Allah -peace be upon him- states in another Noble Saying:

"Scholars are the heirs of the prophets." (Bukhari)

We have explained the statement **"The words of such people are like the words of the prophets, they are the true heroes"** from the Noble Saying by these three prophetic sayings.

Since no rank is higher than Prophethood, no greater honor can be imagined than inheriting this rank.

No nation of any prophet has attained the status of the inheritors of the prophets. This duty has only been entrusted and bestowed upon the Community of Muhammad.

These are those whose every action is for Allah. They expect no payment, no benefit from anyone. All they do is for the sake of Allah; they rely on Allah the Almighty alone.

•

Who are the inheritors of the prophets?

They are those whom Allah the Most High has loved and chosen, whom He has drawn unto Himself, to whom He has entrusted His trust, and upon whom The Messenger of Allah -peace be upon him- has placed His mantle. They are the heirs of the prophets.

Their teacher is none other than Allah the Almighty Himself.

In the Noble Verse, it is stated:

"If you fear Allah and possess piety, Allah will be your teacher." (Al-Baqarah: 282)

Since their teacher is Allah Almighty, their knowledge is not acquired; that is, they do not learn from any teacher or traditional school. Their knowledge is gifted; it comes directly from Allah the Almighty and The Messenger of Allah -peace be upon him-. Thus, they are not dependent on people.

The Messenger of Allah, -peace be upon him-, describes this knowledge and states in his Noble Saying:

"There are such types of knowledge that are like hidden jewels. Only those who are Arif billah (gnostic of Allah) know them. When they speak of this knowledge, those who are negligent of Allah do not understand.

Therefore, do not disdain or belittle the scholars to whom Allah the Most High and Majestic, has granted knowledge from His bounty. For Allah, the Mighty and Exalted, did not disdain them when He bestowed that knowledge upon them." (Arba'in)

As mentioned in the Holy Qur'an, the polytheists said similar things about The Messenger of Allah, -peace be upon him-. They questioned, **"Should prophet hood have been given to so-and-so instead?"** (See, Zuhruf: 31)

In other words, they did not accept the decree and division of Allah the Most High. Why? Because the ego idol says, "Me!" and listens to no one else; it is a false deity.

•

How do we know that they are the inheritors of the Prophet?

They know the Truth most accurately without having received any formal education.

In the Holy Quran, Allah the Almighty says:

“If you do not know, ask those who people of remembrance for your religious difficulties.” (Nahl: 43)

By the term people of remembrance, it is meant the revered saints of Allah.

It is also stated in another Verse of the Holy Quran:

“He taught man that which he knew not.” (Alaq: 5)

They tell the truth without hesitation. Why? Because they are appointed to do so. What matters is the command of Allah; the judgment of creation holds no value.

In the Noble Verse:

"O you who believe! If you fear Allah and protect yourselves with piety, He will grant you a criterion (of judgment between right and wrong) and a light." (Anfal: 29)

It is through that grace and light bestowed upon them that they know all Truths as much as Allah the Almighty has informed them, and they speak the Truth without fear of anyone.

And Allah the Almighty describes them in His Noble Verse:

"They do not fear the blame of any blamer." (Al-Maeda: 54)

•

The Messenger of Allah, peace and blessings be upon him, also states in his Noble Saying:

"Allah the Almighty will send a renewer of religion for this Community at the head of each century to revive its religion." (Abu Dawood)

When the world starts to decay and corruption and turmoil increase, Allah the Almighty sends one of these beloved and chosen servants to eradicate that corruption.

In these times, each day breeds a new divider, each day a fresh discord arises.

Let me present to you this matter of being sent. Jesus, -peace be upon him-, sent two of His disciples to the people of Antioch to call them to Divine Unity. When the people resisted, He sent another disciple after them.

Exalted the Allah reveals this incident in the Holy Qur'an:

"When we sent to them two Messengers, they rejected both of them." (Yasin: 14)

"So we strengthened them with a third." (Yasin: 14)

"Indeed, we have been sent to you," they said. (Yasin: 14)

If you pay attention, outwardly it seems that it was Jesus, -peace be upon him-, who sent them, but Exalted the Allah declares, **"We sent them."** The reason for saying **"We sent them"** is that their being sent by Jesus, -peace be upon him-, was indeed by the command of Allah.

Therefore, if those sent convey the command of Almighty Allah, the people are required to obey them. Because they were sent.

One who rebels against them actually rebels against the sender. Undoubtedly, they will be held accountable for this in the Hereafter. "O My servant! Was my decree not conveyed to you? Did you believe in my decree, or did you believe in your leader?"

Those who follow their religious leader with faith will ultimately find themselves in the depths of hell, for they disregarded the decree of Allah the Almighty.

In the Qur'anic Verse, it is stated:

"We will call forth every people with their religious leader on that Day." (Isra: 71)

During the Battle of Badr, upon the advice of Gabriel -peace be upon him-, The Messenger of Allah -peace be upon him- grasped a handful of sand and threw it towards the polytheists. This act led to their defeat.

In the Noble Verse, Allah the Almighty declares:

"It was not you who killed them, but Allah killed them. And you did not throw when you threw, but it was Allah who threw." (Anfal: 17)

Outwardly, it was the Prophet -peace be upon him- who threw the sand, but Allah states, **"I threw."**

In another Noble Verse, it is conveyed:

"Say: 'O Allah, Owner of Sovereignty, You give sovereignty to whom you will and take sovereignty away from whom you will. You honor whom you will and humble whom you will. In Your hand is all good. Indeed, you are over all things competent.'" (Al' Imran: 26)

The Absolute Actor, His Holiness Allah, enacts His deeds while others appear on the stage.

•

Those who receive a spiritual share in the Prophetic inheritance and a spiritual share in the Saintly inheritance, the Honorable Pride of Creation -peace be upon him- are with the Truth and speak of the Truth.

Allah the Almighty describes them in a Noble Verse:

"Among Our creatures, there is a group who guide by the Truth and establish justice by the Truth." (Araf: 181)

Their knowledge is bestowed by His Holiness Allah and The Messenger of Allah, -peace be upon him-. They strive to lead those fortunate ones toward His Holiness Allah and His Messenger through the paths of Islamic law, spiritual path, Truth, and gnosis.

They acknowledge their own worthlessness because all worth belongs to Allah Almighty.

They see themselves as devoid of authority because sovereignty belongs to Allah Almighty.

None but they know this. Everyone tries to make himself seem significant. But, being annihilated in His Holiness Allah, they perceive Allah alone and see nothing in themselves.

It is stated in the Noble Verse:

"Not a leaf falls without His knowledge." (An'am: 59)

Exalted the Allah is such that even if all creatures gathered together, they could not create a single leaf.

If you cannot find the Exalted the Allah, think deeply, find Him here! For the entire universe is helpless before a single leaf. And He is such an Allah! If you contemplate the Exalted the Allah beautifully, you can feel His presence in every particle.

In His Noble Verse, He says:

"It is not possible for anyone to have faith without Allah's permission." (Yunus: 100)

If the Exalted the Allah does not will it, He does not place faith in anyone's heart. He is just in guiding those whom He leads to guidance and leaving those whom He misguides to their misguidance.

"They are those upon whose hearts Allah has inscribed faith." (Mujadilah: 22)

As stated in the Noble Verse, for whomever He inscribes faith in their heart, through that faith, through that light, He reveals the Truth to them.

"Allah has made faith beloved to you and adorned it in your hearts. He has made disbelief, debauchery, and rebellion detestable to you. These are the rightly guided." (Hujurat: 7)

In accordance with this Noble Verse, whoever is endowed with the love of faith, and that faith is embellished in their heart, it means they are being held by Allah. This is the essence, the fundamental Truth. Salvation comes thus, it is by His grace one finds salvation. We call this "Divine protection and governance".

They know the Truth, but not themselves. They see the Truth, but not themselves.

If they possessed even the weight of a mosquito's wing in existence, or if they saw themselves as possessing any existence, it is still a being before Allah the Almighty.

This state of self-annihilation is unique to them. Because Allah the Almighty declares in His Noble Verse:

"Whatever good comes to you is from Allah, and whatever evil befalls you is from your own self." (An-Nisa: 79)

The Messenger of Allah -peace be upon him- stated in his Noble Saying:

"Seeing yourself as possessing existence is a sin greater than all other sins."

For the only one who truly exists is Allah the Exalted. He is the Existence; He is the Being.

•

Among those who truly seek the truth, nothing exists besides the Truth. They cast off their being to reach the Essence.

The Most Noble Messenger, peace and blessings be upon him, said in a Noble Saying:

"The solitary ones have won the race;

Who are the solitary ones, O the Messenger of Allah?

They are those who immerse their entire existence in the remembrance of Allah, and do not engage in anything else.

This remembrance lightens their burdens, and they will come to the Day of Judgment light and unburdened." (Hakim)

In a Sacred saying, it is said:

"When my servant remembers Me, I am with him." (Bukhari)

For those who exist in the realm of one who knows through Allah, Allah the Most High manifests as He wishes.

He is the Lord of all worlds. When He reveals Himself to His servant, the world becomes through His manifestation.

Allah the Most High says in a Noble Verse:

"They are the ones on whose hearts He has inscribed faith and whom He has supported with a spirit from Himself." (Mujadilah: 22)

Notice, the Exalted the Allah sustains us with the spirit; when He withdraws the spirit, nothing remains. The Exalted Allah, who created the spirit, has also created spirituality. This is an esoteric knowledge. Allah the Most High supports His chosen servants with this spirituality, from which subtle Truths are brought forth. He operates these subtleties as He pleases. It might be one person, or ten, or forty; this is beyond the scope of your knowledge.

Everyone possesses a soul, but they have two. Our aim is to gradually convey to you the people and knowledge of gnosis.

This sacred spirit is found in none but them.

Furthermore, they have been honored by The Messenger of Allah, -peace be upon him-, with the title of **"Fırkai Nâciye"** or **"The Saved Group."** These men of Truth, whose hearts remain alive, have walked the path of The Messenger of Allah, -peace be upon him-, and the path of the venerable companions and righteous predecessors, never straying from the straight path even for a moment. Up until now, through their exalted aspirations, they have protected the seekers of the true path from the misguidance and deceptions of heretics and the errant.

Allah the Most High has demonstrated their righteousness to the believers through His mercy, and the believers have benefited from these great ones, receiving spiritual effulgence from them.

•

And how did these servants draw near to Allah the Almighty?

In a Sacred saying, it is said:

"To whoever draws near to me by a hand's span, I draw nearby an arm's length; and to whoever draws near to me by an arm's length, I draw near by a fathom. And whoever comes to me walking, I come to him running." (Bukhari and Muslim)

Allah the Almighty has chosen these servants for Himself. Those who have drawn close to Allah the Almighty have done so with love. Allah the Almighty has become enamored with them; just as He loves them, these servants are also in love with Allah the Almighty. They harbor no desire other than Him.

"Allah distinguishes with His mercy whoever He wills." (Al-Baqarah: 105)

Thus, Allah the Almighty has bestowed these beloved servants with such grace.

"We strike with our mercy whoever we will." (Yusuf: 56)

Indeed, He has taken these cherished servants into the circle of bliss, elevated them to the center of peace, brought them into His presence, and granted them the highest joy.

"They are in the presence of the Sovereign, Mighty and Powerful, in a seat of Truth." (Qamar: 55)

Just imagine! Allah the Most High, has brought them into His presence. Because they were the dust of that amber, He raised them to the station of Truthfulness.

•

Our Master, The Messenger of Allah -peace be upon him- states in his Noble Saying:

"The attraction of the Most Merciful equals the deeds of humans and jinn." (K. Hafa)

Even if a person lived for a thousand years and wished to draw closer to Allah the Most High, Allah could pull the servant He wishes to Himself in an instant. The distance a person could not cover in a thousand years of their effort, Allah the Most High, can make them cover in an instant if He wills. Why? Because He pulled, His force and His power pulled. That is the meaning of this Noble Saying, and it has thus been explained.

Indeed, Allah the Most High, loved them, chose them, and brought them into His presence.

"We belong to Allah, and to Him we shall return." (Al-Baqarah: 156)

These are the ones who belong to Allah and return to the Most High Allah.

The ones who are graced by divine favor are those.

Truly, these are the servants of Allah the Almighty; they have submitted to Allah the Almighty relinquishing their wills to the will of the Truth. In them, desires do not dwell. What matters to them is the "Divine Decree." They gaze upon the impending Divine Decree. They are in the hand of the Truth, wherever He places them, there they reside. For them, life and death are the same. There is no difference between being in the world and being in the grave. They are the real heroes; this is the "Station of Servitude."

Now, let's all look at ourselves in this mirror of Truth; are we for the Exalted the Allah, for Satan, for the self, or for the world?

•

Allah the Almighty has the name **"Al-Vadud,"** meaning The One who loves His obedient servants greatly, the most worthy of love.

Another name of Allah the Almighty is **"Al-Latif,"** signifying The One who performs the most subtle works, The One who knows the intricacies of all matters, possessing infinite knowledge.

Yet another name is **"Al-Wali,"** meaning the Friend of His righteous servants. Imagine if the friend of a servant were the Exalted the Allah...

In the blessed Verses, it is stated:

"If the deceased is among those brought near to Allah; then, for him is comfort, bounty, and a Garden of Bliss." (Waqi'ah: 88-89)

There are various Noble Sayings stating that such individuals will not have their souls taken until they see their place in paradise, or until a branch from the flowers of paradise comes and they smell its fragrance.

When this glad tiding from the Noble Verse is given to the person, they wish to reach Allah the Almighty. However, Allah the Almighty rejoices far more in their desire to reach Him.

"If he is among those on the right hand, it will be said: 'Peace be upon you, O right hand! Peace be upon you from those on the right!'" (Waqia: 90-91)

The believer whose soul is at the throat receives this peace with utmost joy and is comforted, feeling the warmth of divine friendship.

"But if he is among the deniers, the errant, then he will be welcomed with boiling water and thrown into hell. This is indeed the ultimate Truth!" (Waqia: 92-95)

I have witnessed this boiling water. I was curious about how one is thrown into it for a particular person, so they showed me. He was thrown into the boiling water, and when he came out, I saw that all his bones were stripped, hung up like clothes on a line. Such pain would never be forgotten, even after thousands of years. And after that comes the casting into hell.

<u>The Strange State of the World.</u>

Allah the Almighty states in the Noble Verse:

"Every self shall taste death." (Al' Imran: 185)

Allah the Almighty's creation is like this: imagine a vast sea, and a net cast upon it, capturing all the fish. Yet, the fish do not realize they are captured; they thrash about in every direction. The owner of the net slowly pulls it in, but none of them take heed. Soon, they will be drawn onto the shore, flailing desperately yet their struggle will be in vain. They are all doomed to die.

However, Allah the Almighty possesses an ocean of grace and mercy, one that is boundless and infinite. This ocean reaches the sea of The Most Noble Beloved -peace be upon him-. This sea is the water of grace and life. It then flows to the ocean of the spiritual guide of the time.

Whomever Allah the Almighty takes from the net and places into the water of life -the spiritual grace- of The Messenger of Allah -peace be upon him- will escape the confines of death.

As the Noble Saying proclaims:

"Believers do not die; they merely transfer from one abode to another."

Regarding the Perfect guide, another Noble Saying states:

“In every century, there are those among my Community who precede others. They are called Substitutes and Truthful. Such is the divine favor and mercy upon them that you benefit from it, eating and drinking through their provision. Disasters and calamities predestined for the people of the earth are averted through them.” (N. Usûl)

Those whom He places in this grace can be given life in the water of life if He wills. These individuals focus greatly on earning permissible sustenance, and they dedicate themselves to sincere worship and obedience. Simultaneously, they engage in Struggle in the Path of Allah to defend our faith and homeland.

Who are the "Truthful Ones"?

Allah the Exalted states in His Noble Verse (Verse):

“Be with the Truthful Ones.” (At-Tawba: 119)

The Truthful ones are the Perfect guide who are the beloved servants of Allah the Exalted.

This Noble Verse has not been fully elucidated until now.

These Truthful ones pass through three stages. First, they come as original beings, but believe that they are among the Truthful ones even before being sent to the world; they come as Truthful ones. Second, they ascend back to their original stations under the guidance of a sincere mentor and reach Allah. If Allah the

Exalted wishes to assign them a duty, He brings them down from that station and appoints them to a task.

Allah the Exalted commands to be with them. Because He has emptied that servant's existence and filled it with His own grace. He has made Himself known to them, and He has conveyed that there is nothing that belongs to the creature, everything is from Him and of Him. Then He has tasked them with guidance, saying, "I am sending you, convey what I have informed you." The teacher of these individuals is none other than the Exalted the Allah; this Noble Verse will be frequently mentioned.

Only they can lead to the Truth. The others call to their own paths, draw to their own religions, and act according to their own books.

Only those whom He has assigned are distinguished.

Allah the Exalted elucidates His beloved servants to us in His Noble Verse:

"Know well that there is no fear for the friends of Allah; they will not grieve." (Yunus: 62)

Since the fear of Allah removes all other fears, no other fear remains. They have no sorrows about the past, for the future is more beautiful.

"They are those who have faith and attain piety." (Yunus: 63)

Just as they believe with perfect faith, they accept and affirm all divine commands and rulings. They exert the utmost effort for their fulfillment and execution. They abstain from all forbidden and doubtful things.

"For them are glad tidings in this worldly life and in the Hereafter." (Yunus: 64)

This is Allah's favor and benevolence towards them. They are given the glad tidings in this world and in the Hereafter.

"There is no change in the words of Allah." (Yunus: 64)

No force can alter these glad tidings or revoke His decrees, nor is there any possibility of it. His promises inevitably come true.

"This is indeed the greatest happiness." (Yunus: 64)

The heralding of the Saints of Allah in both this world and the hereafter is such a divine grace that no blessing greater than this can be imagined.

"You are the best community ever raised for humanity; you enjoin what is right, forbid what is wrong, and believe in Allah." (Al' Imran: 110)

These are the ones who come once every hundred years. They are the pioneers of the Community of Muhammad.

"Allah guides to His light whom He wills." (Nur: 35)

When Allah the Almighty brings a servant to His light, all his actions and deeds align accordingly. These are the chosen servants of Allah the Almighty exclusive to none other.

"The Qur'an is clear signs in the hearts of those who are given knowledge." (Ankabut: 49)

With the knowledge granted by the sacred Qur'an, thanks to the beaming light in their hearts, Allah the Almighty reveals and shows as much of the divine secrets to them as He wills. That is why what they know, others cannot comprehend. The outward scholars neither know, understand, nor perceive this. We have distinguished this line for this sacred knowledge of the chest is different from the written knowledge of the outward scholars.

"Is one whose heart Allah has opened to submission, so that he is under a light from his Lord?" (Zumar: 22)

Only through this light granted by the Lord can these divine secrets be known. They are aware of these Truths because they have been informed.

It is for this reason that:

"Allah is the Light of the heavens and the earth." (Nur: 35)

They are thus graced with the secret of this Noble Verse. They see, they know, they speak. All scholars stand in awe of this Noble Verse. Indeed, they do not object to it, because it is a Noble Verse, but their hearts do not fully accept it. However, the people of Truth know this, and they see it with their eyes. Without Allah showing it, it cannot be known through mere knowledge.

In His Noble Verse, Allah says:

"Indeed, Allah is with those who fear Him and those who are doers of good." (Nahl: 128)

For such people, their true protector is the Exalted the Allah. This is an expression of a particular companionship.

"Allah chooses for Himself whom He wills." (Shura: 13)

Pay attention, the Exalted the Allah is describing these individuals. He manifests Himself to these beloved and chosen servants in the manner He wishes and assigns them duties. Each is sent with different responsibilities. This described group are the true sufis.

"The believer is the mirror of another believer."

Our esteemed Prophet Muhammad -peace be upon him- stated in his blessed Noble Saying:

"A believer is the mirror of another believer." (Abu Dawood)

This is a very significant Noble Saying... It can be interpreted in two ways.

Firstly, the believer refers to the heart of the faithful servant; secondly, Allah the Almighty Himself is meant by the believer.

That is, Allah the Almighty attributes His beloved Name to the pious believer.

When Allah the Almighty manifests Himself, He sees Himself in the heart of that faithful servant. This is exclusive to them alone.

It is stated in a Noble Verse:

"Indeed, you are on a straight path, by the command of the Almighty, Most Merciful." (Yasin: 5)

This is because Allah Almighty's Beloved, the Noble Messenger, is His deputy.

The Value of Saintly Servants in the Sight of Allah:

Allah the Most High describes His saintly servants in a sacred saying:

"Indeed, the longing of the righteous to meet me has intensified. Yet, my longing to meet them is even stronger."

Imagine the depth of Allah the Most High's love for them, the immense desire He harbors to reunite with them. They are never separate from Allah the Most High, but He expresses and reveals this to us so that we may understand.

Now, let us present another sacred saying. The Revered One, Truth, the Almighty, says:

"Whoever shows enmity to one of my saints, I declare war against them. The deed that brings my servant closest to me is performing the obligatory acts I have enjoined. Through voluntary acts, my servant continues to draw closer to me until I love them. When I love them, I become their hearing with which they hear, their sight with which they see, their hand with which they touch, and their foot with which they walk. (I become their heart with which they understand, their tongue with which they speak.) **Whatever they ask of Me, I will grant them. Should they seek refuge in Me, I will surely protect them."** (Bukhari. Tecridi Sarih: 2042)

This Sacred saying has never been fully explained until now, and we shall elucidate it with the help of Qur'anic Verses.

Allah the Most High says:

"We raise in degrees whom we will." (An'am: 83)

These are the servants whom He elevates to such high degrees. They are the truly fortunate souls.

Now we shall attempt to disclose this sacred saying.

Allah the Almighty says, **"I become his hearing with which he hears, his sight with which he sees, his hand with which he touches, his foot with which he walks, his heart with which he understands, and his tongue with which he speaks."**

Indeed, this is a profound realization, isn't it? But as we have previously mentioned, these beloved servants of Allah the Almighty perceive and comprehend themselves only as a veil, an attire. They see themselves as a garment they see this with their own eyes. For they are looking with the vision of the Exalted the Allah. They know that the true guide is the Exalted the Allah himself. Now, I am revealing this secret to you.

To better grasp this Sacred saying, we shall present a related topic.

Allah the Almighty states in a Qur'anic Verse:

"We are closer to him than his jugular vein." (Qaf: 16)

He has forsaken all, and has been graced with the divine presence of Allah the Almighty seeing with his own eyes that He is within and closer than all else. Why? Because he sees with the vision granted by Allah the Almighty.

These secrets have not been unveiled to you until now. Pay attention as we validate everything with Qur'anic Verses and Noble Saying. No one can contest our discourse with the permission of the Almighty.

In one of His Noble Verse:

"We are closer to him than you are, but you see not." (Waqi'ah: 85)

Even though He has said this, you do not comprehend, just as you are unable to grasp the knowledge of gnosis or understand the people of gnosis. This is because their teacher is the Exalted the Allah. Allah has manifested within them, showing His nearness to them... No person's knowledge, intellect, or comprehension is sufficient to understand this.

In another Noble Verse:

"Within yourself… Do you not see?" (Adh-Dhariyat: 21)

Can you see even though He asks this?

Indeed, only they who truly see can perceive. They alone have seen, known, and confessed.

We open before you a Sacred Noble Saying... Three Noble Verse have passed.

Allah the Almighty states, **"I am within you... Do you not see?"** Yet you do not see, do you? Why? Because you have not attained that state.

Suppose, for instance, a man constructs a shop from nothing. He fills it with the most exquisite goods and jewels and conducts transactions. You see the shop, you see the treasures and ornaments inside, but you do not see the one who built the shop, who placed the treasures and adorned it, the owner. Is this not a profound blindness?

You see with Him, you hold with Him, you walk with Him, yet you do not see Him. Still, you have not recognized the shop owner, even though you look with Him! All creatures are like this. With Him, you exist; all existence is thus.

By His power, you come into being; when He withdraws His power, you perish, becoming nothing. The cosmos is the same. In His sight, there is no distinction between a human and the universe.

"Without you, there is no strength,

Without you, there is no life,

Without you, there is no existence, there is no existence but Allah.

You are Subhan (the Glorious), you are Sultan (the Sovereign), you are Khaliq (the Creator), you are Raziq (the Sustainer), and you are the most Gracious, the abundant Allah!"

Here in lies the secret.

If you grasp this point, you will have comprehended the greatness of Allah the Almighty but it is not easy.

The Perfect guide:

The Perfect guide is the one who truly knows the Exalted the Allah, sees Him within, and understands that he himself is just a mask.

This is the Perfect guide. The Perfect guide is a portrait, the Perfect guide is a rag, and the Perfect guide is a mask.

These things are spoken about, but not truly understood.

In the Noble Verse:

"Within yourself... Do you not see?" (Adh-Dhariyat: 21)

Allah the Exalted, declares.

Only these are the ones who see within.

In another Noble Verse:

"He says, 'We are closer to him than his jugular vein.' (Qaf: 16)

He declares, 'I am within you, your face is but a mask, your body a garment. I am closer to you than yourself,' he speaks. Yet we have never heard this in life.

In another Noble Verse:

'We are closer to him than you are, though you do not see.' (Waqi'ah: 85)

In every atom, the acts of the Absolute Doer exist, meaning the secrets of divinity are present in every atom. Therefore, from everything to everything, He is near, but humans do not perceive this. This Verse refers to that reality.

Because he has been graced with the manifestation of these three Verses, he sees and knows that the Truth is within. Without the manifestation of these Verses, one cannot be a Perfect guide.

How did he know this? He knew because Allah the Most High, informed him; he saw because He showed him.

In a Sacred saying, the Exalted and Glorious Truth states:

"Then I turn towards them with my face. Do you think anyone can know what I wish to give to someone I turn with my face?"

Allah the Almighty continued to say:

"The first thing I will grant them is to pour the pure essence into their hearts. Just as I tell them about you, they will tell you about me." (Hakim)

A clear statement! Indeed, I inform them about you, and they, in turn, inform you about me.

This sacred Noble Saying tells us that no one can know what Allah the Almighty has granted them, the favor and generosity He has shown them, and that these are known only to those specific individuals.

In a Noble Verse:

"Glory to you, we have no knowledge except what you have taught us." (Al-Baqarah: 32)

•

IF TREES WERE PENS

AND SEAS INK

Allah the Almighty informs us in Noble Verse that even nonbelievers are compelled to confess that the Almighty who created the entire universe is His Exalted Essence:

"If you were to ask them, 'Who created the heavens and the earth?' they would surely say, 'Allah.'

Say: Praise be to Allah.

Yet, most of them do not know." (Luqman: 25)

When people return to their innate nature and consult their conscience, they can see this clear Truth. Despite this, they associate others with Allah the Almighty. They remain heedless despite numerous warnings. Most people do not ponder or reflect. Even if their attention is drawn to this matter, they do not pay the necessary heed.

Since the heavens and the earth are the creations of Allah the Almighty all that is within them undoubtedly belongs to Him.

The Noble Verse further states:

"To Allah belongs whatever is in the heavens and the earth. Verily, Allah is free of need and most worthy of praise." (Luqman: 26)

All praise and glorification belong to Him. Everything is in need of Him. Even if no one praises Him, He is independent of the praises of the praisers and the gratitude of the grateful. The disbelief of disbelievers and the polytheism of polytheists do not affect Him in the least.

In His knowledge and power, there exist boundless subtleties and endless mysteries.

As stated in the Noble Verse:

"If all the trees on earth were pens, and the sea [was ink], with seven more seas added to it, still the words of Allah would not be exhausted.

Undoubtedly, Allah is Mighty and Wise." (Luqman: 27)

Nothing can escape His eternal knowledge and wisdom.

Here, Allah the Almighty speaks of His grandeur and majesty, His glory and perfection, His most beautiful names, His divine attributes, and His perfectly complete words, which no human can ever fully comprehend.

The divine words are infinite. For there can be no limit to His knowledge and wisdom; He exercises His will as He pleases. He enforces His decrees without any restriction or boundary.

These Noble Verse illustrate the flawless and limitless nature of Allah the Almighty's power and eternal knowledge, thereby refuting the denials of disbelievers about resurrection after death.

In another Noble Verse, it is stated:

"Your creation and resurrection are as simple as the creation and resurrection of a single self.

Indeed, Allah hears and sees all." (Luqman: 28)

For when Allah the Almighty wills something to be, He simply says, **"Be!"** and it is.

There is no difference between the creation of one thing and many things. Similarly, there is no difference between the resurrection of one self and the resurrection of millions. All of this is easy for Him, and nothing is difficult for Him.

In His divine Verse, He states:

"Our command is but a single act, like the blink of an eye." (Qamar: 50)

He commands only once. Few or many, it is all the same in His infinite power.

Allah the Almighty highlights the signs of His power and majesty in the external world through His divine Verse:

"Do you not see that Allah makes the night merge into the day and the day into the night? He has subjected the sun and the moon to His command. Each moves for a specified term."

"And surely Allah is fully aware of what you do." (Luqman: 29)

In the days of summer, He blends the night into the day, and the day extends while the night shortens. Once the days are at their longest, they begin to shorten, and then the night starts to lengthen, leading into winter.

The merging of night and day and day and night alludes to both of the world's motions and its rotation from west to east.

The motion of the sun and the moon until a set time is decreed. Both are bound to this decree. There is no deviation in their movement durations.

However, the continuous manifestation of this phenomenon before our eyes causes many to lose their insight. They fail to see this flawless and uninterrupted order.

To declare the true cause of these works of power shown, Allah the Almighty states in the Verses of the Qur'an:

"For indeed, Allah is the Reality. And what they invoke besides Him is surely falsehood.

Indeed, Allah is the Most High, the Most Great." (Luqman: 30)

The One who is above all and to whom everything submits in awe:

"Do you not see that ships sail on the sea by the grace of Allah? Thus, He shows you His signs (proofs of His existence).

In these, there are signs (indications) for those who are very patient and deeply grateful." (Luqman: 31)

Had Allah the Most High, not created a power to buoy ships on water, surely, the ships would not be able to glide through the swelling waves of the sea.

•

"Allah has bestowed upon you abundant blessings, both apparent and hidden."

(Luqman: 20)

THE GLORY OF ALLAH, THE ONE WITH INFINITE GRACE, IS EXALTED

CHAPTER 7

- The Divine Guide is none other than Allah, the Most Exalted. He alone is the Creator, the Bestower of blessings, and The One with Infinite Grace.
- The Physical Existence is subject to five manifestations.
- Sweet and bitter water

The Perfect guide knows and sees that he is but an image.

The Perfect guide perceives his true nature as nothing more than a mere mask.

The Perfect guide recognizes his essence as nothing more than a rag.

These concepts will be explained gradually.

Allah the Almighty's blessings upon a human being are immeasurably abundant. He created you in the best form. He endowed you with countless blessings.

"Allah has granted you His evident and hidden favors abundantly." (Luqman: 20)

Such blessings... Both evident and hidden...

He has adorned and beautified you with these blessings to such an extent that even if the entire world were yours, could you buy the garment of your body? No... Look at the signs upon you! The Creator has lavished blessings upon you. He gave you eyes to see, ears to hear, the ability to speak to communicate. Everything you grasp, every step you take, is through His grace.

He has fixed each of your organs in its proper place and granted you a form. It is through this form that you are seen.

The Noble Verse states:

"He gave you form and made your forms the most beautiful." (Taghabun: 3)

You appear as you were created when your picture is taken. And you say, this is who I am. Yet you are but a mask. How wonderfully He crafted and shaped that mask, adorning it in the finest manner. He assigned you a characteristic.

"Blessed be Allah, the best of creators." (Muminun: 14)

He has granted you every opportunity, so many that they are countless. He made the world subjugated for you.

"He created for you all that is on the earth." (Al-Baqarah: 29)

He brought you onto the world stage to be tested. Every word you speak is recorded. Every move of yours is photographed.

"Surely, Allah is ever an Observer over you." (An-Nisa: 1)

He clearly informs you of what needs to be done in the Quran and Noble Saying. Will you worship and be grateful to Allah the Exalted? Or will you be ungrateful to such a gracious and honored Allah the Exalted and turn into an adversary, worshipping Satan instead?

Yet, Allah the Revered says in His Noble Verse:

"Oh children of Adam! Did I not command you not to worship Satan?" so He declares. (Yasin: 60)

Allah the Almighty is testing you. Yet you are with Him. He knows everything about you. He is aware of all.

"O you who have believed, fear Allah. Let every self-look to what it has put forth for tomorrow. And fear Allah; indeed, Allah is acquainted with what you do." (Hashr: 18)

And again, when Allah the Almighty decrees the end of the time granted to you, He withdraws the blessings He gave. You remain merely a mask. That mask too decays and vanishes. You become just an image. In that image, you see the adornments previously bestowed by Allah the Almighty who is the possessor of boundless grace. But He took away all the blessings He had given you. Where then are you?

If only human beings could grasp this! He has given a unique form to everything in creation, from the flower to the sky, and the earth to the universe. All is but from His command **"Be."**

Let me explain the mask to you thus:

If you were to place here a skull dug from a grave, what worth would it have? How much would it sell for? The skull has eyes that no longer see, a nose that no longer smells, ears that no longer hear, and a mouth that no longer speaks. It has no hair, no eyelashes, no eyebrows, no mustache or beard.

Yet, a moment ago, this skull was yours, and while alive, it was very precious. You carried and collected this value within yourself.

But when His power is withdrawn, you cease to exist. His essence was within you; when He pulled His presence back, and the blessings He had given you were taken away one by one, your body decayed, and you were left as just a skull.

Where were you? You now see it was but a mask! Later, even the skull will decay and turn to ash.

Only He remains. The Body is He, the existent is He...

Everything is not He, yet nothing is without Him. You are a mask, a particle is a mask, and the universe is a mask.

Everything subsists through Him. You seem to place your existence, take it away and you vanish. Thus, always He.

Where were you? No. You existed with Him, appeared with Him. When He withdrew His presence, what remained? A bare skull. You are but a mask.

Let us present this with a Noble Verse. Almighty Truth and High, states:

"O Messenger! They ask you about the soul. Say: The soul is of my Lord's command." (Isra: 85)

The soul is a command of Allah the Almighty. Yet mankind does not comprehend this. You exist, but when Allah the Almighty withdraws His command, what do you become? You become nothing. Thus, man is but a mask.

Brother, why did we not understand this Truth in due time! This is what I strive to convey. Yet, mankind could never fully grasp this. They also did not know that Allah the Almighty's closer to them than their own selves.

Your inability to see the Truth stems from your inability to abandon your own existence. Very few people in the world comprehend this mystery. Those who do are the prophets and saints whom Allah the Almighty has drawn close to Himself. It does not include others. For those who have attained spiritual perfection, this matter becomes quite easy. They know, even before they die, that the mask holds no significance and that the true judgment belongs to Him. Others will realize this after they die.

•

Our Master Prophet Muhammad -peace be upon him- states in a Noble Saying:

"Allah created Adam in His own image." (Bukhari)

Contemplate the Exalted the Allah within man. For just as He manifests Himself in mankind, He also manifests Himself in the universe. Everything that exists in the external world has a sample within man. You are unaware that you are a reflection of the entire cosmos.

"We have certainly created man in the best of stature." (Tin: 4)

You see the sea, you see the mountains, and you see the trees... All these exist within man as well. What exists in the universe is present within man. Allah the Almighty manifests in this manner. When He grants existence, you become you and I become me; when He withdraws it, you become a mask, a nothingness. Everything present in the cosmos exists within you, yet you remain unaware of this.

In Truth, He dwells within you. When the mask is lifted, you will see The One who is closer to you than yourself, and you will know that everything is but a veil.

•

The Master of the Universe -peace be upon him- Our Beloved Prophet states in his Noble Saying:

"In every century, there are forerunners from my Community who are called the substitutes and the Truthful ones. The divine grace and mercy

upon them are so abundant that you eat and drink because of them. The calamities and misfortunes that are destined for the inhabitants of the Earth are warded off and lifted through them." (Nawadir alUsul)

If the deputy of Allah the Almighty's Beloved receives such favors and blessings, then consider what favors and blessings are bestowed upon His Beloved, the Reason for Creation, the Mercy to the worlds, The Most Noble Beloved. Had He not created or sent him, neither you nor the worlds would exist!

In the Noble Verse, it is stated:

"O Prophet! We have sent you as a witness, a bearer of good news, a warner, one who calls to Allah with His permission, and a luminous lamp." (Ahzâb: 45-46)

In the Sacred saying, it is further stated:

"Were it not for you, I would not have created the heavens." (K. Hafâ)

Thus, it is understood that the heavens were not the source; rather, they were created from his light. He is the Reason for Creation and simultaneously a mercy to the worlds.

In the Noble Verse:

"We sent you only as a mercy to the worlds." (Anbiya: 107)

In every particle of the universe, there is life. The reason for this is The Messenger of Allah -peace be upon him-, who is the cause of existence.

As one of the wise saints express it beautifully:

"Ahmed the Chosen was made the light of Allah for the universe."

However, the Exalted the Allah is a known and visible being. The Most Noble Beloved -peace be upon him- is an unknown and invisible being. You could neither know nor see the known and visible the Exalted the Allah, so how can you know The Messenger of Allah -peace be upon him-?

Yet, throughout your life, you always said "I". Not once did you see, know, or recognize Him. He always called out to you from within, saying, "I am close to you," but you never heard.

"We are closer to him than his jugular vein." (Qaf: 16)

To see Him, He must reveal Himself. Whoever the Exalted the Allah bestows this sacred knowledge upon, they know and understand. The people of Truth are those to whom Allah the Almighty discloses. He reveals and informs them of His secrets as He wills.

"Allah gives manifold to whomever He wills." (Al-Baqarah: 261)

The people of Gnosis heard, saw, and comprehended this while still in the world. They declared it to be a mask, for they saw what was within, and understood it to be their own skull.

The people of Gnosis say **"Allah,"** attributing nothing to their ego.

The people of Gnosis reach a point where they believe in the Exalted the Allah and deny themselves. This was the secret.

When the presence of the Exalted the Allah was within you, you thought it was yours. When His presence withdraws, you die, decay, and are reduced to a bare skull. Does that skull have any value or significance?

You gathered all values within yourself. However, they always belonged to The Lord of All Worlds.

That skull, too, will rot and turn to ashes. The existence of Allah the Almighty will remain. You existed, decayed, and became nothing.

Allah the Almighty proclaims in the Verse from the Quran:

"Everything will perish except His Face." (Qasas: 88)

Indeed, He was always there and remains still.

"I take pride in my poverty." (K. Hafa)

This is the ultimate station of the secret within this Noble Saying. When even the skull turns to ashes, this state manifests. It is the one who says, "I own nothing; everything belongs to my Master."

They see that the skull exists and that it will decay in the grave; they also witness the decaying process and understand what it means when it turns to ashes. What significance does that ash hold? This is the most hidden secret.

Thus, first, the being must turn into a skull, seeing it with their own eyes; second, their entire existence must vanish.

While other people will decay in the grave, will cease to exist, and will understand that they are nothing, it is Allah the Almighty and The Messenger of Allah -peace be upon him- who guide them through these stages. Before dying, they know, see, and realize that they are mere ashes, and recognize that all existence belongs to Allah the Almighty. This is the secret of **"El fakru Fahri" (I take pride in my poverty).**

These secrets are indeed rarely understood. I see that even many close disciples ask, *"Is the Messenger of Allah -peace be upon him- talking about the poor?!"* However, the Noble Saying "**I take pride in my poverty**" is the highest station for those who attain true knowledge of Allah. Beyond this, there is no station.

The Messenger of Allah -peace be upon him- said in the Noble Saying:

"Allah was, and there was nothing besides Allah." (Bukhari)

And it remains so.

You too were annihilated, just like the universe.

He said **"Be"** and you appeared, He said **"Die"** and you vanished. You and the universe were like this.

There is no difference between a person and a particle in the sight of the Exalted the Allah. Because everything is a mask. Have we understood this? The secrets of divinity are present in every particle. However, humanity always saw the mask. Not once could they see Him and His secrets. They couldn't recognize that the true guide is the Exalted the Allah.

Our aim in explaining this to you is to show you the Divine Majesty.

Because He says **"Be!"** and you come into existence, He says **"Die!"** and you cease, and even when you are dead, He says **"Be!"** again and you come into existence once more.

•

Here is the proof of resurrection after death:

The people would demand miracles from Isa -peace be upon him-. They would point to the grave of a person who had died centuries ago and say, "Raise this one so we may understand that you are a true prophet!" He too would seek refuge in the Exalted the Allah and upon saying, **"Kum biiznillah! = Rise by Allah's permission!"** he would resurrect those who had died and become mere dust centuries ago.

In the time of Moses -peace be upon him-, a man from the children of Israel was found dead. The perpetrator, to hide his crime, insisted on finding the killer. Despite investigation, the murderer could not be identified.

Allah the Almighty commanded them to slaughter a cow and strike the deceased with one of its limbs to find the murderer. They found a cow matching the specified attributes and slaughtered it. When they struck the dead man with one of its limbs, he was resurrected and revealed his murderer with his own tongue. Thus, Allah the Almighty can give life and take it away at will, and He can bring the dead back to life whenever He desires.

Allah the Almighty states in the Noble Verse:

"He brings forth the living from the dead and the dead from the living, and He revives the earth after its death. So too will you be brought forth from your graves." (Rum: 19)

This means that everything in the universe exists by His command **"Be."** In fact, even the word **"Be"** is more than necessary. Exalted the Allah, the Omnipotent, has power over all things.

"He has power over all things." (Al-Maeda: 120)

•

Another Noble Verse states:

"He is the Al-Awwal and the Al-Akhir, the Az-Zahir and the Al-Batin..." (Hadid: 3)

Allah the Almighty is the **Al-Awwal**, without a beginning. He is the **Al-Akhir**, without an end. He is the **Az-Zahir**, as all visible entities are manifestations of His power. He is the **Al-Batin**, existing beyond all perception.

It is **Al-Batin**; the secrets of divinity reside within every particle. Existence is the realm where the particles of the light of being manifest. It all awaits a command.

"Kun feyekun" ("Be, and it is"), He says, and everything comes into existence. It happens through Him. All is but a body, a garment, a veil.

Knowledge of this is exclusive to what Allah the Almighty imparts. It is given to the most exalted possessors of knowledge. Even the most learned scholar only expresses his conjecture if the Divine does not reveal. Conjecture is invalid; like counterfeit money, it holds no value. This subject is not for those in the realm of Knowledge of Certainty or in the realm of Vision of Certainty, nor for the unseeing eye. It belongs to those who see Allah the Almighty yet do not see themselves. It is the domain of the **People of deep understanding**.

Allah the Almighty creates delicate spiritual faculties from the spirituality of His chosen servant. Only He knows how many He has created, and He sets those faculties in motion, oftentimes without the person's awareness. This is hidden knowledge. These are servants supported by Allah the Almighty with spirituality.

The Noble Verse states:

"They are those upon whose hearts Allah has inscribed faith and whom He has strengthened with a spirit from Himself." (Mujadilah: 22)

These are the servants who see and know Allah the Almighty. For Allah the Almighty gathers the universe at one point. And that point is the perfect human being.

Those who are perfect humans are the true scholars, deriving knowledge directly from the Divine without asking anyone.

"Fear Allah and observe piety, and Allah shall teach you." (Al-Baqarah: 282)

The realm of one who perceives is unique. When invoking **“Kulhüvellâhu Ehad” (Say, He is Allah, The One)** to affirm the oneness of Allah the Almightyhe both sees and knows there is naught besides Allah. Indeed, nothing else exists. Since he is immersed in one who knows through Allah, he is aware that the secrets of divinity permeate every particle. Those unaware of these mysteries remain wholly ignorant of them.

"He sent a messenger, to Himself with Himself."

The Absolute Doer directs that person as He wills. Thus, that person enacts the deeds of the Absolute Doer. In Truth, He is closer to that person than they are to themselves.

"We are closer to him than you are, but you do not see." (Waqi'ah: 85)

The creature holds no significance. He is the Absolute Doer. As He wills, so it is and manifests accordingly. This manifestation pertains to the purest of the purest. It is the task of those who have reached annihilation in Allah. More precisely, it is for those who are assigned this duty.

As stated in a Noble Verse:

"Be colored with the color of Allah! And who is better in coloring than Allah?" (Al-Baqarah: 138)

This Verse too belongs to the perfected human.

Because he is governed by the ordinances of Allah the Almighty or rather, because he is nullified in the presence of the Exalted the Allah, and attired in that spiritual garment, he is then colored with that divine hue.

When our Mother, Exalted the Aisha -may Allah be pleased with her-, was asked about the character of The Messenger of Allah -peace be upon him-, she responded:

“The character of the Prophet -peace be upon him- was the Qur'an.” (Muslim)

In other words, the application of all the rulings in the Holy Qur'an is observed in the life of The Messenger of Allah. In this regard, he is the Noble Qur'an personified.

When they say **“Alhamdulillahi Rabbil alamin” (Praise be to Allah, Lord of all worlds),** they contemplate the Lord of all worlds and see only Him in the universe.

They are the true heirs of the Prophet. Their knowledge is the knowledge of the heart, it is gifted. This knowledge comes to them from the Exalted the Allah and The Messenger of Allah. Their business is with the Truth, they think of the Truth, they are occupied with the Truth. They have no dealings or benefits with the people, nor do they expect anything from them.

Those who are immersed in Allah say **“There is no Allah but Allah”.** They say this with insight and understanding. These are the true Sufis.

Our Master, Master Esad Sir -may his secret be sanctified-, said:

“As long as there exists an object of desire other than the Divine in the heart, or an idol in Sufi terms, saying ‘There is no Allah but Allah’ is difficult, and its acceptance and means of union are uncertain.”

One who is heedless of and forgetful of Allah's blessings, and clings to their ego, deifies themselves. Why? Because they attribute Allah's bounties to their own self.

Man possesses not even a single hair; that too was created by Allah the Almighty. Yet, in every field, man repeatedly claims "I, I, I..." These claims are no more than idols.

However, the Exalted the Allah states in His Noble Verse:

"Wherever you are, He is with you." (Hadid: 4)

I am a worthless creature. I am but a mask, and my self is a worthless being. The Creator and Sustainer is the Exalted Creator.

The people of Gnosis have realized and acknowledged this through the grace of Allah the Almighty:

"This is the grace and bounty of Allah; He gives it to whom He wills." (Al Jumu’ah: 4)

They recognized, knew, and spoke of it while still in this world.

As for you, will you only come to understand this when Allah the Almighty withdraws His presence, when you decay in the grave, when your skull turns to ashes?

The difference between the people of Gnosis and others is like that between the living and the dead.

One has killed his soul while the soul lives on.

"Die before you die." (K. Hafâ)

These have comprehended the secrets of this Noble Saying.

The other's soul has perished; the self-lives, he roams like a living corpse. These are impostors.

Anyone who makes claims of their own self, know that they are firewood for hell.

Allah the Almighty says in the Noble Verse:

"Like beams of wood propped up." (Munafiqun: 4)

<u>Bodily existence is subject to Five Manifestations:</u>

1. Bodily existence,
2. Self,
3. The soul,
4. Spirituality,
5. Allah the Almighty's divine manifestation in the heart.

This divine manifestation is not granted to everyone. Allah the Almighty's manifestation in gnosis is exclusively for The Perfect Human. The manifestation of spirituality is reserved for the Perfect guide.

The heart, soul, secret, hidden, and the most hidden aspects are transcended by the soul, which, upon overcoming the whole self and occupying that realm, becomes dominant over the body. Those who transcend these subtleties become human beings stripped of their animalistic attributes.

The self under the occupation of the soul is either sick or dead, akin to a living corpse.

SWEET AND BITTER WATER

Allah the Almighty in drawing attention to His divine power in creating things in varied forms, states in the Qur'an:

"The two bodies of water are not alike. One is sweet, refreshing, and easy to drink. The other is salty and bitter." (Fatir: 12)

There are many profound reasons behind the various creations of water. Underground waters, such as those from springs and wells, and surface waters, like rivers and lakes, are sweet and refreshing. People drink from these waters according to their needs and derive pleasure from them.

Water is the source of life, one of the essential substances for living. The Qur'an states that every living thing is created from water. In all forms of life, like plants and animals, water is present; without it, they cannot sustain themselves.

The waters in the seas and oceans, however, are exceedingly bitter. The bitterness and extreme salinity burn the throat of anyone who drinks them, tormenting the inner being.

The two seas, one with salty water and the other with sweet, or in other words, the bitter and the sweet waters, are not equal. This Qur'anic Verse symbolizes the difference between a believer and a disbeliever, or between the land of Islam and the land of disbelief.

The believer is illuminated by the light of faith, whereas the other is engulfed in the darkness of disbelief. One is esteemed in the sight of Truth due to their faith, while the other is rejected because of their disbelief. Faith brings benefit in every respect, while disbelief brings harm in every regard.

"Yet, from each you eat fresh fish." (Fatir: 12)

In salty seas as well as in sweet waters, there are fresh fish. Each comes in different types and shapes. Their tastes also vary.

"And you remove your ornaments." (Fatir: 12)

As stated in another Noble Verse:

"From both of them emerge pearl and coral." (Rahman: 22)

Just as Allah the Almighty brings forth grains and fragrant plants from the earth, He also brings forth pearls and corals from the water for humanity. These gems, used as ornaments, are also among the blessings of trade. By reminding His servants of the subtleties of His mercies, Allah the Almighty demonstrates the perfection of His uncountable and innumerable blessings.

"You see the ships cleaving through the sea." (Fatir: 12)

This scene forms a profound spectacle for those who witness it. Though carrying heavy loads and hundreds of people, they do not sink. They navigate by the permission and will of Allah the Almighty.

As stated in another Noble Verse:

"His are the ships raised aloft in the sea like mountains." (Rahman: 24)

By their size, these ship mountains are made subservient to humanity by Allah the Almighty. Thus, people can travel to any desired destination on the sea and manage as they wish.

"This is so that you may seek and find the bounties that Allah has bestowed upon you. Perhaps you will then give thanks." (Fatir: 12)

He has revealed His boundless bounties, and granted you reasons for gratitude so that you may fulfill your duty of thankfulness.

•

Indeed, Allah the Almighty has made all that is in the heavens and the earth submit to His servants as an act of His grace and mercy.

In His Noble Verse, He says:

"Allah merges the night into the day and the day into the night." (Fatir: 13)

He takes from one and adds to the other, or does the opposite. Thus, summer and winter lengthen and shorten. This is a manifestation of His boundless and limitless dominion. No one can deny this since it unfolds before everyone's eyes.

All these give peace and tranquility to hearts.

"He has subjected the sun and the moon to His command; each runs its course for an appointed term." (Fatir: 13)

Their revolutions around their orbits will continue until the Day of Judgment. This is the decree of Allah the Exalted and the All-Knowing.

In short:

"This is your Lord, Allah. Sovereignty belongs to Him." (Fatir: 13)

The entire creation is under His dominion and possession.

"As for those whom you invoke besides Him, they do not own even the membrane of a date seed." (Fatir: 13)

They cannot possess anything from the heavens and the earth, not even the worthless membrane.

"If you invoke them, they will not hear your call." (Fatir: 14)

For they are beings that neither hear nor understand. Worshipping the created instead of the Creator is the greatest folly.

"Even if they were to hear, they would not respond to you." (Fatir: 14)

They have no power to do anything that is asked of them; they cannot fulfill any of anyone's desires.

This is the situation in the worldly life. On the Day of Judgement, the greatest day of fear, Allah the Exalted will make them speak, and they will declare their distance from such aberrations.

"On the Day of Resurrection, they will renounce your association." (Fatir: 14)

Just as it is a great sorrow for one to suffer harm from where they sought benefit, it is equally sorrowful to see expected benefits remain unrealized.

Allah the Exalted declares that such news can only be given by Him:

"No one can inform you like Allah, who is All Informed." (Fatir: 14)

He alone reveals the hidden aspects and outcomes of matters, their Truth and reality.

By announcing that He is not in need of anyone, while all creatures are in need of Him and bowing in humility before Him, He states in His Noble Verse:

"O mankind! You are the ones who need Allah; Allah is Free of need, worthy of all praise." (Fatir: 15)

This message is made to all of humanity to remind them of the boundless blessings of Allah the Almighty.

Allah the Almighty in His essence, is All Sufficient and does not require anyone's gratitude and worship. Neediness is the hallmark of creation; all humans, in every state, are dependent on His grace and blessings.

Allah the Almighty in His essence, is praiseworthy and does not need the praise and glorification of His servants. He is already The One praised. Yet, it is obligatory for the servants to praise Him in response to the blessings He bestows.

To comprehend the extent of His generosity, grace, and mercy, people need to acknowledge this Truth.

"They will be in a seat of truthfulness, near the Sovereign, Perfect in Ability."
(Al-Qamar: 55)

THE PERFECT HUMAN

CHAPTER 8

- The Teacher of the Perfect Human Is Allah Himself
- The Perfect Human
- At the Core of the Perfect Human Is the Presence of Allah

THE MENTOR OF THE PERFECT HUMAN IS ALLAH THE EXALTED HIMSELF

Allah the Almighty declares in the Quran:

“No vision can grasp Him, but His grasp is over all vision.” (An’am: 103)

The earthly eyes cannot behold the Exalted the Allah. However, when He opens the eyes of the heart, one can see Him and what He reveals.

In another Noble Verse, He proclaims:

"Did we not give him two eyes?" (Balad: 8)

Allah the Almighty has granted humanity both an earthly eye and a heart eye.

Our beloved Prophet, the Messenger of Allah -peace be upon him-said in a Noble Saying:

"Every person's heart possesses two eyes. Through these eyes, unseen realms can be comprehended. If Allah wishes well for a servant, He opens the eyes of their heart to perceive what the worldly eye cannot see."

You see the veil and what lies upon it, yet you do not see Him. But there exists one who sees and knows what is within. The one who sees and knows what is within sees only Him. They recognize that the universe, themselves and the veil hold no true power. I, the humble servant, express this in one sentence:

"One who sees Allah the Almighty does not see themselves; one who sees themselves does not see Allah the Almighty."

All secrets lie at this point.

Allah the Almighty declares in a Noble Verse:

“Indeed, insights (the eye of the heart) have come to you from your Lord. Whoever sees does so for their own benefit, and whoever is blind, it is against their own self.” (An'am: 104)

The burden of this falls back on the individual.

Just as **"Seeing"** is for the eyes, **"Insight"** is for the heart.

The faculty that causes the eyes to see is called vision, similarly, the faculty that causes the heart to see is called insight.

Insight is a manifestation of Allah the Almighty’s attribute **“Basar” (All-seeing)** within His servants. Those blessed with this manifestation have the veils lifted from their eyes. Corresponding to the two eyes that see the external world, the heart has an eye that perceives the inner world, often called **"Eye of the Knowledge"** or the **"Eye of the Heart."**

In the second Verse of Surah al-Hashr, Allah the Almighty describes those endowed with insight as **"Ulul Absar"** (those endowed with vision).

Insight is a light that Allah the Almighty places in the heart of the believing servant, enabling them to grasp the Truth.

Verses of the Holy Qur'an that illuminate the Truth are referred to as **"Besair" (Insights)** for this reason. (Araf: 203 and Qasas: 43)

For those whose hearts have been blinded and whose insight is blocked, they are described with terms like **"Blind"** (Al-Baqarah: 18).

In the Noble Verse, it is stated:

"It is not the eyes that are blind, but the hearts within the chests that are blind." (Hajj: 46)

True blindness is not the blindness of the eyes, but the blindness of the heart. The harm from this blindness has no limit, no end.

Allah the Almighty reveals the "Truth" clearly, opens the insight of those He wishes to convey it to, and makes known what He wills, shows what He wills. On the other hand, He does not show it to the eyes of the unworthy, He binds their insight, leaving them in blindness and darkness.

The wisdom of this is explained in a Noble Verse as follows:

"Thus do we explain the signs variously, so that they may say, 'You have studied,' and that we may make it clear to a people who know." (An'am: 105)

The revelation of Allah the Almighty's Noble Verses has caused some people to fall into misfortune. They said to The Messenger of Allah -peace be upon him-, *"You have read and learned these from somewhere else. You want us to listen to them as the 'Word of Allah'!"* Thus, they went astray. For others, it became a source of happiness, and they were honored with the dignity of faith.

Who taught the Prophet? It was none other than the Glorious Allah.

Indeed, the Exalted Instructor, in another Noble Verse, states:

He declares, "If you fear Allah and possess piety, Allah will be your teacher." (Al-Baqarah: 282)

In another Verse, He states:

"You have been taught that which you did not know." (An'am: 91)

I humbly convey in the simplest manner, with the style Allah has inspired in me, that the true guide is Allah the Exalted. It is impossible not to understand, yet you do not comprehend because your mind is not engaged, and your self is not at that level.

As for those endowed with insight, Allah the Most High, has opened their eyes and revealed the Truth.

Indeed, The Messenger of Allah -peace be upon him- in a Noble Saying declares:

"Beware the intuition of the believer, for he sees with the light of Allah, the Mighty and Majestic." (Munawi)

In summary, what we wish to express is this: Outer knowledge is taught by people, inner knowledge is taught by the Truth. As outer knowledge is acquired, a person's information increases, but as Allah the Most High, teaches, a person's knowledge of the Truth deepens.

•

THE PERFECT HUMAN

"The Perfect Human", is known by various names: **"spiritual pole," "spiritual helper a renewer of religion,"** among others.

Some reside in the circle of bliss; others are in both the circle of bliss and the center of salvation. Some stand in the presence of the Exalted the Allah.

In the Noble Verse, it is proclaimed:

"They are in the seat of Truth, in the presence of a Sovereign Omnipotent." (Qamar: 55)

Not even every angel can enter here.

For the Exalted Khatam al-Anbiya (Seal of the Prophets) -peace be upon him- has conveyed in the Noble Saying:

"The believers of complete faith are superior to certain angels in the sight of Allah." (Ibn Majah)

This matter pertains to The Perfect Human. Let's briefly outline their characteristics.

The Messenger of Allah -peace be upon him- stated in a Noble Saying:

"A believer is the mirror of a believer." (Abu Dawood)

Here, the heart of the believing servant is alluded to by the first "believer," while Allah the Almighty Himself is intended by the second "believer."

When Allah gazes upon them, He sees nothing but Himself.

When a scholar of the Truth passes away, the birds in the trees and the fish in the sea mourn. When an enlightened being passes, the entire universe weeps for him.

Allow me to reveal the secret and wisdom behind this. It is because he is the surrogate of **"We have sent you only as a mercy for the worlds"**, for **"The heart of the believer is The Throne of the Most Merciful,"** and **he bears the Divine Trust**, that the universe grieves for him.

"We have certainly created man in the best of stature." (Tin: 4)

This Verse manifests in them.

Exalted the Ali -may Allah honor his face- remarked:

"Thy remedy lies within thee, yet thou knowest not.

Thy ailment too is from thee, yet thou sees it not.

Thou deemest thyself a mere speck,

Yet within thee are enfolded all the universes (and thou knowest it not)."

Why? Because thou art favored by the manifestations of the Divine.

"In this threshing floor, I am but a single grain,

The universe is from me."

He is indeed but a grain. Yet when He manifests, He becomes a cosmos. Allah manifests wherever He wills.

The tree spoke to Prophet Moses. But it was not the tree speaking. Allah had manifested Himself in the tree.

In the Essence of the Perfect Human Lies the Presence of the Exalted the Allah:

Everything has an essence. In the essence of mountains lies the gem. In the essence of the Kaaba lies the Black Stone. In the essence of the perfect human lies the Presence of the Exalted the Allah.

The perfect human gazes upon themselves; just as one sees the shell of an egg as insignificant, believe and trust that they see and know with certitude their own insignificance.

When the particle called Immutable Archetypes breaks apart, what happens? Upon reaching the final stage of the Unity of Being;

“Allah is the Light of the heavens and the earth.” (Nur: 35)

When this Noble Verse's manifestation occurs, this particle, this atom, too, breaks apart. When an atom, that is, a particle, splits, nothing remains in it. Nothing remains within, and it becomes the Great Universe. Why? Because there is nothing left other than Allah the Exalted. Yet, if even a particle remains, it signifies existence. Hence, the becoming of the Great Universe arises from nothingness. Since even a particle is existence, it is necessary to become nothing. Thus, the perfect human becomes the Great Universe.

Apart from Him, there is no existence, no being.

These are the ones graced by the manifestation of this Noble Verse. They see and know that Existence is Him, and being is Him. They recognize that everything comes into being by the command **“Be,”** and that everything is given a form that the secrets of divinity are in every particle, that the universe emerges from the manifestation site of these particles of existence.

In a Sacred saying, it is stated:

"I could not fit into the heavens and the earth, but I fit into the heart of my faithful servant." (K. Hafâ: 2256)

The true adherents of The Unity of Being are only these individuals. For they see the Truth, yet they do not see themselves. The secrets of Divinity are present in every particle, thus He encompasses everything entirely. Everything encompasses everything, yet He alone encompasses all.

"Allah is the Encompasser of all things." (An-Nisa: 126)

Since Allah the Almighty encompasses all things entirely, wherever you look, you shall see Him alone.

"To Allah belong the east and the west, so wherever you turn, there is the Face of Allah." (Al-Baqarah: 115)

These are the select and special servants of Allah the Almighty. They are created for Himself, chosen, and have been taken into His presence.

These are the perfect human beings. They are the ones accepted into the divine presence of the Exalted the Allah.

"In a seat of honor in the presence of the Sovereign, Perfect in Ability." (Qamar: 55)

•

Those who are grateful know Him, the Sublime...

The Sultan who bestows infinite blessings.

Only He is the Creator,

Only He is the Provider,

With limitless grace and abundant generosity, that Creator Sultan...

•

These individuals do not see themselves; they see the Truth. They see and know that everything is from the Truth. They recognize their incapacity to comprehend even a speck of the blessings bestowed upon them. Because they see from Him, and they see Him.

Indeed, these people understand that they are but rags. Exalted the Allah uses these rags as He wills. He ensures that the place He desires is cleansed.

These true Sufis and true adherents of The Unity of Being know, see, and proclaim these Truths while still in this world. What do they know? They understand that they are nothing more than a picture, a mask, or a rag. In summary, they are the rags of the Truth.

The true guide is Allah the Exalted. Genuine sufis and those who speak of the true The Unity of Being see that both themselves and the entire universe came into existence by the command **"Be,"** and they perceive themselves as mere frames. Within that frame, they witness and recognize the manifestations and presence of Allah the Exalted. Henceforth, within them exists the Truth. They see that Truth and understand they are nothing but a frame. Such individuals alone are worthy of spiritual connection.

For the Allah the Almighty has said:

"Within yourself… Do you not see?" (Adh-Dhariyat: 21)

The secrets and mysteries of this Verse are revealed only to these select individuals. They are the keepers of the chamber of secrets.

One who connects to them establishes a direct bond with Allah the Exalted. This is because that person has annihilated themselves in the Truth. No other than Truth exists within them. This state is unique to those who have attained such a realization.

In the Noble Verse of the Holy Qur'an, Allah the Almighty decrees:

"Be with the Truthful Ones." (At-Tawba: 119)

This is a divine command. But to whom is this divine command addressed, and who are its exclusive recipients? To whom should one make a spiritual connection?

•

"O you who believe! Fear Allah and be with those who are truthful."

(At-Tawbah: 119)

WHAT IS SPİRİTUAL CONNECTİON?

AND TO WHOM IS IT DIRECTED?

CHAPTER 9

- What Is Spiritual Connection?
- To Whom Is Spiritual Connection Directed?
- Those Who Make Their Desires Their Allah and Those Who Follow Them
- Truth and Falsehood
- Fertile Soil and Barren Soil

WHAT IS SPIRITUAL CONNECTION?

In the lexicon, the word Spiritual Connection means the connection of two things. In the language of Sufism, it is a spiritual bond facilitating the flow of divine grace between the guide and the disciple. This connection is sometimes explicitly, sometimes implicitly referenced in the Qur'an and Noble Saying.

In a Noble Verse, Allah the Almighty says:

"O you who believe! Fear Allah and be with the Truthful Ones." (At-Tawba: 119)

In the commentary "Bahrul Hakhâyık," it has been stated that "those who are Truthful" refers to the "spiritual guides ".

Allah, the Most Glorious, has charged the people of faith with this Noble Verse, commanding and obligating them to be in the company of a perfected spiritual guide, who is an heir of the Prophets.

Knowing that Allah the Magnificent **would not impose what His servants cannot bear,** when He commands to be with the Truthful, it signifies that He has always provided and made known the existence of such individuals.

The companionship with a guide can be both physical and spiritual, which we can explain through Spiritual Connection. The degree of Spiritual Connection, whether it is weak or strong, depends on the amount of love present; as love increases, so does the strength of Spiritual Connection.

In another Noble Verse, He says:

"Cooperate in righteousness and piety." (Al-Maeda: 2)

Though material aid is necessary for a person, the pivotal aspect is spiritual assistance. For the former is transient, while the latter is eternal.

What could be a more beautiful form of assistance than that of a Perfect guide who channels the divine grace bestowed upon his heart by the Lord into the withered garden of the disciple's heart? This nurtures the tree of faith, allowing it to thrive, spread its branches, and bear the fruit of worship, leading to eternal bliss.

Spiritual Connection is cooperation in line with this divine command.

In another Noble Verse, it is said:

"O you who believe! Fear Allah and seek a means of nearness to Him." (Al-Maeda: 35)

When we closely observe this Verse, we note that along with piety, a means to salvation is also stipulated. The scholars have interpreted this means as a Perfect guide. For the Perfect guide is the inheritor of the Prophet in his era. Just as salvation is unattainable for those who do not follow the Prophet -peace be upon him-, it is also difficult for those who do not follow his inheritor.

The Honored One, the Pride of the Universe -peace be upon him-stated:

"Allah has such saintly servants whose hearts are oceans of divine mercy."

From this Noble Saying, the meaning derived is that one should channel the divine mercy, found in vast oceans within the hearts of the saints, into one's own heart through a spiritual path. This spiritual flow of grace and mercy is termed Spiritual Connection.

•

Exalted the Abd al-Qadir al-Gilani -may his secret be sanctified- stated, **"What you are meant to purchase is clear, and I sell it to you."** That is to say, you can only engage in Spiritual Connection and receive grace to the extent of your love and devotion. I can only give you what is destined for you. The fountain flows, yet you do not hold your pitcher to fill it...

•

Exalted the Master Muhammad Esad Erbilî -may his secret be sanctified- says:

"In the exalted The Noble Path progress and the reception of grace do not solely depend on the abundance of recitations and devotions, but it is well known and apparent to the knowledgeable that heartfelt sincerity and genuine love also have a significant impact. Some of the esteemed Masters have added to the saying 'A single glance from a Master is superior to forty days of trials,' and have accepted that the blessed gaze of a perfect spiritual guide is also a means to attain grace and progress." (Letter 30)

"As it is known, the purpose of Spiritual Connection is to attain grace. It is without doubt that the true source of grace is none other than Almighty Allah. However, as the Beloved of Allah, Muhammad Mustafa -peace be upon him- is also the place of manifestation for Allah's essence and attributes, receiving grace from The Messenger of Allah -peace be upon him- is essentially receiving grace from Allah.

"Adopting the morals of Allah and His Messenger" in compliance with the prophetic command to rid ourselves of base attributes and adorn ourselves with praiseworthy character, those who have attained the sublime honor of Annihilation in the Messenger and more precisely Annihilation in Allah through the feeling of complete annihilation, their Spiritual Connection too:

'Seek to draw near to Him' is commanded to all believers through the Noble Verse. (Al-Maeda: 35)..." (Letter 13)

•

Exalted İmâmı Rabbâni -may his secret be sanctified- regarding the practice of Spiritual Connection, states:

"The spontaneous emergence of Spiritual Connection without forcing oneself is a sign of complete closeness between the disciple and the Master. This closeness allows for benefit and enlightenment. Among the many paths, there is none that brings one closer faster than Spiritual Connection.

How great a blessing it is to be granted this grace.

Exalted Hâce Ahrar -may his secret be sanctified- says: 'Spiritual Connection is more beneficial than the remembrance of Truth.'

In other words, the Master's image is more valuable for the disciple than the act of remembrance. This is because, at the beginning, the disciple does not have a complete closeness with Allah the Almighty. Therefore, he cannot gain much benefit through the path of remembrance." (Letter 187)

"To progress in this noble Path depends on the loving Spiritual Connection with the guiding Master.

He has traversed this path as the chosen one, and has been drawn to these perfections with great power.

His gaze is a cure for the diseases of the heart; his spiritual focus removes inner ailments.

On this path, growth and the cultivation of others occur through reflection. The disciple, bound by the love for their Master, mirrors them at every moment. They are illuminated by the rays of light emanating from the Master." (Letter 260)

•

Imami Shârâni -may his secret be sanctified- describes the etiquettes of remembrance in his book **Nefehât-ül Kuds,** emphasizing that Spiritual Connection, i.e., envisioning the Master's persona, is among the essential etiquettes of remembrance.

The eminent scholar Sayyid Sharif Jürjani, at the end of his Sharhi Mawaqif, also attests to the validity of Spiritual Connection, suggesting it as a means for the disciple to receive divine grace.

In his books titled Tâciye, **Master Tâjuddin Osmani** -may his secret be sanctified- lists the reasons for reaching Allah, indicating that attaching one's heart to a perfect Master is the third reason.

It is stated from AbdulQadir Gilani -may his secret be sanctified- that those who seek the exalted path must engage in Spiritual Connection with the pious saints.

Additionally, scholars like Imami Ghazâli, Imami Suyuti, Master Khalil, Ebul Abbas Al-Mursi, Ibni Atâ, Najmuddini Kubra, and many others have shared this view in their works. (Risâlei Es'adiyye)

•

The divine grace belonging to Allah the Exalted emanates from His Beloved -peace be upon him- and flows into the ocean of the guide of the time.

Those who are included in the eternal allocation must keep their hearts open towards that ocean to receive their share. The water flows perpetually, but you do not hold your jug to the fountain. Holding the jug to the fountain means disconnecting from everything including remembrance and thought, and standing in Spiritual connection to bind the heart to that ocean.

By detaching from everything, the eyes are closed. The head is slightly turned to the right, and the window of the heart is opened and fastened there. One waits this way for fifteen, twenty minutes, or even longer. When one will attract the gaze of the Perfect guide is uncertain. One must always be ready so that if it strikes even once, it revives the heart. The Lord gives as He wills. You also receive your share and walk with it. They can make you leap distances in an instant that you could not traVerse on your own for years. Your inner world entirely transforms. With that grace and abundance, they turn the copper within you into gold. The old becomes brand new. The entire body is revitalized. Since it is uncertain when the manifestation will occur, lean your heart there and always await it with sincerity and loyalty. Do not look elsewhere. Withdraw your hands and eyes from the external world and turn to your inner world. You came from Truth, and you will return to Truth. Therefore, engage with Truth uninterruptedly, with determination, and unwavering perseverance.

•

TO WHOM IS SPIRITUAL CONNECTION DIRECTED?

1. It is directed to those who take pride in the Exalted the Allah. For they have become annihilated in Truth. Not a trace of their existence remains.

As for those who take pride in their ego; they have directly idolized themselves, and those who Spiritual Connection to them connect to the idol of the ego. This is a matter so delicate and subtle, yet it remains unknown.

In the Noble Verse:

"Be with the Truthful Ones." (At-Tawba: 119)

Who are these Truthful ones?

"They dwell in the presence of a Sovereign whose authority and power are unchallenged." (Qamar: 55)

Those who attain closeness to Allah the Almighty are elevated to the station of Truthfulness.

Spiritual Connection is performed only towards these individuals and no one else. They are few in this world.

•

2. Spiritual Connection is performed solely and exclusively towards one who knows and perceives himself to be nothing but a veil.

Our Master, The Messenger of Allah, -peace be upon him- proclaims in a Noble Saying:

"Gazing at the face of a scholar who acts upon his knowledge is like worship." (Munawî)

For he is but a veil. Within him truly resides Truth. Thus, whoever looks upon him is favored with the divine manifestation.

•

3. One makes spiritual connection to those who understand that the body is merely a garment. These individuals see and perceive through Allah the Exalted.

Didn't The Glorious Truth proclaim in the Noble Verse:

"Within yourself... Do you not see?" (Adh-Dhariyat: 21)

These are the only ones who witness and know that Allah the Exalted resides within. They alone are privy to this secret. Spiritual Connection is made exclusively to them; it is not extended to others. In this manner, it serves as a bridge to reach Allah the Exalted, a means, and indeed, the most important one.

These are the ones who attain the secret of **"El fakru fahrî" (poverty is my pride)**. They understand that in the face of the infinite blessings bestowed by Allah the Almighty, they are incapable of comprehending even a single particle. Yet, they see and realize their own helplessness. They know and see simultaneously.

•

In his Noble Saying, The Messenger of Allah -peace be upon him-declares:

"The believer is the mirror of the believer." (Abu Dawood)

Who are endued with these divine manifestations? Why do the objectors raise objections?

In the Noble Verse:

"Within yourself... Do you not see?" (Adh-Dhariyat: 21)

This manifestation is reserved for those who perceive Exalted the Allah within themselves and recognize that exalted the Allah resides in them.

They realize they are merely a mask, their being nothing but a garment, and acknowledge that within them, there is solely and only Allah.

When Exalted the Allah manifests in such a person's heart, they see only Himself alone.

"A believer is a mirror to another believer." (Abu Dawood)

Only those who embody this prophetic saying (Noble Saying) are graced with its secret; it is not applicable to others. For Allah grants them what He bestows upon none else, supporting them with a spirit from Himself.

In His Noble Verse, He states:

"They are those in whose hearts He has inscribed faith and strengthened them with a spirit from Himself." (Mujadilah: 22)

He felt the presence within and saw the Existence, knew it, but did not see himself.

"This is the bounty of Allah, which He gives to whom He wills." (Al-Jumu'ah: 4)

•

Thus, the one who engages in Spiritual Connection does so with this inner presence. Only those who are granted permission for Spiritual Connection are effective in this practice. Why? Because he has annihilated his own existence in the presence of Allah the Exalted. For the true guide is indeed Allah the Exalted.

Those who object do so out of ignorance, as they are deprived of the manifestations of these Noble Verse and these Noble Saying. However, through their objections, they reveal their true ignorance.

The Messenger of Allah -peace be upon him- said in his Noble Saying:

"Knowledge is of two kinds. One is the knowledge of the tongue (which is the apparent knowledge) **and it is Allah's proof against His servants. The other is the knowledge of the heart** (the knowledge of divine gnosis). **This is the useful knowledge for attaining the ultimate goal."** (Tirmidhi)

It is because they are deprived of this beneficial knowledge that they object and deny what they do not understand.

We give you the measure.

1. Those who remain in the apparent realm; they know they are scholars and say, "I am a scholar."

2. Those who pursue the knowledge of the Path; they know and confess they are ignorant.

3. Those who pursue the knowledge of the truth; they know they are nothing.

4. Those who pursue the knowledge of Gnosis; they have reached the presence of Allah, recognize and know the Truth, but do not know themselves.

•

Those who remain in the apparent realm do not know "What is the soul?" do not know "What is spiritual reality?" do not know "What are the subtleties?" In Truth, they do not even know themselves.

Why do they not know?

Because they are not privy to the secret of the Noble Saying:

"Who knows oneself, knows their Lord." (K. Hafa)

They do not know their ignorance, nor do they know their nothingness. Since they have not attained Gnosis, they do not know Exalted the Allah. Yet, they speak of sufism. However, they are imposters.

They see themselves as so great, so arrogant that they consider themselves to be scholars.

Their arrogance is as vast as mountains; they think they are learned, unaware of their ignorance.

However, Allah the Almighty says in His Noble Verse:

"You have been given from knowledge only a little." (Isra: 85)

And I will present to you their calamities.

The Messenger of Allah -peace be upon him- said in a Noble Saying:

"Whoever says 'I am a scholar,' know that he is ignorant." (Munawi)

"Seeing oneself as significant is a sin greater than any other."

"A person's self-admiration can destroy seventy years of worship." (Jami' alSaghir)

•

Although it is a divine command to attach your heart to a friend of Allah the Almighty what evidence do those who deny this divine command hold?

Instead of showing your tongue, show your proof!

For I have silenced their tongues with the Verses of the Qur'an and the Noble Sayings that I have put forth before them.

You prostrate before the Kaaba with the intention of servitude to Allah, and yet you do not accept polytheism!

It was Allah who commanded Abraham to build the sacred Kaaba and commanded that all souls be invited to it. This continues until the Day of Judgment and includes everyone.

Just as the Exalted the Allah commanded Abraham to build and invite, it is also the Exalted the Allah who commands us to be with the Truthful.

Man has constructed his own being, and it is declared that Allah is within him.

"Within yourself... Do you not see?" (Adh-Dhariyat: 21)

"'Be with the Truthful.' This refers to Spiritual Connection. While the House of Allah, encompasses all, being with the Truthful is specific.

Those who receive their share evolve through this means. At the same time, since **'The heart of the believer is the Throne of the Most Merciful** they will receive the gifts and eternal destiny bestowed by Allah the Almighty through Spiritual Connection and love.

All material allocations in the universe come from the material throne. All spiritual allocations come from the spiritual throne, which is the perfect human being. For this reason, those blessed by Allah the Almighty receive their share from there.

Allah the Almighty says in His Noble Verse:

'Seek a means of approach to Him' (Al-Maeda: 35), commanding us to find a way to approach Him.

The means is to persist in Spiritual Connection with complete love.

•

Allah the Almighty says in another Noble Verse:

'O you who believe! Be patient, persevere, remain stationed, and fear Allah that you may be successful.' (Al' Imran: 200)

Master Es'ad Sir -may his secret be sanctified- said:

"If I use this Verse in this sense, I should not be seen as mistaken by the literal scholars. Because;

"The Qur'an has an outward meaning and an inward meaning. Its inward meaning extends up to seven levels.' ***Such Noble Sayings have expanded the scope of interpretation."*** (Letter 45)

You do not consider prostrating before the Kaaba as idolatry, but the meaning of Spiritual Connection:

"Be with the Truthful Ones." (At-Tawba: 119)

Why do you consider this divine command as polytheism? Both are commands of Allah Almighty.

•

Literal scholars express the existence and oneness of Allah the Almighty outwardly. They know His blessed names and strive to describe them.

Why do the literal scholars not know the Truth?

For they are deprived of the knowledge of Gnosis. Their knowledge is of the written lines, and their intellects are limited to practical and eschatological reasoning.

But those of true wisdom strive to reveal and proclaim the very essence of Allah the Exalted.

They proclaim: He is Existence, He is the Present... All entities are but the manifestation points of the particles of the light of existence.

In Truth, there is no existence other than His. One who is with the Truth endeavors to describe the Truth. Those who remain in the apparent, however, are with their egos, truly heedless of Allah the Exalted. They even imagine themselves to be separate from Allah the Exalted.

Our Master, The Messenger of Allah -peace be upon him-, conveys in his Noble Saying:

"There are such knowledges that they are like hidden treasures. Only those who are one who knows Allah understand them. When they speak of this knowledge, those who are heedless of Allah the Almighty do not comprehend them." (Erbaîn)

Thus, it is from their lack of understanding that they object; their knowledge and intellect fall short.

And in the Noble Verse, it is stated:

"Most people do not know." (Mumin: 57)

"They do not use their intellect." (Ankabut: 63)

The knowledge of the enlightened ones is the knowledge of the heart. It comes from Allah the Exalted and The Messenger of Allah -peace be upon him-. Their intellect has been elevated after the Universal Intellect to become People of deep understanding.

In His exalted Noble Verse, The Exalted Truth declares:

“This is Allah’s grace, which He bestows upon whom He will.” (Al-Jumu'ah: 4)

“Allah gives manifold increase to whom He wills.” (Al-Baqarah: 261)

In another Noble Verse, it is stated:

“Allah has not made for any man two hearts within him.” (Al-Ahzab: 4)

For how can one heart hold Allah the Exalted and at the same time hold things other than Allah? If Allah resides in that heart, it is united with the Truth; if worldly matters enter, it is filled with worldly things.

Those who reach this station know that their faces are but masks. They see and know their bodies are but garments. Why? Because they are empowered by a sacred spirit. And they recognize the true guide as being none other than Allah the Exalted. But only they know this.

•

You do not consider bowing down in prostration before The Venerable Kaaba as idolatry, yet why do you consider the Spiritual Connection as such when the divine command **"Be with the Truthful ones"** also comes from Allah the Almighty? Both are ultimately decrees from Allah the Almighty.

The perfect human is nothing more than a veil, a mask. Everything that exists within The Venerable Kaaba also resides within The Perfect Human. There exists a structure created by Him, in its essence is the Truth.The Venerable Kaaba contains the Hacerül esved (Black Stone).

There, within, lies the Altınoluk (Golden Spout), from which those destined since eternity receive their share. What you see in The Perfect Human is merely a mask, a veil. Within, they know and perceive that there is nothing but Him alone.

As stated in the Noble Verse:

"Within yourself... Do you not see?" (Adh-Dhariyat: 21)

Only these individuals truly perceive. Because within them there is only Him, that is why they become the House of Allah. Thus, the Spiritual Connection can only be made to House of Allah.

Allah the Almighty commanded Abraham -peace be upon him- to construct The Venerable Kaaba and ordered the invitation of all souls. This decree is perpetual, extending until the Day of Judgment, inclusive to all.

The same Allah, who commanded Abraham -peace be upon him- to build and invite, also commands being with the Truthful ones.

Man built his edifice, declaring his presence within.

"Within yourself... Do you not see?" He commanded. (Adh-Dhariyat: 21)

The purpose of companionship with the faithful is Spiritual Connection. While the House of Allah is for the masses, being with the faithful is for the select few.

Those graced with this assortment achieve completion through this channel. Moreover, since his heart is The Throne of the Most Merciful, Allah's entrusted grace and predestined fate are received through Spiritual Connection and love.

In His Noble Verse, Allah states:

“Seek the way to come closer to Him,” commanding the quest to draw nearer to Him. (Al-Maeda: 35)

The means are bound to perpetual Spiritual Connection with sincere love.

In sum:

He is but a veil. Only Spiritual Connection is viable for those placed in this condition. These are unique in the world, appearing once in a century.

In a Noble Saying, it is stated:

"Allah the Almighty sends a renewer of religion Path to this Community at the beginning of every century to rejuvenate the faith." (Abu Dawood)

They carry the light and sainthood of the Prophet, and they may have assistants. This does not apply to anyone else. Everyone should know their place and limits.

"O Messenger! Have you seen the one who takes his own desire as his deity? Will you then be a guardian over him? (Will you protect him from polytheism" (Al-Furqan: 43)

And yet, humans do not bow before an idol. The one who makes his ego a deity is indeed an idol. He has turned himself into an idol. Those who make Spiritual Connection to him idolize him. See, there is that self-admiring one, Allah created him from a drop of fluid, manifested His power. He revealed him and placed him on the stage of trial. Soon, he will take away his existence, place him in the grave, and he will become a handful of dust. Then you will understand, but judgment will have already passed against you. You are condemned to burn in hell alongside your ego idol.

Our beginning is weakness and sin.

Our end is death and the grave.

This was a stage, we were sent to be tested. Allah the Almighty does not wrong anyone, but truly, humans are unjust and ignorant.

"For truly, humans are very unjust and ignorant." (Al-Ahzab: 72)

And the Almighty will ask them, "Did they worship you?" When asked this, they will not know how to escape or what to say.

He will also question those who worshiped them, "Did you worship these?" They will be astounded, seeing the Truth, but they will end up in hell with their leaders and religious leaders.

"They and the deviants will be thrown headlong into it. Even all the soldiers of Satan." (Shuara: 94-95)

•

The purpose of Sufism is to realize, "I entered as a great man, knowing I am as insignificant as a speck."

Sufism is entirely for knowing this and reaching this state. This becomes the beginning.

It is understood that unless a person annihilates their existence, they cannot even begin to know their Creator. The secret of **"Men arefe" (He who knows)** manifests here. Only by knowing one's self can one know their Lord.

To know oneself, it is necessary to descend to that drop of despised water from which one was created. That too was created by Him. This is what you are. He is The One who created the despicable water. He is The One who created you, transforming you from state to state, endowing you with His blessings, perfectly placing your members, and showing you with a unique attribute. Thus, to understand The Existent, it is necessary to annihilate one's existence. These are specifics belonging to the traveler on the path of Sufism.

But concerning the Perfect Man, the pure hearted guide's greatness in the world:

"Neither earth nor sky could contain me, but I have found my abode in the heart of a faithful servant."

Such is expressed in a sacred saying.

To abide in the heart of the faithful servant means **to manifest in his heart.** This does not imply that Allah literally enters the hearts of His servants.

In essence, the servant's heart becomes but a veil. That is to say, his existence is merely a veil. The dominion belongs to Allah the Exalted. For within him resides Allah the Almighty. Thus, spiritually, he becomes a Kaaba.

Previously, it was explained that just as diamonds lie in the heart of mountains, the Black Stone in the heart of the Kaaba, so is exalted the Allah presence in the heart of the enlightened human.

Allah the Most High, who commands prostration towards the Kaaba structure made of stone also commands, in keeping with the Quranic Verse **"Be with the Truthful ones,"** the practice of Spiritual Connection with one who contains only Him.

His form is but a veil. Yet, the veil knows that it is both a concealment and merely a mask. For it beholds The One within. It realizes it is a mask. Thus, it perceives and understands. Consequently, the Spiritual Connection is directed at The One within, not at the veil. Yet, the veil was placed by Him and brought forward by Him.

•

In the Kaaba, there is the Golden Spout. Yet Allah the Most High, bestows such a spout through which the ocean of divine grace flows-from the ocean of the Prophet to the ocean of the Perfect guide. The universe receives from that ocean, from that Golden Spout. Therefore, turning toward it is turning toward the Truth. The grace received from it is divine grace. From Allah the Exalted, to His Noble Messenger, from the Noble Messenger to the guide, and from the guide, the divine grace is received.

For example:

“With the Sacred saying ‘I did not fit into the heavens and the earth, but I fit into the heart of my faithful servant,”

And the Verse

‘İn your own selves… Do you not see?’ (Zariyat: 21),

They witness the manifestations of these Truths, seeing the essence within, recognizing it as merely a mask. They also know that the divine guidance flows from the true guide, who is none other than Allah the Exalted, for the true guide is indeed Allah.

In the Noble Verse: ‘Allah has not made for any man two hearts within his breast’ (Al-Ahzab: 4).

Their hearts are solely occupied by Allah the Almighty.

Yet, the existence of one deprived of Truth, whose heart is filled with anything but Allah, becomes an obstacle and the thickest veil in the quest for True Existence. Such a state impedes vision and understanding. Allah the Almighty has not put them in this condition. Those who engage in Spiritual Connection with such people are merely connecting with their ego's idols."

"Peace be upon those who follow the guidance."

(Taha: 47)

•

THOSE WHO MAKE THEIR SELF A ALLAH AND BIND THEMSELVES TO IT

Those who do not see or know The Glorious Truth, who do not avoid sin, and who make their ego an Allah. By binding themselves to it, they essentially worship their own ego. This creates a bond with Satan. Such is the way of it.

The Almighty declares in the Noble Verse:

"They truly believe themselves to be on something. Be aware that they are liars.

Satan has taken hold of them and made them forget even remembrance of Allah. They are the allies of Satan." (Mujadilah: 18-19)

They speak of Sufism while following a different path, tracing the footsteps of Satan, chasing their own desires and goals, filling their pockets, seeking fame.

This is impossible!..

They are nothing but artificial Sufis. Truly deprived of the essence. All their deeds are mere conjecture.

The Noble Verse states:

"Have you seen the one who takes his own desires as his Allah? Will you then be a guardian over him? (Will you protect him from idolatry?)" (Al-Furqan: 43)

Woe to them! They do not know themselves, they cannot see the Truth. They talk about The Unity of Being. They have heard its name and think they understand it. These are the false Sufis and the counterfeit adherents of The Unity of Being.

These are the misleading guides known as "Master devils." They accomplish under the guise of Masterdom what Satan himself cannot. They fulfill all unlawful desires and secure material gains under this guise. They defy Islamic law and attribute it to their supposed greatness. Their disciples think likewise. They say, *"Our master is so great that he might act contrary to Islamic law."* Any act against Islamic law should be seen not as a sign of greatness but as heresy.

If the actions contradict Islamic law, that guide is an imitator, a fake.

Even if you see them flying in the sky, if they act against Islamic law, that is not a miracle but rather a deception, without validation, a "Master devil." Today, they have occupied most of the domain. They act upon conjecture and teach to act similarly. They speak based on assumptions, relying on their ego. Their path holds no foundation.

A true disciple lives in the fear of being expelled. A false Master, however, fears his disciples will desert him, for his authority relies on their devotion.

His disciples call him "Master," and he, in turn, claims, "I am a Master." Do you know what this resembles? Imagine someone in a city with an appointed governor who arrogantly declares, "I am the governor of this land," and usurps the governor's seat. He would immediately be removed and punished accordingly. Just imagine the consequence for someone who dares to occupy a spiritual station without divine appointment!

The Qur'anic Verse states:

"And do not sit on every path, threatening and hindering those who believe in Him, and seeking to make it appear crooked." (Araf: 86)

The people of Allah are appointed by Allah Himself. It is a divine trust, bestowed upon whomever He wills. We do not approve of anyone pursuing this path out of mere desire.

These false pretenders may either select themselves, or be chosen by their parents, or by the public. They are imitators, devils masquerading as Masters. The public elevates them, exclaiming, *"This one is greater! No, this one is even greater!"* In Truth, they are mere highway robbers, deceitful impostors.

The Messenger of Allah, -peace and blessings be upon him-, said in his Noble Saying:

"Liars and deceivers will arise from my Community." (Munawi)

These liars and deceivers are those who outwardly appear to guide and reform people but in reality, they prevent them from adhering to divine commandments.

For they have not been chosen by the Truth. The one who sees themselves as great is truly small.

Imitators act on conjecture, basing nothing on reality and thus leading others away from the truth. Their ultimate destination is hell, dragging those around them into the same fate. Their followers, both in this world and the hereafter, remain united. The righteous will be with the righteous, and the wicked with the wicked.

As the Noble Verse states:

“We will summon every group of people along with their leaders on that Day.” (Isra: 71)

The people of truth are few; they act according to the decree of the Exalted the Allah. They are with the Truth. Their declarations and words are rooted in reality. They speak openly, without fear or reservation. They are dyed in the color of the Truth.

“Among those we created is a group who guide by Truth and give justice according to it.” (Araf: 181)

The imitator may try to resemble such people but is not dyed in that color. They are dyed in the color of Satan. One is dyed in the color of the Truth, the other in the color of Satan. One’s dealings are with the Truth, the others with the multitude. The one in alignment with the Truth has no need for the multitude. The one with the multitude depends on them. Their dealings are not with the Truth. They are soldiers of Satan, for they are counterfeit.

O Ungrateful Human!

Could it ever befit one so boundlessly merciful

To rebel against Allah the Almighty?

Would you not become a Muslim?

•

TRUTH AND FALSEHOOD

Allah the Almighty in His divine wisdom, presents two examples in the Noble Verse to illuminate and distinguish between Truth and falsehood.

"Allah sends down water from the sky, and the valleys flow according to their measure. The torrent carries away the rising froth." (Ra’d: 17)

The persistence of Truth and the dissolution of falsehood resemble the water Allah the Almighty sends from the heavens to the earth. As rain falls, valleys fill to their capacity and overflow. Humans benefit from it in various ways arid lands are revitalized, and water accumulates in the soil, emerging as springs, providing sustenance for people.

Falsehood, however, is likened to the froth that surfaces on the floodwaters. This froth initially rises and attracts much attention, but soon dissipates and vanishes, offering no benefit whatsoever.

Here is a refined translation of the provided Sufi narrative text, touching the heart while staying true to the original:

Another example is the following part of the Noble Verse:

“When they melt metals in the fire to make a jewel or other items, similar scum is produced.” (Ra'd: 17)

For the purpose of making adornments or useful items like utensils, metals such as gold, silver, or copper are melted and poured. The impurities and slag are separated out. Just as foam forms on the surface of a torrent, a similar foam is produced from these metals. The true essence appears in all its simplicity.

“Thus Allah exemplifies the Truth and falsehood.” (Ra'd: 17)

Due to its continuous and steadfast nature, the state of Truth and reality is like the state of pure water that settles on the earth and wholly benefits people. In terms of dissolution and being devoid of benefit, the state of falsehood is like the foam that accumulates on the surface of a flood. Just as foam vanishes in a short time, when Truth and delusion come together; the delusion's possibility of persistence, substance, and reliability vanishes.

That is why Allah the Exalted has said:

“Foam is cast away, while that which benefits people remains on the earth.” (Ra'd: 17)

Just as foam has no impact on water in any way, falsehood is the same; it cannot impact Truth and reality. No matter how high it rises, it will ultimately and inevitably vanish.

As it is with Truth and falsehood, so it is with the people of Truth and the people of delusion.

The people of Truth are with the Truth, deriving their support from the Truth. They guide the populace toward the Truth.

The people of deviation, however, are with Satan, receiving their backing from Satan. They corrupt the populace and drag them toward hell.

"Thus does Allah present examples for the people." (Ra’d: 17)

These examples call on those who use their intellect to align with the Truth and the people of Truth, and to distance themselves from falsehood and the people of deviation.

"For those who respond to their Lord is the best [reward]." (Ra’d: 18)

According to the narration from Abu Moses al-Ashari -may Allah be pleased with him- , our Master, the Messenger of Allah -peace be upon him-said in a Noble Saying:

"The example of the guidance and knowledge with which Allah has sent me is like rain falling upon the earth.

Some of the earth is fertile, accepting the water, and brings forth lush grass and abundant vegetation.

Some of it is barren, holding the water, and through it, Allah makes people benefit. They drink from it, give water to animals, and use it to pasture the animals."

Another part of the earth receives rainfall as well. Yet, that region is flat and slippery, unable to retain water, nor can it nurture any vegetation.

Such is the parable of one who truly understands Allah's religion and benefits from what Allah has sent through me, learning and teaching it to others. Contrast this with one who, out of arrogance, turns away, and rejects the guidance of Allah that was conveyed through me." (Muslim: 2282)

As understood from this Noble Saying, the earth can be categorized into three types, as can people.

Some parts of the earth benefit from the rain, bringing life to what was dry and growing grass. People, animals, and crops benefit from it. Likewise, some people receive guidance and knowledge. When they embrace it, their hearts are revived. They practice it and teach it to others, thereby benefiting themselves and others.

The second type of earth does not benefit itself but retains water, thus providing for people and animals. Similarly, some individuals may not directly benefit from knowledge, but they pass it on to others.

The third type neither benefits from rainwater nor retains it for the benefit of others. So too are some people, possessing neither receptive hearts nor intuitive minds. Though they hear knowledge, it does not benefit them, nor do they retain it for others to benefit.

FERTILE LANDS,

BARREN LANDS

Allah the Almighty while bringing down His mercy, declares through a Noble Verse that plants will grow according to the capacity of the earth:

"The vegetation of a good land emerges by the permission of its Lord, but from a bad land nothing emerges except that which is worthless." (Araf: 58)

Though rain may fall equally, not every soil produces the same abundance; the strength of each soil varies.

In soil that is pleasant and fertile, valuable terrain by Allah the Almighty 's permission, will, and facilitation, abundant and beneficial plants emerge that are useful to people.

In contrast, in soil that is rocky, salty, barren, and infertile, no matter how much rain falls, beneficial vegetation will not grow. Even if anything manages to sprout, it does so with difficulty and bears no goodness.

Here, rain and its blessings are conveyed metaphorically. Just as with lands, people and communities also have their good and bad, believers and nonbelievers. The goodhearted think well, believe, and accept the Truth when they hear it, find life, and give thanks for their blessings. They resemble the fertile land with good vegetation. Conversely, the wicked deny Allah the Almighty's mercy and blessings and are deprived of benefit. Despite hearing the Truth, they do not accept it nor gain from it. Goodness does not emerge from them by Allah the Almighty's will. They spiral into calamity, amidst hardship and deprivation. The stories of past nations bear witness to this Truth.

A good heart is likened to fertile soil in Exalted the Qur'an and Noble Saying while a bad heart is compared to barren land.

"Thus do we explain the signs to a people who give thanks." (Araf: 58)

The mentioning of the grateful is due to their reflection upon Noble Verse, their alignment with its indications, and their direction toward righteousness.

Those who ponder upon the blessings of Allah the Almighty appreciate their value and, consequently, express gratitude. Gratitude emerges from pure hearts.

•

**"Is one whose heart Allah has opened to Islam,
so that they are upon a light from their Lord, [not guided]?"**
(Az-Zumar: 22)

THE HEIRS OF THE PROPHETS

-Peace Be Upon Them-

CHAPTER 10

PRAISE

IS DUE TO HIM ALONE

In a Noble Verse, Allah the Almighty informs us about His exalted being, declaring that **"Praise"** belongs to Him alone, unconditionally, both in this world and in the hereafter:

"Praise be to Allah, to whom belongs all that is in the heavens and the earth. And to Him be praise in the hereafter." (Saba: 1)

For just as He is the benefactor and possessor of all with His blessings in this world, so is He in the hereafter. He is the absolute ruler over everything.

In this world, praise is a duty and an act of worship. In the hereafter, praise will be an experience of pleasure and joy.

As stated in another Noble Verse:

"He is Allah; there is no deity except Him.

All praise belongs to Him in the beginning and the end, and to Him you shall be returned." (Qasas: 70)

This means that everything belongs to Him, and all is under His control and authority.

The inhabitants of paradise will rejoice in the blessings and, due to the delight and peace from the immense rewards they receive, they will offer praise and thanks to Allah the Almighty.

One of His noble names is **"Al-Hamid."** It means The One who is praised and worthy of all praise and recognition. The perfection that necessitates all praise and thanksgiving exists only in Him, and He is worthy of every commendation.

"He is the Wise, the All Aware." (Saba: 1)

He is the only possessor of wisdom. The beauty of His wisdom is clearly evident in all creation.

To know the most hidden states belongs to Him alone. He is the one who knows the inwardness of everything and is aware of all things.

He is so aware that:

"He knows what penetrates the earth, what emerges from it, what descends from the sky, and what ascends therein." (Saba: 2 Hadid: 4)

This Noble Verse reveals the boundless gnosis of Allah the Almighty demonstrating that He is aware of the minutest details of everything.

"What penetrates the earth";

Every raindrop descending to Earth, each particle of rain; the scattered seed, the plant hidden in the soil; the seminal fluid entering the wombs; the bodies buried in the ground...

What is raining? What is being planted? What is buried? What is concealed?

The Noble Verse states:

"Not a leaf falls except that He knows it, nor a grain within the darknesses of the earth, nor anything moist or dry but that it is in a clear record." (An'am: 59)

The phrase "what penetrates the earth" also alludes to the Gnosis that enters the heart of the seeker.

"What emerges from the earth";

Plants that sprout from seeds scattered on the ground come in countless numbers, shapes, and qualities; the water emerging from the depths of the earth, gushing springs; flames and erupting volcanoes...

In the Noble Verses, it is stated:

“Tell me about the seeds you sow in the ground! Is it you who makes them grow, or is it we?” (Waqiah: 63-64)

The phrase “what emerges from the earth” alludes to the unveiling within the heart.

“What descends from the sky”;

Rains and snow... Provisions and blessings... Lightning and thunder... Angels... Commands and prohibitions... So many things descend upon the earth.

In the Noble Verses, it is stated:

“Tell me about the water you drink! Is it you who sent it down from the cloud, or is it we?” (Waqiah: 68-69)

The phrase “what descends from the sky” signifies the divine knowledge that enters the heart from the names and attributes of Allah.

“The Ascending to the Heavens”;

Mists... Spirits... Angels... Sincere prayers, righteous deeds...

In the Noble Verse, it is proclaimed:

“Good words ascend to Him, and He raises righteous deeds.” (Fatir: 10)

The term "ascending to the heavens" also refers to the Word of Divine Unity.

"If there were Allah's besides Allah in the heavens and the earth, they would surely be in a state of disorder." (Anbiya: 22)

As understood from the Noble Verse, whether beings are high above like stars, or on the earthly plane like animals and plants, the fact that they have endured unaltered for thousands of years, in unfailing order and wisdom, definitively indicates that there is no other deity but Allah.

"He is the Most Forgiving, the Most Merciful." (Saba: 2)

HEIRS OF THE PROPHETS

The true spiritual guide, who is also the perfect human, is unique in the world. He is the heir of the prophets. He is the one who receives the divine trust that is poured heart to heart.

The Messenger of Allah, The Most Noble Messenger -peace be upon him- stated in his Noble Saying:

"Whatever Allah poured into my chest, I poured it into the chest of Abu Bakr as it is."

This Noble Saying carries such a profound meaning that it signifies, **"I entrusted the divine trust to him."**

This divine trust, which overflows from heart to heart, continues until the Day of Judgment through the path of the Truthful ones. These are the beloved chosen servants of Allah the Almighty. He created them for Himself.

They see Allah, the Most Gracious. They see and know that they are merely a veil. Allah the Most High, keeps them in the state of a mere rag through His sovereign will. Many matters can't be explained. He cleanses whomever He wills with this rag. Thus, these true spiritual guides see and know that the Real Guide is Allah Himself. They have no sense of self left. Indeed, not a trace of them remains. They know Truth, they see Truth, and they describe Truth.

These are the ones who receive a share of prophet hood and sainthood. They are the deputies of The Messenger of Allah, -peace be upon him-.

From among the distinguished companions of the Prophet, Exalted the Jabir -may Allah be pleased with him- narrated...

"O the Messenger of Allah! What did Allah the Exalted create first?" When he asked this, the Noble Glory of the Universe peace and blessings be upon him replied:

"Allah the Exalted, before everything else, created the light of the Messenger of Allah from His own light. By Allah's permission, that light wandered wherever He wished. At that time, the Tablet, the Pen, Paradise, Hell, Angels, the earths, the heavens, humans, and jinns were not yet created.

When Allah the Exalted desired to create the worlds, He divided that light into four parts.

From the first part, He created the Pen; from the second, the Preserved Tablet; and from the third, the Throne of Mercy.

He then divided the fourth part into four again. From the first part, He created the angels who bear the Throne; from the second part, the Footstool; and from the third part, other angels.

He again divided the remaining part into four parts. From the first, He created the heavens; from the second, the earths; and from the third, Paradise and Hell.

And He divided the final part into four again. From the first, He created the light of the believers' eyes; from the second, the light of the believers' hearts, which is the haven of divine knowledge; and from the third, the light on their tongues. This is the light of 'La ilaha illallah, Muhammadur Rasulallah' (There is no Allah but Allah, Muhammad is The Messenger of Allah)." (AlMawahib alLadunniyyah)

In the Noble Saying, it is mentioned that the last remaining part was divided into four, but the fourth part is not detailed. Let us now explain this and unveil this secret.

The Mighty and Exalted the Allah manifested to His beloved, chosen prophet servants with a special grace. That grace was the light of Muhammad, -peace be upon him-. When they came, they came with that light. From Adam, -peace be upon him-, onward, that light circled upon them, shining on each of their foreheads. Finally, it arrived with the Noble, Beloved, peace and blessings be upon him. It belonged to him from the beginning. Light joined light. Thereafter, that light:

"The scholars are the inheritors of the prophets." (Bukhari)

In accordance with this Noble Saying, the deputies began to embody his essence. The Exalted and Most Holy Lord has bestowed such immense graces upon these luminous deputies:

He has chosen them, drawn them near to Himself, given them the finest of all things, elevated them to the highest degree of piety, and illuminated their hearts with the lights of gnosis.

These are the ones who have inherited both the **prophetic and saintly legacy** of The Messenger of Allah -peace be upon him-. They are not of the apparent scholars; let this not even cross one's mind.

Thus, the one who acts is with his light; that light it is. All virtue lies in that light... Therefore, whoever Allah bestows this light upon, attains that virtue.

•

The true inheritors of The Messenger of Allah -peace be upon him- are on a level akin to that of a child and surpass those who are closer to him in apparent lineage. In terms of spiritual kinship, they are his closest.

They are the elite of the chamber of secrets.

Those who follow the path of Sıddiq-i Akbar -may Allah be pleased with him- and come through Salman-i Farisi -may Allah be pleased with him- are, in essence, his family.

Allah the Almighty chooses to send whom He wills through evident lineage, and whom He wills through spiritual lineage.

Our Master, The Messenger of Allah -peace be upon him- states in his Noble Saying:

"Imam Ali, Fatimah, Hasan, and Husayn are my household. Abu Bakr and Umar are the people of Allah. The people of Allah are more virtuous than my household." (Nawadir alUsul)

The Most Noble Messenger -peace be upon him- declared that Siddiqi Akbar and Umarul Farooq were closer to him, thus announcing that those who are spiritual offspring hold a higher status than those of apparent lineage.

Regarding Selman al-Farsi, The Messenger of Allah -peace be upon him- says:

"Selman is one of us and of the Ahl alBayt." (Tabarani)

This Noble Saying explains the concept of spiritual offspring and lineage. In other words, He sends whomever He wills, whenever He wills, in whatever manner He wills. Those who inherit the spiritual share in the prophetic inheritance and a spiritual share in the saintly inheritance are these alone. They are also those referred to as "the distinguished ones." These individuals are sent at the will of Allah in terms of spiritual lineage.

In brief, they all belong to the progeny of The Messenger of Allah -peace be upon him-. Some come through the Siddiqiyyah path, while others through the path of Exalted the Ali -may Allah honor his face-. Sometimes, both lineages converge in one individual, meaning a person can be connected to Exalted the Ali -may Allah honor his face- through evident lineage and to Siddiqi Akbar -may Allah be pleased with him- through spiritual lineage. These are the ones who possess both the state of prophet hood and the state of sainthood of our Master, the Pride of the Universe -peace be upon him-.

Such closeness exists spiritually that it is even closer than the closest, and this nearness continues along a path until the Day of Judgment. Indeed, not everything can be disclosed to you. Every virtue and every attribute is due to that the light of Muhammad.

And now, I will explain these with Noble Verse and Noble Saying.

In a Sacred saying, Allah the Almighty:

"If it were not for you, I would not have created the heavens." (K. Hafa)

Thus, it is understood that he is not from the heavens; rather, the heavens were created from his light. He is the cause of existence, and indeed the father of spirits. Simultaneously, he is a mercy to the worlds.

In the Noble Verse, Allah the Almighty states:

"We have sent you as a mercy to the worlds." (Anbiya: 107)

Every speck in the universe holds life, and that life is sustained through The Most Noble Beloved -peace be upon him-.

Therefore, if you can perceive it, you will see the inscription: **"The name of the Universe is Muhammad** -peace be upon him-."

Why? Does not The Exalted Truth say in Noble Verse 35 of Surah Nur: **"Allah is the Light of the heavens and the earth"?** How can this be? We perceive it differently. Allah the Almighty created the light of The Most Noble Beloved -peace be upon him- from His own light and adorned the universe with that light. All these secrets are contained within this. However, I speak of these openly, but you cannot possibly comprehend. For there is a need for maturity. If your eye does not see this light, if it is blind, what fault is it of the sun?

As previously mentioned, the Exalted the Allah is a known entity, and everything subsists through Him. Muhammad -peace be upon him- is an unknown entity.

Why?

"His essence is light, his body is Adam,
And indeed, We have honored the children of Adam."

His essence is light, a light that no one comprehends. Although Allah the Exalted has said, **"None knows my saints except me,"** who can fathom His own light?

In the Light of Muhammad[*], the following poem is found:

"He is the light of the Truth

A source of knowledge and wisdom

His essence is of the Truth"

"The word comes from the Truth."

(*) Light of Muhammad -peace be upon him- Ömer Öngüt. Hakikat Publishing

The state of the heirs of the Prophet is a part of prophet hood, and their inner world is a trust from the Khatam al-Anbiya (Seal of the Prophets) -peace be upon him-. All virtue lies in that trust. Indeed, they are united with the Truth and speak of the Truth. Their teacher is none other than Allah the Exalted.

Allah the Almighty describes them in the Noble Verse:

"If you fear Allah, Allah will teach you." (Al-Baqarah: 282)

Their knowledge is divinely gifted. It comes from Allah the Exalted and The Messenger of Allah, -peace be upon him-.

It is impossible for this state to arise through reading and acquiring superficial knowledge. Do not even consider it.

The complete heirs of the Prophet -peace be upon him- surpass even those who are related to him by blood, being closer in terms of spiritual lineage. They are his nearest spiritual kin.

In his Noble Saying, The Most Noble Messenger -peace be upon him- thus commands:

"There are certain sciences that are like hidden jewels. Only those who are one who knows Allah know them. When they speak of this knowledge, those who are heedless of Allah do not understand.

Therefore, do not belittle or despise the scholars whom Allah the Almighty has blessed with knowledge from His own grace. For when Allah, the Glorious, granted them this knowledge, He did not disdain them." (Erbain, from Abu Huraira -may Allah be pleased with him-)

These individuals see the void of their own judgments, for judgment belongs to Allah the Almighty alone. No one else can recognize this Truth. Everyone strives to sell their own existence, yet because these individuals are annihilated in Allah the Exalted, they see Allah the Almighty finding nothing in themselves. They know the Truth, but do not know themselves; they see the Truth, but do not see themselves.

There are also those who **a spiritual share in the prophetic inheritance**: These are equipped with outward knowledge and are worthy of the beneficial knowledge they have been described to possess. They are the true scholars who guide to the Truth and govern by the Truth.

As stated in the Noble Verse:

"Among those we have created, there is a community who guides with the Truth and establishes justice therewith." (Araf: 181)

They expect no benefit from anyone. They never take fees for the knowledge they impart. All their affairs rest solely on the pleasure of the Creator, for the sake of Allah alone. They are described as the people of the Qur'an. They embody the teachings of Exalted the Qur'an, conforming all their actions and deeds to it. They radiate light to the people, guiding humanity. These are the officers of guidance, and their number is very small.

As for those **who a spiritual share in the saintly inheritance**; these are the spiritual guides sent by The Glorious Truth. They are the beloved chosen ones, known as **The Brought Near Ones** They do not engage in guiding others; their stations are exceedingly high. They are always in a state of serenity and devotion before the Divine Presence. They observe the commands and inspirations that come to them, yet they are not officers of guidance.

In the Noble Verse, it states:

"It is advised, 'If you do not know, ask those who people of pemembrance.' (Nahl: 43)

By people of remembrance, it is meant the venerable saints.

Those we mentioned are perfected ones.

They perceive themselves as mere frames and understand that within them is the divine name inscribed with light. This awareness is specific to those endowed with People of deep understanding. It belongs to those who have ascended to those ranks. This recognition is only possible through Allah's revelation. It cannot be achieved through personal knowledge alone.

In the Noble Verse, it is stated:

'Allah expands the heart of whomever He wills for Islam, so they are upon a light from their Lord.' (Zumer: 22)

For they lead people from darkness to light. Their every action and undertaking is by the command of the Truth. They can never act independently. Therefore, they are faithful guides. They are the servants preserved and protected under divine care and governance. Because they are within this divine guardianship and governance, they do not err. They are the safeguarded ones, acting under divine governance.

In summary, whomever Allah the Almighty loves and chooses, to whom He entrusts His trust, and upon whom He bestows the light of The Messenger of Allah -peace be upon him-, these individuals are the heirs of the Prophet.

The Messenger of Allah -peace be upon him- stated in his Noble Sayings:"

"Abu Bakr surpassed others not through the abundance of his fasting and prayers, but through something that was poured into his heart".

The divine trust passed from heart to heart endures until the Day of Judgment.

Regarding the continuity of this source of light, the Noble Messenger -peace be upon him- declared:

"My Community is like the rain. It is not known whether the first or the last is better." (Tirmidhi)

These are the rare ones, they come once in a hundred years.

In a Noble Saying, it is stated:

"In every century, there are pioneers, the forerunners, from my Community." (Nawadir alUsul)

These individuals are the deputies of The Messenger of Allah. Allah the Most High chose, loved, and poured into His dear friend.

Those who wish for their hearts to be revived by this spiritual and mystical grace should present their hearts to the spiritual influence of the friends of Allah.

The companionship with a guide is both physical and spiritual. Through Spiritual Connection and Contemplative Meditation, one can transfer the divine grace from this noble heart to one's own.

The divine effusion belonging to Allah the Exalted flows from the Creator's ocean to the ocean of the Beloved Prophet, -peace be upon him-. From there, it reaches the ocean of the guide of the time. Then it flows into the hearts of those predestined to receive it. Through Spiritual Connection, a connection so profound is achieved that all the attributes of the Perfect guide can be transferred to a disciple. With the love bond in the heart, one becomes enveloped in his essence. Moment by moment, one becomes like him and is illuminated by the light reflecting from him.

•

In a Noble Verse, it is stated:

"Bestow upon us from your presence a protector, bestow upon us from your presence one who will aid us." (An-Nisa: 75)

Some of the esteemed scholars have interpreted this Noble Verse as, **"Grant us a protector from you who will guide us back to you."**

Accordingly, our Beloved Prophet, The Most Noble Messenger -peace be upon him-, has conveyed that Prophet David -peace be upon him- prayed thus in a Noble Saying:

"O Allah! I ask you for your love, the love of those who love you, and the action that will lead me to your love.

O Allah! Make your love dearer to me than my own self, my family, my wealth, and even cool water!" (Tirmidhi)

•

Every prophet is revered, but our Beloved Prophet -peace be upon him- is the most revered.

In the Noble Verse, it is said:

"We favored some of those messengers above others." (Al-Baqarah: 253)

Every community is esteemed, but the Community of Muhammad is the most esteemed.

In the Noble Verse, it is said:

"You are the best nation brought forth for mankind. You enjoin what is right and forbid what is wrong, and you believe in Allah." (Al' Imran: 110)

Every guide is exalted, but the deputy of the Beloved Prophet -peace be upon him- is the most exalted. Why? Because **"The believer's heart is the Throne of the Most Merciful,"** because they embody the divine trust, because they are the deputy of the Beloved Prophet -peace be upon him- These enlightened ones know that they are but a veil. Reflect upon this, if you can decipher the secret:

"Allah is the Light of the heavens and the earth." (Nur: 35)

You too shall be graced with the secret of this Noble Verse.

To grasp this secret is an impossible feat. One must rise to that station to comprehend it.

As our esteemed Prophet -peace be upon him- proclaims in a Noble Saying:

"Allah existed, and there was nothing with Him." (Bukhari)

It remains true to this day.

The true guide is none other than the Exalted the Allah. A perfected guide is but a rag. When Allah desires to cleanse someone's heart, He employs that rag, purifying the heart through it. This is the essence, the Truth of the matter. I witness this with my very eyes.

That is to say, the true guide is the Exalted the Allah, and the perfected guide is nothing more than a humble rag. But these are the rags of the Truth.

The servants supported by the Truth are the perfected guides who have attained Annihilation in Allah.

To convey to you the essence of self-effacement described here, I shall present a Verse by our Master Es'ad Sir -may his secret be sanctified-:

"Neither knowledge nor wisdom did you bestow, nor a lofty status, O Lord!

Praise be to Allah, I have not a speck of pride.

I am but a shadow, a mere apparition in the form of mankind."

True perfected guides are like tattered rags, and it is to them alone that Spiritual Connection is directed; none else is included.

"The world knows Allah the Exalted, the scholar knows his ego, and the scribe only knows his pocket." All these are within the secrets mentioned here.

The true guide described here is Allah the Exalted. All these subjects describe Him. They all aim to declare Him. The true guide is Allah the Exalted.

Our Master, the Master of the Universe and the Reason for Existence peace and blessings be upon him states in his Noble Saying:

"I take pride in my poverty." (K Hafa)

However, the poverty discussed here is not what you understand; it's not about being without money or clothes. It means saying, "My soul, my body, my knowledge, my wealth, and everything I have belongs to my Lord. I possess nothing. I take pride in my poverty."

Because we claim Allah's gifts for ourselves, we fail to recognize this divine generosity. For instance, consider what remains when the soul is taken away? Nothing. The important thing is not to recognize these when they are taken away, but to know them without losing them, to know the Giver. This is the ultimate. **"I take pride in my poverty."**

We have another point to share on this humility.

There was a Caucasian scholar, Hacı Yunus Sir, may Allah have mercy on him, who was our neighbor, a humble and gentle teacher. One day, as I was leaving the house, we encountered each other. He said, *"I was waiting for you."* "Please, Sir!" I replied. *"As I was reading a book, a Noble Saying caught my attention. The Prophet, -peace be upon him-, says,* **'I saw Gabriel** -peace be upon him- **clinging to the cover of the Kaaba in the form of a rag.'** *My mind stood still; I could not comprehend it. I thought if anyone could know its meaning, it would be you."*

At that moment, Allah granted me the knowledge to respond to such an esteemed person's trust in asking this question:

"We said, 'this is very simple, Sir. Gabriel *-peace be upon him-* was in supplication at that moment. Before the divine majesty, he was so annihilated that he regarded himself as a rag and was pleading in that state. The Prophet, -peace be upon him-, captured a vision of him in this manner.'"

The scholar was very pleased with this answer. *"May Allah be pleased with you!"* he said and left. Yet, Allah had bestowed such magnificence upon Gabriel -*peace be upon him-* that when the Master of the Universe, the Reason for Existence, -peace be upon him-, was granted prophet hood, he saw him in his original form with six hundred wings covering the horizon. This first vision frightened him greatly, and he returned to his blessed household trembling(*).

Even though Allah granted him this grandeur, Gabriel *-peace be upon him-* would still behave as a rag before divine majesty in his supplications.

How then will those who find it beneath themselves to perform prostration fare?

Allah the Almighty in His Noble Verse, says of them:

"Wooden planks set against a wall." (Münâfikun: 4)

Unshaped timber...

In Truth, they are but logs or the fires of hell.

(*) 4th Conversation (ADRESSES FAİTHFUL HEARTS), Hakikat Publishing.

"By The One in whose hand is Muhammad's self,
if you were to lower a rope to the lowest part of the earth,
it would descend upon Allah."
(Tirmidhi)

HE IS EXISTENCE, HE IS THE EXISTENT...

CHAPTER 11

- The Sole Knower of the Unseen
- He Is Existence, He Is the Existent...
- The Qualities of the Perfect Guide
- The Character and Attributes of the Guide

THE SOLE KNOWER OF THE UNSEEN

Allah the Almighty declares in His Noble Verse that He is aware of all happenings in the universe, of every secret and every state, and that He will inform everyone in the hereafter of their deeds in this world:

"Do you not see that Allah knows whatever is in the heavens and whatever is in the earth?" (Mujadilah: 7)

To Him, no secret remains hidden, nor any deed done in the open.

One who witnesses the deeds of the Absolute Actor with the eye of certainty understands that He knows all that is in the heavens and the earth.

Nothing can be excluded from His eternal knowledge.

"Wherever three people whisper together, He is the fourth.

Wherever five conVerse in secret, He is the sixth." (Mujadilah: 7)

He knows what they whisper and their state never remains hidden from Him. He is fully aware of their conditions, hears their conversations and whispers.

It makes no difference where they are or where they speak.

"Be they fewer than that, or more, and wherever they may be, He is certainly with them." (Mujadilah: 7)

Here, it is implied that nothing can be hidden from Allah the Almighty and no one can escape Him.

Although Allah the Almighty knows and hears their states, the appointed angels also record the secret conversations.

"Then on the Day of Judgment, He will inform them about their deeds." (Mujadilah: 7)

No one will have anything to say; they will find no words to speak.

The Verse, which begins by speaking of Allah's infinite knowledge, also concludes by speaking of His eternal knowledge:

"Indeed, Allah is All-knowing of everything." (Mujadilah: 7)

Henceforth, people should reflect on this Truth and arrange their actions accordingly.

As stated in other Verses:

"Do they not know that Allah knows their secrets and their private conversations.

And Allah is the All Knower of the unseen." (At-Tawba: 78)

"Or do they think we do not hear their secrets and private conversations?

No! We hear, and our messengers with them write down (all that they do)." (Zuhruf: 80)

•

HE IS EXISTENCE, HE IS THE EXISTENT...

Allah the Most High and Most Sanctified, created the entire universe. It came into being with the command **"Be."** This cosmos is a mirror. When the people of Truth look, they see Allah; when the people of delusion look, they see themselves. A person looks at the glass and sees themselves. A Perfect guide looks at the glass and sees Allah. This occurs only in those upon whom Allah manifests. Truly, the universe is a glass, and it is as He manifests. Sin is like a veil, preventing vision. If there is even a speck of ego within oneself, this cannot happen; instead, one binds to their own ego.

Therefore, the true adherent of The Unity of Being and the false one are discerned from this point.

The Noble Verse proclaims:

"He is the Subtle, the All Aware." (An'am: 103)

Al-Latif: The one who accomplishes the finest tasks, knows the subtleties of all deeds, infinitely gracious.

Al-Khabir: Knowing the inner dimensions of everything, aware of their hidden aspects.

Divine secrets reside in every particle. He encompasses all. Everything envelops everything, yet He envelops all.

"Know that He indeed encompasses all." (Fussilat: 54)

Because Allah the Almighty encompasses everything, wherever you look, you will see only Him.

For:

"Allah is the Light of the heavens and the earth." (Nur: 35)

There exists no being nor existence apart from Him...

Let us elucidate one more point:

The ashes of the mask signify the final stage of Sufism. Although it marks the end stage of Sufism, the divine manifestations have no end. Allah the Almighty the Benefactor and the Generous, bestows as much as He wills to whom He wills.

Allow us to present you with an illustration of this.

Seven or eight years ago, under the illusion of having understood my nothingness, I wished for my death in the blessed garden of the Prophet's Mosque. I had set out with that intention. However, the command was, "We know when to take you. Do not ask for it again!"

Had Allah the Almighty taken me at that time, I would have departed without truly comprehending my nothingness, which would have been the greatest ignorance. Therefore, for a person to understand the existent, they must first comprehend their own nothingness.

In the Holy Qur'an, it is stated:

"All that is on the earth will perish, and the Face of your Lord, full of Majesty and Honor, will abide forever." (Rahman: 26-27)

Those who reach this point of divine knowledge are granted these divine manifestations. They become ashes, and what remains is the everlasting Allah the Exalted.

He is existence, He is the existed... There is no existence besides Him, no reality beyond Him...

All existence is merely the place where the particles of the light of His Being manifest. Everything is not Him, yet nothing is without Him.

Everything is body; He is the spirit.

In another Verse, it is stated:

"I breathed into him of my spirit." (Sa'd: 72)

Everything is a veil, it is truly Him. Everything is a mask, the reality is Him.

And He declares to us:

"Within yourself... Do you not see?" (Adh-Dhariyat: 21)

Even though He has declared that He is nearer to us than anything, we still fail to recognize the true existence.

We tell you; He is existence, He is being... Aside from Him, there is no existence, there is no being...

Yet, you still cannot comprehend this.

As The Messenger of Allah -peace be upon him- said in his Noble Saying:

"By Allah in whose hand is Muhammad's self, if you were to lower a rope to the ground, it would fall upon Allah." (Tirmidhi)

Why it is not understood?

Let me present to you a Verse from the Holy Qur'an:

"Allah is He who created seven heavens and of the earth the like thereof. His command descends between them, that you may know that Allah has power over all things and that Allah comprehends all things in [His] knowledge." (Talaq: 12)

Ibn Abbas -may Allah be pleased with him- said:

"If I were to explain the commentary of this Verse to you, you would surely stone me."

Do not think that what is being conveyed is unknown, yet it is impossible to reveal all of it to you, because your mind cannot grasp it. However, we endeavor to unveil it to you ever so gradually that no objections arise, always presenting Noble Verse and Noble Saying as evidence.

He created the dominion, and you imagine Him within His dominion, while you say, ***"Alhamdulillahi Rabbilalamin" (All praise is due to Allah, the Lord of the worlds).*** What kind of faith is this, what sort of thought? Yet what you see is the smallest portion; only Allah the Exalted knows what He has created.

Why can't you comprehend this?

Because your knowledge remains at Knowledge of Certainty, and your mind is the intellect of livelihood, you cannot comprehend.

The rank of intellect, People of deep understanding, and those whose knowledge is Reality of Certainty accept and comprehend this without hesitation.

Here we strive to convey to you the knowledge that you neither know nor understand nor have heard. Since this knowledge has always been explained to you through the words of Allah, denying it by claiming ignorance leads you to disbelief.

As Exalted the Imam al-Ghazali states in his work Ihya Ulum alDin:

"Never attempt to deny this knowledge by claiming you do not understand it. The downfall of scholars lies in arrogantly overstepping their bounds, thinking they grasp all intellectual sciences. Ignorance is far better than the knowledge that rejects the states of the friends of Allah. Denial of the saints and their miracles equates to denial of prophets and their miracles, and to deny prophets is to completely leave the faith."

For these are the chosen servants of Allah the Almighty.

A Sacred saying declares:

“Sincerity is one of my secrets. I place it in the hearts of those among my servants whom I love. Neither angel can record it, nor can the devil corrupt it.”

If the angel cannot witness it, will you be able to?

Our Master, The Messenger of Allah, -peace be upon him- in his Noble Saying:

"He who is for Allah will find Allah is for him," it is said.

The righteous servants base all their actions on seeking the pleasure of Allah, they do not look beyond Him, and they never stray from the path of His pleasure. They are His chosen servants.

The Noble Saying, which we will now present, has been conveyed to you many times. Our intent in reiterating it is to reveal the existence of a second form of knowledge. Everyone is aware of the first kind, but they are unaware of the second.

The Messenger of Allah, peace and blessings be upon him, says in the Noble Saying:

"Knowledge is of two kinds. One is the knowledge possessed by the tongue (which is the outward, apparent knowledge); it is a proof of Allah the Almighty over His servants. The other is the knowledge held in the heart (gnosis). It is this which is beneficial in reaching the ultimate goal." (Tirmidhi)

Those who attain this goal are the people of gnosis.

Allah the Almighty in the Noble Verse declares:

"Allah gives in abundance to whom He wills." (Al-Baqarah: 261)

Thus, Allah the Almighty who is generous in His grace and bounties, has bestowed unimaginable blessings upon His beloved servants. These are the true sufis.

The Seeing Eye recognizes its Creator, perceives Him through His light, and sees nothing else but Him.

It was previously stated that "Existence is Him, the entity is Him..." This cannot be unraveled. Only if Allah the Almighty wills to make someone aware and elevates them to this point, can He be seen through His light. He is known through His revelation. Apart from Him, there is no other existence, no other entity. It is impossible for you to understand this, for you are either blind or cross-eyed. This pertains to the eye that sees.

When does this truth manifest? When you become nothing, when the veils are lifted, when you see Him through His light, and when you see nothing but Him.

Note that the Perfect guide is well aware that he is nothing.

The Exalted Truth, in His Noble Verse, commands:

"Be with the Truthful Ones." (At-Tawba: 119)

Why? Because that Truthful servant knows very well that he is but a humble particle, seeing himself through his own eyes. All the marks upon him belong to Allah the Almighty; he acts in the name of Allah. For indeed, the true guide is Allah Himself.

That is why our revered Master Es'ad Sir -may his secret be sanctified- stated, ***"The purpose of coming into the world is to find the*** **Perfect guide.*"*** If you find the Perfect guide, you find the Truth; if not, how will you find the Truth?

AbdulQadir Gilani -may his secret be sanctified- addressed the members of the path thus:

"I am not here merely to adorn your outward appearance, but to plant the saplings of gnosis in the fields of your hearts and to water and nurture them. Thus, these saplings of gnosis will grow, branch out, and provide shade and fruits for others to benefit from."

It is of utmost importance to seek a guide. There is a Perfect guide who guides towards righteousness, and there is another who corrupts. For his path is towards Allah, whereas his false Masterness stems from Satan, arising from the idol of ego, destroying both himself and his followers.

Therefore, Allah the Almighty commands, **"Be with the Truthful ones,"** not with Satan or Masters who have become like Satan.

How can one discern this? Only those endowed with the Truth can distinguish it using the measure of divine judgement.

The Qualities of a Perfect guide:

Uprightness, counsel, compassion, and mercy.

Uprightness: He must live by the Holy Qur'an and the Sunnah.

Our mother, Exalted the Aisha -may Allah be pleased with her-, said:

"The character of the Prophet -peace be upon him- was the Qur'an." (Muslim)

In other words, the practice of all the commandments in the Qur'an al-Karim is evident in his life. In this respect, he is Exalted the Qur'an.

A guide must possess these qualities. If not, if even one attribute is missing, he is not a Perfect guide. Here is your measure, here is your scale.

The second attribute is counsel: to rescue a person from a difficult situation, describe the best path with few words and in the shortest way, directing them to Truth, leading them to Truth.

The third attribute is compassion: to help both acquaintances and strangers solely for Allah's sake, sparing no effort in doing so. This applies to humans as well as animals.

The fourth attribute is mercy: to provide someone with a blessing they cannot attain, if you have it, with a joyful heart. The essence of this is profoundly deep.

Consider that The Most Noble Messenger -peace be upon him- our Master, was incredibly merciful and compassionate. This lies beyond human capability. His deputy also inherits this quality.

Thus, without these attributes manifesting themselves, one is not a Perfect guide. As long as you hold these measures, you will not go astray in life.

Ethics and Attributes of the Guide:

Our esteemed Master Es'ad Sir -may his secret be sanctified- states:

"A guide must be adorned with virtues such as righteousness, advice, compassion, and mercy, and must avoid base traits.

The qualities of a guide authorized for guidance:

Acting in accordance with the requirements of the purified Islamic law with steadfastness.

Guiding people to abide by Islamic law and to remember Allah the Most High with presence of heart.

Advising all people as much as possible, showing them the path of piety and integrity, and striving to deter them from all evils.

Viewing all creatures with compassion and mercy, showing mercy to the young and respect to the elders.

Having sufficient knowledge to teach his disciples the necessary tenets of Islamic jurisprudence and the doctrine of Divine Unity.

Covering and concealing the faults of believers that he becomes aware of.

If the guide is endowed with spiritual insight, he recognizes the states and perfections of the heart, the ailments and calamities of the self through that divine revelation. If he lacks this insight, he discerns them through external indications or the conditions that arise in the disciple."

Possessing a wealth of heart and beautiful character, becoming wrathful solely for the sake of Allah.

As for the outcome in the Sufi path for a Master; there is no requirement beyond completely abandoning sin, consistently adhering to obligations and compulsory acts, performing the recommended acts that are easy to accomplish, invoking the name of Majesty as much as possible, and frequently sending blessings upon The Messenger of Allah -peace be upon him-.

•

"I have chosen you for myself."
(Taha: 41)

THOSE WHOM ALLAH LOVES AND CHOOSES FOR HIMSELF

CHAPTER 12

- The Vital Point of Contact Between Allah and His Servant
- Those Blessed by the Verse:"I Have Chosen You for Myself." (Taha: 41)
- True Sufis Paid Close Attention to These Three Things, While False Ones Deviated from These Points

THE VITAL POINT OF CONTACT

BETWEEN THE LORD AND HIS SERVANT

One seeks daily, moment by moment, to annihilate their being. To find the Existent.

The other accumulates existence within themselves. To lean on the idol of ego.

One's work is with Allah, the other's work is with the ego.

In a Noble Saying:

"Whoever is for Allah, Allah is for him," it is said.

One who chooses Exalted the Allah strives to make himself pleasing to Exalted the Allah, in all his deeds and actions.

But one who is self pleasing seeks to please people, in all his deeds and actions. Such a person is not pleasing to Exalted the Allah, for they are people of the world.

A valuable person finds value through the appreciation of Exalted the Allah.

By valuing a valuable person, you enhance their worth.

If you value a worthless person, you inflate his arrogance on one hand, and on the other, you become worthless yourself for valuing the worthless.

O Divine!

You are such a Sublime One that only you know yourself.

You are such a Sovereign that only you know yourself.

You are such a Creator that only you know yourself.

You are such a Provider that only you know yourself.

You are such a boundless Lord of grace, my Allah that only you know yourself.

In short:

Those who choose the Truth are with Truth.

Those who choose the people are with the people.

•

Allah the Exalted states in His Noble Verse:

"Allah is the Light of the heavens and the earth." (Nur: 35)

All the universe is but a body, a veil, a cloak. The one and only omnipotent and creative being, Allah the Exalted, created existence and adorned this veil. In every particle, the secrets of divinity are present. Such an artist, such a creator that all the scholars of the world, if gathered together, would be helpless before even one particle of His creation.

This is Allah.

He adorned the veil of the cosmos with such beings... O human! You are also on this veil, among these beings and upon this veil. For your first creation too was from the earth. He caused you to grow like a plant.

O proud, oppressive, and ignorant human! He created you from the earth. You walk upon the surface of the earth. You tread upon the faces and eyes of those who departed before you. And again, He will return us to the earth.

“He it is who makes you laugh and makes you weep.” (Najm: 43)

“He it is who causes death and gives life.” (Najm: 44)

Nothing created is Allah. Everything has come into existence by His command **“Be!”**

He creates and stages this scene.

In His Noble Verse, it is said:

“He is the one who created death and life to test which of you is best in deeds.” (Mulk: 2)

He tests us to see if we will keep the promise we made before. For this world is a stage of trials.

He is Al-Ahad. There is no Allah but Him. Every particle of existence announces His presence. Humanity failed to understand this and saw itself as separate from the Exalted the Allah. On the stage of the world, humans could not recognize that they exist through Him. Yet, He is As-Samad. He created the universe and adorned it. You also appear on this stage by His mystery. The earth, the sky, inanimate objects, plants, animals all are in need of Him. Everything knows it is in need of Him and praises Him. They acknowledge and remember His greatness.

Allah the Almighty states in the Noble Verse:

“There is nothing except that it glorifies Him with praise, but you do not understand their glorification.” (Isra: 44)

O heedless human! He created you from a despised fluid. You were once in three layers of darkness in the mother's womb. He protected you from water, heat, and light. Then He shaped you and brought you forth from the mother's belly.

He honored you. He adorned and embellished you in the most beautiful form. He provided you with the most exquisite blessings. He subjugated the entire universe for your service.

A day will come when He will take account of every particle of these boundless blessings. Yet, humanity failed to know and recognize Him.

As stated in the Noble Verse:

"The extent of their knowledge is but this." (Najm: 30)

Their grasp of knowledge is limited. The ignorant person attributed this divine grace to their own selfish ego and declared, "I." Moreover, they became hostile towards their Creator, the benefactor of all blessings. They failed to grasp the Truth and did not find Allah.

Yet every entity came into existence by the command, **"Be!"** and appeared on the stage of existence. When He wills, He will obliterate everything.

He has announced that He will bestow endless blessings upon those who serve and glorify Him; Conversely, He has warned that ungrateful and doubting humans and jinn will be cast into a hell whose fuel is men and stones.

"I HAVE CHOSEN YOU FOR MYSELF."

(Taha: 41)

THOSE HONORED WITH THIS VERSE

In a Noble Saying The Messenger of Allah -peace be upon him- stated:

"There is a knowledge akin to concealed jewels. Only those who are one who knows Allah can comprehend it. When they speak of this knowledge, those who are heedless of Allah do not understand.

Therefore, never disdain the scholars upon whom Allah the Exalted, has bestowed knowledge from His grace. For Allah the Almighty did not scorn them when He granted them this knowledge." (Erbaîn)

All who are deprived of this knowledge are heedless of Allah the Exalted.

This is affirmed by the following sacred saying:

"Then I turn my face towards them. Do you think that anyone will know what I intend to grant to the one towards whom I turn my face?"

Allah the Exalted, continues:

"The first thing I will bestow upon them is to pour it into their hearts. Then, as I inform them, they too will inform about me." (Hâkim)

This divine sacred saying reveals that what Allah the Almighty bestows upon them is beyond anyone's knowledge, and that He grants them gifts not given to others. It is made known to us that only these individuals have true gnosis of Allah the Exalted.

Allah the Exalted, discloses here how He grants this knowledge. He declares that it remains a secret between Him and the servant.

According to another Sacred saying, Allah the Most High informs the dwellers of the heavens, and the angels inspire love for that person in the hearts of the people of truth on earth.

According to a narration from Abu Huraira -may Allah be pleased with him- The Messenger of Allah -peace be upon him- said:

"When Allah the Most High loves a servant, He commands Gabriel, 'I love this person, so you should love him as well.' Gabriel then loves him and proclaims to the inhabitants of the heavens, 'Allah loves this person, so you too should love him.' Thereupon, those in the heavens love him, and his love is then placed in the hearts of those on the earth.

Similarly, when Allah the Most High detests a servant, He commands Gabriel, 'I detest this person, so you should detest him as well.' Gabriel then detests him and announces to the inhabitants of the heavens, 'Allah detests this person, so you too should detest him.' Consequently, they detest him, and animosity and hatred for that person arise among those on earth." (Muslim)

•

Allah the Most High states in His Noble Verse:

"The Qur'an is composed of clear signs that reside within the hearts of those endowed with knowledge." (Ankabut: 49)

Thus, Allah the Most High pours the essence of the Holy Qur'an into his heart, transforming his heart into a Qur'an. Such a person no longer needs a guide or a teacher.

These individuals know Allah the Most High and are aware that this knowledge comes from Him, attributing nothing to themselves.

External scholars, however, imprint what they take from texts onto their self. Hence, they proclaim, *"I am a scholar!"* The self transcribes all knowledge onto a blackboard, and as it reads, it sees itself and becomes arrogant. It perceives itself as grand to the extent of its arrogance, believing it knows everything, unaware of its true ignorance.

Indeed, a revered individual once said, *"I have been trying to erase the ink I licked in the madrasa (Islamic school) for forty years, but still, I have not managed to entirely cleanse it from my heart."* This means: for forty years, I have been striving to eradicate the pride myself felt during the acquisition of external knowledge from my heart, but I have yet to succeed.

We mentioned that "a purified heart is exempt from distractions." Similarly, this revered individual expresses that his heart has been preoccupied with striving against such distractions for forty years.

During the journey of The Noble Path, numerous divine manifestations occur, making a person believe he knows everything. Since he perceives these divine mysteries with his soul, he thinks he knows it all. However, when the study of The Noble Path reaches completion and the study of truth begins, he realizes he knows nothing. Upon entering Gnosis, he sees and understands his own nothingness. Here, he attains proximity to the Truth and, through Truth's manifestation, perceives reality.

Allah the Almighty states in the Noble Verse:

"Is one whose heart Allah has opened to Islam, so that he has received a light from his Lord (like one whose heart rejects it)?" (Zumar: 22)

Now, Master of the Universe, Reason for Creation, explains in a Noble Saying:

"Beware of the insight of the true believer, for he sees with the light of Allah, the Mighty and Majestic." (Munawi)

This means that it is highly likely he will discover your secrets through the divine light in his heart.

The path of the ascetics is rooted in the self. All outward sciences, including the knowledge of the path, fall within this realm. Both its acquisition and manifestations accompany the self. Up to this point, the external aspect of the exalted path continues. Since it partakes of the self, it arrogates itself and believes it knows everything, deeming itself superior to others.

Indeed, such individuals ignore the prophetic statement:

"Whoever claims 'I am a scholar,' know that they are ignorant." (Munawi)

Why is this? Because the self-claims, *"I am a scholar!"* It says, *"I!"* recognizing no one else.

Had they believed in this Noble Saying, they would renounce their ego. However, they neither believe nor relinquish their ego, thus failing to attain maturity.

Yet the Allah the Almighty declares in a Noble Verse:

"Of knowledge, you have been given only a little." (Isra: 85)

But the self does not acknowledge this. It insists, *"I am a scholar!"*

The path of the Gnostics lies within the heart. Knowledge penetrates the heart's core. When one passes into this realm, they pierce the blackboard and shield of the self. This transition alone achieves this. Outward knowledge remains here. Even the knowledge of the path remains, but through remembrance of Allah, one gradually purifies their heart of the stains imposed upon it.

However, as one ascends to the ranks of the one who knows, knowledge permeates the heart. With the passage to the reality, the esoteric aspect of The Noble Path begins, shedding all attachments to the self.

Let us illustrate this with an example: While in the world, you claimed everything as yours; but upon entering the grave, you are stripped of it all.

Here, one divests from all worldly attachments, confessing to know nothing and acknowledging one's ignorance. Why? Because the transition is made from the external to the internal, from the manifest to the hidden.

"Die before you die." (K.hafa)

This is where the secret of this Noble Saying begins to manifest.

The path of the initiated is within the soul. Those taken into this station recognize their insignificance. One cannot ascend to this place, but rather is taken there.

Here, neither reason nor knowledge works as they would in other contexts. This realm belongs to the People of deep understanding. These are the ones who directly encounter the Exalted the Allah.

Allah the Almighty imparts knowledge as he wills, and they see as He wills. They truly see and understand their own nonexistence with their own eyes. For he who reaches The Glorious Truth sees the Divine and not himself. He believes in the Exalted the Allah and denies himself. Such is this station. And this is the essence of esoteric knowledge.

Allah the Almighty declares in His Noble Verse:

"Whomsoever Allah guides, he is the rightly guided one." (Araf: 178)

Because He has bestowed the grace of guidance, He keeps them on the path of His consent. And He reveals the Truth. These are the chosen servants, whom He holds under His command, protection, and divine management.

A second Noble Verse clarifies this further:

"I have chosen you for myself." (Taha: 41)

From this, it is understood that these are His beloved servants, chosen and drawn towards Him.

All mysteries stem from here.

Allah the Almighty describes these servants in a Sacred saying as follows:

"Allah the Almighty and His angels, the inhabitants of the heavens, the earth, even the ants in their dens and the fish in the sea, all pray for the forgiveness of those who teach goodness to people." (Tirmidhi)

Now, pay close attention to this Noble Saying. Allah the Almighty; to His angels, to all inhabitants of the heavens, to the ant in its hole, and to the fish in the sea, they have all heard it. Yet how heedless is man toward them? Here is the Noble Saying: Everything recognizes it and prays for its forgiveness.

According to a narration from Abdullah ibn Abbas -may Allah be pleased with him-, when it was asked to the Prophet -peace be upon him-, "What should we do when we encounter an issue not addressed in the Quran and Sunnah?" He replied:

"Ask it from the righteous and present it for their consultation." (Tabarani)

Allah the Almighty the Mighty and Majestic, says in a Sacred saying:

"Do not deem my knowledgeable servants among the people of paradise or hell until I have decreed a judgment among them!" (Deylemi, from Exalted the Ali -may Allah be pleased with him-

Allah the Almighty's greatest favor to His servants, after faith, encompasses two gifts: one is gnosis, and the other is Divine Love.

Divine Love is the love of Allah. It is a fire that consumes all other loves apart from Allah. It is the victory of the soul and the source of its joy.

Gnosis, however, is a more delicate station than Divine Love.

Where does this subtlety and delicacy come from? In Divine Love, you exist because you are the one who loves. In gnosis, only He exists, and you do not. Neither you nor your love remains.

In this regard, although many explanations have been offered by various individuals, my humble opinion is that to be in Truth, one must completely efface oneself.

The Sacred saying, **"Do not make them amongst the people of paradise or hell,"** is meant for the noble angels, as Allah the Almighty confides in them before sending them to their stations.

True knowledge is one's ignorance and nothingness existing where the knowledge of Truth is. This is Gnosis. One who dwells in this sees Allah Most

High but does not perceive their own self. They cannot possess knowledge because they do not exist. The exalted status of Allah signifies that one possesses gnosis concerning Him. This means knowing that only He exists. To regard all values and merits as insignificant in comparison to the transcendence of Allah's merit and to see no other worth beside His majesty is a trait belonging to those who are Verse in Gnosis.

The Messenger of Allah, peace and blessings be upon him, states in his Noble Saying:

“In every century, there are forerunners among my Community who are called the substitutes and the Truthful ones. The divine grace and mercy upon them are so vast that through them you receive sustenance and drink. Disasters and calamities that could occur to the people of the earth are averted because of them.” (Nawadir alUsul)

These figures are sent once every hundred years. Allah the Almighty loves them so much that He grants all the blessings to the people of the earth for their sake, and all humanity benefits from them. When He intends to send a calamity to the earth, He refrains from doing so out of respect for them.

As it is in this world, so shall it be in the hereafter, on the Day of Judgement, and on the bridge of Sirat.

“They have witnessed the resurrection and gathering here,

Before the Trumpet is blown.”

When the angels in paradise ask these selves, ***"Can you describe the scales and the bridge for us?"*** they respond, ***"No, we have seen no such thing."***

Just as Allah made a path through the sea for Exalted the Moses, He makes a path over Hell for these beloved servants.

•

Reflect on the supplication of Exalted the Demirci (the Blacksmith Saint). He implores, ***"Make my body so large that only I enter Hell, and let no other member of the Community of Muhammad do so."***

When Bâyezidi Bestamî -may his secret be sanctified- was curious about to whom the spiritual leadership was given, Allah directed him to Exalted the Demirci. Upon hearing this plea from Exalted the Demirci, he remarked, **"Then I understood that these saints are those who say 'My community, my community,' and not 'Myself, myself."**

These lovers continue until the Day of Judgment; it is not limited to Exalted the Demirci alone.

This is a divine mystery. Individuals like these will act as bridges for the Community of Muhammad on the Day of Resurrection. You benefit from their blessings unknowingly. Through them, Allah the Almighty lifts calamities and tribulations without your awareness, and you will pass the bridge over Hell without seeing it.

•

The beloved servants of Allah are described by The Messenger of Allah -peace be upon him- in the following nine Noble Sayings that will be presented to you:

"My Community is a blessed Community. [Although the Companions, the Followers, and the Followers of the Followers are exceptions] It is not known whether the best of this Community's men are those who came earlier or later." (Tirmidhi)

"On the Day of Judgment, as the believers cross the Sirat Bridge, the Hellfire will say: 'Pass, O believer! Your light extinguishes my flames,' and thus, it addresses the perfected believer." (Jami' alSaghir)

In the Noble Saying **"The believer is the mirror of the believer,"** the 'first believer' signifies the heart of the believing servant, and the 'second believer' refers directly to Allah Himself. What harm can befall him if he falls into hell?

"The chosen ones of my Community are like rain; it is not known whether the earlier or later saints will benefit people more." (Tirmidhi)

This second Noble Saying explains the first Noble Saying. It's a very subtle matter, and it's impossible to explain all. Imam Rabbani -may his secret be sanctified- has elucidated this subject in a letter of his.

"A perfected believer is superior to some angels in the sight of Allah." (Ibn Majah)

"Show respect and honor to scholars who practice what they know. For they are successors to the prophets in conveying the divine rulings. Whoever honors those honors both Allah and His Messenger." (Bukhari)

"The scholar who teaches good deeds to people and forgets his own self is like a candle that burns itself to illuminate the world." (Jami' alSaghir)

For they were not created for their own selves.

“He who shows respect to a scholar who acts with knowledge honors Allah the Exalted.” (Munawi)

“The sleep of a scholar, with the intention of restoring health and devoting it to worship, is itself an act of worship, and his breath is a form of glorification.” (Munawi)

“To gaze upon the face of a scholar who acts with knowledge is akin to an act of worship.” (Munawi)

Did we not tell you, that person is a mask? He knows and sees that he is a mask. Through looking at that mask, if one can see beyond, one can also see what lies within. Thus, gazing upon that mask becomes one of the greatest acts of worship, because within it resides He, the true guide, Exalted the Allah.

When explaining the concept of Spiritual Connection, we touched upon this matter; give it much contemplation.

"He who knows himself knows his Lord." (K. Hafa)

This Noble Saying is presented to you, yet you do not comprehend it.

Many secrets have been revealed to you. What has been disclosed? The true guide knows himself to be merely an image. The true guide recognizes himself as nothing but a tatter. The true guide sees himself as a mask. The true guide perceives himself as a mere drop of tainted water. When Allah the Exalted, with His grace, dissects the particle known as Immutable Archetypes, one sees that there is only He. For within that particle reside the secrets of divinity. This is the essence of **"Men arafa" (he who knows)**. Being the greater world stems from this understanding. In summary, only He exists.

It becomes clear that the true guide is Exalted the Allah.

•

True Sufis have paid close attention to these three things. The false ones, however, have deviated in these three areas:

1. For existence, Allah the Exalted suffices, yet they chose creation. Despite being brought into existence from nothing and drowned in blessings, forgetting the Giver and becoming a servant to Satan, worshiping the world, and separating from Truth is profoundly sorrowful.

2. For adornment, exalted the Qur'an suffices, yet they chose luxury and ornamentation.

Our Mother, Exalted the Aisha - may Allah be pleased with her - said: **"The character of the Prophet -peace be upon him- was the Qur'an."** (Muslim)

Whoever adopts his character and aligns their nature with his, there is no greater adornment.

However, people abandoned this adornment and leaned towards materialism, luxury, and ornamentation.

The Most Noble Messenger -peace be upon him- has a curse for such people:

"May those who are slaves to wealth, silver, silk, and velvet fall on their faces and be destroyed." (Bukhari. Tecridi Sarih: 1218)

In one of his Noble Saying, he states:

"Love for the world is the greatest of all major sins." ((Jami' alSaghir)

For you were created not for the world, but for the Creator.

3. Islam itself is enough for honor, but they abandoned Islam and turned to division.

For it is said:

"Indeed, the religion in the sight of Allah is Islam." (Al' Imran: 19)

However, those who caused division strayed from Islam and diverged into various paths. Is there a greater honor than Islam?

Our revered Abraham Hakki -may his secret be sanctified- states:

"What should the servant do with wealth and power?

Is it not enough that we have found a sovereign like you?

May He grant us union with Him in Allah?

Make us among those who die before death."

The people of Allah have chosen this, what did others worship?

•

"And among the people are those who dispute about Allah Without knowledge, guidance, or an enlightening book."

(Luqman: 20)

WHO CAN SPEAK OF THE UNİTY OF BEİNG?

CHAPTER 13

- The Conditions Necessary for a Person to Discuss the Unity of Being
- The Criterion of the "People of Truth" and the "People of Action"
- Thief of the Unity of Being

WHO CAN SPEAK OF THE UNİTY OF BEİNG?

As for the concept of The Unity of Being; only the knowledgeable should speak on this matter, not others.

The Noble Verse proclaims:

"Among people, there are those who argue about Allah without any knowledge, guidance, or illuminating scripture." (Luqman: 20)

To convey something appropriately, one must speak with knowledge of its essence; otherwise, it is falsehood. These conditions will be clarified for you through various Noble Verse.

Allah the Almighty bestows understanding of life to whom He wills, and they know as much as they live. Others, however, write about that life based on assumptions. They then attempt to explain to the public as though they know and live it. This can be likened to the difference between the living and the dead. One has a living spirit, having subdued their ego; the other's ego is alive, but their spirit is dead. Yet humanity often cannot distinguish between the two.

For instance, there are two kinds of reeds: one produces molasses when squeezed, and the other is a broomstick reed, which remains empty no matter how hard you squeeze, for it is hollow inside.

Now, we will illustrate this with a Noble Verse.

When Pharaoh's magicians cast their spells onto the ground, Moses -peace be upon him- threw down his staff, and it began to swallow the magicians' illusions.

The Noble Verse says:

"Thereupon, Moses threw his staff, and it began swallowing their conjured illusions." (Shuara: 45)

The Noble Verse we present to you will similarly swallow their enchanted pens.

"I boast in the presence of Allah the Exalted

Yet, I am ashamed of my own existence.

I am a creature without authority or value

Authority and value belong to my Lord."

Without Sufism, there can be no The Unity of Being. Know well that the ultimate stage of Sufism marks the beginning of The Unity of Being.

Now, we shall present to you the innermost secrets and measures of this path. Pay close attention to these measures, for you shall learn much.

To speak of The Unity of Being, it is essential to personally experience the manifestations of the Noble Verse we shall present.

How can one who has not yet shed their animalistic traits, who has not freed themselves from ignoble morality, speak of The Unity of Being?

It was said earlier that "The Noble Verse we shall present will have swallowed their magical pens."

•

And now, we move to the Verses of the Qur'an:

"Within yourself... Do you not see?" (Adh-Dhariyat: 21)

What has happened now? Examine your inner selves, who exists there? These proponents of The Unity of Being speak without understanding. When Allah the Almighty says**, "I am within you, do you not see?"** they pause. It seems that this Verse has consumed all these arguments.

If a person truly sees and says, "I see, my Lord!" they have been graced with the secret of this Qur'anic Verse; it does not apply to others. It is the work of those who say, ***"I am not myself; there is an essence within me."*** It is not merely words.

In other words, they have annihilated themselves, seeing only the Truth, not themselves.

In His divine Verse, The Exalted Truth states:

"O people of reason and insight! Take heed." (Hashr: 2)

•

In one of the Noble Verse, it is stated:

"Allah is the Light of the heavens and the earth." (Nur: 35)

Can you perceive that the heavens and the earth are light? If you cannot, how can you talk about The Unity of Being? You speak of The Unity of Being, yet you see yourself, mountains, stones, and the sea; thus, you contradict yourself. Your own existence prevents you from seeing the Truth and knowing the reality.

In another Noble Verse, it states:

"Only those endowed with sound intellect reflect deeply." (Rad: 19)

The matter of The Unity of Being is not the business of every saint. These are rare individuals. It is not at all the concern of the apparent scholars or the ignorant. This must be clearly understood.

•

Allah the Almighty states in a Noble Verse:

"We are closer to man than his jugular vein." (Qaf: 16)

This is not exclusive to followers of The Unity of Being; now let us turn to ourselves. Allah the Exalted says, **"I am closer to you than yourself."** How is it that we have not felt this closeness, why have we not seen it, why have we not known it? Before us stands a Noble Verse.

In another Noble Verse, He says:

"My Messenger, when my servants ask you about me, tell them I am near." (Al-Baqarah: 186)

Allah the Exalted is close to everything and in all things; can you see Him in everything? He is closer to you than yourself; can you feel Him within? Or are you still veiled? If you feel this, you must recognize and see that you are but a mask. If you cannot see this, if you have not reached this state, how can you speak of The Unity of Being?

Speaking of these matters without having attained this state means oppressing oneself.

Allah the Exalted says in a Noble Verse:

"And among them is he who wrongs his own self." (Fatir: 32)

Do you know what kind of oppression this is? It is an abyss without any barrier, casting one into hellfire. For he knows nothing of The Unity of Being yet glibly speaks of it with his pen and tongue.

•

Allah the Almighty says:

"He is the Al-Awwal and the Al-Akhir, the Az-Zahir and the Al-Batin..." (Hadid: 3)

With this Noble Verse, He declares to you that He is manifest in all things. He is the Al-Batin (Hidden), yet you still see yourself, you see the tree, the rock, the sea, but you cannot see Him!

Those who do not experience this manifestation only reveal their ignorance in the presence of those who know the Truth.

One who sees only himself is in no way qualified to talk about The Unity of Being.

The one who knows he is nothing, who sees himself as an insignificant particle, sees the Truth, and only he can speak of The Unity of Being. If Allah the Almighty wills, He reveals His secrets to such a one. However, these individuals are exceedingly rare in this world. It is not the task of every saint.

If someone is elevated to the station of the Righteous Ones, and Allah wills it; He annihilates that person's selfhood and establishes His own presence. He sees, nobody else does, and he sees only because the Exalted the Allah shows him; he cannot see by his own means.

Yet, you notice that the display windows are filled with books discussing The Unity of Being. All these are written out of ignorance, for profit, or spoken based on assumptions.

If one has not even experienced the manifestation of a single Verse of these Noble Verses, all his talks are in vain. The Truth can only be disclosed and conveyed by the Exalted the Allah.

For in His divine Verse, He declares:

"This is Allah's grace and bounty; He bestows it on whom He wills." (Al-Jum'ah: 4)

This is the work of divine manifestations, not mere talk.

•

Allah the Most High, in His divine Verse, commands:

"Be with the Truthful Ones." (At-Tawba: 119)

The true guide is Exalted the Allah. Since these individuals are students of Allah the Most High, they know Him. They know and perceive what Exalted the Allah has taught and shown them; they alone can resolve those mysteries and strive to reveal them. They guide towards Exalted the Allah, none else.

In the Noble Verse:

"If you fear Allah and are pious, Allah will be your teacher." (Al-Baqarah: 282)

These are the Perfect guides appointed by the Exalted the Allah. They bestow their wisdom upon those predestined to receive it.

How do they bestow it?

Our noble Prophet -peace be upon him- said, "The heart of a believing servant is The Throne of the Most Merciful Allah."

Because it is the spiritual throne of Allah the Almighty whatever is entrusted to this spiritual throne is given to those who are destined to receive it. Others do not possess this power.

Just as in Sufism, one cannot attain Annihilation in the Master without first achieving "Annihilation in the Messenger", and "Annihilation in the Messenger" cannot be attained without "Annihilation in Allah", so too, one cannot reach "The

Unity of Being" without achieving "Annihilation in Allah." In Annihilation in Allah, one becomes nothing and realizes their nothingness.

Here, a person sees the primordial nature known as Immutable Archetypes. This is but a particle, an atom. What significance does this particle possess? None.

Both the existence and the creator are the Exalted the Allah. The concept of The Unity of Being begins thereafter. After this state of nothingness, if Allah the Almighty wills, He makes the person aware of His existence to the extent He desires.

This awareness is granted only to those who see and comprehend that there is no existence other than Allah the Almighty.

A Sacred saying states:

"Then I turn my face to them. Do you think anyone can know what I wish to give to a person to whom I have turned my face?"

(Allah the Almighty continued :)

"The first thing I will bestow upon them is the light flowing into their hearts. At that time, as I inform them about myself, they will also inform others about me." (Muslim-Hakim)

"This is Allah's grace and benevolence; He gives it to whom He wills." (Al-Jumu'ah: 4)

From this, it is understood that the final stage of Sufism is the initial step of The Unity of Being. Since this is the first stage, many more manifestations and stages exist. Each of these stages possesses a Noble Verse that can be understood and known through these Verses.

•

"Within yourself… Do you not see?" (Adh-Dhariyat: 21)

The secret of this Noble Verse is that when they speak of The Unity of Being, to put it plainly, they see Allah the Exalted. Internally, they perceive that there is no other existence or entity besides Him. With Allah the Almighty's guidance, they know The Unity of Being to the extent He wishes.

"Allah guides whom He wills to His light." (Nur: 35)

These are the individuals He draws to Himself and envelops in His light. This is another manifestation in The Unity of Being.

•

"We are closer to him than his jugular vein." (Qaf: 16)

A person who speaks of The Unity of Being sees and knows this within himself, through the revelation of Allah the Almighty. He is privy to all manifestations.

"We are closer to him than you are, but you do not see." (Waqi'ah: 85)

That is, we are closer to everything than everything else, yet you do not see this.

•

And I will reveal to you where The Unity of Being culminates.

"Everything will perish except His presence." (Qasas: 88)

We are talking about the Immutable. When the manifestation of this Divine Verse happens, those Immutable Archetypes too are shattered. Even atoms are split here. I have explained the final stage to you. However, it is impossible for me to explain what follows from this point onward.

•

These proponents of The Unity of Being manifest which Divine Verse that they speak of The Unity of Being!

For someone who has not yet been granted entrance through the gate of virtue, who has not stepped on the path of Sufism, to speak of The Unity of Being is a great ignorance and misguidance.

Let my testament to you be this: Do not speak of The Unity of Being. These are special servants of Allah the Almighty. They are those who are subject to divine manifestations. These individuals are exceptional. There is no one among you who is to speak of this. Whoever takes it up with assumption, either by pen or tongue, should know well that they not only destroy themselves but those around them. Just as they poison themselves, they also poison those who read and listen.

Let us open up the inner Truth of what we said, "These individuals are exceptional. "Allah the Almighty has created them for Himself. These are the ones towards whom He directs His face in actions. These are the ones chosen by the Truth, and they are the ones who choose the Truth. They are directly the inheritors of The Messenger of Allah.

And now, let us close this subject with a sacred saying:

"Indeed, the righteous have an intense longing to meet me, and indeed, my longing to meet them is even stronger."

Allah the Almighty created them for Himself. They look at Allah, through Allah, and see Allah the Exalted with Allah's light. Because Allah shows them through His own light. These matters are not to be known with the eyes or through knowledge.

There are the beloved servants of Allah the Exalted, who are enamored with Him. Then there are those He created for Himself, known as the "Ebrar" servants. They are not only in love with Allah the Exalted, but He also loves them in return. Here is the Sacred Noble Saying. These are the exceptional servants. These are the ones upon whom Allah the Almighty turns His face. They are chosen by the Truth, and they are the ones who choose the Truth. They are the inheritors of the prophets.

Yet, due to their ignorance, people sought to deny them.

These are the possessors of Reality of Certainty. Their teacher is Allah the Exalted.

"If you fear Allah and are pious, Allah will be your teacher." (Al-Baqarah: 282)

This is why this knowledge eluded them and led them to denial. These possess the knowledge of the heart, which others cannot see or comprehend.

"Whomsoever Allah grants wisdom, to him indeed is given much good. But none will grasp this save those with sound understanding." (Al-Baqarah: 269)

It becomes clear that Allah the Exalted bestows this grace upon whom He wills.

Therefore, The Exalted Truth declares in the Noble Verse:

"Follow those who ask of you no fee, and who are rightly guided." (Yasin: 21)

Observe here a sign; they are on the righteous path. These individuals are devoted to Truth, they do not seek the favor of the masses. All their needs and tasks are personally overseen by Allah, they are not dependent on anyone.

In the Noble Verse, The Glorious Truth declares:

"He manages the affairs of the righteous." (Araf: 196)

Because others are unaware of this knowledge, they are left stunned in its presence. But if we had not confronted the divisive with this knowledge, neither you nor they would have understood their misguidance... This is the reason behind the mystery.

This knowledge has not emerged in vain. In this time, each day, a new dissenter arises.

Allah the Almighty states in a Noble Verse:

"O you who have believed, if you fear Allah and are reverent, He will grant you a criterion to distinguish between right and wrong." (Enfâl: 29)

Since this is the knowledge of gnosis bestowed by Allah the Almighty, you do not comprehend it. As seen here, as clearly indicated by the Noble Verse, their instructor is none other than Allah the Exalted.

"If you fear Allah and are reverent, your instructor will be Allah." (Al-Baqarah: 282)

For someone to discuss the concept of The Unity of Being, certain conditions must be met:

"Allah encompasses everything." (An-Nisa: 126)

One must be endowed with the secret of this Noble Verse. Consider this:

Think of a fig! It contains numerous particles. The Creator, Allah, has encased it with a skin. As you see this, until you perceive that Allah encompasses all worlds similarly, until you realize that all beings exist within Allah's essence and subsist through Him, no one has the authority to speak about The Unity of Being. One who speaks does so from conjecture. And conjecture has no value in the face of Truth.

"They indeed think that they stand on something. Verily, they are the liars.

Satan has overpowered them and made them forget the remembrance of Allah. They are the party of Satan. Truly, the party of Satan is the loser." (Mujadilah: 18-19)

Just as Exalted the Allah does not reveal this Truth to every saint, He discloses it only rarely to those He wills, as much as He wills. To these individuals, He reveals and makes known the secrets of all these Noble Verses. This knowledge is a special knowledge granted by Allah the Almighty, a gift He bestows upon whom He wills.

"This is the grace of Allah, which He bestows upon whom He wills." (Al-Jumu'ah: 4)

This knowledge comes from Him. He speaks, knows, and conveys only the Truth.

"Then I turn my face towards them. Do you think anyone else can know what I wish to give to the one I turn my face to?"

(Allah the Exalted continued.)

"The first thing I will bestow upon them is to pour light into their hearts. At that moment, just as I reveal to them, they too reveal about me." (Hakim)

These are they, only they speak of Allah the Exalted. True existence belongs to Him, and He is the existent. They see and know that all created beings are manifestations of particles of the light of existence. They speak with this understanding. The reason you cannot grasp this is that your knowledge is mere conjecture. For your teacher is a human, and your intellect is concerned with mundane affairs, making comprehension impossible. This is the task of the People of deep understanding, as their teacher is directly Allah the Exalted. He has elevated their knowledge and intellect to the level of the People of deep understanding.

“Fear Allah and be pious, and Allah will be your teacher.” (Al-Baqarah: 282)

Allah the Exalted teaches them directly. They know, see, and speak as much as He wills. These are the true adherents of The Unity of Being.

Just as there are counterfeits for everything, those who have not attained this state are impostors and thieves of this Truth.

•

To better lodge this subject in your mind, Noble Verse and Noble Saying are presented repeatedly. So that you may not be confused.

The Criterion of the "People of Truth" and the "People of Action":

The People of Truth seek only the pleasure of Allah; every action they undertake is solely for the sake of Allah. They work purely for Allah, expecting nothing from others, and seeking nothing for worldly gain. They declare, "Our reward belongs to the Lord of all worlds." They persist in acts of worship and piety, striving thereby to draw nearer to Allah. Their efforts are dedicated to attaining the pleasure of Allah.

In a Sacred saying Allah the Almighty describes their qualities, making it known to the believers:

"To whoever shows enmity to my saint, I declare war. My servant draws nearer to me with nothing more beloved than what I have made obligatory upon them. And my servant continues to draw near to me with optional acts of worship (nawafil) until I love them. When I love them, I am their hearing with which they hear, their sight with which they see, their hand with which they grasp, and their foot with which they walk. (I become their heart with which they understand and their tongue with which they speak.) If they ask of me, I will surely grant it, and if they seek refuge in me, I will surely protect them." (Bukhari. Tecridi Sarih: 2042)

The People of Action, on the other hand, focus on being close to the people and have no real connection with Allah.

Allah the Almighty says in His Noble Qur'an:

"There are some people who say, 'We believe in Allah and the Last Day,' but they do not believe." (Al-Baqarah: 8)

"They think to deceive Allah and those who believe, but they deceive only themselves and are not aware." (Al-Baqarah: 9)

Allah the Almighty refutes their claims. While they attempt to deceive the believers, in Truth, they deceive only themselves, bearing the greatest loss.

THE THIEF OF THE UNİTY OF BEİNG

Allah the Almighty states in the Holy Qur'an:

"Say: He is Allah, The One and only. Allah, the Eternal, Absolute; He begets not, nor is He begotten." (Ikhlas: 12)

Existence is He; being is He. Apart from Him, there is neither existence nor being. All beings are mere manifestations of the particles of His light. Yet, you are caught in the created, failing to know the Truth, presuming you do.

If only you cast off the garment of existence, He stands revealed. When you don the garment of existence, you stand. How then will you see Him?

Suppose the whole universe is a tray, laden with numerous bounties. You perceive only as much of the tray as you can see. You also see the bounties upon the universal tray.

However, you do not see the Creator of these bounties, The One who holds the tray. In **"No"**, you remain lost in the created. And without shame, you boast of The Unity of Being. Is this not a grand falsehood?

For He declares **"The One"**. Apart from Him, there is no other being.

He is one. He created everything, and all things need Him. For He creates, He sustains life, He takes it away, and He resurrects. Yet, you did not see Him.

You say **"Kulhüvallâhü ehad" (Say, He is Allah, The One)**, but you remained with the name, the words; still, you did not see Him.

From the particle to the globe, everything encompasses everything. Some are enveloped by a membrane, others by skin, and some by a shell…

That is to say, Allah the Most High has encircled every particle with something. This is true for the earth and the heavens as well. With the Throne of the Compassionate, He has encompassed all. Allah the Exalted has encircled everything, woven around all realms.

"He encompasses all things." (An-Nisa: 126)

You lingered at **"No"**, and you saw the heavens and the earth.

Yet Allah the Most High proclaims in His Noble Verse:

"Allah is the Light of the heavens and the earth." (Nur: 35)

Those whom He reveals it to see this and know it to be so. But you saw the earth, you saw the heavens. You could not see that they are His Light.

However, Allah the Almighty declares in His Noble Verse:

"He is the Manifest." (Hadid: 3)

He who says, **"I am the Manifest."**

Despite this declaration, have you seen Him? You have not. Yet, those whom He has shown and informed know this reality. They see that there is no existence apart from Him.

And again, He states:

"We are closer to man than his jugular vein." (Qaf: 16)

He tells you that He is closer to you than yourself. Have you been able to see this? But those whom He has informed and shown both see and know this Truth. How will you see and know these things? Because within you resides yourself, and there exist the idols of masiva (all that distracts from Allah). How will you comprehend this Truth?

Allah the Almighty also declares:

"We are closer to him than you, yet you do not see." (Waqi'ah: 85)

That is to say, Allah the Almighty is close to everything and everyone. Can you perceive this? Those whom He reveals this to, know and see this Truth.

All of these are exclusive to the servants whom Allah the Almighty informs. Only they can see and know this reality. For they see The Glorious Truth and see nothing else but Him.

He knows... The Existence is Him, the Being is Him...

Yet after such blindness, you speak of The Unity of Being.

You thief of Allah, false claimant of The Unity of Being! How can you speak of these matters without experiencing the enlightenment of Noble Verses?

It is clear from here that Allah the Almighty is closer to you than you are to yourself. Close to everything and everyone. It is He who declares this. Yet you, unable to see Him, imagine He is in the heavens or elsewhere. With your limited understanding, you think He is still within possession, and you speak of The Unity of Being.

He, however, declares that He encompasses the entire universe:

“He encompasses all things.” (An-Nisâ: 126)

But you did not see the Creator; you saw the created.

But in His Noble Verse, He says:

"Within yourself... Do you not see?" (Adh-Dhariyat: 21)

He declares, "I am within you!" Yet, have you perceived Him within yourself? I know well that you have not. For within you resides yourself. You clung to the idol of yourself, imagined you saw Him, and made Satan your guide.

As it is said in another Noble Verse:

"Surely, Satan commands you to do evil and indecency, and to say about Allah what you do not know." (Al-Baqarah: 169)

You presume to tread the path of Truth, yet you befriend Satan. And one day, you will awaken from your slumber and realize who is with you.

And you will say:

"O Satan! I wish there had been a distance as far as the east is from the west between you and me. What an evil companion you are." (Zukhruf: 38)

How will you know and see these divine secrets? For your intellect is the intellect of worldly matters, and your knowledge is mere conjecture. You thought you knew, your arrogance made you believe you were a savant. But a day will come when you truly understand your ignorance.

Allah the Almighty declares:

“Indeed, you were heedless of this. Now we have removed your veil, so your sight today is sharp.” (Qaf: 22)

But there is no turning back.

The ear of the heart must open to hear the Truth. Yet yours has not.

The eye of the heart must open to see the divine secrets.

Knowledge must reach “People of deep understanding” for these Truths to be learned. But you remained in speculation, in Knowledge of Certainty.

Your intellect is of the intellect of livelihood. After The intellect of livelihood, there is the intellect of the afterlife, the luminous intellect, and the Universal Intellect. Those who reach People of deep understanding hear through what Allah the Almighty has conveyed. They see whatever He has shown. This is attained only when one moves from outward knowledge to the path, from the path to the knowledge of Truth, and from the knowledge of Truth to the gnosis. He bestows this only upon whom He wills. Those among the Rabbanî (those devoted to Allah) whom He has informed know it alone, for their teacher is none other than Allah the Exalted.

Your heart's lock is sealed, the eye of your heart blind, and the ear of your heart deaf. You are unaware that such knowledge even exists. For your knowledge is but the ignorance of knowledge of ignorance, mere conjecture. You make meaningless noise! And you do not realize that this is a grave responsibility.

In the Noble Verse it is stated thus:

"Say: Those who fabricate lies about Allah will surely not succeed." (Yunus: 69)

O thief of The Unity of Being!

Reflect, as the garment you wear is to your body, so is the body's garment to the Divine Presence of Allah.

The universe is likewise. You remained fixated on the outer garment. You presumed what you saw and knew. You deified your own existence.

Why these people are called thieves of Allah? Because they do not even know their own selves. They attempt to describe the Creator of all worlds. And by doing so, they write books and earn money. Is this not deceit?

The Noble Verse states:

"Among the people is he who disputes about Allah without knowledge and follows every rebellious devil." (Hajj: 3)

This Truth is known only to those whom Allah the Almighty has chosen to reveal and make heard. Even among those who come once in a century, He rarely discloses this secret, and only they know it. For a person to know, Allah the Almighty must have:

1. Unlocked the heart's lock.

2 The heart has opened its ear.

3 The heart has opened its eye.

4 It has poured forth its light.

5 It has engraved all its secrets onto the heart.

This has been disclosed and communicated only to its select servants, the The Devout. For their teacher is none other than Allah the Exalted.

However, the thieves of Allah remain ignorant of the existence of these beings. They have never heard of them in their lives and possess no knowledge about them. They do not even know themselves. This is because they are deprived of the secret of **"Men arefe" (He who knows himself knows his Lord)**. How can those who do not know themselves, who are unfamiliar with the knowledge of gnosis, understand these? Yet, they foolishly endeavor to describe the Lord of the worlds. Without a doubt, this is the doing of the scholars of the last age who will appear at the end of times.

In a Noble Saying reported from Exalted the Ali -may Allah be pleased with him- , the Noble Messenger -peace be upon him- said:

"A time will come upon people when only the name of Islam will remain, and only the outward form of the Qur'an will endure. The mosques will be full in appearance, but they will lack guidance within.

Their scholars will be the worst under the heavenly dome. Discord emerged from them and will return to them." (Bayhaqi)

Thus, they demonstrate through their actions how they have ended up in this condition.

•

"Indeed, Allah is with those who are mindful of Him (Taqwa) and those who are doers of good."

(An-Nahl: 128)

TRUE SUFIS

AND CHARLATANS

CHAPTER 14

"O you who believe! If you fear Allah and are mindful of Him (Taqwa), He will grant you a criterion (Furqan) to distinguish between right and wrong, and bestow upon you light and understanding."

(Al-Anfal: 29)

The differences between those to whom Allah the Exalted has given esoteric knowledge and those to whom He has not:

Regarding those endowed with esoteric knowledge, He proclaims:

"The Qur'an is comprised of clear signs shining in the hearts of those endowed with knowledge." (Ankabut: 49)

Allah the Almighty opens the heart of whomsoever He wills to Islam; only such a person hears the Truth and makes it known to others.

Those to whom He has not made the Truth known speak, but they do not truly understand; they merely talk aimlessly.

And in this matter, Allah the Almighty says in a Verse:

"If Allah opens a person's heart to Islam, such a one is illuminated by a light from their Lord." (Zumar: 22)

If a person can illuminate their inner self by consuming lawful sustenance, performing worship with sincerity, and consistently adhering to obligatory and voluntary acts, then Allah Almighty, if He wills, bestows wisdom upon them, enabling them to speak with wisdom.

Allah the Almighty says in another Verse:

"Allah grants wisdom to whom He wills, and whoever is granted wisdom has indeed been given much good. Only people of understanding take heed." (Al-Baqarah: 269)

However, artificial sufis are deprived of all these Truths; they have no connection with Allah, and all their actions are mere show.

Yet, those who know the Truth say, "We do not live Sufism, nor do we know its Truth." They are aware of the existence of Sufism and try to describe how its practitioners live. For it is a divine grace; He grants it to whom He wills. Those who declare this speak truly.

But artificial sufis, no matter how much they try to present themselves as masters of this path, if you pay attention to these Verses, you will come to understand their true nature and distinguish Truth from misguidance.

The people of Truth are those whom Allah the Almighty has informed. He reveals His secrets to them as much as He wills and informs them.

In the Noble Verse, Allah says:

"Allah gives manifold to whom He wills." (Al-Baqarah: 261)

However, artificial Sufis are deprived of these Truths and remain ignorant.

Indeed, the knowledge that is not found between the lines of books but is hidden in the hearts and deep within those close to Allah is the knowledge of divine understanding.

Those who follow His path and worship with divine reverence, sincerity, and honesty, Allah the Almighty liberates from all doubts and difficulties. He makes them possess innate wisdom, teaches them without formal education, and makes them knowledgeable without learning.

The Messenger of Allah, -peace be upon him- stated in his Noble Saying:

"Whoever acts upon what he knows, Allah teaches him what he does not know." (K. Hafa)

From this, it is evident that if a person clings to all the commands of Allah the Exalted and continues worship with sincerity, Allah the Exalted informs them of what they do not know. However, this never occurs without worship, obedience, piety, and sincerity.

•

The beginning of wisdom is the fear of Allah. Above all, one must be in awe of Allah the Almighty and act as commanded.

Indeed, in the Noble Verse, He commands:

"Be upright as you have been commanded!" (Hûd: 112)

Without fully adhering to all His commands and avoiding everything He has forbidden, a person can never truly become one of the people of Truth.

In another Noble Verse, Allah the Almighty declares:

"Those who conceal the clear proofs and guidance we have revealed, after we have made it clear for the people in the Book, they are cursed by Allah and cursed by those who curse." (Al-Baqarah: 159)

Anyone who denies or obstructs the Truth, or who conceals it through alteration and confusion, is deserving of this curse.

In yet another Noble Verse, He states:

"O you who believe! If you fear Allah and are mindful of Him, He will grant you a criterion, a discernment to distinguish between right and wrong, and will forgive your sins." (Enfâl: 29)

Notice that the concept of gnosis is always mentioned alongside "piety", signifying that it is impossible to attain gnosis without piety.

•

Indeed, when a person turns their entire heart with sincerity and a sound heart to Allah the Exalted, Allah the Almighty may reveal many secrets to them.

As stated in the Noble Verse:

"He taught man what he did not know." (Alaq: 5)

Thus, it becomes evident that these Truths and mysteries can only be known through the teaching and revelation of Allah the Almighty. They are sustained by His disclosure.

Allah the Almighty describes them in the Noble Verse as follows:

"Indeed, Allah is with those who fear Him and those who are doers of good." (Nahl: 128)

However, by merely reading books or quoting others, the essence of this knowledge cannot be grasped, and the Truth remains elusive. Their understanding is based on assumptions, and they do not attain the genuine Truth.

To achieve this, one must first purify their own self. Ascending from The commanding self to The reproaching self, from The reproaching self to The inspired self, from The inspired self to The Tranquil Self, from The Tranquil Self to The content self, from The content self to The pleasing self, and finally to The Purified self, so that:

"He who purifies his self indeed succeeds." (Ash-Shams: 9)

May they be graced with the manifestations of this divine Verse?

This is not a matter of mere words. It is sustained by Exalted the Allah's enlightenment and guidance and is achievable by traversing the aforementioned "Stages of the self" one by one.

Yet some, in the face of the Truth:

"They became blind and deaf." (Al-Maeda: 71)

•

If a servant strives to fulfill all the commands and prohibitions of Allah to gain divine approval, and if they endear themselves to Allah, and if Allah loves them in return:

"Allah chooses for Himself whom He wills." (Shura: 13)

But now, to be on the path, to follow the trace of the devil, to chase after ambitions and desires, to fill one's pockets, to seek fame, and yet to speak of Sufism... This is impossible!

These are merely artificial Sufis, bereft of true reality. All their actions are based on conjecture.

Allah the Almighty states clearly in the Noble Verses:

"They truly think they have something worthwhile. Be aware, they are liars.

Satan has overtaken them and caused them to forget Allah's remembrance. They belong to the party of Satan. Indeed, the true losers are those allied with Satan." (Mujadilah: 18-19)

The teacher of the people of Truth is none other than Allah the Almighty, while the teacher of these individuals is Satan.

We prove this through these Noble Verses.

For Allah the Almighty has drawn these beloved servants to Himself, illuminated their hearts, purified them from all base morals, and granted them noble qualities:

"Allah guides whom He wills to His light." (Nur: 35)

In accordance with the Noble Verse, that servant has attained the light and grace of Allah the Almighty.

These are the ones who are truly beloved by Allah the Almighty. His gaze has fallen upon them, He has bestowed all His favors upon them, and elevated them to the station of the Truthful.

These are the chosen servants of Allah the Almighty. In His Noble Verse, He describes them thus:

"They will be amidst gardens and springs, in the seat of Truth, in the presence of the Sovereign, the Omnipotent." (Qamar: 55)

However, as for the artificial sufis, they are indeed in the lap of Satan.

•

Allah the Almighty states in His Noble Verse:

"And among those we created there is a community who guide by Truth and establish justice therewith." (Araf: 181)

According to this Noble Verse, Allah the Almighty declares that He sends true Sufis, known as Perfect guide, specifically for guidance. They work solely for the pleasure of Allah the Almighty and strive to connect the people to Allah the Almighty and His Messenger.

They strive to rescue humanity from all kinds of division and defilement, guiding them towards Allah the Almighty and The Messenger of Allah. For this reason, they are those who lead people to Truth.

For them, there exists a glad tiding:

"All praise is due to Allah, and peace upon His chosen servants." (Naml: 59)

A true Sufi must be trained and educated under the guidance of a Master for a long period to achieve spiritual refinement and reach "Annihilation in the Master". Following "Annihilation in the Master," one must attain "Annihilation in the Messenger", and after "Annihilation in the Messenger" transition to "Annihilation in Allah".

This spiritual refinement consists of three stages.

In "Annihilation in the Master," one sees their existence; in "Annihilation in the Messenger," their nonexistence; and in "Annihilation in Allah," their complete nullification.

Which university and professor taught this sacred knowledge to these artificial sufis, or did they obtain it from America? From where did these pretenders, who speak of Sufism, acquire this knowledge?

Those of “the Unity of Being” are the "Ascetics." Those of unity of witnessing are the "Gnostics." As for those of unity of the observed, they see nothing apart from the Truth, and none but Allah the Almighty can make this known.

Are these synthetic sufis aware of these secrets? If they are aware, how can they explain and prove them? To which divine mysteries do they have access?

Every Noble Verse has its own manifestation, every sacred saying has its unique manifestation, and every Noble Saying has its particular manifestation.

I disclose these Truths in my lifetime, so if they speak the Truth, they should prove it with these Noble Verse and these Noble Saying. I always conVerse with Noble Verse, I always seek Noble Verse and Noble Saying, and I absolutely do not accept mere words, for they always have mere words.

As we previously presented; one must be endowed with "a spiritual share in the prophetic inheritance", one must also be endowed with "a spiritual share in the saintly inheritance", and one must be endowed with both "a spiritual share in the prophetic inheritance" and " a spiritual share in the saintly inheritance" to be graced by the divine mysteries.

Indeed, the instructor of these matters is none other than the Exalted the Allah Himself, and this light, this authority, comes directly from our master, The Messenger of Allah -peace be upon him-.

"If you fear Allah and are pious, Allah will be your teacher." (Al-Baqarah: 282)

However, the work of pseudo sufis is mere empty words. According to the people of truth, this is highly peculiar.

•

For those who mislead others, Allah the Almighty states in His Noble Verse, addressing the believers:

"And do not sit at every path, threatening and hindering those who believe from the way of Allah, seeking to make it appear crooked." (Araf: 86)

This Verse is a divine admonition. We elucidate all these Verses so that they may understand, see the truth, repent, and save themselves and those around them from the torment of hellfire. For indeed, the punishment of the Exalted the Allah is severe. To attain salvation, it is imperative to fear Allah and adhere to His commands.

As stated in the Verse:

"Yet, those who repent, make amends, and openly declare the Truth are spared from being cursed. I accept their repentance and indeed, I am the most accepting of repentance, and I am merciful." (Al-Baqarah: 160)

We harbor no malice towards anyone, yet we strive to distinguish between Truth and falsehood. I endeavor to discern this.

The Venerable Allah says in His Verse:

"Align yourself towards the faith pure and upright, the innate religion Allah has placed within humanity. There is no altering Allah's creation. This is the straight and stable religion, but most people do not know." (Rûm: 30)

Thus, they hold onto their conjectures as their core belief, imagining and asserting that this is the truth. They believe that only they know the Truth and that no one else does.

In doing so, they lead both themselves and others astray. Why? Because they disregard the Verses and ordinances of the Exalted the Allah, relying solely on their assumptions.

Nonetheless, Allah, Exalted be His Name, states in His Verses concerning such people:

"For those who strive with all their might to invalidate our signs, there awaits a loathsome and grievous torment." (Saba: 5)

•

Allah the Almighty has servants whom He sends once every century. These are the individuals who stand as a barrier between Truth and error, revealing reality to those who attempt to distort the faith or stray into misguided paths. Allah the Almighty sends them for this purpose.

Their actions are with the Truth. They follow the Sunnah (practices) of The Messenger of Allah, -peace be upon him-. They perform the divine commandments as much as they can, engaging in worship and devotion. They expect no benefit from the people and evade all forms of worldly wealth and fame.

For they are with the Truth, showing no regard or attention to the people. They act solely as commanded, fearing none.

Among these, The Messenger of Allah, -peace be upon him-, described their attributes, saying:

"In every century, from my Community, there are forerunners referred to as the Substitutes and the Truthful ones. Divine grace and mercy upon them are so abundant that because of them, you eat and drink. The calamities and tribulations destined for the people of the earth are averted because of them." (Nawadir alUsul)

In those who one who knows through Allah His manifestation is as He has willed.

He is the "Lord of the worlds." When He manifests to His servant, that servant becomes through His manifestation.

How Does a Saint Become "Worlds"?

When they say, **"Alhamdulillahi Rabbilalamin" (All praise is due to Allah, Lord of all worlds)**, not a trace of themselves remains. **"Rabbilalamin" (Lord of all worlds)** manifests.

Just as a snowflake dissolves into nothingness when it falls into the sea, so too do they become nothing when they utter, **"Alhamdulillahi Rabbilalamin,"** through the divine manifestation of Allah the Almighty, and thus, they become **"Worlds"**. However, when a piece of iron falls into the sea, it does not dissolve. A scholar who cannot pierce through the shell of the ego cannot comprehend these Truth. Even if you throw an egg itself, it won't dissolve. It deteriorates but does not melt away.

Allah the Exalted says in the Noble Verse:

"They are the ones upon whose hearts He has inscribed faith, and whom He has supported with a spirit from Himself." (Mujadilah: 22)

Everyone has one soul, but they have two souls. How can the pseudo Sufis be aware of this? This is a divine grace.

Those who are supported by the sacred spirit, who pierce through the ego's shell, are like snowflakes falling into the sea. Their essence is different. This is because they come from **"Rahmatan lilalamin"**. The dust of that Light, the powder of amber, truly partakes in the secret of **"Al-faqru fakhri".**

Exalted the Allah loved and chose them, drew them to Himself, and made their faces reflect His own. He granted them whatever He willed.

In a Sacred saying, The Exalted Truth states:

"Then I turn my face toward them. Do you think anyone else can know what I intend to give to the one I turn my face to?"

(Allah the Almighty continued to say :)

"The first thing I will give them is to pour enlightenment into their hearts. Then, as I have informed them about me, they will inform others about me as well." (Hâkim)

See here how what is given, is given in this manner.

•

They are those whom the Messenger -peace be upon him- Our Master describes thus:

"Whenever Allah takes a scholar from this Community, a gap is created in Islam and it will not be filled until the Day of Resurrection." (Deylemî)

Why does that gap remain unfilled? Allah the Almighty bestows unique duties upon each servant He sends. Just as the duties are distinctive, so are the manifestations. Because what He gives to one He does not give to another, and what He takes He does so with the gifts bestowed, the place remains vacant.

It is thus understood that Allah the Almighty sends each of His servants every century with unique manifestations. Because a scholar is not sent again with the same light and knowledge, it is declared that their place will remain empty until the Day of Resurrection.

Our Master, Prophet Muhammad -peace be upon him- describes them in another Noble Saying as follows:

"The scholars of my Community are like the prophets of the Children of Israel." (K. Hafa)

From this Noble Saying, it is understood that these individuals are special servants of Allah the Almighty. They are His beloved chosen ones.

Allah the Almighty states in a sacred saying:

"Persist in hunger and you will see me, withdraw from people and you will meet me."

Thus, it becomes clear that He can be seen.

In a Noble Verse, He says:

"I have chosen you for myself." (Taha: 41)

It is evident from this that those whom exalted the Exalted Truth created for Himself, loved, chosen, and drawn close to Him, are His special and exclusive servants. How could the superficial Sufis be aware of this? Their beliefs are nothing but dry assumptions and empty words; their faith is merely outward, and their knowledge is based on conjecture.

Allah the Almighty states in the Holy Qur'an:

"We gave each of them distinction over the worlds." (An'am: 86)

Exalted The Exalted Truth made them known to all the realms, declaring their virtue and excellence.

These are the perfect humans, those whom Allah the Almighty has accepted into His divine presence.

"They will be in a position of Truth, in the presence of a sovereign omnipotent." (Qamer: 55)

Both the Sacred saying and the Noble Verse explain and prove this to you.

This grace is not common to all saints but is specific. That is, He chooses whom He loves; He draws near whom He selects. Only those whom He loves and selects are admitted into the divine presence.

Those who reach this station are admitted into the divine presence. They cast off the mask of their faces, the garment of their bodies, and become nothing. Their intellect and bodies turn to ashes. What remains is truly manifest. The Holy Spirit remains eternally.

He now gazes at Allah the Almighty with the light granted by Exalted the Allah. He looks at Him, he sees through Him.

"This is Allah's grace and bounty; He bestows it upon whom He wills." (Al-Jumu'ah: 4)

•

Exalted the Truth has bestowed such great favors upon these bearers of divine light; He has drawn them towards Himself, granted them the finest of all things, elevated them to the highest station of piety, and illuminated their hearts with the lights of gnosis

In return, they have bound their hearts to Allah the Almighty, awaited His decree, remained in a constant state of supplication, and have been devoted to divine grace and blessings from Al-Samad.

Allah the Almighty's guidance is their companion. Freed from discord and conflicts, from opposition and disagreements, they gaze upon all creation with eyes of compassion and mercy.

Their knowledge is the science of unveiling and witnessing, a wisdom founded upon divine inspiration. It is affirmed through both traditional and rational proofs. It is impossible to confine their states, their wisdom, and their knowledge within mere words and forms.

Truly, they are the ones who have found the path of Allah. Their journey is of utmost beauty. The way they tread is the most correct. Their character is the purest of characters. And why is that? Because they have adopted the character of Beloved of Allah -peace be upon him-, taken on his nature, been dyed in his color, essentially becoming one with him.

Let me explain this to you. When a hypocrite enters the company of unbelievers, he says, *"I am one of you,"* and takes on their color. When a hypocrite joins the freemasons, he says, *"I am one of you,"* and adopts their color. Similarly, when a Muslim mingles with other Muslims, he declares, *"Alhamdulillah, I am a Muslim,"* and one who has reached Annihilation in the Master becomes lost in the Master. Those who have attained Annihilation in the Messenger are enrobed in the color of The Messenger of Allah -peace be upon him-. Likewise, those who have reached Annihilation in Allah are dyed in the color of Allah the Almighty. Nothing of themselves remains.

Those who harbor enmity against them or entertain baseless doubts about them will inadvertently bring about their own ruin. This is because there exists a vigilant Exalted the Allah who watches over them with care. They are blessed with the help and support of Allah the Almighty. These individuals are the true sufis.

Allah the Almighty states in a Noble Verse:

"By those who spread the seeds of truth!" (Mursalat: 3)

•

"Those deeply rooted in knowledge say,
'We believe in it; all of it is from our Lord.'
But none will grasp the message except those of sound understanding."
(Al-Imran: 7)

TRUE UNITY OF EXISTENCE PRACTITIONERS AND THE COUNTERFEITS

CHAPTER 15

- What Is the Unity of Being? Who Attains This State?
- Those Who Are Deeply Rooted in Knowledge
- A Person Cannot Know or Witness "Being" Without Annihilating Their Own Existence
- False Followers of the Unity of Being See Only Themselves
- False Followers of the Unity of Being Are Not Favored by Any Verse's Manifestation
- The Believing Servant's Heart Is the Throne of the Merciful Allah
- Continuing the Explanation of Verses That Allude to the Unity of Being

Allah, who elevates the trivial to the peak and casts it into the sea as He wills.

What happens when that drop falls into the sea? It ceases to exist. It came from the sea and returned to the sea.

Thus, the one who understands this truly becomes nothing, while Allah the Almighty remains. Only those who reach this state can speak of The Unity of Being; others lack the authority.

Because The Messenger of Allah -peace be upon him- our Master, says in his sacred saying:

"Allah existed, and there was nothing else besides Allah." (Bukhari)

And it remains so.

Pay close attention to this Noble Saying, for it will clarify future discussions. Our entire aim is to let you grasp the presence of the Exalted the Allah.

From this Noble Saying, it is evident that the only existence is the Exalted the Allah. Those who recognize and perceive this can speak of The Unity of Being. However, those who do not reach this state cannot even recite The Word of Divine Unity, and do not even know how to utter it; they remain at **"No"**.

Why? Let's explain this to you:

None of the created is Allah. If a person does not see the Exalted the Allah but sees only the creation, they remain at **"No"**. The Creator of everything is the Exalted the Allah. Yet, if you cannot see Him, and do not recognize His presence within yourself, you see only the creation and think of Him as within His created realm. This is why you remain at "**No**". And yet, you speak of The Unity of Being.

In the Noble Verse:

"Allah gives the light to whom He wills, and whoever is not given His light, there is no light for him." (Nur: 40)

However, the Essence is Him, the existence is Him... You do not see or know that the whole universe is a place for the manifestation of particles of the light of existence, yet you speak of The Unity of Being.

How can you know and speak of this? Moreover, you think He exists within His dominion. You do not see and know that He is closer to you than you are to yourself. You believe you are separate from Allah the Almighty, yet you speak of The Unity of Being. This is such a profound blindness, and yet you are unaware. You do not know yourself, yet you try to make the Creator known to the entire universe.

Allah the Almighty states in the Noble Verse:

“The blind and the seeing are not equal, nor are the darkness and the light, nor the shade and the heat.” (Fatir: 19-20-21)

“Nor are the living and the dead equal. Indeed, Allah makes whom He wills hear, but you cannot make those in the graves hear.” (Fatir: 22)

They neither perceive nor understand.

What is The Unity of Being?
Who Attains This Vision?

The Unity of Being is exclusive to those who see and know that there exists nothing other than Allah the Almighty. Others cannot comprehend it. Even if they speak, they speak falsehoods and inaccuracies.

One who speaks of The Unity of Being must know the Greatest Name of Allah.

Do you wonder about the Greatest Name? When you say Allah and you see that there is no existence other than Him, you have spoken it.

"There is no Allah but Allah" is also the Greatest Name, but only when you truly see that there is no existence other than Him... It can indeed be seen! At that moment, you have genuinely proclaimed the Word of Divine Unity. This is perfect faith. Faith reaches its perfection when you see nothing but Him.

This divine secret has only been revealed to those among the people of gnosis whom He chooses, and not even to every beloved servant. It has been unveiled to some of the servants He sends once every hundred years. This is why this matter is known by very few.

Even those informed have manifested their understanding based on their individual experiences, as the manifestations differ for each person.

Such individuals are few, yet their manifestations are distinct from one another.

The Deep Scholars:

When Allah the Almighty lifts comprehension and understanding from a person, they cannot grasp the apparent meaning or the true essence. Only those to whom Allah the Almighty grants understanding can grasp the inner meaning, which lies beneath the surface.

In His Noble Verse:

"Why do they refuse to understand any word?" He declares. (An-Nisâ: 78)

However, the Arab society at the time the Qur'an was revealed understood the outward meaning of the Qur'an, but they could not grasp the intended inner meanings of that address. Thus, Allah the Almighty reproaches them for not comprehending this inner meaning.

Why? Because they are deprived of the beneficial knowledge of gnosis... Both they and these, are unaware of the Truth because they lack this knowledge.

Allah the Almighty states in a Verse:

"Those deeply rooted in knowledge say, 'We believe in it; all of it is from our Lord.' Only those with sound reason ('Ulûl-elbâb) understand this subtlety." (Al' Imran: 7)

Allah the Almighty explains that only those deeply rooted in knowledge, those whose intellect has reached the level of "People of deep understanding," can grasp these truths.

This Verse contains deeply profound meanings. Therefore, its explanation is not possible at this moment.

However, let us offer this much: Allah the Almighty has opened the lock of the heart, granted "Closeness" and " Truthful", informed whom He wills, and has made the Truth known and shown. They, the "People of Allah," know and speak only as much as He shows them. Those to whom Allah the Almighty has not revealed these truth's only speak falsehood and inaccuracies.

The matter of The Unity of Being is not a topic that can be understood from an external perspective. It is a truth that can only be known and seen by those who perceive inwardly.

And this is only for those who can say:

"I am not myself,

I have an inner self beyond myself."

It is not shareable with others.

The poor one says:

"My Allah! Without you, there is no strength, there is no existence, there is no being; la mawjud illa Allah (there is nothing existent except Allah).

You are Subhan (Glorious), You are Sultan, You are Khaliq (Creator), You are Raziq (Provider), You are Gani (immensely Rich), my Allah!"

Do those who speak of this The Unity of Being understand what we are saying? Of course not. For this can only be known by those who are allowed in through the door of Allah's virtue. For the lock of the heart is also opened from the inside.

Those who look from the outside see the veil and remain there.

They:

"He is the Manifest." (Hadid: 3)

They cannot comprehend or recite this Noble Verse.

This is the task of the "People of deep understanding". When an individual ascends through spiritual progress from the "The intellect of livelihood" to the “the intellect of the afterlife”, from the “the intellect of the afterlife" to the “The luminous intellect”, and from the “The luminous intellect” to the “The Universal Intellect”, then:

"All that is on the earth will perish, but the face of your Lord, full of Majesty and Honor, will remain forever." (Rahman: 26-27)

This Noble Verse finds its full manifestation.

O false proponent of The Unity of Being! Come, explain the true manifestations of this Noble Verse!

For the one blessed with this manifestation, both his intellect and self-become universal, devoid of anything pertaining to worldly existence. Allah the Most High, elevates someone to the status of "People of deep understanding" through His revelation and vision. This cannot be achieved through mere knowledge or worship. Here, the creature has no rule. The Being that emerges is Exalted the Allah Himself. He is the existence, and He is the existent... This subject is a divine secret known only to those who understand and perceive that “all of existence is the manifestation of particles of His luminous essence,” and no one else can comprehend it. Others might have heard the name, and might imagine it exists.

Until One Annihilates All Existence They Cannot Know or See the Reality:

Until one annihilates all existence, they cannot know or see the Reality. For the existence they believe is theirs obstructs the path to finding the Reality. This matter is the domain of those with perfect. Those whose faith is merely superficial and whose knowledge does not go beyond conjecture only reveal their ignorance.

Allah the Almighty states in the Noble Verse:

"They truly think they are upon something. Be aware that they are liars.

Satan has taken over them and has made them forget the remembrance of Allah. They are the party of Satan. Be aware that the true losers are the allies of Satan." (Mujadilah: 18-19)

According to a narration from Anas -may Allah be pleased with him- , The Messenger of Allah -peace be upon him- said:

"Indeed, there are those among people who are close to Allah."

The noble companions asked:

O The Messenger of Allah! Who are these people? He asked.

He replied:

"They are the people of the Qur'an, the people of Allah, and the chosen servants of Allah." (Ibn Majah: 215)

These are the ones who say:

"I am not me,

There is a self within me that is beyond me."

He, however, does not yet know himself, attempting to describe his Creator. He has taken the idol of the self into his hands and set out to guide with that idol. On the Day of Resurrection, he will stand before the Divine Presence with this idol of the self. Then he will see whom he truly worshipped, and upon seeing, he will awaken.

For The Messenger of Allah -peace be upon him- said in a Noble Saying:

"People are asleep; when they die, they awaken." (K. Hafa)

They will awaken in due time.

•

In the holy Noble Verse, Allah the Almighty declares:

"Allah encompasses all things." (An-Nisa: 126)

From the smallest particle to the grandest sphere, everything envelops everything else. Some are shrouded in a membrane, some in skin, some in a shell... In short, Allah the Almighty has encompassed every particle with something. This is true for both the earth and the heavens. He has encompassed everything with the Throne of the Most Merciful. The Most High has encompassed all things; this is the Greatest Name of Allah.

Unity of Being. There is no existence or presence apart from Him. He is Al-Khabir, the All Aware, cognizant of everything.

In another holy Noble Verse, it is said:

"Allah knows what is before them and what is behind them, but their knowledge cannot encompass Him." (Taha: 110)

Do those who speak of The Unity of Being comprehend these Truths?

In yet another holy Noble Verse, He declares:

"Your deity is Allah, there is no Allah but Him. His knowledge encompasses everything." (Taha: 98)

False Advocates of The Unity of Being See Themselves:

We shall distinguish true adherents of The Unity of Being from the false ones through Noble Verse and Noble Saying. It is important for you to know the Truth and not fall into misguidance. True adherents of The Unity of Being see only the Exalted the Allah, not themselves. This is the state of those who have reached Annihilation in Allah. Didn't we say moments ago, "He elevates the speck to the peak and then lets it fall back into the ocean? What significance does that speck hold?"

False proponents of The Unity of Being see only themselves and not the Exalted the Allah. They search for the Exalted the Allah within the realm of the created and speak of The Unity of Being. These are impostors.

In a Noble Verse, Allah the Almighty says:

"They became blind and deaf." (Al-Maeda: 71)

They act on assumptions. They have heard the name of The Unity of Being and think they understand it.

Yet, this is Allah's grace and bounty, bestowed only upon whom He wills.

In another Noble Verse, Allah the Most High, says:

"This is Allah's grace and favor; He bestows it upon whom He wills." (Al-Jumu'ah: 4)

This Noble Verse and the Noble Saying, **"Elilmü ilmâni..."** have often been mentioned together. Let me explain the reason and the secret behind this.

This knowledge cannot be attained through study and worship alone. Allah the Almighty draws close to whom He loves, and to whom He draws close, He bestows His grace and bounties. It is exclusively the favor of Allah the Almighty and is established by knowing the "Beneficial Knowledge." Not even every saint can attain this. If Allah the Almighty wishes, He reveals this secret to some of those sent once every hundred years, and only they know it.

As we presented, they know Allah the Almighty. They know, see, and say that "Existence is He, the present is He..." But look at the displays! You will find many books written on The Unity of Being. They themselves know very well that they do not understand its reality.

Regarding the Noble Verse, Allah the Almighty says:

"Indeed, those who conceal the clear proofs and guidance We revealed, after We made it clear for the people in the Book, are cursed by Allah and cursed by those who curse." (Al-Baqarah: 159)

They have dared this for material gain, benefit, and fame.

Especially those who have not even learned about themselves, who do not know what the self is. Such people speak of The Unity of Being while deprived of the secret of **"Men arefe" (He who knows himself).**

In the eyes of the people of truth, this is very laughable.

Those False Assertors of The Unity of Being Deserve No Divine Manifestation of Any Noble Verse:

Those who speak of The Unity of Being, to which Noble Verse do they claim a manifestation?

Our revered Prophet -peace be upon him- states in a Noble Saying:

"Seek knowledge before those who conjecture start speaking." (Bukhari)

This is a command of the Prophet. Now, look into this mirror of Truth and see your own state. For all Truths are indicated by Noble Verse. We will use this Noble Verse as a mirror to those false assertors of The Unity of Being:

"Allah is the Light of the heavens and the earth." (Nur: 35)

Can they explain the essence of this Noble Verse? Or are they blind in the realm of Truth? How can one speak of the Exalted the Allah without knowing the secrets here? How can one prove what they claim to know, and how can they speak if they do not know? This is indeed a profound ignorance.

•

“Surely, man is ever unjust and ignorant.” (Al-Ahzab: 72)

He oppresses his own self and, in his ignorance, misguides humanity, diverting them from the Truth along seventy-two divergent paths. This is a spiritual massacre, making him both unjust and ignorant. He wrongs himself while simultaneously wronging humanity.

Now, the Noble Verse proceed one by one.

Allah the Almighty declares:

“We are closer to him than his jugular vein.” (Qaf: 16)

Can you feel this? Can you see this? How can you prove what you feel? And how would you describe it? An explanation is needed.

The second divine Verse immediately follows.

Allah the Almighty declares:

"Within yourself... Do you not see?" (Adh-Dhariyat: 21)

Behold the divine address! **"I am within you, do you not see?"** proclaims Allah the Almighty.

Can he perceive this? Or is he preoccupied with loves that are placed within his heart as idols, apart from Allah? What can one who occupies and busies the heart, the divine sight, with such distractions understand of The Unity of Being, the concept in Sufism that all of existence is one and divine? He does not even know himself, has not purified and cleansed his inner self, yet he speaks of The Unity of Being!

These people are superficial and speak with unfounded assumptions. In reality, they are deprived of Truth, and they are unaware of their deprivation.

Why do they not know the Truth? Because the teacher of the people of Truth is Exalted the Allah Himself, and this knowledge is the knowledge of the innermost. Their teacher, on the other hand, is human, and their knowledge is the literal knowledge there is a vast difference between the two. They have either received it from written lines or have heard it and assumed its existence. Hence, they are truly blind to the reality.

That is why Allah the Almighty says in His Noble Verse:

"Will you destroy us for what the foolish among us have done, O Allah?" (Araf: 155)

Indeed, the audacity of these foolish ones in speaking of Sufism and The Unity of Being has truly angered Allah Almighty.

•

Allah the Almighty declares in His Noble Verse:

"He is the Al-Latif, the Al-Khabir." (An'am: 103)

Allah the Almighty is Al-Latif; the one who performs the most delicate tasks and knows the intricacies of all matters.

Yet you still search for Allah the Almighty within the realm of His creation while speaking of The Unity of Being Is this not verily a sign of deviation and ignorance?

In another Noble Verse, He says:

"No one can inform you like The One who is acquainted with everything." (Fatir: 14)

The entire secret stems from here; how will you comprehend these Truths?

But you forsake the decree of Allah the Almighty and act upon your own assumptions, ignorant of the divine decree.

It is thus evident that only those whom Allah the Almighty has informed and enlightened understand these divine secrets. The rest speak from their hollow suppositions.

As The Messenger of Allah -peace be upon him- states in the Noble Saying:

"There are certain types of knowledge akin to hidden jewels. Only those who are one who knows Allah know them. When they speak of this knowledge, those who are heedless of Allah do not understand.

Therefore, do not disdain or belittle scholars whom Allah, exalted and sublime, has endowed with knowledge from His bounty. For Allah, mighty and majestic, did not scorn them when He granted them such knowledge." (Erbaîn. Narrated by Abu Hurairah -may Allah be pleased with him-)

These One who knows Allah are truly the people of gnosis. They have acquired their knowledge directly from the Truth. But from whom did these ignorant ones obtain their knowledge? Their teacher is none other than Satan.

Let us elaborate on this Noble Saying. What is being explained to you are among the hidden jewels. You cannot comprehend it because your knowledge is Knowledge of Certainty and your intellect is the intellect of livelihood. For both knowledge and intellect have degrees.

The noble Qur'an states:

"Above every possessor of knowledge is one more knowing." (Yusuf: 76)

Allow me to elucidate this further. Imagine a large diamond. If someone says, "We are selling this for a hundred thousand lira, will you buy it?" someone who doesn't understand its value might say, "What am I to do with this stone? Are you trying to deceive me? Do you think I would fall for it?" This too is a type of intellect. However, when the same diamond falls into the hands of a knowledgeable person, they might cut it into pieces and sell it for millions. This is another kind of intellect because they understood its value and used their knowledge accordingly.

This is a parable, and within it lie hidden secrets. Know well that not every person is just a stone. There are those who are diamonds among them, but who possesses such a jewel is not always apparent.

“The Heart of a Faithful Servant,

Is the Throne of Allah, the Merciful.”:

As mentioned earlier, everything has an essence. The essence of mountains is diamond. The essence of the sacred Kaaba is the Black Stone. Within the essence of man lies none other than Allah the Exalted.

This is why the Perfected Human is considered the Greater Cosmos.

Evidence of this can be found:

Allah the Most High says in a sacred saying:

“Heaven and earth could not contain me, but I am contained in the heart of my faithful servant.” (K. Hafâ: 2256)

In another:

“The heart of a faithful servant is the Throne of Allah, the Merciful.” (K. Hafâ: 2/130)

The people of gnosis recognized the Truth, knowing the reality through the manifestation of the Truth.

As for those who proclaim, "I am a scholar, I know," they understood only their self and followed its desires. Truly, they could not comprehend Allah the Exalted, in His true essence, for the lock on their hearts was not opened. Outward knowledge remains external, while the knowledge of gnosis is poured into the heart.

Previously, we provided a parable and said:

Outward knowledge is the outer shell of an egg, the knowledge of the path is the white, and the gnosis of Allah is the yolk. Those who are supported by the Holy Spirit, when they attain the knowledge of gnosis, pierce the shell of the ego, realize their nothingness, and soar into the realm of representations.

All these graces, virtues, and excellences arise from Allah the Exalted's, support of that person with the Holy Spirit. They reach the station in this world and enter the assembly of prophets;

“They are those in whose hearts Allah has inscribed faith and supported them with a spirit from Him.” (Mujadilah: 22)

These graces all stem from there.

To be granted these secrets, it is essential for Allah the Exalted, to inscribe this knowledge in the heart and support it with a second spirit, as seen.

In the Noble Verse:

"It is proclaimed, 'If you fear Allah and embrace piety, then your teacher shall be Allah." (Al-Baqarah: 282)

For Allah the Most High, has poured His light into their hearts, inscribed knowledge upon their hearts, and supported them with a spirit from His grace.

It is evident here that the Exalted the Allah personally attends to them, teaching them what they do not know. This is why their teacher is the Exalted the Allah.

Allah the Most High, declares in the Noble Verse:

"O you who believe! If you fear Allah and embrace piety, He will grant you a discerning insight, a light by which to distinguish between right and wrong." (Anfal: 29)

This indeed revolves around these two gifts: an insight, a light...

These are the chosen servants of Allah the Most High.

Yet they preferred darkness over Light and remained in darkness, deprived of light. Consequently, they mislead the people. This is a grave responsibility in the sight of Allah the Most High.

•

"Truly, Allah is with those who are pious and those who are muhsin (doers of good)." (Nahl: 128)

Just as understood from this Noble Verse, piety is essential on this path. Piety means avoiding all that is prohibited and dubious. It is impossible to achieve piety without abstaining from such things.

That is why both outward and inward knowledge are necessary. Outward knowledge establishes external order, while inward knowledge establishes internal order. The inward knowledge that ensures internal order is the knowledge of gnosis.

Our master, The Messenger of Allah -peace be upon him-, states in a Noble Saying:

"Knowledge is of two kinds. One is that which is on the tongue (this is the outward knowledge), **which is Allah's proof against His servants. The other is that which is in the heart** (the knowledge of gnosis); **this is the beneficial knowledge that leads to the ultimate goal."** (Tirmidhi)

If this beneficial knowledge is not acquired, it remains on the blackboard. For what the self reads outwardly remains outside the heart. Hence, the self thinks it is knowledgeable by merely reading these words.

However, Allah the Glorious and Exalted through the light He pours into the heart, reveals His mysteries, makes oneself aware of Him, and unlocks the heart's lock, and grants proximity and Truthfulness. Therefore, this is the truly beneficial knowledge. Because it has moved from the apparent to the reality, it has learned that it knew nothing.

While in the outward, a person always claims to know. But upon reaching reality, they penetrate inwardly and admit knowing nothing. By attaining gnosis, they realize they are nothing. For they have achieved the status of closeness and Truthfulness. In Truth, the only being that exists is Exalted the Allah. Upon finding the Existent, their own existence perishes; they learn they are nothing and are not left in ignorance.

"Whoever is for Allah, Allah is for him."

This is the shortest path.

Because the self always seeks its share, asserting its presence. However, the people of Allah speak only of Allah.

"We are among those who turn and bind their hearts solely to Allah." (At-Tawbah-: 59)

The people of Truth are with Truth. They recognize that every grace and benevolence is from Him.

For it is said:

"Whatever of good reaches you, is from Allah, but whatever of evil befalls you, and is from your own self." (An-Nisa: 79)

Since all evils stem from the self, those who unwittingly speak of The Unity of Being have followed their egos; they dare to speak as if from the Exalted the Allah for material gains and benefits; they speak and write books.

Allah the Exalted states in the Noble Verse:

"But they threw it away behind their backs and purchased with it some miserable gain! How wretched is what they received in exchange!" (Al' Imran: 187)

The concept of The Unity of Being is reserved for the rare servants whom Allah the Almighty reveals it to. Yet he, far from grasping The Unity of Being, does not even know himself. He attempts to describe the Exalted the Allah and searches for Him within this realm, and goes on to speak of The Unity of Being.

All this stems from ignorance and misguidance, as his faith is superficial and his knowledge mere conjecture. He is misguided and seeks to mislead others. That is why we present these Noble Verse to them. If they are people of Truth, they must explain the manifestations of every Noble Verse. However, they cannot do this because they lack the knowledge of gnosis.

Their knowledge is nothing but conjecture. They grasp no Truth. I openly declare this during my lifetime so that you may know the Truth and understand the people of misguidance.

If they are Truthful, let them respond to our writings. But we will only accept this through the manifestations and explanations of the Noble Verse. Mere words, never! They only deceive themselves.

Do they live in piety? Do they avoid all commands and prohibitions of Allah the Almighty? Look at their lives and take heed. Compare their words with the life they live!

Allah the Almighty states in the Noble Verse:

"Allah has endeared faith to you and beautified it in your hearts and has made disbelief, wickedness, and disobedience hateful to you.

These are the rightly guided." (Hujurat: 7)

Such are the people of Truth, but the people of mere action are not like this.

The Messenger of Allah -peace be upon him- in his Noble Saying, proclaims:

"Seeing oneself as significant is a sin so enormous that it cannot be compared to other sins."

Allah the Almighty in His Noble Verse states:

"Most people do not know." (Mumin: 57)

These doubters speak without understanding. They appear knowledgeable. Yet, this is a major sin in the presence of Allah the Almighty, and they do not recognize its gravity.

Indeed, Allah the Almighty in His Noble Verse says:

"O you who believe! Why do you say what you do not do? Saying what you do not do is greatly detested by Allah." (Saf: 23)

Continuing the Elucidation of Noble Verse Indicating the Unity of Being:

"We are closer to him than you are, but you do not see." (Waqia: 85)

You speak of The Unity of Being; how do you interpret this Noble Verse? How can you prove your awareness of The Unity of Being? One who can prove it speaks the Truth. One who cannot is indeed a liar, misleading both themselves and humanity.

Such people are utterly unaware of the whirlpool of ignorance they are caught in.

In the Noble Verse, it is stated:

"When it is said to them, 'Do not cause corruption on the earth,' they say, 'We are only reformers.'" (Al-Baqarah: 11)

Allah the Most High sternly refutes their response in His Noble Verse:

"Be aware that it is they who are the corrupters, but they do not comprehend." (Al-Baqarah: 12)

•

Allah the Most High says:

"Everything on earth will perish, but the face of your Lord, full of majesty and honor, will endure." (Rahman: 26-27)

How can you interpret this Noble Verse? How do you explain The Unity of Being here?

You haven't yet annihilated your own existence... You've heard the name, thought you found it!

Now, go ahead and explain the manifestations of this Noble Verse, so we can see whether you are among the Truth seekers or the deceivers.

For only the people of Truth understand this. They are the ones who are privy to the secrets of all these Noble Verses. They know only as much as Allah the Most High has revealed and made known. They see only as much as He has shown. They speak with knowledge and vision.

But as for you, you speak as though you comprehend the Majesty of Allah based on falsehood and deception, unaware of the grave sin this entails.

Allah the Most High says in His Noble Verse:

"They have not assessed Allah with the assessment due to Him." (Hajj: 74)

And The Messenger of Allah, peace and blessings be upon him, said in his Noble Saying:

"I swear by Allah, in whose hand Muhammad's self rests, that if you were to lower a rope into this base earth, it would fall upon Allah." (Tirmidhi)

This Noble Saying clearly contains the essence of The Unity of Being. Try to explain it if you are truthful!

However, if you cannot explain and prove it, know that you are truly mistaken and have fallen into great ignorance and error!

Allah the Almighty states in the Quran:

"This is my straight path, so follow it. Do not follow other paths, for they will lead you away from His path." (An'am: 153)

Notice how we continuously enlighten you with the words of Allah the Almighty and the Noble Sayings of The Messenger of Allah -peace be upon him-. We repeatedly present you with Noble Verse and Noble Saying, clarifying the subjects for you one by one. If you believe in these!

Allah the Almighty states in another Noble Verse:

"Do not pursue that of which you have no knowledge. Indeed, the hearing, the sight, and the heart all of those will be questioned." (Isra: 36)

•

To help you better understand the sacred saying, we present the following Verse from the Qur'an:

"No one can inform you like Allah, who is Aware of everything." (Fatir: 14)

In the Sacred saying, the Exalted the Allah says:

"Then I turn my face towards them. Do you think anyone knows what I intend to give to a person when I turn my face towards them?

Allah the Exalted continues:

"The first thing I will grant them is that I will pour light into their hearts. It is then, as I inform them, they will also inform about me." (Hakim)

From this Sacred saying, it is evident that only such persons truly know Allah the Exalted. For He has bestowed His secret and mysteries solely upon those whose hearts He has illuminated with His light. Allah the Exalted also indicates that no one other than these individuals can know these secrets.

Pretending to know and speaking of these matters, without true knowledge, is indicative of great ignorance and deviation on your part. It is also a sign that you deserve a severe punishment for your falsehood. Repent and strive for salvation! For I convey to you what Allah the Exalted commands through His Verses and sacred sayings.

In the Verse, He says:

"Who does greater wrong than one who turns away after being reminded of their Lord's signs? Indeed, we will exact retribution from the criminals!" (Sajda: 22)

Every affection other than the love for Allah is a hindrance, a hook, an obstacle to reaching the Divine Presence of Allah.

Every being is also a veil. Truly, both in reaching and seeing the Truth, it is an obstruction. If someone speaks of their own existence or puts forth their own knowledge, this is indeed a great deviation. They have not transcended their self to know or speak of The Unity of Being!

We set down the speech of Allah the Most High as a boundary for these bewildered ones to know their limits!

If they hold fast to this Noble Verse, they will repent and be saved. But those who do not believe and are too arrogant to accept it have no connection with Exalted the Allah. They are those who exceed the limits. They are the false adherents of The Unity of Being.

•

In another Noble Verse, Allah the Most High says:

"And among those we created is a community which guides by the Truth and thereby establishes justice." (Araf: 181)

This community is comprised of those servants upon whom Allah the Exalted has poured His light into their hearts, imparting the Truth, making His presence known, and sending them to convey the Truth. The path of Allah is not mere talk!

Each Noble Verse manifests differently. Are those who speak of The Unity of Being aware of these manifestations? How can they explain and prove these Noble Verse separately, to claim they understand The Unity of Being and are people of Truth?

Yet, our Master, The Messenger of Allah -peace be upon him- describes them in his Noble Saying thus:

"In every century, there are pioneers from my nation who are called substitutes and Truthful ones. The divine care and mercy for them is so abundant that you also partake in eating and drinking through them. Calamities and misfortunes foreseen for the earth's inhabitants are averted and lifted through them." (Nawadir alUsul)

I divulge these points while I am still alive, in hopes they will answer. For I never wish to grant a path to those in misguidance, to prevent Truth from mixing with falsehood.

Thus, everyone should know their limits and not incline towards corruption.

These Noble Verse and Noble Saying serve as boundaries to prevent transgression. Will they deny these, or claim to know and then explain them? The explanation must be with the intrinsic meanings of Noble Verse and Noble Saying. Mere words are not accepted.

•

Allah the Exalted declares in His Noble Verse:

“It is Allah who created seven heavens and from the earth, their like. His command descends among them, so you may know that Allah is over all things competent and that Allah has encompassed all things in knowledge.” (Talaq: 12)

The concept of The Unity of Being is explained here in plain terms. If they claim to speak the Truth, let them elucidate this Verse of the Qur'an!

Those who grasp the reality assert:

"Whether it pertains to Sufism or The Unity of Being, it belongs to its adherents. We merely recount what we have seen in the books of these people of Truth. But in reality, we have not lived this life. And because we have not lived it, we cannot claim to truly know it."

Those who confess this truth are indeed few. And these are the ones who speak frankly.

Yet those who are not of this station but attempt to portray themselves as among the followers of Sufism and The Unity of Being should read our statements with heed. For the true Sufis and the heralds of The Unity of Being’s teachings have as their real teacher none other than Allah the Almighty. This is not something that can be attained by ordinary people.

Our Master, The Messenger of Allah -peace be upon him- states in his Noble Saying:

"When Allah takes a scholar from this Community, it leaves an opening in Islam that will not be filled until the Day of Judgment." (Deylemi)

Such individuals are seldom sent. This Noble Saying is frequently referenced, and indeed, each Noble Saying has distinct meanings.

Why does that gap remain unfilled? Because Allah the Almighty assigns different duties to each servant He sends. Just as the duties are different, so are the divine manifestations. Since He does not bestow the same to one as to another, and when He takes one with what He has given, the place remains vacant.

These are the perfect human beings, those accepted into the divine presence of Allah the Almighty.

“They will be amid gardens and rivers, in a seat of Truth near the omnipotent Sovereign.” (Qamar: 55)

For, in the Noble Saying, our Master, The Messenger of Allah -peace be upon him- says:

“The scholars of my Community are like the prophets of the Children of Israel.” (K. Hafâ)

When we examine these Noble Saying, it is revealed that such individuals are rarely sent to the world. Each is endowed with distinct duties, unique knowledge, and different manifestations. Because what is given to one is not given to another, their absence is deeply felt.

Paying attention to the second Noble Saying, we see that these individuals are the bearers of The Messenger of Allah's -peace be upon him- al

Light, inheritors of divine trusts, and are referred to as **“Kalbülmümin Arsh al-Rahman” (the heart of the believer is The Throne of the Most Merciful).** This status belongs to those who inherit either the spiritual share in the saintly inheritance, the spiritual share in the prophetic inheritance or both.

As stated, even among those who come once in a century, many have not focused on The Unity of Being. Those who have, present their own unique explanations and manifestations. These will be elucidated to you.

As it is stated in the Noble Verse:

“You are the best nation produced for mankind. You enjoin what is right and forbid what is wrong and believe in Allah.” (Al' Imran: 110)

It was said:

"All beings are the manifestation of the particles of the light of existence. Everything is not Him, yet nothing exists without Him."

Those who speak of The Unity of Being claim to have knowledge of it; how do they explain and prove this?

In the Noble Verse, it is stated:

"I have breathed into him of my spirit." (Sad: 72)

Thus, you subsist in the presence of Exalted the Allah. Everything is a veil, the essence is Him; everything is a mask, the reality is Him.

Do those who speak of The Unity of Being understand these words?

You do not understand any of this. And I know very well that you do not understand. How can you speak of The Unity of Being? You do not even know yourself yet, and you try to speak of Allah the Exalted. You perceive your own body as your existence, unaware that you exist through Him.

•

"Allah is the Light of the heavens and the earth."

(Nur: 35)

HE IS BOTH HIMSELF,
FROM HIMSELF

CHAPTER 16

Allah the Almighty presents to our awakened eyes the beauties that testify to His power and greatness, to His endless and boundless blessings, in His Noble Verses:

"Do you not see that Allah sends down water from the sky, and the earth becomes green because of it?

Indeed, Allah is Al-Latif and Well-acquainted with all things." (Hajj: 63)

He sends the winds, raises the clouds, and causes rain to fall on the earth; the earth, once lifeless, is revived, turning lush and green after its dryness and barrenness.

Rain descends from the heaven that belongs to Allah the Almighty upon the earth, which also belongs to Him. He is the owner of everything in the heavens and the earth.

"To Him belongs whatever is in the heavens and whatever is on the earth; indeed, Allah is Free of need, and Worthy of all praise." (Hajj: 64)

In no way does He ever need anyone. Whether one praises Him or not, all praise belongs solely to Him.

"Have you not seen? Allah has subjected to your service all that is on the earth and the ships that sail through the sea by His command." (Hajj: 65)

Everything on earth has been made subservient to humankind, granting them the ability to use and manage these blessings wisely.

Ships move across the sea through His facilitation and subjugation. They float upon the waters by His power and will for the benefit of humanity.

"He holds up the sky that it may not fall upon the earth except by His permission." (Hajj: 65)

The existing order is established by divine power, and it will be disrupted by this same divine manifestation. The day He permits, it will be impossible for the sky to remain without falling; this will occur when the Day of Judgment arises.

"Indeed, Allah is very kind and merciful to people." (Hajj: 65)

He has opened many doors of benefit for them and endowed them with the ability to utilize these blessings, so that in appreciation of these favors, they may offer their gratitude to Him.

•

HE IS BOTH THAT AND FROM HIM

On earth, there are fountains of Allah the Almighty. Every seeker's portion stands beside these fountains, in accordance with eternal decree and apportionment.

The fountain is His... Even the fountain cannot draw anything from that ocean. If it stands for a thousand years, it cannot flow unless the water arrives.

The fountain here symbolizes the Perfect guide of the time. Allah the Almighty and Glorious, pours His divine favor from the ocean of the Beloved Prophet to the ocean of the guide of the time. From the guide's ocean, the divine favor is given to those who are destined to receive it.

Allah the Almighty also has amplifiers, and when He manifests through them, they speak. Can an amplifier speak on its own, even if it stands for thousands of years? Only those whom Allah the Almighty manifests through can fulfill the duty of the amplifier. What He makes them flow or speak...

Despite this, if someone attributes these manifestations of exalted the Allah to themselves, saying, *"I am the fountain"* or *"I am the amplifier,"* or if they pretend to have such manifestations without it, trying to show as if they possess it, they are in deviation. They poison both themselves and their surroundings.

When do these divine mysteries manifest?

This state never arises until a person sees with their own eyes that everything they own is akin to the filth rolled by the dung beetle named Cubullâ. Such a person is not authorized to speak of The Unity of Being.

The secret here is this: An individual cannot see that their essence is but a drop of filth. Another eye is needed to reveal this. That eye is the light of Allah's grace. With that light, He shows one their essence. At that time, that eye is no longer theirs. But those who can see these secrets with their own eyes are rare in this world.

Now we will explain The Unity of Being to you in such a way, confirmed with Verses from the Qur'an that you will have no doubts remaining.

In the Qur'anic Verse:

"Allah is the Light of the heavens and the earth." Thus it is revealed. (Nur: 35)

There is not a single atom without Him. Yet, He is unseen as the corporeal form veils Him. In Truth, everything is lifeless.

For instance, Prophet Adam -peace be upon him- was but clay before the soul was breathed into him. The soul is His command, His essence. When He gave it, Adam came to life and began to move.

When the human soul is bestowed, one accomplishes everything. One acts through His presence. When Exalted the Allah withdraws the soul, nothing remains. Therefore, what exists is Him alone.

Knowing Him is only possible through spiritual education.

Just as there are primary, secondary, and higher education levels in the apparent world, there are also spiritual sciences and spiritual studies.

This spiritual education consists of three stages:

1– Knowledge of Certainty, "Knowing."

2– Vision of Certainty, "Seeing."

3– Reality of Certainty is “Becoming.”

Those at the stage of Knowledge of Certainty are the “Ascetics,” those at the stage of Vision of Certainty are the “Gnostics,” and those who reach the stage of Reality of Certainty are the “Witnesses.”

The Truth cannot be understood because one knowledge cannot access another. There are vast differences between the stages.

There are three kinds of eyes:

1– The blind eye: It has fallen into the darkness of nature and sees nothing else.

2– The squinting eye: It looks at both itself and its Creator, seeing double.

3– The Seeing Eye: It sees with the light of Allah the Almighty. It understands and knows that everything exists through Him. It does not see itself.

This is the secret of the unresolved and unknown The Unity of Being. It is a subject that those who have attained Reality of Certainty can know. It has been debated without understanding. He is the Doer, yet others are seen behind the veil.

Shaykh al Akbar Muhyiddin Ibn Arabi -may his secret be sanctified- said, **“Everything is He.”** Imam Rabbani -may his secret be sanctified- said, **“Everything is from Him.”**

Since the manifestations are distinct, these two revered figures present separate statements, which has led to a significant conflict in Islam. And this conflict continues until now. With the permission of Allah, we are resolving and removing this conflict and will prove it to you with a Noble Verse.

Both statements are true. The humble one unites their declarations into a single sentence and says:

"Allah the Almighty created everything; all things exist through His presence."

Thus, we eliminate this dispute, alhamdulillah (praise be to Allah).

Therefore, He is both it and from it. His presence exists in every atom. Everything is a body; He is the soul. Just as you have a body, you exist with the order and soul of Allah the Almighty. The universe is the same. What value can a body without a soul have?

"Yes, He is both it and from it."

As for the Noble Verse:

"Praise belongs to Allah, the Lord of all worlds." (Al-Fatiha: 1)

We prove our statement with this Noble Verse. Why do you try to separate when you say **"All praise belongs to Allah, the Lord of all worlds"** and then say "He is" and "He is from"? For He is both it and from it. Because He is the Lord of all worlds. He is Subhan (Glorious), He is Sultan (Sovereign), both the Hâlık (Creator) and the Râzık (Sustainer).

The Truths presented to you are by the notification and manifestation of Allah the Almighty; undoubtedly, they do not belong to the creatures.

"All praise be to Allah, and peace be upon His chosen servants." (Naml: 59)

"All praise be to Allah, who guided us to this. We could not have found the way if Allah had not guided us." (Araf: 43)

I am here today, gone tomorrow. Allah the Almighty places this light in your hands. When you encounter followers of falsehood, if you reveal this light, none shall dare speak. For our explanation is always through Noble Verse and Noble Saying. We present to you the light of Allah the Almighty and His Messenger, The Messenger of Allah -peace be upon him-. How blessed you are that Almighty Allah discloses these truths to you.

When Does Such Divine Mysteries Manifest?

Truly, a human's essence originates from a vile drop of fluid. It is essential for one to descend into that impurity. When the entire being is annihilated, evaporated into nothingness and void, should Allah the Almighty will, He unveils the Divine Majesty. Upon witnessing the Divine Majesty, one realizes their utter insignificance and minuteness. This recognition marks the beginning of The Unity of Being.

The Messenger of Allah -peace be upon him- declared in a Noble Saying, **"I recognized my Lord through my Lord."**

However, one who does not descend to this state and does not see through the light of Allah the Almighty, how can they speak of The Unity of Being? Such individuals are not even qualified to discuss the concept of The Unity of Being.

When one descends to the origin of a drop of sperm and sees their fixed archetypes, and when the manifestation of Allah the Almighty occurs, they realize that only He exists. He is the being, and He is the existence.

Allah the Almighty, in His divine Verse:

"Allah is the light of the heavens and the earth." (Nur: 35)

And this, The Messenger of Allah -peace be upon him- explains to us through a Noble Saying, yet we do not comprehend it because we are not graced with that manifestation.

He states:

"By Him in whose hand is the self of Muhammad, if you were to lower a rope to the nethermost depths, it would fall upon Allah." (Tirmidhi)

Observe how the Messenger of Allah -peace be upon him- perceived and explained the just mentioned divine Verse. In other words, I attempt to elucidate the Verse with this Noble Saying.

To perceive both this impurity and the eternal verities, only the light of Allah the Almighty's grace is necessary.

The Exalted and Glorified One declares in His divine Verse:

"Whomsoever Allah wills to guide, He opens his heart to Islam; such a one is upon a light from his Lord." (Zumar: 22)

The Messenger of Allah, -peace be upon him-, in his Noble Saying, says:

"Beware the insight of the believer, for he looks with the light of Allah, the Al-Aziz and Al-Jalil." (Munawi)

Only those who possess this light can perceive it, others cannot; it is not comprehensible to others because it is not their gaze. They look with a divine light. With it, they see Him. Yet, in this world, such individuals are very few. These are the ones who are blessed with Allah the Almighty's divine manifestations. They are the people of Reality of Certainty.

Allah the Almighty says in the Qur'anic Verse:

"Within yourself... Do you not see?" (Adh-Dhariyat: 21)

These people see that Allah the Almighty is within themselves, and they see none other than Him. When a person sees Allah the Almighty, they cannot see themselves. Those who are graced with this divine address are the ones mentioned here.

Whoever does not see this should refrain from discussing the matter.

The Qur'anic Verse states:

"We are closer to them than (their) jugular vein." (Qaf: 16)

How could one speak of The Unity of Being without knowing it? If you pay attention, we strive to explain and prove the unity of being to you using both explanations and Noble Verse. In one of the Noble Verse, it is stated:

"He is the Al-Awwal and the Al-Akhir, the Az-Zahir and the Al-Batin..." (Hadid: 3)

Allah the Almighty is the **Al-Awwal**, eternal from the beginning.

He is the **Al-Akhir**, beyond the end.

He is the **Az-Zahir**; every visible existence is a manifestation of His power, sustained by His being.

He is the **Al-Batin**; the secrets of divinity are present in every particle, and existence itself is the manifestation place of the particles of the light of existence. It looks to a command to come into being. **"Kun fayakün."** (**"Be,"** and it is.) It all happens with Him. All is but a body, a garment, a veil.

Yet, He is closer to everything than anything else.

In His Noble Verse, He proclaims:

"We are closer to him than you are, but you do not see." (Waqiah: 85)

In one Noble Verse it is stated:

"O Messenger! They ask you about the soul. Say to them: The soul is of my Lord's command." (Isra: 85)

When the soul is given to you, you seem as if you exist. When it is taken back, you cease to be. You are like this, and so is the universe.

Our Master, the Pride of the Universe -peace be upon him- took a handful of sand upon the advice of Gabriel -peace be upon him- at Badr and threw it towards the polytheists. This action led to their defeat.

In the Noble Verse, it is stated:

"My Beloved! You did not throw, but Allah threw." (Anfal: 17)

Outwardly, our Master, the Pride of the Universe -peace be upon him- threw it, but Allah says, **"I threw it!.."**

Only those who attain this state can speak of The Unity of Being. Yet those who attain this state do not speak, they remain silent. There is this too. The knower did not reveal this secret, the ignorant spoke endlessly. And this is a poison; if one speaks about this matter without knowledge, they poison themselves and those around them.

One should speak on matters they are knowledgeable about and remain silent on those they are not, lest they reveal their ignorance.

Who Speaks on This Matter?

1. Those who are one who knows through Allah speak only of Truth. They have no dealings with the public, nor do they need the public. Such individuals never focus on material gains, status, or personal interests. For they are truly annihilated in Truth. They observe how Allah the Almighty manifests and decrees. Their knowledge is bestowed, coming directly from Truth.

2. The scholar's knowledge is acquired, deriving from texts. Unable to reach Truth, the scholar seeks approval from the public and is always self-interested. Though they provide service, it is entangled with desires, aims, and benefits due to their ego.

3. The writer, on the other hand, considers his pocket. He might write extraordinary pieces, yet before penning a word, he calculates his profit. Even the most significant matters will not be disclosed if they harm his earnings.

We tested them during the Gulf War. We presented the writing, but no newspaper published it. Later, after time had passed, one newspaper did.

For spiritual education, one must progress through the stations of Annihilation in the Master, Annihilation in the Messenger, and ascend to Annihilation in Allah. In Annihilation in the Master, existence is annihilated. In Annihilation in the Messenger, even the nonexistence is annihilated. In Annihilation in Allah, even the state of nothingness is annihilated. Essentially, one begins to witness their own nothingness, with the divine majesty of Allah manifesting. Without annihilating oneself in the Master, one cannot attain Annihilation in the Messenger. Without annihilating oneself in The Messenger of Allah -peace be upon him-, one cannot attain Annihilation in Allah. Any other form of spiritual education is but a fantasy. This matter belongs to those who have reached Annihilation in Allah and only they will understand it.

"Within yourself... Do you not see?" (Adh-Dhariyat: 21)

This Verse manifests in them, and no one else. They see, others do not. Without Annihilation in Allah, it is absolutely incorrect for anyone to speak on this matter. How can you discuss these Truths when you do not perceive them? Writing about it, or even reading it, is incorrect unless you have reached that state. Do not read the books of the people of Truth. They see, know, and speak. You do not see, do not know, yet you speak. If someone, who has not passed through these stages of advancement, picks up the pen thinking they understand this matter, they should know they will mislead, not guide. Because they do not know or see the Truth. Furthermore, there are those specifically nurtured by masons and Christians to corrupt the true religion. They aim to distort, alter, and deny the commands of Allah the Almighty and the explanations of The Messenger of Allah -peace be upon him-. These individuals have significantly infiltrated today. What a great suffering this is! Blasphemy is freely at play. Yet, those who hold positions are merely puppets, incapable of any intervention.

The Messenger of Allah -peace be upon him- our Master, says in a Noble Saying:

"Islam began as something strange, and it shall return to being strange as it started. Blessed are the strangers!" (Muslim)

Even though the concept of The Unity of Being is elucidated through Noble Verse and Noble Saying, Why does not everyone understand?:

Even though The Unity of Being has been explained to you with the words of Allah the Almighty, you still do not understand. The Messenger of Allah -peace be upon him- will respond to you with a Noble Saying, and in this mirror of Truth, you will see yourselves.

Some outwardly denying scholars reject these sciences because they are unfamiliar with them, or rather, because they do not know. Just as they deny Sufism, they also deny these sciences due to their ignorance, yet remain unaware of it.

Thus, I convey and unveil these matters to you as it is.

I present the Noble Saying once more:

"Knowledge is of two kinds. One resides in the tongue (which is external knowledge), and it is a testament from Allah the Almighty upon His servants. The other resides in the heart (gnosis knowledge). This is the one that benefits in reaching the ultimate goal." (Tirmidhi)

The Messenger of Allah, -peace be upon him- states that this heart based knowledge is the one beneficial for reaching the goal. What is this goal? It is to reach Allah the Almighty.

To reach Allah, a person must be trained in "Annihilation in the Master, undergo training in "Annihilation in the Messenger", and then ascend to "Annihilation in Allah". There is no other way. Thus, denying this Noble Saying is equivalent to denying this Truth.

External knowledge establishes external order, while inner knowledge illuminates the inner being. They deny this knowledge because they are unaware of it. Why? Because they cannot penetrate its essence, are unfamiliar with the Truth, and, more precisely, because they have not rid themselves of bad morals…

They remain in the shell of egotism and thus commit this ignorance.

Once, we used the metaphor of an egg, and today we will attempt to use it again. External knowledge is the shell, knowledge of the path is the white, the Truth is the yolk, and the chick's emergence is gnosis. Think does the shell hold any importance once the chick emerges?

The shell, in fact, belongs to Him; that is, external knowledge is also a grant from Allah the Almighty, the white is His grant, the yolk is His grant. The chick's emergence and the knowledge of Allah, gnosis, are also His grace and generosity.

However, those who fail to attain this attribute the blessings conferred by Allah the Almighty to their egos, trying to showcase and sell them as if they are their property.

It is because they ascribe divine trusts to the idol of ego that they neither recognize themselves as liars, hypocrites, nor impostors.

In the Noble Verse:

"All the good that comes to you is from Allah; all evil is from your own self." (An-Nisa: 79)

This is something man cannot perceive; he claims to know, saying, "I did it, I am doing it."

•

When outer scholars delve inwardly, they can reach certain profound points to some extent, reaching the level of The İnspired Self. However, those who cannot penetrate within remain on the outside, sounding hollow, thinking no one else knows anything, yet they are truly ignorant. This is the case. Additionally, there are some ignorant followers of the Path who say, *"I am not in Islamic law, but in path,"* thus automatically departing from the religion.

There are some ignorant light followers who say, *"We are not in path, but in the truth."* How strange! They have not stepped through the door of virtue yet consider themselves at the threshold of Truth; indeed, they are in ignorance.

These are situations of inward penetration. Allah the Exalted grants outward knowledge to whom He wills and grants both outward and Path knowledge to whom He wills. He grants both outward, Path, and Truth knowledge to whom He wills. However, what is beneficial for reaching the ultimate goal is this.

If Allah the Exalted loves and chooses a servant, He supports him with a sacred spirit unique to that servant. Just as a chick emerges from its shell, that spirit reaches the realm of similitudes, enters the assembly of the saints, enter the lofty assembly. All of this is due to Allah the Exalted's grace and favor, for they are supported by that sacred spirit.

And now, we will strive to explain this topic with a Noble Saying.

The Messenger of Allah -peace be upon him- said:

"People are doomed, except for the scholars. Scholars are doomed, except for those who act upon their knowledge. Those who act upon their knowledge are doomed, except for those who are sincere. Even the sincere are in great danger." (Kashf al-Khafa)

Let everyone see themselves in this mirror, all of us, to be precise... Where are the egos now?

In His divine Verse, Allah the Most High, says:

"If you fear Allah and have piety, Allah will teach you." (Al-Baqarah: 282)

They denied this divine Verse because they did not understand it. Why? Because their teacher is Satan... They are entirely unaware of the knowledge of the heart.

As Abu Hurairah -may Allah be pleased with him- said:

"I received two vessels of knowledge from The Messenger of Allah. I have shared one, but if I were to share the other, this throat would be cut." (Bukhari)

They deny this Noble Saying as well because they do not know it.

Here is the knowledge imparted to you. This is called the Reality of Certainty. Some of the revered individuals who spoke of this knowledge were either respected by scholars or persecuted by tyrants. A learned man, out of ignorance and jealousy, might say, "Let it be eradicated." I will present a few exemplars to you.

The esteemed Shaykh al-Akbar Muhyiddin Ibn alArabi -may his secret be sanctified- is an entire universe in himself. At that time, they did not understand, and thus they hanged him and buried him in a dump. What great ignorance, isn't it?

The venerable Sayyid Nasimi was flayed alive simply for saying 'Allah.' Look at this cruelty. And it was those who considered themselves scholars who did this.

The venerable Hallaji Mansur was dragged through prison, enduring untold suffering. Why? Because he proclaimed 'Truth'.

Others were poisoned to death.

There are hundreds of such instances. Yet, to offer a lesson, I will present one more.

One day, I was in Skopje. A subject was brought up. They said, *"There is a veil over Skopje, which never lifts."* And they narrated as follows: One night, the people were struck with great panic, thinking a fire had broken out. Even the governor of that time rushed out in his pajamas. When the people approached the supposed fire, they saw it was not flames but a radiant light emanating from the house of the venerable Ismail Hakki. The governor, upon comprehending the situation, dispersed the crowd and entered the blessed house. He found the venerable Ismail Hakki in a small room, under the light of a candle, expositing the Verse **"Allahu nurus samawati wal ard"**. Realizing the situation, the governor apologized and left.

The incident spread throughout the city the next day. But, as mentioned, they did not understand and grew envious. Some superficial scholars, devising a plot, accused, *"This man is a heretic; he has The Throne Verse in his shoe."* They inspected and found The Throne Verse, and subsequently exiled this venerable figure from Skopje. His wife, who was pregnant, looked back involuntarily as they were leaving the city, and Skopje perished. That veil descended, never to be lifted again.

They say that Allah did not sustain the local inhabitants here anymore. Foreigners honored the place, and henceforth, it has been possessed by outsiders.

Why? Because they removed this divine light from there. This is a lesson. At the time, they could not understand this Truth when it was revealed. The learned ones were envious, and the oppressors, well, they executed their tyranny, inflicting oppression. Know well that attempting to destroy these beloveds of Allah the Almighty is akin to the Jews' destruction of their prophets.

But what does The Messenger of Allah -peace be upon him- say in his revered Noble Saying?

"The scholars of my Community are like the prophets of the children of Israel." (K. Hafâ)

Pay attention to this Noble Saying, is it not a great ignorance what they have done? They faced these circumstances because they spoke of the knowledge of Allah.

And here, this knowledge is being conveyed to you, take heed.

•

The grace and bounty of The Glorious Truth are not exclusive to the Muslims of the early periods. It is an evident Truth that all Muslims who adhere to divine commands in every era will benefit from such blessings. Allah the Almighty sends whomever He wills, whenever He wills.

The Messenger of Allah -peace be upon him- mentions in his revered Noble Saying:

"My Community is like the rain. It is not known whether the first or the last of it is better." (Tirmidhi)

I will give two meanings for this Noble Saying the apparent meaning is: It is unknown whether the previous community or the community that will come in the end times is better. The hidden meaning is: It is unknown whether the earlier saints or the saints who will come later are better.

Therefore, since that The Messenger of Allah has said **"It is unknown!"** one should not impose personal opinions or exert one's intellect on this matter.

Thus, some of this knowledge is revealed to you. You are astonished by this knowledge. However, since we present it always with Noble Verse and Noble Saying, no one can object.

Indeed, Allah the Almighty says in a sacred saying:

"Then I will turn to them with my face. Do you think anyone else can know what I intend to give to the one I turn to with my face?

(Allah the Almighty continues.)

The first thing I will grant them is to pour light into their hearts. Then, as I inform about them, they will also inform about me." (Hakim)

Only those who speak of The Unity of Being can understand these matters; no one else can know.

Allah the Almighty says in the Noble Verse:

"This is Allah's grace; He gives it to whom He wills. Allah is the possessor of great bounty." (Al-Jumuah: 4)

•

A Saint who is the inheritor of prophets possesses both the state of prophecy and sainthood of our Master, the Respected Khatam al-Anbiya (Seal of the Prophets) -peace be upon him-. We call this **"The Share of Prophecy and Sainthood."** For the state upon him is a part of prophecy, and his inner realm is a trust from the Khatam al-Anbiya (Seal of the Prophets) -peace be upon him-. All virtue lies in that trust.

Attaining this state through reading and acquiring outward knowledge is impossible; it is inconceivable.

The true inheritors of the Prophet -peace be upon him- are esteemed as children and surpass even those who are close to him in outward lineage. In terms of spiritual lineage, they are the closest.

Why you do not understand will now be answered by The Messenger of Allah -peace be upon him- in a Noble Saying:

"There is indeed a certain knowledge that is like hidden jewels. Only those who are one who knows Allah know it. When they speak of this knowledge, those who are heedless of Allah do not comprehend.

Therefore, do not scorn or belittle the scholars to whom Allah grants knowledge from His grace. For when Allah granted them this knowledge, He did not belittle them." (Forty Noble Sayings. Narrated by Abu Hurairah -may Allah be pleased with him- .

In a Verse of the Holy Qur'an:

"He says: 'I breathed my spirit into him." (Sad: 72)

These are the servants directly supported by Allah with His divine, sacred spirit.

And in the Noble Verse, He says:

"They are those whom Allah has inscribed faith upon their hearts and has strengthened them with a spirit from Himself." (Mujadilah: 22)

This is the source of virtue.

Allah creates subtle elements from the spirituality of the servant He wills. He knows how many He has created, and He activates them, sometimes even without the person's awareness. This is a hidden knowledge.

These are the servants Allah has reinforced with spirituality and sacred spirit.

The Noble Verses say:

"They are those whom Allah has inscribed faith upon their hearts and has strengthened them with a spirit from Himself." (Mujadilah: 22)

"We strengthened him with the Holy spirit." (Al-Baqarah: 87)

"Allah supports whom He wills with His help." (Al' Imran: 13)

Our beloved Prophet, peace and blessings be upon him, prayed for Hassan bin Thabit, -may Allah be pleased with him- one of the noble Companions, saying:

"O Allah! Support him with the Holy spirit!" (Bukhari)

The spirituality of such servants is always vigilant.

The physical body's sleep or wakefulness does not affect the spirituality. Since it is perpetually awake, Allah the Almighty creates subtle influences from that spirituality and sets them in motion.

By Exalted the Allah's grace and permission, he helps those who seek spiritual aid from him, whether they are near or far...

He meets and converses with angels who come to visit him or with people in the unseen world. Just as if another person were nearby, his spirituality interacts with them. The servant might not even be aware of this. If Allah wills, He informs him, and if not, He does not.

"My eyes sleep, but my heart does not." (Bukhari)

We learn beautifully the distinction between spirituality and materiality from the Noble Saying.

Whether in life or after transitioning to the hereafter, by divine permission, he aids those who seek assistance from him.

The proof of this is the following Noble Saying:

"In times of difficulty, seek help from the people of the graves." (K.hafâ)

This occurs only in servants who are supported by Allah the Almighty with spirituality and a Holy Spirit; it does not manifest in others.

•

"Be devoted servants of the Lord because of what you have taught of the Book and what you have studied."

(Al' Imran: 79)

THE DEVOUTS

CHAPTER 17

"They are the ones upon whose hearts Allah has inscribed faith and whom He has strengthened with a spirit from Himself."
(Al-Mujadila: 22)

THE DEVOUTS

"The Devouts" are the teachers appointed by Allah the Almighty. They receive their knowledge from their Lord.

In a Noble Verse, The Exalted Truth, says:

"Be The Devouts, since you teach the Book and you study it." (Al' Imran: 79)

This Noble Verse is related to the inner meaning, not the outward aspect. Allah the Exalted gives this command to His own disciples.

To "Be The Devout" means to become devoted servants of the Lord, scholars associated with the Lord, listeners with the ears of the heart and viewers with the eyes of the unseen. This is a matter of the inner realm.

This point has now changed. They perceive "with the eyes and ears of the mind," whereas these perceive "with the eyes and ears of the heart."

They are under the guidance of the Almighty, He governs them and bestows knowledge from His own presence.

They know the Truth, see that they are from the Truth, and do not recognize themselves. These are the ones annihilated in the Truth. For they are the people of Gnosis.

The true meaning of The Devouts is that Allah exists within their essence. Their words are solely of Allah and His Messenger.

The Exalted and Glorified One declares in a Noble Verse about such people:

"Allah supports with His aid whom He wills." (Al' Imran: 13)

These are individuals directly supported by the help of Allah the Almighty. Though they appear as ordinary beings, within them reside Allah the Almighty and The Messenger of Allah.

In another Noble Verse, it is stated:

"This is Allah's grace; He bestows it upon whomever He wills." (Al-Jumu'ah: 4)

That is to say, this is not something achieved through mere reading and writing.

In summary:

They became pure servants to their Lord, while the others became pure servants to Satan.

Externally, we possess physical eyes and ears, which help us comprehend the external world a world that is minuscule and utterly insignificant.

However, Allah the Almighty has also created the eye and ear of the heart. If He chooses to open a servant's heart eye, the realm of the unseen becomes visible.

Those who can see with the eye of Truth, if Allah the Almighty wills, may observe entire worlds and read the secrets inscribed in the Preserved Tablet. The inner world encompasses all realms.

If one opens the ear of the heart, they will hear what they desire. True hearing is this.

One perceives Truth to the extent it is revealed. The unseen world is seen as much as one is shown.

You hear what is conveyed to you. If the eye of your heart is opened, you see what is presented.

In the essence of the righteous (The Devouts), there is Allah the Almighty and The Messenger of Allah -peace be upon him-, and in their words, there is again Allah the Almighty and The Messenger of Allah.

In your essence, there is the ego, and in your words, it is always "I!" It is all that "I"!

When they enter hell, they will say, "If only I had awoken in the world!"

Yet Allah the Almighty commanded for people to awaken in the world:

"Be with the Truthful Ones." (At-Tawba: 119)

If you had obeyed this command, if you had awakened, if you had been with the truthful, you would not have this regret.

But you cast aside this divine command, choosing the companionship of Satan instead, and now you are with the devils.

Indeed, Allah the Exalted describes their condition in His Noble Verse:

"Shall I tell you on whom the devils descend? They descend on every sinful liar.

They give ear (to deception), and most of them are liars." (Shu'ara: 221-222-223)

The devils plant in them delusions and suspicions, aiming to lead them on the paths of falsehood and rebellion.

Yet Allah the Exalted declares in His Noble Verse:

"Allah has not made for any man two hearts within him." (Al-Ahzab: 4)

That is, so you cannot dedicate one heart to the love of Allah and the other to the love of worldly things (mâsiva). If one heart harbors Allah, worldly things cannot enter it. However, if worldly things have entered, the Presence of Allah will not manifest there. Two loves cannot coexist in one heart.

"ASK THIS OF ONE WHO KNOWS!

(AL-FURQAN: 59)

EXPLANATION OF THE DIVINE VERSE

Without needing any intermediary, knowing both the manifest and the hidden, devoid of any imperfection and endowed with the highest attributes, Allah the Almighty states in His Noble Verse as follows:

"It is He who created the heavens and the earth and all that is between them in six days.

Then He established Himself on the Throne. (From there, He governs His dominion.)

He is the Ar-Rahman. (His mercy envelops all creatures. Existence and life are the manifestations of His mercy. From Allah's Throne, life and existence are bestowed upon the entire universe.)" (Furkan: 59)

This divine declaration is meant for His servants to comprehend, yet in essence, it is always He.

"Allah, there is no deity but He, the Ever Living, the Sustainer of all existence." (Al-Baqarah: 255 Al' Imran: 2)

He is such an Allah that there is no Allah other than Allah, nor any being but Him. He gives life to everything; everything exists through Him.

The divine The Throne of the Most Merciful is indeed like this. Therefore, seeking or presuming the presence of Allah the Almighty within this realm or on the throne is nothing but speculative knowledge.

Undoubtedly, those whom Allah the Almighty has granted vision and understanding are aware of these Truths by direct observation. However, it is impossible for them to convey these realities. Both knowledge and intellect are not at that point; therefore, comprehension is unattainable.

As Allah the Almighty declares:

“Ask someone who knows! (They will truly explain it to you.)” (Al-Furqan: 59)

For He has imparted to them as much as He wished. He has revealed His grandeur and has shown that all creatures are but a particle.

Those particles existed in the realm of exemplars. Since the particles desired to know their own innermost essence, they were sent to the world. They were unveiled. They saw their origins. The decree was communicated to them. And again, their origin is merely a particle. For they will reanimate with that particle and will be accountable for the commands they were obliged to follow.

Creation; though it consists of simply willing and bringing into existence by saying **"Be!"**, He created all these not all at once, but developed and matured them with His divine wisdom. The All-powerful who is capable of creating the seven layers of the heavens with such height and breadth, and this dense and wide earth in an instant, has measured and allotted each in due time with precision.

The days referenced are not the twenty-four-hour days of the earth, but stages and periods whose duration only He knows.

"Then He established Himself upon the Throne. (From there He governs His dominion.)" (Al-Furqan: 59)

The 'Throne, encompassing other entities, is an entity itself. Its name is given due to its height or its resemblance to the throne of a sovereign.

In the Noble Verse, there are around eighteen Verses where the 'Throne is attributed to Allah the Almighty.

In one Verse, it is stated:

"Lord of the heavens and the earth, and Lord of the 'Throne, exalted is He above what they ascribe to Him." (Zukhruf: 82)

Some Verses speak of the 'Throne being grand, valuable, and honorable:

"He is the Lord of the great 'Throne." (At-Tawba: 129)

In some other Verses, the term **"Dhul'Arsh"** which means **"Owner of the Throne,"** is used:

"Say:

If there were other Allah's besides Allah, as they claim, then they would try to find a way to the Owner of the 'Throne." (Isra: 42)

From this Noble Verse, it is understood that there is no deity but Allah. He encompasses all of His creation.

The Great Throne is carried by four angels, and on the Day of Judgment, the number of these angels will be eight.

The Noble Verse states:

“On that day, eight angels will bear the Throne of your Lord above them.” (Haaqqa: 17)

The Great Throne is the largest of all the bodies created by Allah the Almighty. It even encompasses the Footstool.

Some angels encircle the Throne and perform ritual circumambulation, glorifying and praising Allah the Almighty.

The Noble Verse states:

“You will see the angels surrounding the Throne, glorifying their Lord with praise.” (Zumar: 75)

The Throne existed before the heavens and the earth were created.

The Noble Verse proclaims:

"It is Allah who created the heavens and the earth in six days. Before this, His throne was upon the water." (Hud: 7)

In seven instances in the Qur'an, it is mentioned that the heavens and the earth were created in **"six days."** These days are not to be understood as twenty-four-hour earthly days but as phases and periods known only to Allah the Almighty.

The entire universe, with all its contents, was created in an instant by the majestic command **"Be!"** by the exalted and magnificent Allah.

"When He decrees a matter, His command is only to say to it, 'Be,' and it is." (Yasin: 82)

In the 7th Verse of Hud's Surah, there is a subtle indication of the significance of water.

As in another Noble Verse:

"And we made from water every living thing." (Anbiya: 30)

•

As for Allah the Almighty's **"establishment on the Throne"**;

"Establishment" means to rule. From the "The Throne of the Most Merciful ". He continues to exercise His command over all creatures.

From the earth to the heavens, and from the heavens to the Throne, all beings exist under His decree and management, changing moment to moment, from state to state, form to form, cycle to cycle, through creation and annihilation, diversity and similarity.

He, with perfect dominion and absolute ownership, possesses an unparalleled grandeur above all particles and spheres, souls and bodies, powers, sovereignties, and authorities. From there, He creates, sustains, governs, provides sustenance, and brings death.

This Noble Verse not only describes the concept of The Unity of Being but also elucidates how He governs all creation, and from where.

Other Noble Verses reveal:

"He executes His command." (Yunus: 3)

From His Throne to His earth, He personally manages and directs the affairs of all creatures with wisdom and purpose. He ordains while knowing and oVerseeing the beginning and the end. None can obstruct any of His plans. His sovereignty is unconditional and eternal.

"He directs the affair from the heaven to the earth; then it will ascend to Him in a day, the measure of which is a thousand years of your reckoning." (Sajda: 5)

He governs the world's affairs by descending them from above. His management is in accordance with His wisdom and will.

An order, an act, or an event that is subject to the decree of Allah the Almighty sometimes concludes over a span of a thousand years; for Him, a single day can encompass such a vast cycle.

There are also instances where it spans fifty thousand years:

"The angels and the spirit (Gabriel) ascend to Him in a day the measure of which is fifty thousand years" (Al-Ma'arij: 4)

This fifty thousand years is from Sidrat al-Muntaha (the Lote Tree of the Utmost Boundary). In an instant, it descends and ascends.

In one of His revered Verses, He proclaims thus:

"This is your Lord, Allah" (Yunus: 3)

For He is Al-Ahad, As-Samad; everything exists by His being. Everything is in need of Him.

Although Allah the Almighty declares that He created the heavens, the earth, and everything in between in six days, you still search for Him within His created realm and suppose that He resides there!

How can you grasp the Truth with such an assumption?

The Throne of the Most Merciful encompasses all other entities. It, in turn, is encompassed by the divine.

"Allah surrounds everything." (An-Nisa: 126)

•

In the continuation of the 59th Verse of the Surah Furqan, it is stated:

"He is the Ar-Rahman." (Al-Furqan: 59)

His mercy envelops all existence. Being and life are manifestations of His mercy. From the throne of Allah, life and existence permeate the entire universe.

Just as Allah the Exalted, bestows existence and life from the Throne upon all humans, spiritual life also stems solely from **"Rahmatan Lil'Alamin" (Mercy to the worlds)**, the Prophet Muhammad, Allah's Messenger, -peace be upon him-. Whatever spiritual gifts are granted to an individual come through the Light of Allah, which is His Messenger, -peace be upon him-. Without receiving the life-giving water from that spiritual fountain, a person cannot truly live.

The Verse states:

"All praise is due to Allah, the Lord of all worlds." (Al-Fatiha: 1)

He is the Lord of the Worlds. He creates the worlds. He is within them. Mankind thinks that he exists by himself and attempts to see Him. How contrary is this idea!

In Truth, both man and the cosmos are nothing but veils. Lift the veil, and He is there. He commands, **"Be!"** to the veil, and it becomes a veil. He is the Creator. Meaning, He is within, you are without. You are outside seeking The One within, striving to see Him through the veil. This is impossible. You are merely a veil, as is the cosmos. Lift the veil, and He is there.

In the Surah Al-Ikhlas, Allah the Almighty says:

"Say: He is Allah, The One and Only; Allah, As-Samad." (Ikhlas: 1-2)

He is one; He creates, and His creations are within Him. You look at Allah from the outside, whereas the people of Truth look at Him from within. They say, **"He encompasses everything, and I am within Him."** When they say **"Ahad" (The One),** they see none but Him.

Imagine, for argument's sake, a cup. The cup is insignificant; its significance depends on what is placed inside. He is **"As-Samad",** and everything needs Him. Because He creates, everything is in need of Him.

He gives you life; you exist through Him. Yet you still think He resides within the realm of your possessions.

In various Verses of the Holy Qur'an, Allah the Almighty declares His creation of everything, His encompassing of all, His adornment of the cosmos, and that everything is in need of Him.

Everything visible is a veil to Him.

He is the Az-Zâhir. He is Zâhir, yet no one sees Him; they see the veil. It is He who creates that, and everything exists through Him. You exist through Him, and the veil He created exists through Him. Mankind does not know this.

•

Just as He envelops the child in the womb with three distinct membranes, He has covered all realms with His mercy. He, the Absolute Sovereign, has encompassed everything.

In the Noble Verse, He states:

"He creates you in your mothers' wombs, creation after creation, within three veils of darkness." (Zumar: 6)

Allah the Almighty protects the baby from heat, light, and water with three separate membranes, thus sustaining it there. When the time comes, He takes it out and brings it into the test arena of the world, nurturing it with various provisions. Additionally, He subjects it to trials and, from there, passes it again into the realm of Barrier.

Do you have any involvement in these matters? No. Therefore, you should step aside, and let the Creator remain.

You see that He always enacts His will.

And at this point, we will offer you a comparison.

When Moses, -peace be upon him- was addressing his people, he was asked, "Who is the most learned among the people?" He replied, **"I am the most learned."** Because he did not say **"Allah knows best,"** Allah the Almighty was displeased with his response and sent him to Khidr -peace be upon him- to teach him the Truth. (Bukhari)

However, the Master of the Universe and the Cause of Creation, The Messenger of Allah -peace be upon him-, said:

"I take pride in my poverty." (K. Hafa)

"I am poor, I possess nothing. My soul, my body, my knowledge, my wealth everything He has granted and gifted belongs to my Master. He gave everything; I possess nothing."

Those who contemplate these subtleties will understand only as much as they grasp this delicacy. Know well that there remains beyond what they perceive.

For Allah the Almighty states in His Noble Verse:

"Above every possessor of knowledge is one more knowing." (Yusuf: 76)

For whatever He has given to anyone, it is what exists.

And again, it is stated in the Qur'anic Verse:

"Say: If the sea were ink for (writing) the words of my Lord, the sea would be exhausted before the words of my Lord were exhausted, even if we brought another like it as a supplement." (Kahf: 109)

No creature can comprehend the majesty of Allah.

"O Allah! You are such an Allah that only you know yourself and only you praise yourself. I acknowledge, being insignificant and mere dust, that throughout my life I have not once been able to mention you or worship you as you deserve."

Hypothetically, the knowledge Allah (a term for Allah in Islam) grants humans is but a drop in the ocean. Yet, even that drop belongs to Him. What do you possess that you claimed *"I!"* and said, *"Mine!"* and declared *"I know!"* failing to see that by this you have entered a form of hidden polytheism?

The secret of the Truth; it only emerges when you see that nothing belongs to you, and recognize that all is His, only then will you be a vessel for such divine manifestations.

It mentions in the Second Book: "The Existence is He, the Being is He... When you wear the garment, you are there; when you remove the garment, He is there."

You are like this too, and so is the universe. But because man cannot strip away the garment, he sees himself and, failing to see his Creator, says *"I!* "You assume that you are you. Relying on the idol of the ego, you declare *"I!"*

However, only He who can annihilate the garment of existence sees and knows this Truth.

This holds true for both humanity and the cosmos.

•

Yet, all His creations know Him, recognize Him, and glorify their Creator.

"The seven heavens and the earth, and all that is within them, proclaim the praises of Allah; there is not a thing but celebrates His praise. But you do not understand their praise. Verily, He is Ever Forbearing, OftForgiving." (Isra: 44)

From this Noble Verse, it is evident that whether on earth, in the heavens, or on the Throne of Mercy, everything He has created glorifies Him.

Existence is divided into two categories: those with intellect and those deprived of it. Beings with intellect acknowledge, with words and language, the oneness and eternity of the Most High Truth. In contrast, things devoid of intellect, according to tradition, confess and witness His oneness and freedom from all flaws and imperfections through the language of their very state.

For it is clear and undeniable, through definitive evidence, that an expertly crafted cosmos, brought into existence from nothing, necessitates a masterful artist and a grand Creator who is worthy of worship and reverence, embodying the perfect attributes of oneness and self-sufficiency.

"Were there Allah's in the heavens and the earth besides Allah, they both would have been in disorder." (Anbiya: 22)

That is to say, Allah the Exalted proclaims His being **"Ehad" (The One)** through numerous Noble Verse.

As understood from the Noble Verse, regardless of whether entities reside in the skies like stars or on earth like animals and plants, their constant and unchanging existence for thousands of years under a steadfast principle and wisdom, definitively indicates that there is no deity other than Allah.

In the Noble Verse, it is stated:

"All that is in the heavens and the earth glorifies Allah, the Sovereign, the Holy, the Almighty, and The Wise." (Al-Jumu'ah: 1)

While all beings know and glorify Him, ungrateful humans neither could comprehend nor find Him, becoming His explicit adversaries instead.

However, you exist through Allah, yet you still fail to realize this. When will you comprehend? Only when He withdraws His power and might from you?

Every particle contains secrets of divinity. He encompasses everything. Everything envelops everything, and He encompasses all.

"Allah encompasses all things." (An-Nisa: 126)

Because Allah the Exalted surrounds all things, wherever you look, you will only see Him.

•

And even if they are read aloud countless times, knowing the Truth of Allah the Almighty is impossible without Divine revelation. Because true understanding does not arise merely from words.

Why is this being told to you if you cannot comprehend it?

At the end of the 59th Verse of Surah Al-Furqan, Allah the Almighty states:

"Ask one who is well Versed in it! (He will surely explain its Truth.)" (Al-Furqan: 59)

Indeed, there are those who are knowledgeable about these subtleties.

Follow and adhere to such a person's path.

This Verse explicitly both emphasizes and elucidates the concept of The Unity of Being.

Allah the Almighty reveals this divine secret to whom He wills and elucidates it to whom He chooses. They possess this knowledge. However, whether they choose to disclose it or not is up to them.

As indeed stated in the Noble Verses:

"He is the Knower of the unseen, and He discloses His unseen to none." (Jinn: 26)

"Except to a messenger whom He has approved, and indeed, He dispatches guard(s) before him and behind him." (Jinn: 27)

However, He reveals as much as He wishes to His chosen servant. Outside of this, no created being possesses knowledge of the Divine.

"So that it may be known that they have conveyed the messages of their Lord. And He has encompassed whatever is with them, and has enumerated all things in number." (Jinn: 28)

Allah the Exalted conveys through revelation to the "Nabi" and through inspiration to the "Saint" as He pleases. Since His teacher is the Exalted the Allah, it is He who teaches him.

The Messenger of Allah -peace be upon him- has said in his Noble Saying:

"Among the nations before you, there were people to whom Allah the Exalted gave inspiration. If there is one among my nation, it is undoubtedly Umar." (Bukhari)

The knowledge that arises from divine inspiration is called the Divine Knowledge.

Just as this encompassed Exalted the Omar -may Allah be pleased with him- , such individuals will always be present among the Community of Muhammad until the Day of Judgment.

All these blessings, virtues, and merits stem from Allah's support of that individual with that sacred spirit. They ascend to lofty ranks while still in this world, entering the assembly of prophets;

"They are those whose hearts Allah has written faith and whom He has supported with a spirit from Himself." (Mujadilah: 22)

These blessings all originate from there.

To attain these secrets, it is essential for Allah to inscribe this knowledge upon the heart and support with an additional spirit, as observed.

In the Noble Verse it is stated:

"If you fear Allah and are pious, He will teach you." (Al-Baqarah: 282)

For Allah has poured light into their hearts, inscribed knowledge within them, and supported them with a spirit from His grace.

Here, it is seen that Allah the Almighty personally attends to them, teaching them what they do not know. This is why their teacher is Allah the Almighty.

In the Noble Verse, it is stated:

"O you who have believed, if you fear Allah and have Piety, He will grant you a criterion (to distinguish between right and wrong), a light." (Anfal: 29)

Indeed, it is always these two things: **"A criterion, a light..."**

These are the chosen servants of Allah the Almighty.

However, those who prefer darkness over Light remain in darkness and are deprived of the light. Thus, they mislead the people. This, in the sight of Allah the Almighty, is a grave responsibility.

Do not be amazed by those who speak of such divine mysteries. For these are the people of Allah, and their teacher is Allah the Almighty.

Do not try to comprehend these mysteries, for they cannot be solved with ordinary intellect, nor with the intellect of the Hereafter, nor with the enlightened intellect, nor even with Knowledge of Certainty. Allah the Almighty grants these insights only to His righteous servants to the ears that hear and the eyes that see. This is the realm of People of deep understanding, those endowed with mature intellect, the knowledge of Reality of Certainty. This Truth is known through the divinely taught and bestowed knowledge.

The Messenger of Allah -peace be upon him- states in a Noble Saying:

"There is such knowledge that it is like hidden jewels. Only those who are one who knows Allah understand it. When they speak of this knowledge, those heedless of Allah cannot comprehend.

Therefore, do not scorn or belittle the scholars to whom Allah the Most High has granted knowledge from His grace. For when the Most Gracious granted them this knowledge, He did not demean it." (Erbain)

Allah the Most High declares the unknowable and states that this knowledge is exclusive to them because only they possess this mystery.

"I then turn my face towards them. Did you think that anyone could know what I wish to bestow upon those towards whom I direct my face?"

Allah the Most High continues:

"The first thing I shall grant them is to pour light into their hearts. At that moment, just as I inform them, they also inform about me." (Hakim)

As seen from these Noble Saying, Allah the Most High reveals this Truth only to those He wills. He has communicated this mystery exclusively to them and has declared that only they can understand it.

To summarize: Who knows? They know. How do they know? Because He makes them know. And the one who knows speaks knowingly. This means there are those whom He informs and who are conveying it to you. This is said so you know there are those whom He informs.

Only the one whom He informs knows this. Regardless of whether they are scholars or pilgrims or teachers, no one else can know."

In the 59th Verse of Surah Furqan, Allah the Exalted informs us that there are those who know this Truth. And I convey this to you as well. It means that those who are informed know everything that is conveyed.

Those who know, are aware of this Truth.

In a Sacred saying, Allah the Exalted states:

"At that time, as I inform about them, they also inform about me." (Hâkim)

Here, I am informing you.

For a person to comprehend this secret;

It is necessary to grasp the secret of **"Men 'arafa" (He who knows himself knows his Lord).** This secret does not manifest until one sees and acknowledges their own insignificance and worthlessness. That is, one must realize that without self-annihilation, it is impossible to understand or solve these divine mysteries without knowing that wisdom and judgment belong solely to Allah the Exalted.

In other words, those who know Him understand that they are insignificant, worthless creatures.

Secondly, comprehending the secret of **"Al faqr fakhri" (Poverty is my pride)** is also essential. Such individuals see with their own eyes that they possess and own nothing, recognize their insignificance, and proclaim it.

While everyone else takes pride in their ego, these individuals take pride solely and exclusively in the Exalted the Allah. This is because only they know there is no other existence or presence apart from Him.

While everyone else says, *"I, I, I!"* these individuals say, *"Allah, Allah, Allah"* and boast of the Exalted the Allah.

For they know the Exalted the Allah and see that there is no other existence apart from Him.

"They see a sign within yourself... Do you not see?" (Adh-Dhariyat: 21)

They are endowed with the secret of this Noble Verse.

Whether within themselves or throughout the entire universe, they know only He exists.

And these individuals:

Say, ***"I am not I, there is a self within me deeper than me."***

These individuals have transcended their ego, annihilating their self. For they see The One. Within themselves He is, within the universe He is.

But how can one who does not know himself, who cannot see the purpose of his creation, come to know and find Allah the Almighty?

•

"Only those with sound intellect truly reflect."

(Ar-Ra'd: 19)

THE INTELLECT AND ITS DEGREES

CHAPTER 18

- The Intellect Is of Four Types:
    1. The intellect of livelihood
    2. The intellect of the afterlife
    3. The luminous intellect
    4. The Universal Intellect
- People of deep understanding
    - The Two Types of *People of deep understanding*

THE INTELLECT AND ITS DEGREES

The reason you cannot comprehend these subjects, the reason you cannot grasp them fully, is because you lack that level of intellect.

The Exalted Truth says in a sacred saying:

"I have an important matter with jinn and humans! I create, yet others are worshipped besides me! I provide sustenance, yet gratitude is shown to others!" (Taberânî)

Taking this Sacred Noble Saying into consideration, we will explain the degrees of intellect from the beginning to the end.

One of the greatest blessings Allah the Almighty has bestowed upon His servants is intellect. Nevertheless, without the light of revelation, without the light of prophets, one cannot know the Truth or find the right path.

The intellect can only earn Truth's love by following the religion of Islam, by fulfilling Allah the Almighty's commands and avoiding His prohibitions, and by adhering to the commands and path of the Messenger of Allah -peace be upon him-.

Allah the Almighty declares in the Holy Quran:

"Say, O Muhammad, to the people: If you love Allah, follow me; Allah will love you and forgive your sins." (Al' Imran: 31)

The Messenger of Allah -peace be upon him-, states in his Noble Saying:

"The believer who adheres to my Sunnah practices and will enter Paradise." (Munawi)

In other words, divine love from Allah is attained solely by following The Messenger of Allah -peace be upon him-, otherwise, there is no benefit!..

Intellect is categorized into Four Parts:

1. (The intellect of livelihood)

2. (The intellect of the afterlife)

3. (The luminous intellect)

4. (The Universal Intellect)

Allah the Almighty admonishes some, advises others, opens His table to some, and embraces others.

Now, let's explain the four levels:

1. The intellect of livelihood

These intellect holders are in a state of spiritual numbness.

In the Noble Verse:

"Among them is he who wrongs his own self." (Fatir: 32)

Although Allah the Almighty created us to know Him and worship Him, these people, overcome by their egos, have misused the divine trust of intellect. They have forgotten The One who bestows grace and blessings, conformed to Satan, worshipped the world, and thus altered their path.

Allah Almighty, who is exalted, has named those who forget Him, neglecting remembrance and thought, as "Transgressor ".

In the Noble Verse, it is stated:

"Do not be like those who forgot Allah, so He made them forget their own selves. They are the rebellious transgressors." (Hashr: 19)

May Allah protect us from being among them.

"They prefer the worldly life over the Hereafter." (Nahl: 107)

As declared in the Noble Verse, those engrossed in worldly the intellect of livelihood are solely attracted to the earthly life. They worship the world, devoting themselves entirely to it.

Our noble Prophet -peace be upon him- declares in his Noble Saying:

"Love for the world is the greatest of all sins." (J. Saghir)

That is why Allah the Exalted, to caution His servants, states in His Noble Verse:

"O people! Indeed, the promise of Allah about the Day of Judgment is true. So do not let the worldly life deceive you, nor let the great deceiver (Satan) delude you about Allah." (Fatir: 5)

He also says:

"The time for people's reckoning has drawn near, yet they remain in heedlessness, turning away from pondering it." (Anbiyâ: 1)

They have followed the desires of the self, indulged in pleasure and luxury, believing that true life is this worldly life alone; thus, they squander their lives, unaware that real life begins after death.

However, it is stated in the Noble Verse:

"Fear Allah as much as you can." (Taghabun: 16)

•

The Messenger of Allah -peace be upon him- says in his Noble Saying:

"People are asleep, and they wake up after death." (K. Hafa)

Why are people asleep? They have deviated from the Truth, worshipped their egos, and pursued Satan. In doing so, they have strayed from the Truth and reality.

Allah the Exalted, says in His Noble Verses:

"But whoever turns away from the remembrance of Allah, Ar-Rahman, We appoint for him a devil to be an intimate companion." (Zuhruf: 36)

"Indeed, the devils divert them from the right path while they think that they are rightly guided." (Zuhruf: 37)

"Until, when he comes to us, he says, 'Oh, that between me and you were the distance of the two easts' how wretched a companion." (Zuhruf: 38)

Allah the Exalted, in His great compassion and mercy towards His servants, warns them in His Noble Verses to protect them from the enmity of Satan:

"O children of Adam! Did I not enjoin upon you not to worship Satan, for he is to you a clear enemy, and that you worship me? This is the straight path." (Yasin: 60-61)

This is a divine command.

In another Noble Verse, He says:

"Indeed, Satan is an enemy to you; so take him as an enemy. He only invites his followers to become companions of the blazing Fire." (Fatir: 6)

•

One should not keep company with people who have embraced evil.

In the Holy Quran, Allah the Most High states:

"Do not incline towards the wrongdoers, or the Fire will touch you." (Hud: 113)

Our beloved Prophet Muhammad peace and blessings be upon him also advises in his Noble Sayings:

"Do not associate with anyone except the true believer." (Tirmidhi)

"Beware of sinful and rebellious friends, for it will be assumed that you are one of them." (Jami' alSaghir)

Our revered Shahi Naqshband -may his secret be sanctified- also beautifully expressed this matter:

"If you benefit from someone you meet, it is obligatory to meet them; if you are harmed, it is obligatory to part from them." For the state of the person you associate with transfers onto you.

Indeed, meeting with the rulers increases one's pride, meeting with the scholars increases one's knowledge, meeting with the righteous increases one's sincerity, and meeting with the wicked increases one's wickedness. Meeting with the worldly increases one's desire and love for the world, sitting with women increases one's lust, and sitting with children is a waste of time.

Those consumed by the intellect of living are driven by greed for money and pursuit of pleasures. Some worry about their children; others follow the path of lust.

But a day comes when life comes to an end. The hope for a long life is extinguished. Everyone is subjected to questioning. Some attain eternal happiness, while others destroy themselves. For they did not understand their purpose; they worshipped the world so much that they thought they were sent for it.

However, the Exalted and Exalted the Allah decrees:

“He who created death and life to test which of you is best in deed.” (Mulk: 2)

The Most Noble Messenger -peace be upon him- explains this Verse through his Noble Saying, saying:

“It is to test you, to see which of you is best in intelligence, most cautious in avoiding what Allah has forbidden, and fastest in pursuing His obedience.” (Suyuti)

Allah the Most High, sent us to this worldly stage to test us. Although in His infinite knowledge, He already knew what each of us would do. He had decreed our fate while we were still embryos. Yet He sent us to the stage so we could witness for ourselves. Had He not sent us, we would raise claims and objections.

But on this stage, there is such a condition: every moment of a person is photographed, every word, every sentence is recorded.

Allah the Almighty states the following in His Noble Verses:

"Be well aware that there are Noble Scribes assigned over you. They know and write down all that you do." (Infitar: 10-12)

And when a person faces death, they will witness this unfolding before them, seeing their ultimate destination either eternal bliss or eternal misery.

If one is destined for bliss, they will yearn to leave as if they could fly. After the soul departs, it ascends through the seven heavens and meets Allah the Almighty. But if one is bound for wretchedness, they will resist departure. Allah the Almighty will also not desire to meet them; the gates of heaven will not open for them. They will be sent back from the lowest heaven.

This is a very delicate matter.

Those who filled their hearts with worldly distractions turned the divine abode of the heart into a rubbish heap, corrupting both mind and soul.

However, The Most Noble Messenger, peace and blessings be upon him, states in a Noble Saying:

"Very few of my community live to the age of seventy years." (Jami' al-Saghir)

In another Noble Saying, he also says:

“Remember often the death that spoils one's pleasures,” they say. (Tirmidhî)

One who often reflects on death cannot commit evil. Just as a good friend leads one to guidance, a bad friend urges one to rebellion.

Therefore, one must use their intellect in this matter.

The Glorious One states in His Noble Verse:

“Most of them do not use their intellect.” (Ankabut: 63)

Many who were on the righteous path became victims of their companions, losing their eternal lives and falling into hell.

Allah the Almighty warns us about this and declares:

“On that Day, the wrongdoer will bite his hands and say, 'Oh, I wish I had taken a path with the Messenger. Woe to me! Would that I had not taken so-and-so as a friend! Surely, he led me astray from the reminder after it had come to me. And Satan is ever a deserter to man in the hour of need.'” (Al-Furqan: 27-28-29)

Allah the Almighty created our bodily structure, adorned it with infinite blessings, and made it unparalleled in the world. If we tried to count the apparent blessings in our bodies, we would fail. Furthermore, there are spiritual blessings that are endless. He has placed the eternal Truths within us and will revive us again. Yet, we remain in heedlessness, unaware of all these. We have never truly understood the purpose of our existence.

In the Noble Verse, it is stated:

"They will say, had we but listened or used our reason, we would not be among the companions of the blazing fire." (Mulk: 10)

Remorse is abundant, yet it avails nothing. For everything is left behind.

In the Noble Verse it is stated:

"The Day whereon neither wealth nor sons will avail, except him who comes to Allah with a sound and pure heart." (Shuara: 88-89)

In the Hereafter, the only currency that will hold value is a sound heart.

•

Allah the Exalted clarified the reason for our creation and said:

"I have created jinn and mankind only that they may serve me." (Adh-Dhariyat: 56)

Those who do not know Allah the Almighty cannot truly worship Him. I speak plainly: above all else, it is essential to know Allah the Almighty. And to know Allah the Almighty, one must first know one's own self.

Anyone who shows ingratitude in the face of such grace and favor has plainly doomed themselves.

By allowing enemies to inhabit the body granted by His grace that is, by placing love for things other than Allah in one’s heart one deviates from Truth and reality.

For, as the Noble Verse states:

“Allah has not placed two hearts within any person’s breast.” (Al-Ahzab: 4)

That one heart may be devoted to the love of the Lord, and the other to the love of all else.

The heart, being the divine mirror, was created by Allah the Almighty for Himself. Thus, if the love of Allah the Almighty resides in that heart more precisely, if Allah the Almighty Himself resides in that heart then anything else besides Him cannot enter.

Money should remain in the treasury or the purse, possessions in the shop or at home, yet they must not enter the heart. If they do infiltrate the heart, they corrupt it, and the love of the Lord cannot reside there.

Those devoid of Truth dedicate that divine structure to the self and to Satan, thus corrupting the graces bestowed by Allah. Just as an enemy ravages a house upon entry, these two foes corrupt the heart and the entire body. Such a person, appearing human, acts like an animal, or even fifty degrees worse. For even that animal knows its Creator and praises Him.

Everything on earth and in the heavens, both animate and inanimate, glorifies Almighty Allah. Among them, it is mostly inanimate objects, followed by plants, animals, and humans.

In the Qur'anic Verse, the Exalted Truth declares:

"There is nothing that does not glorify Him with praise, but you do not understand their glorification." (Isra: 44)

Among humans, there are those who, through remembrance and contemplation, draw closer to Allah, surpassing even some angels in proximity.

As stated in the Noble Saying:

"Perfect believers are more virtuous than some angels in the sight of Allah." (Ibn Majah)

Creation is divided into two categories: those endowed with intellect and those deprived of it.

Beings with intellect glorify Allah the Almighty with words and speech, while those lacking intellect do so solely through the language of their state.

What becomes of a person who persistently dwells in rebellion?

For:

"We are indeed Allah's servants (in this world), and to Him shall we return (in the afterlife)." (Al-Baqarah: 156)

There is no way for us to escape. He created us in the most beautiful form, gave us the best appearance, allows us to live in His dominion, and declares:

"Indeed, we have honored the children of Adam with dignity and nobility." (Isra: 70)

He has provided us with the most splendid blessings. The jinn (a class of supernatural beings) form a separate nation, and they are numerous; their food consists of dung and bones. As for the animals, you are well aware of their sustenance.

May Allah make us among those who worship Him with the utmost sincerity and the best deeds in response to His magnificent blessings.

•

Those guided solely by practical reason exhibit animalistic traits, which are very frightening. If these traits are not eradicated, the person will appear in animal form in the afterlife due to such despicable conduct. Because each base morality has its own corresponding animal trait.

Allah the Exalted has written the destiny of everyone on their foreheads, yet we cannot read it.

In the Noble Verse:

"We have fastened every man's deeds to his neck." (Isra: 13)

Everyone's human attributes or animalistic traits are evident, yet we cannot read them. When the veil is lifted, everything will be seen clearly, one's true nature will be revealed alongside their actions. When will this happen? When we shed the garment of the body and don the other garment... Then, everything in the universe will be unveiled.

"Read your book!" it will be said. When everyone reads their book, they will see all their deeds. The book of this world is now closed, and the book of the realm of Barrier is opened.

Allah the Almighty says in the noble Qur'an:

"O you who believe! Fear Allah as He should be feared, and die not except in a state of Islam." (Al' Imran: 102)

Take great heed! In face of this Noble Verse, not only the scholars, not the saints, not even the Truthful ones, but the prophets also feared.

Joseph -peace be upon him- has a supplication:

"O Allah! Cause me to die as a Muslim and join me with the righteous." (Yusuf: 101)

The last words of Sıddıkı Ekber -may Allah be pleased with him- were these.

In one of His Verses, Allah the Almighty instructs us on how to seek refuge in Him:

"Our Lord! Take us unto yourself with the righteous." (Al' Imran: 193)

Our Master, The Most Noble Messenger -peace be upon him-, states in his Noble Saying:

"Remembrance of Allah the Almighty is a cure for heart diseases." (Münâwî)

The most beautiful remedy for salvation is to embrace Allah the Almighty and His Messenger in our hearts, to engage in remembrance of Allah, to expel the inner enemies, and to attain divine love.

In another Noble Verse, Allah the Almighty declares:

"He who purifies his self is successful." (Ash-Shams: 9)

And in yet another Noble Verse, it is stated:

"Nevertheless, there is no doubt that I am indeed most forgiving to those who repent, believe, perform righteous deeds, and remain steadfast on the path of Truth until death." (Tâhâ: 82)

This is the last opportunity for us to return to the presence of Almighty Allah.

2. The intellect of the afterlife

These individuals possess a mind that is half-conscious and half dormant. If they find a guide leading to the Truth, they awaken; if not, they remain in a state of sub consciousness.

In the Noble Verse, it is stated:

"Some are justly balanced." (Fâtır: 32)

Indeed, the world is for a temporary period; its days are limited, it is not trustworthy, and it is transient, unworthy of attachment.

However, since it is the sowing field for eternal life, it is of great value and immensely respectable.

In the Noble Saying, the Prophet -peace be upon him- has stated:

"The world is the field of the hereafter," they say. (Munâwî)

If a person truly understands the purpose of their creation, they would strive day and night to sow in this field. Thus, they attain both worldly happiness and eternal salvation, protecting themselves from the flames of Hell.

Allah the Almighty, in His Noble Verse, instructs us on how to seek refuge in Him:

"O our Lord! Grant us goodness and beauty in this world, and goodness and beauty in the hereafter. Protect us from the torment of Hell." (Al-Baqarah: 201)

The hereafter is earned through the world. When used for this purpose, the world becomes a vessel that keeps one afloat. If used otherwise, it drags one to the depths of Hell.

A Noble Saying states:

"Be aware that the world is accursed, and everything in it is accursed, except for the remembrance of Allah the Almighty and acts that please Him, and the learned and their teachings." (Tirmidhî)

Other people also sow, but they are engrossed in the accursed part of the world, rendering their lives meaningless.

The Messenger of Allah, -peace be upon him- in his Noble Saying, said:

"As you do, so shall it be done to you," He says. (Bukhari)

If it is good, good shall befall you; if it is evil, evil shall befall you.

And in the Noble Verse, it is stated:

"Man shall have nothing except what he strives for." (Najm: 39)

It is necessary to work day and night, for this world is like a field. We have come to sow for an eternal life. We are faced with either everlasting bliss or eternal catastrophe.

From here, it is understood that worldly life is very important, and we must be very cautious.

•

The Messenger of Allah -peace be upon him- says in his Noble Saying:

"Leave the wealth of this world to its rightful owners. For whoever takes more than what suffices, unknowingly destroys themselves." (Jami' alSaghir)

"Every nation has a trial that leads to its destruction. The trial of my nation is the love of worldly possessions." (Hâkim)

"Beware of the world. For it has a bewitching nature surpassing even that of Hârût and Mârût." (Tirmidhî)

"Detach your love from the world and its enticing goods." (Munâwî)

"The world is a prison for the believer and a paradise for the disbeliever." (Tirmidhî)

No matter how much comfort a believer may find in this world, it feels like a prison compared to the blessings Allah the Almighty will bestow in Paradise. Yet, regardless of the suffering a disbeliever endures, the world seems like a paradise compared to the torment of hellfire.

The Messenger of Allah, -peace be upon him-, said in a Noble Saying:

"On the Day of Judgment, the distance between the shoulders of a disbeliever will be the equivalent of a three-day journey for a swift rider." (Bukhari. Tecridi Sârih: 2053)

This vast breadth of the body is for the sake of intense punishment.

In another Noble Saying, he states:

"On the Day of Judgment, the one who suffers the least in Hell is he who has two burning coals placed in the hollows of his feet. These cause his brain to boil like a brass kettle or pitcher." (Bukhari, Tecridi Sarih: 2055)

May Allah make us among those who understand why He sent us and not among those who worship the world.

•

In Truth, Allah the Almighty, the Most Merciful of the merciful, never imposes suffering on His servant, nor does He cast them into His Hellfire. However, if a person forsakes the Truth, idolizes the self, follows Satan, and indulges in worldly affairs... Then, because of their own injustice to themselves, they will be thrown into Hell alongside Satan.

In His Exalted and Sublime Majesty, Allah states in His Noble Verses:

"Indeed, it is we who created man, and we know what his self-whispers to him. And we are closer to him than his jugular vein." (Qaf: 16)

"On his right and on his left sit two recording angels, capturing his deeds." (Qaf: 17)

"Not a word does he utter, but there is a watcher beside him ready to record it." (Qaf: 18)

"And the intoxication of death will bring the Truth; 'This is what you tried to escape!' will be said." (Qaf: 19)

"The trumpet is blown, and here is the Day that was promised." (Qaf: 20)

"Everyone comes forward accompanied by a driver and a witness." (Qaf: 21)

"It is said to him, 'indeed, you were heedless of this, and now we have removed your veil, so your sight today is sharp.'" (Qaf: 22)

"And his companion will say, 'This is what I have ready with me." (Qaf: 23)

"Allah will say, 'Throw into Hell every obstinate disbeliever, every hindrance to good, transgressor, and doubter!" (Qaf: 24-25)

"The one who set up another Allah alongside Allah. Throw him into the intense punishment!" (Qaf: 26)

"His companion will say, 'Our Lord, I did not lead him astray, but he was in far error himself!" (Qaf: 27)

"Allah will say, 'Do not argue before me! I had already given you the warning." (Qaf: 28)

"My word cannot be changed, and I am not unjust to the servants." (Qaf: 29)

"On that Day, We will say to Hell, 'Have you been filled?' And it will say, 'Are there more?" (Qaf: 30)

"Heaven will be brought closer to those who are conscious of Allah. It will not be far." (Qaf: 31)

"They will be told, 'this is the paradise you were promised. It is for those who turn to Allah, follow His commands, fear Ar-Rahman (The Merciful) though unseen, and come with a devout heart. Enter it in peace!" (Qaf: 32-33-34)

"There, they will have whatever they desire. And with us is more." (Qaf: 35)

As one must fear greatly, so must one avoid falling into despair.

Our beloved Prophet -peace be upon him- elucidates the vastness of Allah's mercy in His Noble Saying:

"Allah is more pleased with the repentance of His servant than a person who was in a perilous desert with his camel carrying his water and provisions, lays down to sleep, and upon awakening finds his camel gone. Desperate and stricken by heat and thirst, resigned to his fate, he returns to his former place. Falling asleep again briefly, he awakens to find his camel standing beside him." (Bukhari. Tecridi Sarih: 2143)

It suffices for the servant to recognize why he came, to turn towards Allah, and to persist in worship and obedience.

As another Noble Verse states:

"My Messenger! Inform My servants that I am indeed the All Forgiving, Most Merciful, but my punishment is a painful punishment." (Hicr: 49-50)

In another Noble Verse, the path to salvation is illuminated:

"Indeed, he succeeds who purifies his self, and he fails who corrupts it." (Ash-Shams: 9-10)

Those who cleanse their selves of sins and cultivate piety are truly the ones who attain genuine salvation.

•

We continue with the intellect of the hereafter.

Now, we present to you three Noble Verse:

"O you who believe! Fear Allah. Let every self-look to what it has sent ahead for tomorrow. Fear Allah, for Allah is well aware of all that you do." (Hashr: 18)

"Wherever you may be, Allah is with you." (Hadid: 4)

"We are closer to man than his jugular vein." (Qaf: 16)

The first Noble Verse speaks to the general public.

The second Noble Verse addresses a specific group.

The third Noble Verse is directed towards the choicest of the chosen.

Those possessing the intellect of the afterlife ponder both worldly life and the afterlife, thus their numbers are fewer compared to those with the intellect of livelihood. They have been somewhat refined. They engage in worship but also commit faults.

According to a narration from Ibni Mas'ud -may Allah be pleased with him- , The Messenger of Allah -peace be upon him- said in a Noble Saying:

"When Allah the Almighty created the intellect, He said to it, 'Come!' and it came. Then He commanded, 'Return!' and it returned. Upon this, Allah addressed the intellect:

'I have not created anything more beloved to me than you. I will place you upon the most beloved of my creation to me." (Razin)

True intellect is that which wholeheartedly obeys the commands of Allah the Almighty and The Messenger of Allah -peace be upon him-.

In the Noble Saying:

“Obey Allah, so that you may be deemed wise." (munawi)

Those who possess the intellect of the afterlife belong to the class of ascetics. They act by distinguishing between good and evil, and persist in worship and obedience. However, in every righteous deed they perform, the self-interferes and takes its share.

If they find good friends, they persist in goodness and increase their worship and devotion. But if they associate with bad friends, they can be led astray quickly, for they are not yet spiritually strong.

It has been said, **“Refik sümmet’tarik = Find a friend, then the path.”**

•

We shall present an illustration of how important a friend is.

There was an executive officer in Düzce. He retired and opened an office across from our shop. He was a person who performed his prayers, very polite, refined, and clean. However, sometimes he played backgammon. I found it unbecoming of him. One day, I took the book Kanz'ulIrfan (Treasure of Knowledge). I opened the page containing the Noble Saying about backgammon and placed it in front of him. “May Allah be pleased with you, I have never received such courteous guidance in my life,” he said.

He then narrated with embarrassment:

"In my youth, I was very pious. I would recite the Ezanı Muhammedî (Islamic call to prayer) in mosques and read the Mevlidi Şerif (ceremonial poem honoring Prophet Muhammad) in Circassian. Meanwhile, I entered into public service. My friends would revel each night, inviting me as well, but I never went. One day, it seems the devil must have tempted me, as I decided to see what they were up to. I found them seated around the table, living a very corrupt life. I tried to escape, but they would not let me. They pinned me down and forced a sip past my throat. From that moment, I too began to drink, and for years and years, I drank.

I have only recently freed myself from this filth. Thanks be to Allah the Almighty He delivered me."

This, indeed, is what a friend can lead one to. But if one finds a righteous friend, they can attain eternal happiness. As we mentioned at the beginning, "When the reason engages with a good friend, it awakens.”

Allah the Almighty states in the Noble Verse:

“Only those gifted with sound intellect truly ponder.” (Ra'd: 19)

If one finds a Perfect guide, and if they are destined, they receive their share day by day. Depending on the struggle with their lower self, with Allah's permission, one day they will achieve victory.

•

In the works of many great scholars of Islamic law and Sufi orders, such as Abd al-Qadir al-Gilani_-may his secret be sanctified- and Muhyiddin Ibnül Arâbî -may his secret be sanctified-, it's frequently expressed and stated:

"One who has no Master, has Satan as their Master." And the Truth of this meaning has been confirmed by many Noble Verse.

"O children of Adam! Did I not command you not to worship Satan?" (Yasin: 60)

From this divine command, it becomes clear that a person cannot resist Satan when alone.

Saying 'I am a Muslim' is one thing, living as a Muslim is another. Living as a Muslim is fundamental. Some people create divisions, and others pursue the customs of disbelief. They idolize their selves, thus straying from the path.

•

The necessity of the exalted path is proven by the Verses of the Qur'an.

Allah the Almighty proclaims:

"For each of you, we have made a divine law and a clear way." (Al-Maeda: 48)

Look at how beautifully Allah the Almighty declares. How He describes the ways. Why? For our salvation.

In another Verse, He says:

"Be with the Truthful Ones." (At-Tawba: 119)

Following this noble command, seek a Perfect guide in the universe.

Those who initiate allegiance resist the command of Satan, as they gain strength through the spiritual assistance of the venerable beings present in The Noble Path. By this strength, they free themselves from Satan's domination.

"Whoever joins a group becomes one of them." (Abu Dawood)

As indicated by this Noble Saying, if a person joins a group with love, they are counted among them and will be gathered with them on Judgment Day.

For The Messenger of Allah -peace be upon him- said in a sacred tradition:

"A person will be with those whom they love." (K. Hafâ)

Undoubtedly, it is essential to fully adhere to Allah Almighty's law, which means meticulously performing the prayers, which are a sign of faith, and fulfilling acts of worship such as almsgiving, fasting, and pilgrimage.

Masters of paths without Islamic law and prayer are Satan in the guise of a Master. Under that mask, they do what Satan cannot.

However, one must seek a Perfect guide who has attained Annihilation in Allah, and by obeying his commands and showing loyalty with love, one can advance spiritually. Otherwise, one cannot. May The Exalted Truth never leave the people of Divine Unity hopeless from spiritual doctors until the Day of Judgment.

The Noble Verse states:

"Who is better in speech than one who calls to Allah, works righteousness, and says, 'Indeed, I am of the Muslims'?" (Fussilat: 33)

Calling to Allah is the path of the prophets and their heirs.

Allah the Almighty commands His mercy prophet, the Khatam al-Anbiya (Seal of the Prophets), to declare to the people:

"Say, 'this is my way; I invite to Allah with insight, I and those who follow me. Glory be to Allah, and I am not of the polytheists." (Yusuf: 108)

Just as the exalted prophets invited their communities to Allah's path with unequivocal evidence, so too do the select heirs of the prophets among the Community call the people to the Truth, reinforcing divine laws. Their proclamations are always based on clear evidence, making it impossible to dismantle or refute them. Those who oppose them with mere conjecture always end up humiliated.

Another Noble Verse states:

"Let there be a community among you who invite to what is good, enjoin what is right, and forbid what is wrong. Those who do this shall attain true salvation." (Al' Imran: 104)

These are the healers of the world of one who knows through Allah who, by Allah's permission, resurrect dead souls and cleanse them from animalistic traits, so they can live and pass away in human nature, liberating them from vile morals.

If a person does not find salvation, they remain in an animalistic state and will be resurrected in the same manner upon death.

A Noble Saying states:

"As you live, so shall you die, and as you die, so shall you be resurrected."

Just as those afflicted by physical illnesses must visit a doctor, take their medicine, and adhere to a diet, it is essential to consult the physician of the spiritual realm to treat spiritual ailments and eliminate vile characteristics.

If a patient does not take their medicine and follows a diet strictly, they will not recover; similarly, if a person acts against the Islamic law, if they place loves higher than the love of Exalted the Allah in their heart, and if they associate with people entrenched in heedlessness and hardness of heart, they will lose their divine grace and remain stagnant on their path.

We need to ponder these matters deeply.

Allah the Almighty says:

"O wisdom and insight possessors! Take heed!" (Hashr: 2)

This Noble Verse commands us to take heed.

Thus, it is essential to ponder deeply, do well, and avoid evil.

The Most Honorable of the Universe -peace be upon him- states in his Noble Sayings:

"Faith is two halves. Half is in patience and half in gratitude." (Jami' alSaghir)

Patience is to avoid all evil, while gratitude is to fulfill every divine command with joy.

"Peace be upon those who follow guidance." (Taha: 47)

3. "The luminous intellect"

Those who possess an enlightened mind understand their purpose, turn towards Almighty Allah, and strive inwardly within the universe.

Through Contemplative Meditation, one welcomes the divine manifestations into the heart, and the light of Divine Beauty reflects on the mirror of the heart. It is through this that one may attain serenity, vision, and companionship. True closeness is found solely in the Universal Intellect.

The Most Noble Messenger -peace be upon him- states in a Noble Saying:

"The believer is the mirror of another believer." (Abu Dawood)

In this context, the heart of the first believer refers to the heart of a perfect believer, while the second believer refers to Allah the Almighty Himself. 'Al-Mu'min' is one of the sacred names of Allah the Almighty.

When Allah the Almighty manifests in one's heart, divine knowledge begins to emerge. This emergence relies on a mirror like reflection in the heart.

As stated in another Noble Saying:

"Indeed, in the body, there is a piece of flesh. If it is good, the entire body is good. If it is corrupt, the entire body is corrupt. That piece of flesh is the heart." (Bukhari)

And in the Noble Verse, it is decreed:

"Is one whose heart Allah has opened to Islam, so that he has received light from his Lord, (not better than one hardhearted)? Woe to those whose hearts are hardened against the remembrance of Allah! They are manifestly astray." (Zumar: 22)

Our noble Prophet, peace and blessings be upon him, elucidates in his sacred saying:

"Beware the insight of the true believer, for he looks with the light of Allah, The One who is Al-Aziz and Al-Jalil." (Munawi)

This means it is highly probable that the secrets of your heart will be uncovered through the divine light within his heart.

Indeed, Allah bestows such favors upon His beloved servants.

The Noble Verse declares:

"To whomsoever Allah grants wisdom, to him He has indeed given much good. Yet none remembers except those endowed with understanding." (Al-Baqarah: 269)

Whosoever acts upon their knowledge, Allah the Exalted, teaches them what they do not know.

And the Noble Verse further states:

"If you fear Allah and are pious, Allah will be your teacher." (Al-Baqarah: 282)

If one uses their intellect wisely to draw near to the Ar-Rahman Allah, Allah Most High will also unite them with His divine essence.

In the Noble Verse:

“Allah unites whom He wills with His divine essence.” (Nur: 35)

The remains of their bodies, though in the ground, will not decompose. For they have shed their animalistic traits, embodied the human form, and become light. These individuals will be resurrected in the form of humans.

Indeed, The Messenger of Allah -peace be upon him- has said:

On the Day of Judgment, when crossing the bridge of Sirat, the fire of Hell will say:

"Pass, O believer! Your presence extinguishes my flames!" addressing the perfect believer. (Jami' alSaghir)

What would happen even if this person were to fall? The fire would not burn them.

In another Noble Saying, it is said:

"Believers do not die. They are merely transferred from one abode to another."

Let me offer an example of this. One day, I was wandering in the blessed city of Damascus. My path brought me to a shrine. The saint there was known as Cotton Uncle. Intrigued, I entered and inquired. Two people were conversing inside. One said, *"This man is a Saint, a beloved servant of Allah."* The other responded, *"Can this man be a Saint?"* At that moment, the revered saint raised his foot. It remains suspended as it was, its color unchanged. They have covered it with cotton. Visitors come to pay their respects.

This means that the body of such a person in the universe does not decay by the earth.

In the Noble Verse, Allah the Almighty says:

"Beware! Certainly, no fear shall overcome the friends of Allah, nor shall they grieve." (Yunus: 62)

Therefore, let those who work, work for this; let those who live, live for this.

A human can surpass the angels in virtue, or fall fifty degrees below an animal.

•

Now, let us reveal the states of those who attain eternal happiness through

Noble Verse.

In the Majestic Surah Rahman, Allah the Exalted declares:

"For those who fear standing before their Lord, there will be two gardens. Which of your Lord's favors will you deny?" (Rahman: 46-47)

"Both are filled with all kinds of trees. Which of your Lord's favors will you deny?" (Rahman: 48-49)

"In them, there are two flowing springs. Which of your Lord's favors will you deny?" (Rahman: 50-51)

"In both gardens, there are pairs of every fruit. Which of your Lord's favors will you deny?" (Rahman: 52-53)

"There, they recline on carpets lined with thick brocade, and the fruits of both gardens are within easy reach. Which of your Lord's favors will you deny?" (Rahman: 54-55)

"In those gardens are maidens devoted, restraining their glances only for their spouses. Before them, neither man nor jinn has touched them. Which of your Lord's favors will you deny?" (Rahman: 56-57)

"They are like rubies and coral. Which of your Lord's favors will you deny?" (Rahman: 58-59)

"Is there any reward for goodness other than goodness? Which of your Lord's favors will you deny?" (Rahman: 60-61)

"Beyond these two paradises, there lie two more. So which of your Lord's favors do you deny?" (Rahman: 62-63)

"They are deep green. So which of your Lord's favors do you deny?" (Rahman: 64-65)

"In both, there are two springs flowing incessantly. So which of your Lord's favors do you deny?" (Rahman: 66-67)

"In them are various fruits, date palms, and pomegranate trees. So which of your Lord's favors do you deny?" (Rahman: 68-69)

In Surah Al-Waqi'ah it is said:

"They will recline on couches adorned with gold and jewels, facing each other. Eternal youths will circulate among them with vessels, pitchers, and cups filled from a flowing fountain of wine. This wine will neither cause headaches nor intoxication." (Waqi'ah: 15-16-17-18-19)

"They will have fruits of their choice and flesh of birds they desire. And in return for their deeds, there will be fair maidens with large, dark eyes, like hidden pearls." (Waqi'ah: 20-21-22-23-24)

"They will hear no futile talk nor sinful speech, but only the greeting 'Peace, peace'." (Waqi'ah: 25-26-27)

"Those who receive their records in their right hand oh, how blessed they are! They will be amid thorn less lote trees, banana trees laden with fruit, in extended shade, by flowing waters, amid abundant fruits, unfailing and unrestricted, reclining on high, raised couches." (Waqi'ah: 28-29-30-31-32-33-34)

"We have created the women of Paradise as a new creation. Thus, they remain perpetual virgins, devoted to their spouses, and all of them are delicate, in the same age." (Waqi'ah: 35-36-37)

"These are for those who receive their records in their right hand." (Waqiah: 38)(*)

Allah the Exalted, has bestowed such blessings and bounties upon His servants.

The Noble Messenger -peace be upon him- states in his Noble Saying:

"If a woman from the houris (beautiful maidens of Paradise) were to gaze upon the inhabitants of the earth, surely she would light up everything between heaven and earth and fill it with a pleasing fragrance. The veil on her head is more valuable than the world and all that is in it." (Bukhari, Tecridi Sarih: 11-82)

We have become infatuated with the world, even worshiped it. Yet, true life and happiness lie there. This is the divine feast Allah the Exalted, has prepared for those with luminous intellect

4. "The Universal Intellect"

Those who possess this intellect are the beloved and chosen servants of Allah the Exalted.

In the Noble Verse, He proclaims:

"I have chosen you; listen to what is revealed to you!" (Tâhâ: 13)

"Allah chooses for Himself whom He wills." (Shura: 13)

"I have chosen you for myself." (Tâhâ: 41)

(*) For the explanations of these verses, the relevant sections of our work **'Human, World, and the Hereafter'** can be consulted.

And The Messenger of Allah Muhammad -peace be upon him- said in his blessed Noble Saying:

"One attraction from the Ar-Rahman equates to the deeds of humans and jinn." (K. Hafâ)

Such a delicate matter is best presented to you through an analogy.

Suppose one person sets out on foot for the Ka'ba, while another travels by airplane. The same is true on the path of spiritual journey. Some people, depending on their portion, walk a certain distance. Others, having received a greater share, progress further. Those whom Allah the Almighty has favored with miraculous gifts; some fly like birds, alighting wherever they wish. Then, they walk and join the assembly. Some even travel through transcending space; Allah the Almighty makes the earth move for them, and they reach their desired destination in a single step.

Those who journey with the heart arrive in an instant.

How they arrive in an instant, I will prove to you with a Noble Verse.

When Solomon -peace be upon him- asked who could bring the throne of Bilqis, a jinn, Ifrit, said, *"I will bring it to you before you rise from your place."* However, Khidr -peace be upon him- claimed he could bring it in the blink of an eye.

This matter is depicted in the Noble Verse as follows:

"The one who had knowledge from the Book (Khidr) said, 'I will bring it to you within the twinkling of an eye.' When Solomon saw it placed firmly before him, he said, 'This is by the grace of my Lord! To test whether I give thanks or act with ingratitude. Whoever gives thanks benefits his own self, and as for whoever acts with ingratitude, surely my Lord is Self-Sufficient, Most generous." (Naml: 40)

From this Noble Verse, it is understood that the throne was transported from one land to another in an instant. Allah the Almighty is capable of transporting not just a throne but the entire universe from one place to another in a blink, let alone a human being! Does your mind accept this now? Has your doubt been cleared? Why? Because the Noble Verse proves it.

It means that when Allah the Almighty draws a beloved and chosen servant near, they arrive at once. Not just to the Great Kaaba, but trust that they reach the divine presence at once. He loved and chose them, and because He chose them, He drew them close.

Allah the Almighty draws His chosen servant to Himself. These beloved servants, who use their intellect, reach Truth through three paths: Love, Affection, and Self-annihilation.

"This is Allah's grace; He grants it to whom He wills." (Al-Jumu'ah: 4)

Allah the Almighty has granted, with His grace, the opening of the spiritual vision of the believers' hearts, bringing them to the knowledge of the divine, reaching them to His satisfaction, the contentment of the Creator.

No saint has grown without divine attraction; know this. For a servant to reach Truth, it is necessary for Truth to draw that servant towards Himself. No one can reach Truth by their own means.

Divine attraction stirs the hearts of the enlightened; it is the sustenance of lovers and the joy and solace of travelers on the path of Truth. Undoubtedly, this is sustained by love. For everything is made possible through love. Such is the grace of love that it defies expression. Since it comes from Truth, it leads back to Truth.

Self-effacement too, is such a divine favor that it unites one with Allah the Almighty for those to whom it is granted, it lifts the veils between the Creator and the created, and consumes all attributes and desires.

Love is fire, love is pleasure, and it is the source of strength to reach Truth.

Exalted the Mawlana Jami -may his secret be sanctified-said:

"Even if love and affection are metaphorical, do not turn away from them, for they are means, bridges leading to true love."

One who is in love must grow accustomed to trial and tribulation. For the beloved does not want the lover to be occupied with anyone else.

•

Let me present this delicate point with an analogy. A nobleman had no children and greatly desired one. Finally, Allah the Almighty bestowed him with a child. Inevitably, he grew attached to this child.

One day, after the Morning Prayer, he had a dream in which he wandered among the beautiful palaces of the Supreme Paradise. *"Whose palace is this?"* he asked. **"It belonged to a certain person, but it was taken away because of his affection for his child,"** they replied.

He asked about a few more palaces, and it turned out that all those palaces belonged to him. When he heard that they had also been taken from him, he was deeply saddened. *"I don't want that child, I don't want that child!"* he said repeatedly. His wife replied, *"Master, wake up, our child fell from the roof and died."*

Allah the Almighty is most jealous of everyone. First, He took him out of his heart, then took his child. He does not desire His beloved servant's heart to turn elsewhere. Although what is loved causes pain and hardship, the sincere lover must welcome these with a gracious heart.

"Everything the Beloved does is endearing."

The sweetest thing for a lover is to burn for their beloved. Indeed, spiritual nourishment is connected to love of Allah and Divine Love. Those who attain the perfection of love and affection think of nothing but being with their True Beloved and serving Him.

•

These are the travelers of Truth who reach Allah through the path of wisdom. It is the station of the perfect human. Such a person has reached Allah and has become annihilated in Him. They are called **"those who have reached Allah."** They have attained the secret of Word of Divine Unity. Until then, they ponder their own and the universe's nonexistence, praising Allah the Almighty's existence; but upon reaching this station, they perceive the true nature of both themselves and the universe. It turns out everything is Him. There is nothing else.

Infinite thanks to Allah the Almighty who opens the eyes of the believers' hearts, allowing them to attain divine knowledge and the pleasure of the Creator.

When Allah the Almighty manifests, everything perishes. When the lights of the Divine Essence manifest, human qualities melt away completely into nonexistence. This is such a manifestation that all other lights in creation are annihilated.

As the Noble Verse states:

“Everything besides His existence is destined to perish.” (Qasas 88)

On the other hand, when Allah the Almighty manifests Himself in someone, only the Truth remains. Neither the self nor the intellect endures. He is present, and nothing else exists.

In another Noble Verse, it is stated:

“Allah effaces what He wills and establishes (what He wills).” (Ra’d 39)

After this state, the holy soul remains everlasting. He observes with the divine Eye of Allah the Almighty. Seeing through Him, seeing from Him, and seeing by Him.

It means Allah the Almighty bestows such gifts upon a servant! He does this for a servant as a grace and benevolence.

Now, we present three Noble Verses.

Exalted The Exalted Truth says:

“Among them, a portion, by Allah’s permission, are foremost in good deeds. That is the great grace itself.” (Fatir 32)

"Those who excel and win in the good deeds' competition are also the frontrunners there. They are the ones brought closest to Allah and are in the Gardens of Bliss." (Wâqi'a: 10-11-12)

"Then, We made those whom we choose from among our servants inherit the book." (Fatir: 32)

•

People of deep understanding:

It is an intellect which arises from Allah's declaration and demonstration. Beyond the “The Universal Intellect”, the intellect does not operate independently. The intellect that follows comes from Allah's pronouncement and guidance. This is known as "People of deep understanding."

The Messenger of Allah -peace be upon him- said in a Noble Saying:

"There is such knowledge akin to hidden gems. Only those who are one who knows Allah understand it. When they speak of this knowledge, those who are heedless of Allah do not comprehend it.

Therefore, do not disdain or belittle the scholars to whom Allah, in His grace, has granted knowledge. For the Almighty did not disgrace them when He bestowed this knowledge upon them." (Arba'in, from Abu Huraira -may Allah be pleased with him-.)

This Noble Saying has been mentioned frequently. This knowledge comes directly from the Exalted the Allah and is revealed to specific individuals; it is not comprehensive for others.

Those described by Allah the Almighty as **"those who delve deeply into knowledge"** are indeed these individuals, and the truly beneficial knowledge is this.

The Messenger of Allah -peace be upon him-, in another Noble Saying, states:

"Knowledge is of two kinds. One is that which is merely on the tongue (this is outward knowledge) and it serves as Allah the Almighty's argument against His servants. The other is the knowledge that resides in the heart (gnosis, spiritual knowledge). The latter is the beneficial knowledge that leads one to the ultimate goal." (Tirmidhî)

We learn this second described path, the illuminated path, through this Noble Saying.

The first is "literal knowledge" This knowledge is learned by hearing and reading. Then there is the knowledge that Allah the Almighty instills in the heart, known as "knowledge of the innermost" also referred to as "gnosis knowledge". Those who achieve this goal and possess this beneficial gnosis knowledge have become akin to birds with two wings, enabling them to soar in both the outward and inward realms of existence.

Knowledge of the innermost is particular, whereas literal knowledge is general.

Knowledge of the innermost pertains to states, whereas literal knowledge pertains to deeds.

Knowledge of the innermost is for contemplation, whereas literal knowledge is for transaction.

The knowledge of the innermost is the science of proof, while the literal knowledge is the science of expression.

The knowledge of the innermost is the science of guidance, while the literal knowledge is the science of narrative.

The knowledge of the innermost is to know, in Truth, that there is no other evidence of Him except Himself, while the literal knowledge is to observe the artistry of Allah the Almighty in the universe.

Our Master The Messenger of Allah -peace be upon him- stated in another Noble Saying:

"When Allah wishes good for a servant, He unlocks the seal of his heart. He causes certainty and honesty to emerge from it. He makes the heart a container that protects what enters it and renders that person's heart sound, his tongue Truthful, his character upright, his ears hearing, and his eyes seeing." (Râmuz)

What does **"the unlocking of the seal of the heart"** and **"the emergence of certainty and honesty in the heart"** mean in the Noble Saying? These terms need explanation.

Those who possess outward knowledge inscribe all the knowledge they derive from texts onto a blackboard. As they read them, they see themselves. They cannot stop themselves from saying, "I am a scholar!" A person who remains at the outward level of The Noble Path observes many things and says, "I see."

One says, "I am a scholar!" but does not realize they are ignorant.

Upon reaching the Truth, one learns that they know nothing. Then they exclaim, "Alas! I knew nothing; yet I thought I knew everything." This is because the seal of their heart has not been unlocked; all their inscriptions were on the door of the heart. Seeing these, they kept saying, "I know, I know!" If they penetrate deeper, gaining the gnosis, they realize their nothingness.

Here lies the entire secret, in unlocking the heart and diving into inner knowledge.

Allah the Almighty lifts the veil as much as He wills from His servant and reveals His mysteries to them.

Allah the Almighty proclaims in the Noble Verse:

"Those deeply grounded in knowledge say, 'We believe in it; all of it is from our Lord.' Only those with sound understanding can comprehend this subtlety." (Al' Imran: 7)

Thus, Allah the Almighty declares that only those who are profound in knowledge and have the intellect of People of deep understanding can grasp the Truth; others cannot.

People of deep understanding are of Two Kinds:

1. Zâhirî (Exoteric)

2. Bâtınî (Esoteric)

Zâhirî (Exoteric): Those whom Allah the Almighty has deepened in knowledge are the ones grounded in knowledge.

Bâtınî (Esoteric): There are those servants whom Allah the Almighty has deepened in Himself; these individuals are enlightened by the Truth and gain insight into the Divine Presence.

Among them, some are Versed in knowledge, while others are acquainted with the Truth. Some He has steeped in scholarly depth, and others in His Sacred Essence.

•

It has been narrated from Abu Dardâ -may Allah be pleased with him- that our Noble Messenger, -peace be upon him- said:

"Allah the Almighty addressed Jesus -peace be upon him- saying:

'O Jesus! After you, I will bring forth a community who, when they encounter something they love, will praise and thank Allah. When they confront something they dislike, they will remain patient and seek reward from Allah. These people will lack knowledge and forbearance.'

Jesus -peace be upon him- inquired:

'O my Lord! How can these actions emanate from them if they possess neither knowledge nor forbearance?'

The Glorious Truth:

"'I bestow upon them from my knowledge and my forbearance.' He said." (Ahmad ibn Hanbal)

Indeed, this is the secret of gnosis. Allah the Almighty bestows upon them His own knowledge and forbearance. Hence, those among People of deep understanding receive these as divine gifts. They are the inheritors of The Messenger of Allah -peace be upon him-. Just as Allah the Almighty grants His chosen prophets what He wills, similarly, divine knowledge is a gift, not attained through mere effort or study.

It is through Allah the Almighty inscribing faith upon the heart,

Pouring divine light into the heart,

Allowing the inner ear to hear,

Enabling the eye of the heart to see, that this divine gift is bestowed. Allah the Almighty inspires these individuals through His grace.

Therefore, we clarify the terms **“those deeply rooted in knowledge”** and "People of deep understanding" in this manner.

"By the passage of time,
indeed, mankind is in loss,
except for those who have believed, done righteous deeds,
advised each other to truth,
and advised each other to patience."
(Asr: 1-3)

SURAH AL-ASR

AND ITS EXPLANATION

CHAPTER 19

- The Apparent, Inner, and Mystical Meanings and Explanations of Surah Al-Asr
    1. Verbal Gratitude
    2. Practical Gratitude
    3. State of Gratitude

THE NOBLE SURAH AL-ASR

EXTERNAL, INTERNAL, DIVINE

MEANING AND EXPLANATION

The Most High and Exalted Lord declares:

"By the time, indeed, humanity is in a state of loss, except those who believe and perform righteous deeds, and advise each other to Truth and advise each other to patience." (Asr: 1-3)

The Messenger of Allah -peace be upon him-, said, **"All of humankind is destroyed."** Likewise, Allah the Most High swears that people are truly in a state of loss. What a great calamity this is for us! O Allah, forgive us for the sake of the righteous.

It is evident here that all people are in a state of loss, except for those who believe.

Yet, The Messenger of Allah -peace be upon him-, said in his Noble Saying:

"My community will divide into seventy-three sects after me, all of which will be in the fire except one."

– Who are they, O the Messenger of Allah?

"Those who follow my path and that of my companions." (Abu Dawood)

The Noble Saying that indicates people are doomed is general, while this specific Noble Saying pertains to the Community of The Messenger of Allah -peace be upon him-.

Seventy-two sects will enter hellfire. Which sect might we belong to? Reflect on this!

These divisive elements, they've torn apart both religion and the nation.

In a Noble Verse, Allah Most High declares:

“No matter how ardently you desire it, most people will not believe.” (Yusuf: 103)

To these divisive elements, even if you speak the Truth genuinely, or present the reality, they neither recognize the Truth nor accept it.

And thus, seventy-two sects became destined for hellfire.

Now, only one sect remains for us to align with. Everything we refer to as outward, inward, and profound knowledge belongs to this one sect.

Another Noble Verse says:

"Most people do not know." (Mümin: 57)

What couldn't they understand? They couldn't grasp the Truth, and because they couldn't comprehend the Truth, they couldn't find the Divine; instead, they sided with the founders of false religions and thus became conduits for their own ruin.

Let us present a single example:

A divider emerges and says, *"Interest is permissible!"* Another divider claims, *"It is permissible to the extent of inflation!"* Yet another says, *"I buy coal with interest, I buy this, I buy that!"* No divider leaves interest untouched. Everyone distorts it according to their own book and consumes it.

When we say "book," you might ask, "Is their book different?" Yes, it is different.

Because the Almighty says in Surah Al-Mu'minun, Verse 53:

"But people have divided their religion among them into sects, each faction rejoicing in what it has."

Allah the Almighty severed their ties with Islam.

And test them. Say, "Friends! I have fifty million, a hundred million, five hundred million, but I don't touch it because it involves interest, what should I do?" See how they will try to reconcile it with their own religion, their own scriptures.

Let me present to you an example we often encounter.

A brother came from Kayseri and said, "My Lord, I brought five thousand Marks." We asked, "Why are you giving this money?" He replied, "I have some doubts about this money." I said, "Brother! I cannot put the money you doubt into the treasury." He had come all the way from Kayseri to give five thousand Marks, but no, by Allah, that money is worth not a penny to me, for this is the house of Allah.

And so the brother took the money back, we did not accept it.

We are building waqf (a charitable endowment under Islamic law) buildings. For these waqf buildings, not a single penny is demanded from anyone. We do not beg from anyone, we do not fleece anyone. Because this is the house of Allah. That is why everyone comes here as if it were their own home, they eat, they drink, and they leave. May it be permissible and blessed. For it is indeed their own home.

Also, Allah the Exalted has made us wealthy by His grace, making us in need of nothing and no one. If He wills, other buildings can also be built. This, by Allah, is purely from His grace, not from labor.

Our income comes from selling books. We sell books, calendars, and tapes. With this revenue, Allah the Glorious enriches us. For wealth is in blessing, not just in earnings.

•

Let us continue with our subject:

Allah the Almighty in the surah of al-Asr informs us that those who believe are saved from loss. Thus, explaining the conditions of faith is necessary.

In the Noble Saying of The Messenger of Allah -peace be upon him- he declares:

"Faith is two halves. Half of it is in patience, and the other half is in gratitude." (Jami' alSaghir)

Outward patience:

1 Being patient when you are angry.

2 Being patient when affliction befalls you.

3 Abstaining from everything that Allah the Almighty has forbidden, not crossing the boundaries He has set, being patient to avoid committing that sin.

•

Allah the Almighty also informs us that after those who believe, those who perform righteous deeds are also saved from loss.

The Messenger of Allah -peace be upon him- says in a Noble Saying as follows:

"Faith is bare; its garment is Piety, its ornament is modesty, and its fruit is knowledge." (Bayhaqi)

Faith resembles a candle burning in the open, easily extinguishable by a wind. Especially today, the opposing winds blow with great intensity.

If a lantern is placed over that candle, it cannot be extinguished. That lantern is Piety. Those who act with Piety have saved their faith. However, Piety is the fruit of inner knowledge.

What does Piety mean? Outwardly, it means abstaining from what is forbidden; inwardly, it means abstaining from anything doubtful. Without abstaining from these, you cannot save your faith.

The adornment of faith is modesty. Piety is also preserved by modesty.

In another Noble Saying, The Messenger of Allah -peace be upon him- says:

"Modesty and faith are intrinsically linked; one cannot exist without the other. When one is lost, so is the other." (Jami' alSaghir)

In yet another Noble Saying:

"They declare, 'The paucity of modesty is a sign of disbelief.' (Munawi)

It implies that in lacking modesty, we unwittingly incline towards disbelief. Unaware of this, we put our faith in jeopardy. Therefore, to avoid this ignorance and to understand these Truths, knowledge is essential.

In a Noble Saying it is stated:

'There is a way for everything; the way to Paradise is through knowledge.' (Jami' alSaghir)

Without knowledge, we wouldn't comprehend that removing modesty also removes faith. Blindly, nothing happens indeed, knowledge is indispensable.

Thus, it becomes clear that piety, modesty, and knowledge complement each other.

•

When it comes to knowing the Truth:

Both its outward and inward aspects will be presented."

"Verrâsihune fil-ilmi = those who are deeply rooted in knowledge"

This aspect is external. It pertains to knowing only what one sees with the physical eyes and hears with the physical ears. However, they have not truly submitted to the Truth; they harbor many desires and, despite their deep knowledge, they contemplate their own self. These are the teachers of the common people.

The internal aspect, however:

"Those who are deeply rooted in knowledge say, 'We believe in it; all is from our Lord.' But none will grasp the Message except men of understanding." (Al' Imran: 7)

Here, the term 'men of understanding' is “People of deep understanding”. Those who possess this wisdom comprehend it; others do not.

"Verrâsihune fililmi = those who are deeply rooted in knowledge." From the inner meaning, Allah the Almighty draws His servant closer to Himself and reveals as much of Himself to them as He wills. Such a person knows Allah the Almighty, perceives that everything is from Him and belongs to Him, and sees nothing of themselves.

And this manifestation is infinite.

Whatever Allah the Almighty has instilled in their heart, whatever He has shown to their inner eye and revealed to their inner ear, they know. They harbour no desires or will of their own in these matters. Whatever He decrees and however He wills, so it is... These are those who have submitted to the Truth.

•

Understanding the Divine in another sense is knowing Allah;

Everything is the body, while Allah the Almighty is the soul. It should be understood in this way.

A body without a soul is like a picture. This world, which you see, is not a mere picture.

Inanimate objects, plants, animals, humans... Everything extols Allah the Almighty.

Indeed, Allah the Almighty found such pleasure in the remembrance of David -peace be upon him- that He commanded:

"O mountains and birds! Glorify with him!" (Saba: 10)

When David -peace be upon him- engaged in remembrance, the mountains and the birds would all join in glorification.

In another Noble Verse it is stated:

"The seven heavens and the earth and all that is within them extol Allah's glory. There is nothing that does not proclaim His praise, but you do not understand their glorification. He is indeed Forbearing, Of Forgiving." (Isra: 44)

For all creations know and revere Truth.

Through the remembrance of Allah, a human being ascends to such heights that, as stated in a Noble Saying:

"A true believer, one who achieves perfection in faith, holds a higher status with Allah than some angels." (Ibn Majah)

Those devoted to Truth comprehend Truth and act in accordance with Truth. Their every deed and action align with the decrees and judgments of Allah the Almighty, meticulously adhering to divine commands. They know the Truth and never stray from reality, for they are the chosen servants of Allah the Almighty.

Earlier, it was mentioned that "They are the educators of the people." Now, we shall discuss the teaching role of Truth and His students.

In a Noble Verse from the Quran, Allah the Exalted and Glorious proclaims:

"If you fear Allah and are conscious of Him, your teacher shall be Allah." (Al-Baqarah: 282)

Allah the Almighty instructs His students, and in a Noble Verse from the Quran, He decrees:

"Be devotedly pious scholars of the Lord by virtue of your teaching of the Book and your study of it." (Al' Imran: 79)

To be The Devout means to become a pure servant to Lord, to belong to the learned ones in relation to Lord, to be listeners with the ears of the heart, and to gaze with the eyes of the unseen.

According to the narration from Anas -may Allah be pleased with him- , The Messenger of Allah -peace be upon him- said**: "Surely, there are those among people who are close to Allah."**

The Companions:

"O the Messenger of Allah! Who are these people?" they asked.

He replied:

"They are the people of the Qur'an, the people of Allah, and the chosen servants of Allah." (Ibn Majah: 215)

What does it mean to be a person of the Qur'an? When our mother, Exalted the Aisha -may Allah be pleased with her- was asked about the morality of The Messenger of Allah, she responded, ***"His morality was the Qur'an."*** Those who are of the Qur'an have aligned all their morals with Exalted the Qur'an.

•

We have spoken about outward patience; now we will discuss inward patience.

He surrenders all his will to Truth. He submits his opinion to Allah the Almighty. From now on, he can have no desire or want. He is preemptively content with every decree that will come from Allah the Almighty. These are the ones in the **"Station of the Innocent."** This is the **"Station of Servitude."** The most crucial inner patience is required here.

Whatever the ego desires, with the grace of Allah the Almighty, it has long since been extinguished, reined in, surrendered to Truth, and no desire remains.

These are the people of Allah, those who are under divine protection and directed by divine will.

Allah the Almighty declares in the Noble Verse:

"They are those upon whose hearts Allah has inscribed faith and whom He has supported with a spirit from Himself." (Mujadilah: 22)

Science and intellect do not function here. Let me explain the reason.

No one but those whom Allah the Almighty has supported with a sacred spirit can comprehend these divine secrets.

For it is that spirit that perceives the work, it is that light that perceives the work. Everyone sees the person. Let me speak plainly; it is the spirit supported by Allah the Almighty that perceives the work, it is the light of The Messenger of Allah -peace be upon him- that perceives the work. This can only be found in the heir of the prophet. For they are together with the ever-present Allah the Almighty.

Allah the Almighty declares in the Noble Verse:

"Allah is with the patient." (Al-Baqarah: 153)

Allah the Almighty is only with these servants.

•

Gratitude also has three kinds; we will focus on the outward gratitude.

1: Verbal Gratitude:

Those who practice this gratitude abstain from the forbidden.

a) They say, *"Praise be to Allah, the Creator, who brings into existence out of nothing, who adorns us with the blessings of the body, who raises and forms us in the best manner from the beginning to the end."*

b) They say, *"Endless gratitude to Allah, who keeps us in His domain, who subjugates the universe, who provides us with sustenance from His blessings within His dominion."*

c) They say, *"Endless gratitude to Allah, who honors us with the dignity of faith, who ennobles us with Islam, who sent down the Quran to distinguish between good and evil, who sent the true Guide (Prophet Muhammad)."*

In the Noble Verse, it is stated:

"Indeed, Allah is gracious to humankind, but most people do not render thanks." (Mumin: 61)

Reflect! Have you ever contemplated this and expressed gratitude even once in your life?

2: Active Gratitude:

Now, let's delve into the inner aspect.

The Exalted Truth says in a sacred saying:

"I declare war against anyone who harbors enmity towards one of my friends. My servant draws nearer to me through nothing more beloved than fulfilling what I have enjoined upon him. He continues to draw nearer to me through voluntary acts of worship until I love him. And when I love him, I become his hearing with which he hears, his seeing with which he sees, his hand with which he grasps, and his foot with which he walks. (I become his heart with which he perceives, his tongue with which he speaks.) Should he ask something of Me, I would surely grant it to him, and should he seek refuge in Me, I would certainly protect him." (Bukhari, Tecridi Sarih: 1042)

This Sacred saying arouses curiosity in everyone. If Allah the Almighty bestows His grace, we will explain it succinctly as it is. We will also disclose and reconceal many similar secrets.

To further soothe your minds, we present yet another sacred saying:

"I then turn my face towards them. Can you imagine anyone knowing what I wish to bestow upon the one I face?"

Allah the Almighty continued:

"The first thing I will grant them is to pour light into their hearts. Then, as I inform them about myself, they will also inform others about me." (Muslim-hakim)

In the Sacred saying, He states, "They know me and, in turn, convey knowledge of me."

Now, I shall convey to you news from Allah the Almighty.

Why does Allah the Almighty declare war on those who oppose His beloved servants? Because such a saint has become annihilated in Truth; they have become ashes, dissolving in the divine mysteries. Within themselves, they see and know only the presence of Allah the Almighty, perceiving nothing of their own existence.

Do you need evidence for this?

Allah the Almighty proclaims in the Noble Verse:

"Within yourself... Do you not see?" (Adh-Dhariyat: 21)

He was a manifestation of this Noble Verse.

Allah the Almighty says, "I am within you, look and you will see me!" But where are those eyes that see?

Yet, Allah the Almighty declares, **"There are those who know me."** I am informing you now, informing you through Noble Verse and informing you through sacred saying.

Since He is within, He becomes the ears that hear, the eyes that see. He becomes the hands and feet. The heart understands through Him, the tongue speaks with Him. All the mysteries and secrets lie in Allah the Almighty being within. But when you look, you will see an idol. Thus, we must empty ourselves.

Now, I will present a very important Noble Saying.

The Messenger of Allah -peace be upon him- said:

"By Him in Whose Hand is the self of Muhammad, if you were to lower a rope to the lowest earth, it would fall upon Allah the Almighty." (Tirmidhi)

He swears to the Truth of this matter. Is it so? Now I will explain.

These are secrets manifested in the Noble Verse, **"Praise be to Allah, the Lord of all the worlds."** (Al-Fatiha: 1)

These individuals embody the secret of the Noble Verse **“Say: He is Allah, The One.”** (Ikhlas: 1)

This is a distinction granted only to those who see and know that both themselves and the universe are mere veils. They alone understand that the true guide is none other than Allah Himself.

These are the chosen servants of Allah the Almighty.

Thus, the Noble Saying has been explained to you. Mark my words, all my explanations come either from the Noble Verse, the Sacred saying, or the Noble Saying.

The Messenger of Allah -peace be upon him- says:

“There is such knowledge that it is like hidden treasures. Only those who are aware of Allah know it. When they speak of this knowledge, those who are heedless of Allah cannot comprehend it.

Therefore, do not look down upon the scholars whom Allah, in His bounty, has favored with knowledge. For Allah, the Generous, did not disdain them when He granted them that knowledge.” (Arbain, narrated by Abu Huraira, -may Allah be pleased with him-.

Why do only those who are aware of Allah know it? Because He has informed them.

Now we will delve into a Noble Verse. This Noble Verse has been mentioned often, but it is very mysterious.

Allah the Almighty states:

"Allah is the Light of the heavens and the earth." (Nur: 35)

Indeed, one who sees themselves and the universe as a mask is a recipient of the manifestation of this Noble Verse.

•

Esoteric knowledge arises through inspiration, when Allah the Almighty's light infuses the heart and reveals what He wills.

Our Master, The Messenger of Allah -peace be upon him- says in his Noble Saying:

"I have moments with Allah that no close angel nor any prophet or messenger can intrude upon." (K. Hafa)

In another Noble Saying, he says:

"Whatever Allah poured into my chest, I have poured into Abu Bakr's chest just as it is."

If you pay attention to these two Noble Saying, you will unlock all these mysteries.

The divine trust, Amanatullah, poured from heart to heart, continues until the Day of Judgment. Here lies the essence of the secret, from which all mysteries and all hidden aspects are born.

The types of outward knowledge are numerous. The varieties of inward knowledge surpass even those. The knowledge of faith, the knowledge of Islam, the knowledge of excellence, the knowledge of repentance, the knowledge of asceticism, the knowledge of piety, the knowledge of righteousness, the knowledge of ethics, the knowledge of self-awareness, the knowledge of the heart, the knowledge of self-purification, the knowledge of heart purification, the knowledge of spiritual unveiling, the knowledge of divine unity, the knowledge of attribute manifestation, the knowledge of essence manifestation, the knowledge of spiritual stations, the knowledge of union, the knowledge of annihilation, the knowledge of subsistence, the knowledge of spiritual intoxication, the knowledge of spiritual sobriety, the knowledge of gnosis, and similar forms of knowledge.

Scholars fall into three groups: One group knows the outward knowledge. The second group knows the inward knowledge. The third group knows both outward and inward knowledge. The latter are very few.

In describing them, I have stated that: “Those who inherit the Prophetic portion,” “Those who inherit the sainthood portion,” and “Those who inherit both the Prophetic and the sainthood portions.”

The term “heir” itself signifies that such knowledge is not attained through effort. Allah the Almighty has inscribed His light directly on their hearts, supported them with a Holy Spirit, and transferred the trust of the Prophet Muhammad to them. All secrets converge at this point.

•

We have discussed verbal gratitude, and practical gratitude; now we shall explain spiritual gratitude.

3. Spiritual Gratitude:

They love Allah the Almighty more than their own selves, eyes, hands and feet more than anything He has bestowed upon them. For they know that He is the creator and provider of everything. All belongs to Him and comes from Him. They cherish Allah the Almighty above all gifts given to them. They see Him and see that He is the source. This state is gratitude.

Their will does not live in them. They have bound their will to the will of Allah the Almighty. They are subject to His decree and act according to His divine judgment.

They worship until dawn, then implore forgiveness with tears for their acts of worship; they pray and supplicate for pardon and for the acceptance of their worship and obedience. For they know Allah the Almighty and are acutely aware of their own shortcomings. They burn with the fire of love, choosing to be with Allah the Almighty above all else.

In a Sacred saying, it is said:

"When My servant remembers Me, I am with him." (Bukhari)

What I relate to you are pearls and diamonds taken from the divine treasury, but you see them as stones because you do not understand.

It will not be long before Allah the Almighty sends a great elephant. When it sees these divine jewels scattered, it will search with its trunk to see if there is anyone who has been blessed with these pearls.

•

Yet, it is evident that Allah the Almighty conveys His message to whom He wills.

And if you notice, I have never studied knowledge. This knowledge that I present is “Knowledge of Allah”. I know only what Allah the Exalted teaches me, and I speak only what He makes me speak. I did not know this knowledge, nor did I ever read books about it, for such knowledge is not found in books. That is why I say, "I did not know it to speak of it, and it is not in books that I might read it."

These do not belong to me. When I introduce myself, I say, "I am a worthless creature; judgment and value belong to the Exalted the Allah and the Messenger."

Whatever my Lord has taught, whatever He has poured into my heart, I reveal to you as it is.

Without a doubt, many great personalities have come, and they knew these, but they were not permitted to share them; instead, this poor one was permitted, and you benefit from these.

•

"Does man not see that we created him from a mere sperm-drop, yet now he becomes an open adversary?"

(Ya-Sin: 77)

THOSE DESTROYED

AND THOSE WHO ATTAIN SALVATION

CHAPTER 20

"He is The One who created death and life to test which of you is best in deeds."
(Al-Mulk: 2)

AN EXPLANATION OF THE NOBLE SAYİNG: 'ENNÂSÜ KÜLLÜHÜM HELEKETÜN'

WHO AMONG THE PEOPLE DESTINED FOR DESTRUCTION WILL BE SAVED?

The Master of the Universe, the Reason for Existence peace and blessings be upon him, says in his Noble Saying:

"People have perished, except for the scholars. The scholars have perished, except for those who act according to their knowledge. Those who act according to their knowledge have perished, except for those who are sincere. And even the sincere are in great peril." (K. Hafa)

According to this Noble Saying, the situation is truly terrifying. This terror will be more clearly illustrated by the second Noble Saying we will present.

Who are these perished ones? How many are they? In this regard, The Messenger of Allah peace and blessings be upon him says in his Noble Saying:

"On the Day of Judgment, Allah the Blessed and Exalted will say, 'O Adam!' He will respond, saying, 'Yes, my Lord! I am at your service, awaiting your command. Bliss and all goodness manifest through your decrees.'

Allah the Exalted will say, 'Select those who will go to Hell.' Prophet Adam will ask, 'What is the number of those to be sent to Hell?' Allah the Exalted will respond, 'One out of every thousand to Heaven, nine hundred ninety-nine to Hell.'

When Allah thus addresses Prophet Adam, children who hear this will grow old, and every pregnant woman will miscarry her child.

At that moment, you would think the people at the gathering were drunk, though they are not drunk at all. Yet, the punishment of Allah is indeed severe." (Bukhari, Tejrid alSarih: 1373)

This announcement is such that it is proclaimed to Adam -peace be upon him- to the people, and at the same time, the Day of Judgment ensues. It is indeed such a moment.

When an earthquake occurs, we are bewildered. This, in fact, is the breaking of the apocalypse. It is necessary to recount this apocalypse specifically, which requires time.

Let us now delve into the detailed explanation of the Noble Saying:

1. **"All people are doomed."**

Why are they all doomed? The ego said, "I," and the infidel self openly declared its blasphemy. It opposed Exalted the Allah, did not see or recognize the Truth, thereby becoming one of the polytheists and turning into an enemy of Allah the Exalted.

This is why Allah the Exalted states in the Noble Verse:

"Does man not consider that we created him from a mere drop of semen, and now he stands as an open adversary?" (Yasin: 77)

These are the ones blinded, falling into the darkness of nature.

In this world, they boast, "I have this, I have that, I did this, I did that!" Unaware of the true Creator, the bestower of gifts, unable to see the bestowed blessings and favors, they die.

However, when the Creator withdraws His favor, takes back His blessings, and scatters everything to the ground, it is then that they realize He was always with them. But mankind did not understand this, and thus, was doomed. Moreover, he became arrogantly proud.

However, Allah The Most High says in His Noble Verse:

"Allah does not love the arrogant." (Nahl: 23)

He does not bestow His forgiveness and mercy upon those who, out of pride, reject Truth and Reality, and distance themselves from adhering to divine commandments.

Our Master, The Messenger of Allah -peace be upon him- states in his Noble Saying:

"Seeing yourself as significant is a sin greater than any other sin."

What is the wisdom behind this?

I will delve into the essence of this Noble Saying a bit further.

Your origin is but a despised drop of water. He shaped this despised drop in any way He wished, developed it day by day, placed it in the form of a fetus, bestowed a soul upon it, and attached each organ in its place.

"Blessed is Allah, the best of creators!" (Muminun: 14)

But you have forgotten all of this, asserting "I!" You deny Allah the Almighty and show ingratitude for the blessings He bestowed, moreover, you ascribe divine grace to your ego. A greater sin than this cannot exist, nor can it be compared to any other sin.

There is another grave sin:

"Love of the world is the greatest of all sins." (Jami' alSaghir)

This is declared by The Messenger of Allah -peace be upon him- in his Noble Saying.

Did the world create you? Did you come for the world? Yet, the world is merely a stage of trial.

Allah the Almighty says in the Noble Verse:

"He who created death and life to test which of you is best in deed." (Mülk: 2)

Just a stage, that's all... But mankind failed to understand even this; mankind grew rebellious. I fear this rebellion greatly and seek refuge in my Allah.

The reason: indecency, alcohol, gambling, usury, dance, football, and many other similar vices are rampant today. We have adopted all the customs of disbelief.

We have become so accustomed to it; a man performs the prayer, leaves the prayer, goes to usury, leaves the prayer, goes to football, and attends a ball. Is this possible? Yes, it is. Why?

"Surely, the prayer prevents immorality and wrongdoing." (Ankabut: 45)

Yet, he does this. Now, let us understand this. The Messenger of Allah -peace be upon him- said in his Noble Saying:

"A person's prayer without khushu (reverence and humility) cannot be accepted, and its promised benefit cannot be expected." (Munawi)

However, as stated in the Noble Verse:

"The believers have succeeded, who are humble in their prayer." (Muminun: 1-2)

In reality, the doomsday has already commenced for every deceased person, as their spirit enters either a garden from the gardens of Paradise or a pit from the pits of Hell. Nonetheless, Allah the Almighty will display His wrath twice.

While committing these transgressions, we have audaciously rebelled against Exalted the Allah; He grants us respite akin to that of a parent's patience. But at the moment of doomsday, such an immense wrath will be unleashed that a terrifying noise will suddenly fill the air, the order of the heavens and the earth will disintegrate, the skies will be violently torn apart, the stars will fade and scatter, the sun will fold up, its light extinguished, the earth will be shattered with dreadful sounds, all seas will boil and merge into a single ocean, mountains and stones will scatter like fluffs of wool borne aloft, and the graves will overturn, exposing their contents.

Now, imagine the state of humans at that time!

Allah the Almighty says in His precious Verse:

"O mankind! Fear your Lord! Indeed, the tremor of the Hour is a tremendous thing.

On the Day you see it, every nursing mother will discard her infant, and every pregnant woman will abort her load. And you will see the people as if they are intoxicated, but they are not intoxicated. However, Allah's punishment is severe." (Hajj: 1-2)

They look but have no comprehension of their actions. In the face of the terrifying scenes they witness plainly, their eyes have become humble and desolate.

The moment when Allah the Almighty decides to unleash His wrath for the second time will be when the people are gathered for Judgment Day. At that time, the sun of the Hereafter will be brought close, about a mile away. People, drenched in sweat from the intense heat, will be submerged in their sweat according to the extent of their sins: some up to their ankles, some up to their knees, some up to their necks, and some will be completely covered by sweat. There is no help from anywhere.

On the Day of Gathering, everyone will have a wait that is long or short depending on their rank and status in the sight of Allah. When this waiting becomes unbearable, they will seek an intercessor to commence the trial. They will approach the messengers of great resolve, starting with Adam -peace be upon him-, then Noah -peace be upon him-, then Abraham -peace be upon him-, then Moses -peace be upon him-, and then Jesus -peace be upon him-. Each will respond, **"Our Lord, the Exalted and Glorious, is beyond furious today, a wrath unprecedented and never to be seen again."** They will each present an excuse, stating they cannot intercede.

Finally, they will turn to Muhammad -peace be upon him-, the mercy to all worlds, and ask him to intercede on their behalf.

He will approach under The Throne of the Most Merciful and prostrate himself, beseeching for the commencement of the final reckoning. Allah the Almighty will bestow His favor upon him, accept his prayer and intercession, and the judgment will begin.

These are terrifying moments indeed.

•

We continue with the explanation of the Noble Saying:

2. **"All people are perished except the scholars. And the scholars are also perished except those who act according to their knowledge."**

This point is indeed very alarming.

Scholars who remain on the surface are also engulfed in ego. They constantly say, "I know!", "I speak!", "I guide!"

There is a Verse in the Qur'an. Allah the Almighty says:

"Allah has not made for any man two hearts within his breast." (Al-Ahzab: 4)

That is, to devote one heart to the love of the Divine and the other to the love of what is worldly. Two loves cannot reside in one heart.

The hidden meaning of that "I!" is that Allah the Almighty is not in that heart; existence and ego are. They have linked Allah Almighty's grace to the ego. Since they tied it to the ego, the ego says, "I!" and denies Allah Almighty. This is the clear meaning.

Many indeed believe they are guiding others, yet they unknowingly misguide. Why is this so? It is because they do not know the Truth. They are not taken inwardly; they remain outside the house, calling from outside. Their knowledge stays in the mind and does not descend to the heart. The Qur'an has not descended below the throat. It has not permeated within. Therefore, they do not know the Truth, though they think they know everything and consider themselves scholars, when in reality, they are ignorant.

A person always says, "I... I!" and accumulates ego. These gatherings of ego belong to the self. A person in this world constantly claims, "I have this, I have that, I did this, I did that!" After entering the grave, all those claims remain. Nothing is left except a shroud.

To progress from the outward to the Truth, it is necessary to complete the knowledge of the path; I say this openly. After reaching the Truth, it penetrates the heart. Then they see and say, "Alas! I thought I knew something, how have I accumulated this ego all this time, how have I associated partners with the Exalted the Allah?" At that moment, they realize they know nothing, not even themselves; the veil of Truth opens, and they begin to seek forgiveness for all the ego they gathered and continue this throughout their life.

A person of wisdom even said:

"For forty years I have been trying to remove the ink I licked in the madrasas (Islamic schools), and still, I have not succeeded."

What does this mean? It means that the pride the self-acquired during the pursuit of knowledge is something he still cannot erase from his heart. Yet, this person is someone of spiritual insight.

This is why scholars perished. Because they were unaware of the spiritual journey. For this reason, their hearts did not soften, they were not successful in softening.

Allah the Most High says in the Noble Verse:

"Has the time not come for those who have believed that their hearts should become humbly submissive at the remembrance of Allah?" (Hadid: 16)

They turned towards the world and turned away from the teachings of the Qur'an al-Karim.

"Only a few of my servants are grateful." (Saba: 13)

•

3. For this reason, the condition of those who cannot attain Annihilation in the Messenger is very dangerous. They do not know Allah truly, nor do they know The Messenger of Allah -peace be upon him- genuinely.

The reason:

Because they have not attained Annihilation in the Messenger, they do not know The Messenger of Allah -peace be upon him-; and because they have not attained Annihilation in Allah, they do not know Allah. Holding the idol of ego in their hands, they embark on guidance, but when they pass to the hereafter with this idol, they will see the reality.

For in the Noble Verse

"Indeed, those who purify their selves succeed, and those who corrupt them fail." (Ash-Shams: 9-10)

Those blessed with the secret of **"Al-faqru fakhri" (poverty is my pride)** despise those who hold onto ego, but they say nothing to anyone.

Those who act upon their knowledge, why are they in danger?

However much they are permitted inside, they have penetrated within. In other words, it has descended from the mind to the heart, infiltrating within. They realized and confessed that they knew nothing and began to seek forgiveness. Yet, they do not know they are nothing. Because, for them to know that they are nothing, the knowledge of gnosis is required.

Even those who know they are nothing are in great danger. This Noble Saying is a very deep filter!

Why are they in danger?

As long as they hold on, they won't perish, but if they let go for a moment, it will lead to their downfall. As long as Allah holds you, you won't perish, but if He releases you, you will perish. For you possess nothing of your own. We do not even own a single feather. I do not refer to an eye, a hand, or a foot; we do not own a single feather, yet we said "I!"

He is the Creator, The One who bestows blessings, The One who gives life, and The One who takes life away.

•

We will explain this summary with a representation in three points.

1. Those who remain on the surface engrave at the door of the heart, they are at the mosque door.

2. Those who have grasped the Truth have penetrated into the heart, they are in the courtyard of the mosque.

3. As for the people of Gnosis, they have been admitted into the mosque. They have found the Truth, and they are with Truth.

These chosen servants, if He wills, He brings them closer to His Essence, if He wills, He distances them, if He wills, He holds them, if He wills, He casts them away. The creature has no significance. It is evident here that even the sincere ones are in great danger. I do not speak of the common people; even the saints are in great danger. There are indications in books about the slipping of many saints.

Even in the Noble Verse, it is stated:

"Allah forgives whom He wills and punishes whom He wills." (Al-Baqarah: 284)

In another Noble Verse, it is stated:

"He punishes whom He wills, and shows mercy to whom He wills, and to Him you will be returned." (Ankabut: 21)

Nothing belongs to the creature. How significant is this Noble Saying that indicates the destruction of people. May Allah not leave us to ourselves, and may He not separate us from the grace of His favor.

•

We always say: I am a being without judgment or value; my judgment belongs to my owner, and value belongs to my Allah. Measure what I mean from here.

While these subtle secrets are being discussed, I ask you to hold on to Noble Verse, Sacred saying, and Noble Saying, because the places being proposed are ones where your intellect does not function.

•

One of the favors Allah the Almighty has bestowed upon this humble one is:

Informing me that I am without judgment and value, and protecting me from hidden polytheism and self-praise.

For hidden polytheism makes a person a polytheist.

Ah… You will see this in the hereafter; we speak of it having seen it.

•

"Everything will perish except His essence."
(Al-Qasas: 88)

THE SECRET OF ANNIHILATION

IN ALLAH AND BEKÂ BI'LLAH

CHAPTER 21

THE SECRET OF ANNIHILATION IN ALLAH AND SUBSISTENCE WITH ALLAH

- The Secret of *annihilation in Allah*
- The Secret of *subsistence with Allah*
- Explanation of the Noble Saying: "A believer is the mirror of another believer."

THE SECRET OF ANNİHİLATİON İN ALLAH

A drop of impure water is the creation of Almighty Allah. When you see this single drop rolling, you witness its essence. Yet, that vision does not belong to you; it is the grace filled light of Allah the Almighty.

Within that single drop exists a particle known as Immutable Archetypes.

He has encompassed all of creation's essence and fate within this particle. As with every particle, divine secrets dwell within it.

When Allah the Almighty manifests His grace, causing even that particle to annihilate;

"All things perish, except His Face." (Qasas: 88)

One who witnesses this becomes the manifestation of this Verse. This is the secret of Annihilation in Allah.

Man continually says, "I, I, I!" and gathers possessions; whereas, those who possess true knowledge begin to disperse these possessions. They spread them until ultimately, they too disperse this last particle. After it departs from them, this Verse becomes manifest.

To reach this state and attain this point, every saint has a plea and supplication to Allah the Almighty.

As Abraham Hakki -may his secret be sanctified- says:

"What can a servant do with wealth and fame?

Is it not enough that he found a king like you?

Grant him Annihilation in Allah

Make him one who dies before he dies."

These states arise because they are the chosen servants of Allah the Almighty.

And pay attention to this sacred saying:

"Sincerity is a secret from my secrets. I place it in the hearts of those among my servants whom I love. Neither the angel can write it, nor can the devil corrupt it."

These are the chambers of Allah the Almighty's mysteries; Allah the Almighty has entrusted them with His secrets.

Even an angel cannot access the knowledge He grants, let alone human beings!

The secret to this is that Allah the Almighty chooses and draws His servant unto Himself.

As He says in the Noble Verse:

"Allah chooses His servant unto Himself." (Shura: 13)

THE SECRET OF SUBSISTENCE WITH ALLAH

The essence of Annihilation in Allah; knowing the Truth.

As for subsistence with Allah; finding the Truth, being with the Truth.

I thought I was myself, but it turned out to be Him. When one sees this, one does not see oneself. It turned out that everything subsists with the Truth. One sees and knows this. This is the final station a saint is raised to.

As for the Noble Verse of this station, Allah the Exalted says:

"Whatever is on the earth will perish, but the face of your Lord, full of majesty and honor, will endure." (Rahman: 26-27)

Welcome to the "Station of Truthfulness".

"THE BELIEVER IS THE MIRROR OF ANOTHER BELIEVER."

Explanation of The Noble Saying

"The believer is the mirror of another believer." (Abu Dawood)

When and where does the true essence of this Noble Saying manifest?

It manifests when your inner self and outer self both embody faith, when you see that nothing exists apart from Him.

The entire cosmos is but a body; He is the soul. All the worlds are like a sheet of glass. When you observe Him in the glass, you witness the Truth. At that moment, you too become a glass, and the entire cosmos turns into a glass.

In the Noble Verse, it is said:

"He is the Al-Mu'min, Al-Muhaymin." (Hashr: 23)

Thus, Allah the Exalted bestows the sacred name He has attributed to Himself upon His devout servant as well.

Therefore, the manifestation of the sacred name "Al-Mu'min" in the Perfect Human is concealed within The Word of Divine Unity.

"There is no Allah" implies the nullity of all existence. The universe is a mere body, brought into being by the command **"Be!"**

Here, you are merely a body, as fragile as glass. The universe and all realms are the same.

In a divine sacred saying, Allah the Exalted says:

"I neither fit into the heavens nor the earth, but I fit into the heart of my faithful servant."

When He manifests, all else remains within **"No."**

He is in a constant state of new manifestation.

In the Noble Verse:

"He is every day upon some labor." (Rahman: 29)

Exalted the Allah manifests in myriad ways, issuing new decrees and creating anew in every moment. All of these stem from the noble command **"Be!"** Every particle, every single thing alters constantly. No one knows this except for those He informs, shows, and allows to perceive.

Divine manifestations occur at every moment, yet people remain unaware, entangled in events.

Cells within you change, as does everything in the universe, rising and falling, coming to life and fading away. Death occurs in one place while life springs forth in another.

In short: He is every day upon some labor.

When one says **"Illallah" (Only Allah remains),** He alone is visible in the glass. It is then that the veil is lifted. This means nothing but He exists. You are no more, nor is the world; all is but a shell. **"Illallah" Only He is**. It's not like looking through glass to see a person. You are the glass, a mere vessel. He is the spirit, the essence of both the cosmos and all realms.

The Believer, and you a believer. There is nothing except the Believer because He has manifested within you. When you annihilate your self, only the Believer remains.

When the Exalted the Allah manifests, He sees Himself within the heart of the believer.

These:

"I have chosen you for myself." (Taha: 41)

As revealed in this Verse, they are the chosen servants whom Allah the Almighty has created for Himself, loved, selected, and drawn near to Himself. He reveals Himself to them, and they see only Allah.

They see Him within and see Him without, recognizing that there is no existence apart from Him. Indeed, there is no existence other than Him. He is The One reflected in the mirror and The One within you... remove yourself, and let the Creator remain.

This mystery is unique to them. They are the rare ones, **The Initiates**. They are the ones with the Seeing Eye.

In a Sacred saying Allah the Almighty:

"Persist in hunger, and you will see Me. Withdraw from people, and you will reach me."

Thus, it is apparent that He can be seen.

Exalted the Abu Bakr -may Allah be pleased with him- said, **"I saw my Lord; I saw nothing else."**

Exalted the Ali -may Allah be pleased with him- said, **"I do not worship Allah that I do not see."**

They worship Allah the Almighty.

This is a special knowledge, granted from the divine knowledge of the Exalted the Allah. He bestows it upon whom He wills.

"This is Allah's grace and favor, He grants it to whom He pleases." (Al-Jumu'ah: 4)

The incident between Moses -peace be upon him- and Khidr -peace be upon him- is significant as an example in this context.

After Moses -peace be upon him- conVersed with Allah the Almighty at Mount Tur on the appointed time, he said:

"My Lord! Show yourself to me, that I may look upon you!" (Araf: 143)

Allah the Almighty replied:

"You cannot see me. But look at the mountain! If it remains firm in its place, then you will see me." (Araf: 143)

Furthermore, the Noble Verse states:

"When the Rabbi manifested Himself to the mountain, He made it crumble to dust, and Moses fell unconscious. When he awoke, he said, 'O Allah! Glory be to You, I repent to you, and I am the first to believe.' (Araf: 143)

Even though Allah the Almighty loved and chose Moses -peace be upon him-, He sent him to Khidr -peace be upon him- to impart true knowledge.

In the Noble Verse, it is said:

"Then they found one of our servants, to whom we had given mercy from us and taught him knowledge from our own. Moses said to him, 'May I follow you so that you may teach me the guidance which you have been taught?" (Al-Kahf: 65-66)

When Khidr -peace be upon him- met Moses, -peace be upon him- he said:

"I am proceeding with the knowledge given to me by Allah, which you do not know. And the knowledge that Allah has taught you is unknown to me." (Bukhari. Tecridi Sarih: 102)

Allah the Almighty bestows upon whomever He wills. This knowledge is granted; there is nothing inherent in the person.

Except for those whom Allah the Almighty has loved, chosen, drawn close to Himself, and disclosed His secrets to, no one else can grasp this mystery.

Why do we present these? Those who are destined will receive their portion, and they will take as much as they are destined to take.

The second group consists of the **One who knows.** The Messenger of Allah -peace be upon him- mentioned in his Noble Saying:

"When any of you stands for prayer, he is conversing with his Lord. Certainly, his Lord is between him and the Sacred Direction." (Bukhari)

This is intended for those who do not see Allah the Almighty.

When they stand for prayer, they perceive the Exalted the Allah between themselves and the Sacred Direction. They recognize that the Exalted the Allah is present everywhere and is aware of all their states. In Truth, He is closer to you than even the Sacred Direction.

The Messenger of Allah -peace be upon him- stated in his Noble Saying:

"Spiritual excellence is to worship Allah as if you see Him. Even if you do not see Him, know that He sees you." (Muslim)

These are the ones with "crossed eyes." They do not see the Exalted the Allah. Yet, they have faith. They stand in the Divine Presence, striving to worship. They do not see, but they believe that Truth sees them.

Those of the third rank are the **Ascetics**.

As stated in the Noble Saying:

"Their Sacred Direction will be their wives." (beyhaqi)

They turn toward the Sacred Direction, but their hearts are filled with everything other than the Divine with everything other than Allah. They have wives, wealth, and possessions. Their bodies are in prayer, but their hearts are elsewhere. How can such people know or see the Divine?

Most ascetics are like this. They have become Muslims and perform their prayers, but they are blind of heart.

In a Noble Saying, it is stated:

"The mosques will be outwardly flourishing, but deprived of guidance within." (Bayhaqi)

This is their condition. Its cause is forbidden food.

These are those who turn towards the Sacred Direction; we do not even consider the others.

•

"Within yourself… Do you not see"
(Adh-Dhariyat: 21)

MÂHIR THE ARTIST

CHAPTER 22

"And among His signs is the creation of the heavens and the earth,
and the diversity of your languages and your colors."
(Ar-Rum: 22)

If you present a well-dressed doll to a small child and inquire,

"Is this doll beautiful, or are you?"

"The doll is beautiful," the child will reply. Why does the child say, "The doll is beautiful"?

Because the child sees and loves the doll but does not see themselves.

If you ask those who are heedless of Truth,

"Are you beautiful, or is the one within you beautiful?"

They will say, "I am."

Throughout their life, they have always said, "I am." Why? Because in Truth, they are blind to reality.

"Within yourself... Do you not see?" (Adh-Dhariyat: 21)

Because he has not been graced with the manifestations of this divine Verse.

He considers himself a scholar of great wisdom, yet in Truth, he is blind and ignorant. Why? Because he lacks the knowledge of Gnosis and is deprived of it. Consequently, he could not grasp the Truth and persistently said, "I." Not having seen or known Allah the Almighty, he made his ego his deity and proclaimed, "I."

"Have you seen the one who takes his own desires as his Allah? Will you then be a guardian over him?" (Al-Furqan: 43)

Those ignorant of this knowledge have deified their egos and slipped into disbelief. The thickest veil before Allah the Almighty's one's own existence. If a person begins to gradually remove their own existence and reduce it to nothingness, the existence of Allah the Almighty comes into being. One in such a state sees both Allah the Almighty and himself.

One's existence is a hindrance to finding the Existent. If he obliterates his existence, he will see that the universe is merely a veil.

The Messenger of Allah -peace be upon him- said in a Noble Saying:

"Knowledge is of two kinds. One is the knowledge of the tongue (which is the outward knowledge), a proof of Allah the Almighty upon His servants. The other is the knowledge of the heart (gnosis). It is this knowledge that is beneficial for reaching the true goal." (Tirmidhi)

If he had known himself and seen the Creator, he would have said **"No"** to the creations. Those who attain this awareness are the ones who have stripped off the vestment of the flesh.

Those unaccustomed to this knowledge are like infants. Why can't you recite the Word of Divine Unity no created thing is Allah. When you say, **"There is no Allah"**, you do not understand its meaning. Where is your faith?

The divine Verse says:

"One of His signs is the creation of the heavens and the earth and the diversity of your languages and colors." (Ar-Rum: 22)

In every particle, divine mysteries are present. He measured and shaped everything, revealing His form through those shapes. His might and exemplary volition are evident in every speck.

The entire cosmos is like a veil embroidered by a master artist.

Consider a single grain! Imagine a single leaf!

All the people in the world, including those claiming strides in science and art, would be impotent in trying to create even one grain or one leaf. Given this impotence, contemplate this deeply. Recognize and find the Creator. Reflect upon the Creator of the cosmos.

Within a seed, He contained an entire tree: its branches, leaves, and fruits. He has decreed for whom it will bear fruit. And yet, you still do not recognize the Almighty Allah!

Think of a fruit! Its fragrance, taste, and color are each distinct. With His might and craftsmanship, He also placed its seed within. Human intellect fails to grasp even a particle of the Creator's mysteries and becomes powerless. The entire universe stands helpless before a single particle. His creations are displayed for you to see. Yet, you still look inward, ignoring His works.

All that we see are creations of the Exalted the Allah, manifestations that point to His existence. He created the veil of the universe, adorned and embellished it with His signs. Truly, He is the most magnificent artist! Everything is His. Yet, many remained lost in the creation, unable to recognize and find the Creator. All these are signs and evidence of The One who exists. He is the owner of infinite generosity and grace. There is no entity that grants existence except Him.

"O Lord! I am incapable of comprehending even a fraction of the beings you have created and bestowed. For you are the Lord of all worlds, the creator of all beings. Every blessing and adornment you have granted is an expression and manifestation of your power."

Most of the creatures He created do not know or see this. They look at and attempt to imitate many of His creations. In front of each existence, each particle, they find themselves helpless. It is due to this helplessness that they cannot see or find the magnificence of the Divine; they cannot unravel this mystery. Yet, in every particle, the mysteries of divinity are present. They cannot see or know it.

In the veil of the universe, His mark is present. You see His mark in every particle, see the veil. But you cannot see who made the mark. This universe you see is a veil. This entire realm you see is an illustration. Lift that veil and look at the Artist. Yet, you cannot see Him. This faith is a mere surface faith.

Perfect faith is this:

La ilaha illallah (There is no deity but Allah); you created, you adorned. Yet none of what is adorned is divine. You too are a veil, and the universe is a veil. Lift your own veil, and you will see that the universe is a veil. Do not remain in the grain, in the veil; find Him.

It is stated in the Noble Verse:

"Then we bring you forth as a child" (Hajj: 5)

From this stage onwards, a human, once lifeless, becomes alive, once mute, becomes speaking, once deaf, becomes hearing, once blind, and becomes seeing.

The essence of man, a mere drop of disdainful water, was mingled by the Almighty with the soil of destiny, the seed of judgment was planted, life was infused with water, **"Be!"** He said, and it was. The rest are merely details. Yet, we simply say, a child is born. Most see the shell; few perceive the core.

Allah the Exalted has granted man great honor by breathing into him from His own spirit. Thus, life effectively commenced within man.

"He gave you hearing, sight, and hearts. Little do you thank!" (Sajda: 9)

Allah the Exalted enumerated the ear, the eyes, and the heart in sequence so that first, one hears the Truth, then sees what is heard with the eyes, and finally contemplates with the heart what is seen.

Finally, when the time comes, after 280 days, an extraordinary infant is born into this world.

In another Noble Verse:

"Then He brings you forth as an infant, then [lets you grow] to reach full strength, and afterward to become old men though some of you will be

caused to die earlier, and some will be kept back till a later term so that possibly, you may understand.” (Mu’min: 67)

From the stages of beginning with clay and sperm to becoming a clot of blood, a chewed lump of flesh, and finally taking the human form, every phase of creation reflects the exalted power of the Exalted the Allah. These signs are evident in all living beings.

In the Noble Verse:

“There are indeed signs in the creation of the heavens and earth, and in the spreading of creatures, for people of firm faith.” (Jathiyah: 4)

Just as the creation of humans, the creation of animals, their nourishment, birth, and reproduction also indicate the might and grandeur of Allah the Almighty.

Although Allah the Almighty has the power to create a human instantaneously, the extended period until a human form is achieved holds countless benefits and wisdoms.

Though once unworthy of mention, weak and powerless, Allah the Almighty nurtures this insignificant drop, forms its skeleton, breathes its soul, and sends it forth as a human being on earth.

He declares in His Noble Verse:

“Has there not been a long period of time when man was nothing worth mentioning?” (Insan: 1)

After Adam -peace be upon him- was fashioned from clay and readied, he was left in that form for a while before the soul was breathed into him, allowing him to reach the state suitable for the infusion of the soul.

The cosmos and the creatures on Earth existed long before Adam -peace be upon him-; in that era, he had neither name, form, nor marker.

As for humankind;

Before coming into the world, a person existed as a cell in their father's loins and was a despised fluid known only to Allah the Almighty. A certain time passed while they had no trace on Earth; then Allah the Almighty brought them into the realm of existence, transforming them from an unknown entity into a recognized being.

"When He decrees a matter, He only says to it, 'Be!' and it is." (Yasin: 82)

For any matter, He gives but a single command, needing no repetition. Whatever He commands **"Be!"** to necessarily come into existence.

Allah the Almighty declares that the creation of the heavens and the Earth, whether initially or through resurrection, is grander than creating humans and that there are no difficulties or ease in this for Him:

"The creation of the heavens and the Earth is indeed greater than the creation of mankind, but most of mankind do not know it." (Mu'min: 57)

Such insights signify the insightfulness of the heart, whereas failing to see them indicates a heart's blindness.

"Not equal are the blind and the seeing, nor those who believe and do righteous deeds and those who do evil."

"How little you think!" (Mu'min: 58)

Most people think very little and do not take lessons or admonishments to heart.

In essence;

Those who do not truly know Almighty Allah, who creates from nothing, adorns with blessings, and reveals with His form, become hostile towards Him and say, "I."

"Does man not see that we created him from a drop of despised fluid? Yet now he is an open adversary!" (Yasin: 77)

Allah the Almighty began the human creation from a lowly fluid. He who created man from this weak drop is surely capable of resurrecting him after death.

From time to time and through various writings, we strive to make those heedless of Truth aware of Truth's existence. So that humankind may know that the creation of themselves and the universe is a mere command of **"Be."** There is none other than Him. He is the Existence; He is the Being.

But these are explained to you because you consider yourself separate from Him. That is, when He says **"Be,"** He creates what He wills, and when He says **"Die,"** He kills and brings into being what He wills. Yet, you remain unaware even of this.

He is such an Allah that He knows Himself alone and praises Himself alone.

Why are these statements presented?

Allah the Almighty says in the Noble Verse:

"Within yourself... Do you not see?" (Adh-Dhariyat: 21)

In essence, this means "I am within you!" But, in Truth, he is blind and does not see. Do you see? You do not.

Allah the Almighty states in another Noble Verse:

“We are closer to him than his jugular vein.” (Qaf: 16)

“I am nearer to you than yourself, nearer than your jugular vein.” Despite this declaration, in actuality, he remains ignorant and oblivious. Do you see? You do not.

Allah the Almighty reveals in another Noble Verse:

“We are closer to him than you, but you do not see.” (Waqi’ah 85)

"Despite saying, **'I am closer to everything than everything is to itself,'** he neither sees nor hears. In reality, he is both blind and deaf, yet he is unaware of his condition. He does not hear the divine call and does not realize his ignorance. Do you see? No, you do not.

Exalted the Allah proclaims and makes you hear His voice.

Yet, he imagines himself a scholar, baffled whether to deny or affirm these Truths.

If he denies, there are the Noble Verses that he would be denying, thus becoming known as an unbeliever. If he affirms, his reason and knowledge fall short. What shall this man do now?

It was previously mentioned that:

In a Noble Saying:

'The heart of a believer is the throne of the Ar-Rahman,' it is stated. (K. Hafâ: 2/130)

Since the Perfect guide is the spiritual throne of Allah the Almighty, he bestows to those destined whatever has been entrusted to the spiritual throne. Others lack this power.

The Perfect guide knows and perceives himself as nothing more than a reflection."

A Perfect guide recognizes and sees himself as nothing but a rag.

A Perfect guide recognizes and sees himself as nothing but a mask.

We have addressed this matter before.

For they see the Truth and do not see themselves. These statements are not for those who consider themselves learned and erudite, who see their own ego and do not see the Truth.

My address is to those who do not see themselves but see the Truth.

Our goal in repeatedly presenting various representations of the Exalted the Allah, the true Creator, is to convey and impart the divine grandeur and to endeavor to introduce the Creator, the Exalted the Allah.

It is He who bestows guidance to whom He wills.

"Allah grants wisdom to whom He wills. And whoever is granted wisdom, he indeed is given much good. But none will grasp this except people of understanding." (Al-Baqarah: 269)

•

"WITHIN YOURSELF... DO YOU NOT SEE?"

(ADH-DHARIYAT: 21)

EXPLANATION OF THE NOBLE VERSE

Allah the Exalted, declares in His Noble Verse:

"Within yourself... Do you not see?" (Adh-Dhariyat: 21)

Now, before presenting this Noble Verse, I sought to fill you with it. Allah the Exalted, addresses us: **"I am within you... Do you not see?"**

This Noble Verse will be explained in three distinct ways and categorized according to different levels. Let each person recognize their level here and see themselves in this mirror.

1. Allah the Exalted, states in His Noble Verse:

"Allah has not made for any man two hearts within him." (Al-Ahzab: 4)

That one's heart be devoted to the love of the Lord, another's to the love of the world.

The heart is singular. If the manifestations of the Exalted the Allah have appeared therein, nothing besides Him can reside. But if worldly matters have entered that heart, Allah the Almighty is absent from it.

Suppose a mosque has been occupied, turned into a marketplace, filled with images, and you are obliged to perform prayer there.

In the Noble Verse:

"Prayer prevents shamelessness and wrongdoing." (Ankabut: 45)

Although Allah the Almighty has decreed this, why does our prayer not avert us from all evil? Because our heart is occupied by the self, having turned it into a marketplace. In such a place, how can one pray with serenity?

However, The Messenger of Allah -peace be upon him- states in the Noble Saying:

“A prayer without khushu (concentration and humility) is not worthy of acceptance, nor can its promised benefit be expected.” (Munawi)

What is most important is tranquility. Because in the Noble Verse, Allah the Almighty says:

"Those who perform their prayers with humility and reverence are saved from the torment of the Hereafter." (Mu'minun: 1-2)

Indeed, the prayer performed with tranquility and humility prevents one from all evils.

As for the situation of those who do not pray... The Messenger of Allah, -peace be upon him-, said in his Sacred saying:

"Between a person and disbelief is only the abandonment of prayer. (In other words, abandoning prayer brings one closer to disbelief.)" (Muslim)

And such a heart is truly diseased, heedless of the Truth. For the heart is the divine gaze's abode. This heart, turned into a marketplace, must be emptied and purified. This is achieved through a serious struggle with the ego.

The Messenger of Allah, peace and blessings be upon him, said in his sacred Noble Saying:

"Remembrance of Allah is the cure for hearts." (Munawi)

In other words, your heart is ailing, diseased, and its cure is to implant the remembrance of Allah in it.

The Exalted and Almighty One says in His Noble Verse:

"He who purifies his self is saved." (Ash-Shams: 9)

In his Noble Sayings, The Messenger of Allah -peace be upon him-says:

"The mosques will be splendid in appearance, but they will be devoid of guidance within." (Bayhaqi)

If you pay attention, you’ll see domed mosques with lush green carpets, filled inside... But what did The Messenger of Allah, -peace be upon him- say? **"They will be devoid of guidance within!"** How sorrowful this is!

This is the situation for most who remain on the surface. Why? Because they cannot transition from the apparent to the hidden.

2. Above all, the one who rescues and purifies their heart from this marketplace and these appearances, who illuminates their heart with the remembrance and thoughts of Allah the Almighty, becoming a heart at peace, is graced with this divine favor:

"The Day when neither wealth nor sons will benefit, except him who brings to Allah a clean heart." (Shu'ara: 88-89)

These are the ones who are saved.

"Make clean the palace of your heart

"If a sultan were to come to you."

3. Another devoted self has become annihilated in Truth, entirely nullified. Such a one does not see the self but beholds the Exalted the Allah and declares, "The body is Him, the existence is Him..."

The prayer performed with the Exalted the Allah... Here are those who observe this prayer.

Allah the Almighty states:

"Within yourself... Do you not see?" (Adh-Dhariyat: 21)

It is they who are blessed with the grace bestowed by this Noble Verse. They deserve this divine favor because they are followers of The Messenger of Allah -peace be upon him-, attaining both his prophet hood and sainthood.

Allah the Almighty asserts in Noble Verse:

"You are indeed on the path of someone who has been sent down by the Most Exalted and Most Compassionate Allah." (Yasin: 5)

Why so? Because they carry the mandate of The Messenger of Allah -peace be upon him- embodying his struggles and walking his path.

Pay close attention to this Noble Saying:

"The scholars of my community are like the prophets of the Children of Israel." (K. Hafa)

All this virtue and excellence are because they carry the representation of our beloved Prophet Muhammad, -peace be upon him-. This unique station they hold is conferred by the Exalted the Allah. Whoever is endowed with this unique station, indeed, contains within them the essence of everything... but in reality, nothing belongs to the individual.

It is due to his virtue and excellence that Allah the Almighty made the Prophet Muhammad, -peace be upon him-, the master of this house, while all the other Prophets, peace be upon them, were guests of this house.

Do you seek proof? Exalted the Allah says in a sacred saying:

"Were it not for you, I would not have created the heavenly spheres." (K. Hafa)

Because the universe was created from his essence, and from that light all of creation was adorned.

In a Noble Verse, it is proclaimed:

"We sent you as a mercy to the worlds." (Anbiya: 107)

The Exalted Truth states in his Noble Verse:

"Above every possessor of knowledge, there is one more knowledgeable." (Yusuf: 76)

As can be understood from this, everyone has stages and ranks, and their manifestations are distinct. This is a divine blessing; know how to benefit from it! Only these people recognize that the true guide is the Exalted the Allah, no one else does. But only they know. Previously, the guide was classified into three types: perfect, complete, and imitative, and explained as such.

• The false guide: Uses religion as a tool for worldly gain, committing all kinds of deceit and unspeakable offenses under this guise. These are the ones who have overrun the world today. They are the reason people detest the Truth. Some engage with women, some with children, and others with all sorts of schemes to secure worldly benefits. They do all this under the cloak of being a Master. What Satan couldn't achieve, they execute under the mask of sheikdom. These impostors are the ones who distance people from the Truth, darkening and suffocating the spiritual atmosphere.

• Then, there are those who have received lessons from a guide. They have grasped the Truth to some extent and have read some texts. These are the ones who proclaim, "I am a guide." Beware of them as well. Although they avoid the forbidden, do not encroach on the Truth, and uphold the boundaries of divine decrees, they still wish to sell the Truth to people as if it belonged solely to them. This stems from the fact that their actions and practices are intertwined with their ego. They remain with the created, unable to see the Creator. They do not truly know Truth and the reality. They tell their followers to walk, but they lack the power to guide them forward.

• However, those who have attained Annihilation in Allah and are among the Gnosis do not see themselves and know they are nothing. True guides see and know that the real guide is the Exalted the Allah. Only these individuals know the Truth. They are aware that there is no existence or presence except for Him.

No other existence or presence can be seen or known except by them. These are the rare ones who appear in the world occasionally. Sometimes there is one, other times there are deputies. The ones who know that the true guide is the Exalted the Allah are these individuals, and it applies to no one else.

•

The body is a garment. What keeps it standing is the soul. When the soul departs, the garment has no significance.

Mankind has never been able to truly grasp his own insignificance. Because he couldn't, he also failed to find his Allah.

He who knows this pursues a great amount of knowledge. Those who cannot penetrate these two Truths remain outside the realm of true wisdom.

There are few who pursue this, and even fewer who wish to. Why so few, you may ask?

Man works only if there is a benefit for him. No one works at a task that is both exhausting and fruitless. This is evident in worldly matters. In spiritual pursuit, however, one must shed existence and erase himself. The self never wants to approach this. It always seeks to assert its own existence. It can never say, "This belongs to Allah." the Exalted the Allah denies such existence and never loves it.

In the one who obliterates his existence, the Exalted the Allah manifests. Just as there are very few inclined to this pursuit, there are very few who draw near to the people of Truth.

The people of Truth speak with Truth. They know they are worth less than a speck of dust and that originally, they were but a drop of despised water. Exalted the Allah created him from that despised water. And then, in that created form, existence manifested itself.

•

The luminous path is often referred to as the school of beneficial knowledge and wisdom.

As we have previously stated, The Noble Path is the school of knowledge and wisdom. It is a hospital for cleansing oneself from vile habits. It is a marketplace for trading one's life and wealth with the Exalted the Allah. An army for waging struggle in the way of the Exalted the Allah and His the Messenger of Allah. And only these struggle for the Exalted the Allah and His the Messenger of Allah, disregarding their lives and possessions. For they are soldiers in the army of the Exalted the Allah and His the Messenger of Allah.

In a Noble Saying:

"The true struggler is the one who strives against his self-commanding to evil." (Munawi)

These are the true strugglers.

"Indeed, Allah has purchased the lives and wealth of the believers in exchange for Paradise." (At-Tawba: 111)

Those who strive to be graced by the secret of this Noble Verse are these individuals. For they trade with Almighty Allah.

•

Now, let us present to you the reward and recompense of this struggle and battle in the sight of Allah through a story:

There was to be a war between the Muslims and the disbelievers. The commander came forth and, to extol the virtues of struggle in the way of Allah, he recited the following Noble Verse:

"Indeed, Allah has purchased the lives and properties of the believers for Paradise in return. They fight in Allah's way, so they kill and are killed. It is a promise binding upon Him in the Torah, the Gospel, and the Qur'an. And who is truer to his covenant than Allah? So rejoice in the transaction you have concluded. That is the great triumph." (At-Tawba: 111)

A young man present there said, "Commander! With your permission, let me explain this Noble Verse to my brothers." His initiative pleased the commander, who granted him permission.

The young man explained the Noble Verse and said, "My parents have passed away and left me great wealth. From this moment on, I am donating all my wealth to the army and joining the battle myself."

The commander responded, "Son, you are very young. If you survive the war, you will be left poor." The young man objected, "No! I have made a covenant with Allah the Almighty. Did I err by disclosing it?" He then handed over all his wealth and joined the battle.

In his excitement, he moved to the vanguard. After conducting the necessary reconnaissance and inspections, he sat under a tree to rest and await the army's arrival, and he fell asleep. He had a dream, which I will narrate to inspire you and highlight the virtues of struggle and endeavor.

In his dream, he entered a sublime garden in Jannah. In the center of the garden was a vast pool surrounded by numerous houris (heavenly maidens). The houris cheered, "The master of Âyı merdiyye is coming!" Approaching them, he greeted them and asked, "Which one of you is Âyı merdiyye?" They replied, "We are her servants, she is further ahead."

He proceeded to a second garden, more beautiful than the first, with a larger pool and more houris, who were even more stunning. They also clapped and said, "The master of Âyı merdiyye is coming!" He approached them, greeted them, and inquired about Âyı merdiyye. They, too, said, "We are her servants, she is further ahead."

Arriving at the third garden, so beautiful that he could not imagine a higher place, he heard the congratulations and glad tidings from the houris there. After greeting them, he asked about Âyı merdiyye. This garden was the most magnificent of all, with a pool of milk. "Go further, she is ahead," they told him.

Finally, he crossed a river and reached the fourth garden, far surpassing the previous ones in beauty, with even more houris. The pool here was of honey. He approached them and greeted them, asking, "Which one of you is Âyı merdiyye?" They pointed to a palace and said, "She is in that palace!"

At the palace door, he saw a houri with her arms extended over the doorway. He greeted her and asked, "Are you Âyı merdiyye?" She replied, "No, I am her gatekeeper. She is inside."

Looking in, he saw Âyı merdiyye seated on a red ruby throne. He wished to approach her, but Âyı merdiyye said, "No! You will come to me in the evening." The young man awoke to find the army had arrived. He told the commander about his dream. The commander said, "Son, you will be martyred and will attain that houri, blessed by Allah the Almighty."

When the battle began, the young man was among the first to attack. He fought until evening, killed nine men, and was eventually martyred.

Therefore, the reward for one who sacrifices their life and possessions for Allah is this.

In one Noble Verse it is stated:

"Believers are those who have faith in Allah and His Messenger, then have no doubts, and strive with their wealth and their lives in the way of Allah. They are the Truthful ones." (Hujurat: 15)

These are those who will inherit the highest paradise. However, those who are graced with His perfect beauty are those who have reached Annihilation in Allah, and have attained union with the Truth. They are with the Truth in this world and in the Hereafter. They are the inheritors of the paradise of bliss.

Even though they engage in struggle in the Path of Allah, these are the people of paradise. The servants chosen by Allah the Almighty, supported by the Holy Spirit and the divine elevations, honored with His perfect beauty, are the people of the vision of Allah.

•

In the Noble Verse:

"Within yourself... Do you not see?" it is said. (Adh-Dhariyat: 21)

Many hear this divine address. Very few understand and know it. For this secret is understood through the knowledge of the innermost. Only those who possess the knowledge of the heart can know and see. Since their teacher is Allah Himself, they both know and see as much as is shown to them. This knowledge is called the knowledge of gnosis.

At the same time, the secret and manifestations of this Noble Verse can only be known, seen, and deciphered by the people of Allah.

The people of the outer knowledge:

"Allah is the Light of the heavens and the earth." (Nur: 35)

They read this Noble Verse and consider themselves scholars. Yet, they remain ignorant in the face of this knowledge. For one takes from the heart, the other from the script.

The Messenger of Allah -peace be upon him- said in his Noble Saying:

"Knowledge is of two types. One is on the tongue (this is the outward knowledge), which is Allah's proof upon His servants. The other is in the heart (the knowledge of gnosis). This is the beneficial one for reaching the real purpose." (Tirmidhi)

The knowledge that The Messenger of Allah -peace be upon him-described as beneficial is the knowledge of gnosis. This is also called "divine knowledge". Those who possess this knowledge can see, know, and speak. However, those who think they are scholars have no understanding of this matter.

Let us elucidate and prove this:

Even though Allah the Almighty says, **"I am within,"** can one see what is inside? Does one not see, right?

Though he knows not, he cannot refrain from claiming, "I am a scholar!" For within him lies his self. One person carries Allah within, while another is driven by their self. This, he does not know.

Yet in the Noble Verse, it is said:

"We are closer to man than his jugular vein." (Qaf: 16)

Despite this divine declaration, he remains devoid of this knowledge and awareness. Meanwhile, his self incessantly asserts, "I am a scholar!" and he cannot break free from this pride.

In the Noble Saying:

"Whoever claims to be a scholar, know that he is ignorant." It is said. (Munawi)

This ruling applies to such individuals. All these arise from their failure to perceive Exalted the Allah within them.

Those who are aware and perceptive unravel the mysteries in this address, reading and understanding with ease. However, those who remain oblivious only comprehend according to their presumptive knowledge. They grasp to the extent of their intellect and believe it to be true.

And yet, we have conveyed that there are five levels of intellect:

Those who possess **"The intellect of livelihood"** are engrossed solely in the life of this world, worshipping it as their idol.

Those who possess **"the intellect of the afterlife"** contemplate both the worldly life and the afterlife. They engage in worship but also commit faults.

Those endowed with **"The luminous intellect"** have understood the reason for their creation. They turn towards the Exalted the Allah and strive to purify their inner selves through struggle.

The selected servants whom Allah the Almighty loves and chooses possess **"The Universal Intellect"**. They have reached the Truth and are wholly absorbed in it. Beyond "The Universal Intellect"," the intellect ceases to function.

There is also an intellect granted through Allah the Almighty's inspiration and guidance, known as **"People of deep understanding"**.

Your intellect is "The intellect of livelihood," whereas these topics pertain to "People of deep understanding," the fifth level of intellect.

The self, too, has seven levels:

"The commanding self" is the self that compulsively drives a person towards evil. When the human spirit, still in the "commanding" state, feels remorse for its sins and misdeeds and begins self-reproach, this condition is termed **"The reproaching self."**

With increased worship, remembrance, and ascetic practices, if another veil over the heart is lifted through intense struggle, the self ascends to the third station, known as **"The inspired self"**.

"The Tranquil Self" refers to the self that has found peace and contentment, free from polytheism, doubt, rebellion, and error.

The state of the self whose entire effort and desire is to win the favor of the Lord is called **"The content self"**

The self that is pleasing to Allah is **"The pleasing self"**

There is also **"The Purified self"** a self that has been purified. It now resides in the hand of the Truth. It knows the Truth and attributes everything to the Truth.

Your self is "The commanding self", and this knowledge belongs to those who ascend to the seventh level of the self, which is " The Purified self."

Everyone comprehends this knowledge according to their level of the self.

As mentioned in the Noble Verse:

"Above every possessor of knowledge, there is one more knowing." (Yusuf: 76)

•

"By those who separate truth from falsehood,
reality from delusion,
and right from wrong!"
(Al-Mursalat: 4)

THE BARRIER BETWEEN TRUTH AND MISGUIDANCE

CHAPTER 23

- The Explanation and Levels of the Barrier
- Human and Animalistic Traits
- The True Cry
- How Did the Seventy-Two Sects Become Doomed to Hell?
- The Door to Salvation

THE EXPLANATION AND DEGREES OF THE BARRIER

In the Noble Verse of Allah the Most High, it is stated:

"He has let loose the two seas, meeting together. Between them is a barrier; they do not transgress." (Rahman: 19-20)

I had once elucidated the esoteric meaning of this to the humble. Allah the Most High has also let loose the Truth and the error. However, between them stands the Perfect guide, preventing them from mixing.

Here, Allah the Most High is revealing His power. With His command of **"Be!"** a veil is created, with His order of **"Do not mix!"** the sweet and salty waters remain separate. It is He who places this obstacle.

In His Noble Verse, He declares:

"I swear by those who separate (with clarification) between right and wrong, Truth and falsehood, straight and crooked!" (Mursalat: 4)

His power is so profound that this veil becomes His decree. He has so willed, and He has erected this Barrier. It is impossible to surpass this Barrier. Truth remains on one side, and error remains on the other. His decree is enforced, becoming a barrier, becoming a veil. Yet, in appearance, it is a veil. In reality, there is no veil; there is the decree of Allah the Most High.

In another Noble Verse, it is stated thus:

"It is Allah who merged two seas: one with sweet, thirst-quenching water, and the other with salty, bitter water, placing a barrier between them to prevent mixing." (Al-Furqan: 53)

Allah the Exalted entrusts His secrets to the Divine Throne, distributing them from this spiritual throne to whomever He wills.

The sweet sea waters the thirsty, cleanses their hearts, provides sustenance, satisfies, and guides them on the path. These are the true Sufis.

The other, however, is salty and bitter. It offers no benefit. Those beyond this barrier are the people of error. They appear to have water, yet it neither quenches thirst nor satisfies.

The true barrier is His command and judgment. When His command and judgment are enacted, Truth and falsehood do not intermingle.

The water of Truth comes from Him. This is known as divine grace. This divine grace flows from Allah the Exalted to The Messenger of Allah -peace be upon him-. From him, it reaches the Perfect guides of the time. Only those predestined to receive this grace from eternity can take from this water. If granted to other guides, it comes from there. If not, it appears to exist but does not.

Those who receive, take from Him; it is impossible to take from anywhere else. Those who turn sincerely with a pure intention receive their share; those who do not, receive nothing.

There is no source other than the Cause of Creation peace and blessings be upon him. He is the fountain of knowledge and wisdom. True life comes from Him. The extent of what comes reflects in the individual. If nothing comes, nothing is present.

Since the knowledge and wisdom come from that fountain to the ocean of the Perfect guide, the Perfect guide possesses that knowledge.

In a Noble Saying, our Master, The Messenger of Allah -peace be upon him- says:

"Whatever Allah has poured into my heart, I have poured it all into the heart of Abu Bakr."

This pouring continues until the Day of Judgment, but it goes only to his representative.

Though there were many noble Companions, all esteemed, it was into his heart that it was poured.

This means that until the Day of Judgment, this knowledge will be transferred from one heart to another, and this transferred knowledge is of this nature. It is a chamber of secrets.

"Its essence is the Truth." Here lies the secret of Surah Yasin. But it is not possible for me to disclose this.

"Its words come from the Truth." Only those nourished by that water find life because it comes from Allah. Other waters bring not life but death.

Allah the Almighty states in the Noble Verse:

"They are those in whose hearts Allah has inscribed faith and supported them with a spirit from Him." (Mujadilah: 22)

All of these stem from the light He bestows. The one who crafts is that spirit, that light.

"If Allah does not grant someone light, they will have no light." (Nur: 40)

The true guide is the Exalted the Allah.

In another Noble Verse, He states:

"Is one who was dead and we gave him life, and provided him with a light by which to walk among people, like one who remains in darkness, from which he cannot emerge?" (An'am: 122)

Anyone whom Allah the Almighty does not guide remains in perpetual darkness.

Whomever He guides and perfects their faith along with His guidance, He gives them a light. They then embrace the path of Truth, parting ways with misguidance. Can they ever again be one with those lost in delusion?

HUMAN AND ANIMALISTIC ATTRIBUTES

Humans possess animalistic attributes, and these are varied and extensive.

There are some people who are like animals whose meat is not eaten. Their self has not believed. Apparently, they engage in very good deeds, but because their self has not believed, their intentions are corrupt.

Then, there are others who are like animals whose meat is eaten. Their self has believed, but they have not reformed it. Therefore, they remain in an animalistic state. Whatever animal form they are in, they will appear in that form on the Day of Judgment. Their forms will reveal their true selves.

There are also those who, having shed their vile manners and purified themselves from animalistic attributes, are in human form. On the Day of Judgment, they will be resurrected in human form. Even the earth does not decay the bodies of those who have entirely illuminated their beings with light. Let those who work, work towards this; and those who live, live for this.

Moreover, there is the perfect human; they are the devoted servants of Allah the Almighty.

Animalistic attributes are only seen and known by the showing of Allah the Almighty. When Allah the Almighty shines that spotlight on someone, they see every characteristic, every animalistic attribute of the other person. Otherwise, they cannot be seen.

I am giving you a secret.

How would someone whom Allah the Almighty has not shown, know whether the other is in a human state or in an animalistic state? Or how would they see themselves if they wished to?

If they are indulging in forbidden, they are in an animalistic state. Make your judgment, but do not tell anyone.

If they are not just avoiding forbidden but also shun the slightest doubtful matters, they are human.

Only this much can be said: one cannot discern which animalistic attribute one possesses, nor can their knowledge unveil it.

Those who attack everyone bear the attribute of a dog, those who harbor enmity have the attribute of a snake, the deceitful possess the attribute of a fox, thieves have the attribute of a mouse, the ungrateful own the attribute of a cat, and the indifferent carry the attribute of a pig. There are many such animalistic attributes. Today, the most prevalent forms are those of the dog and pig. We offer you these examples.

However, those with attributes of animals whose meat is permissible to eat are different. Some are like oxen, some like roosters. Those who possess the attribute of a sheep are very few; it is necessary for them to ascend to the state of the inspired self.

Even if two are brothers, those who heed their wives and those who do not are distinct from one another.

For instance, under a brooding hen, there may be both a duckling and a chick. Yet, when a duckling sees water, it immediately dives in, whereas the chick does not.

Let each person examine themselves. Where do I stand? Whether closest kin or friend, this serves as a measure.

Whichever animalistic attribute a person has adopted and acted upon, such an attribute is present within them. They will die with that attribute and be resurrected with that attribute.

The Messenger of Allah -peace be upon him- said in his Noble Saying:

"Every person will be resurrected in the state in which they died." (Muslim: 2878)

When the veil is lifted, everyone's true essence will become apparent and visible, along with their deeds.

In another Noble Saying, it is stated:

As you live,so shall you die; as you die, so shall you be resurrected.

Whichever animalistic attribute a person dies with, Allah the Almighty will bestow that animal's form upon them in the afterlife, and everyone will recognize who they truly are.

•

To help you better understand what animalistic attributes are, we will present two examples. We wish to underscore the importance of doing whatever is necessary to eliminate these attributes.

One day, a woman came and recounted a dream. *"I was sitting in an elevated place. I noticed a long tailed rat coming from below. They told me, 'This is your husband.' As I exclaimed 'How could this be my husband?' I looked closely at its face, and indeed, it resembled him."*

"Yes, yes, dear lady," we said, "such is the nature of animalistic attributes. When a person sheds this bodily garment tomorrow, their true form will emerge. These attributes exist in everyone, except for those who have eliminated them."

•

Let us present another parable. There was a man who constantly obsessed over the thought, *"Ah, if only I were Khidr!"* One day, Khidr -peace be upon him- appeared before him and asked, *"If you were Khidr, what would you do?"* The man replied, *"If you gave me your role for just one hour, you'd see what I would do!"* Khidr -peace be upon him- said, *"Very well. I am Khidr, and for one hour, I give you my role. Do as you will."*

At that moment, a veil lifted from the man's eyes. What did he see among the countless thoughts? He saw all humans as animals.

He encountered an old ragman in human form and said to him, *"I am Khidr. Ask whatever you wish of me!"* The ragman took no notice and answered, *"I have no need."* The man then met two more individuals in human form and made the same offer, but they too paid no heed and asked for nothing.

Before the hour was even up, the man began to eagerly wait, thinking, *"Let him come so I can return this burden!"* Finally, Khidr -peace be upon him- came and asked, *"What did you do?"* The man explained, *"My aim was to help people, but I couldn't see any humans to help. Take back this burden from me and relieve me."*

Indeed, this is the state of people.

•

Everyone succeeds and is enabled according to the direction in which they exercise their will. In other words, they follow a path that suits their condition, whether in guidance or misguidance. Thus, those who walk on the path of guidance attain their rewards, while those who tread the paths of misguidance also reach their deserved punishments. Everyone will be recompensed for their deeds.

The Qur'anic Verse states:

"Say: Everyone acts according to his own disposition. But your Lord knows best who is rightly guided." (Isra: 84)

Here, it is reminded that everyone will face reward or punishment based on the path they follow and the deeds they perform, urging people to turn toward the path of guidance.

THE REAL CRY

When a person is dying, Allah the Almighty makes him witness the movie of his life as he lived it. In an instant, he sees all his actions and also his place in paradise or hell.

The Noble Verse states:

"The agony of death will truly come. 'This is what you tried to escape from,' it will be said." (Qaf: 19)

A person who has lived with animalistic attributes is laid in the coffin like an animal. Until that moment, they have refused to hear the divine decrees, turning a deaf ear to the commands of Allah the Almighty.

When placed in the coffin, it is said:

"You were certainly heedless of this. Now We have removed from you your veil, so your vision is sharp this Day." (Qaf: 22)

As revealed in the Noble Verse, Allah the Almighty lifts the veil from his eyes.

And he begins to wail, for he sees where he is headed. Such a pain envelops him that the Noble Master of the Universe -peace be upon him- has described this situation in a Noble Saying:

"When a dead person is placed in the coffin and carried, if he was a good person, he says, 'Take me to my place quickly!'

If he was a bad person, he says, 'Woe to me! Where are you taking me?' he cries out.

Every creature hears this voice except humans. If humans could hear it, they would immediately faint." (Bukhari. Tecridi Sarih: 658)

For the veil has lifted, and those who bear him are his friends.

He writhes in the coffin. Believe me, I can almost see his contortions.

Until that moment, he paid no heed to divine commandments, listened not. Though told again and again, he refused to hear. Now, no one listens to his cries. His lament is eternal, an everlasting "Woe!" His wails neither benefit him nor soothe his pain.

It was always "I, I!" that you cared for. When in the grave, your ego dissolves, your mask decays, and no trace of your self remains, then what will you say, O cruel and ignorant self! Have you ever pondered this point?

Indeed, all true sufis know and see all this even before they die, while still in this world.

"Die before you die." (K. Hafâ)

They are endowed with the secret of the Truth of this Noble Saying. These individuals are privy to these Truths. Some they reveal, some they do not.

They know and see that everything is from Him and belongs to Him. Thus, they speak with knowledge and vision.

For them, there is no death.

Allah the Almighty states in the Noble Verse:

"Do not think of those who are killed in the way of Allah as dead; they are alive." (Al' Imran: 169)

The Messenger of Allah -peace be upon him-, says in the Noble Saying:

"Believers do not die. They merely move from one abode to another."

However, the false ones are not like this. They will only understand after they have died, decayed, and disintegrated.

•

SEVENTYTWO SECTS

HOW DID THEY BECOME DENIZENS OF HELL?

Allah the Exalted states in the Noble Verse:

"No! Whoever ascends to the echelon of excellence, completely surrendering their self to Allah, their reward is with their Lord.

They shall have no fear, nor shall they grieve." (Al-Baqarah: 112)

These are the perfect believers, and this faith is called Islam. The religion in the sight of Allah is this very Islam. The essence of the faith that Muhammad -peace be upon him- conveyed is this.

This Noble Verse hints at the one group that will persist until the Day of Judgment.

The Messenger of Allah -peace be upon him- in his Noble Saying states that **his community will split into seventy-three sects, with seventy-two deviating and destined for Hell, except for one sect that will be saved.** (Abu Dawood)

How do the seventy-two sects slip into Hell, and from where does the one sect find salvation?

Because those who faltered claimed "I know!... I do!...", constantly asserting "I!" in all their actions, they slipped for they made their egos into deities. Not just ordinary people, even superficial scholars stumble at this point.

Allah the Exalted states in His Noble Verse:

"The Trumpet will be blown. That is the promised Day.

Every self will come forth with a driver and a witness.

It will be said to him, 'You were heedless of this. Now we have removed your veil, and today your sight is sharp.'

His companion will say, 'This is what I have ready with me.'

Allah will decree, 'Throw into Hell every stubborn disbeliever, every ungrateful denier who hindered goodness, who was aggressive and aroused doubts,

The one who set up another deity besides Allah. Cast them into severe punishment!'

His companion will say, 'Our Lord! I did not lead him astray, but he was far astray himself!'

Allah said, 'Do not argue in my presence! I had already warned you of this.

In My presence, words cannot be altered, and I do not wrong my servants.' (Qaf: 20-28)

Indeed, those who declare "I!" and make their desires their deity are led astray.

They are doomed to the hellfire; all who sow discord, follow sects, or chase after any religious leader will gather and wrestle in hellfire.

They said "I!" and perished, "Küllühüm finnar..." (They are all in hellfire.)

But those who reform their "I," and purify their self, reaching such a state where they rise to the level of "The Tranquil Self", are promised paradise by Allah even in this world.

That is how the one saved from this group escapes.

Our declarations are in accordance with the Noble Verse. Despite this, the judgment belongs to Allah the Almighty. He saves whom He wills.

In His Noble Verse, He says:

" Allah forgives whom He wills and punishes whom He wills." (Al-Baqarah: 284)

THE GATE OF SALVATION

The Noble Path is a school of knowledge and wisdom. To comprehend that this path is a school of knowledge and wisdom, it is necessary to thoroughly examine the "stages of the self."

Just as enrolling in a school is meaningless if one does not attend and pass classes, so too is mere affiliation with the exalted path; without progressing through its stages, one cannot purify the self, shed animalistic attributes, or traVerse the degrees.

One must complete the stages and advance through the degrees to don the attributes of a human being.

After reforming the "The commanding self", when one progresses to the reproaching self, significant internal struggles occur. When advancing to the inspired self, one becomes calm, adopts the attributes of a sheep, performs righteous deeds, and to some extent, attains the pleasure of the Creator. During this phase, although infrequent, some inspirations also come. Now, this person is a traveler. A traveler to where? To Truth.

Should one advance another degree, they become The Tranquil Self. Here, those who are saved find their salvation. Divine union originates from here.

We are describing to you the gate of salvation belonging to a certain group.

Allah the Almighty proclaims in His Noble Verse:

"He who purifies and refines his self has undoubtedly found salvation and liberation. But whoever defiles and conceals it is surely doomed to loss. (Ash-Shams: 9-10)

"Their mark is on their faces from the trace of prostration."

(Al-Fath: 29)

THE ILLUMINATED

AND

THOSE LEFT IN DARKNESS

CHAPTER 24

- Attaining Light
- The Light of the Believers
- The Darkness of the Hypocrites
- The Outer and Inner Paradise
- The Pious (*Muttaqeen*)
- The Righteous (*Abrar*)
- The Brought Near Ones (*Muqarrabeen*)

To Become Light:

In His Noble Verse, The Exalted Truth states:

"Their mark is on their faces from the trace of prostration." (Fath: 29)

Their signs are upon their foreheads. The radiance of their continual prostrations bestows upon their faces an exceptional beauty."

The Messenger of Allah -peace be upon him- said in his Noble Saying:

"Those who maintain frequent night prayers will have radiant faces during the day." (Ibn Mâjah)

It is He who bestows that visage and grants that light. The light He gives reflects upon the face.

If the bee ceases to make honey, what good is the hive? You are merely a hive. It is He who will fill you with light.

•

Exalted the Omar's -may Allah be pleased with him- son, Abdullah -may Allah be pleased with him- says:

"In the Age of Happiness, whenever someone had a dream, they would come and narrate it to The Messenger of Allah -peace be upon him-. I deeply wished to see a dream and relay it to The Messenger of Allah -peace be upon him-. At that time, I was very young and often slept in the mosque during the time of the Messenger -peace be upon him-

*One night, I dreamt that two angels took hold of me and brought me to Hell, which appeared as a stone well with two horns. Inside, many familiar people were suffering. **"I was terrified and began to seek refuge in Allah from Hell".** At that moment, we encountered another angel who told me, **'Do not be afraid!'***

I recounted this dream to my sister, Mother of the Believers Hafsa -may Allah be pleased with her- . When she conveyed it to The Messenger of Allah -peace be upon him-, he remarked:

'Abdullah is a good boy. If only he would get up and pray at night!'"

After this incident, I began to sleep very little at night." (Bukhari)

The midnight prayer is a means of enlightenment and a path to salvation.

The humble narrator says:

Those who perform the midnight prayer are like people who have bathed in a hamam (Turkish bathhouse), while those who perform the prayer of glorification are akin to those who have bathed and scrubbed in the hamam.

Exalted the Ali -may Allah be pleased with him- our master, says:

"One early morning, The Messenger of Allah -peace be upon him-suddenly visited me and his daughter Fatimah -may Allah be pleased with her-. He asked, **'Are you not waking up for midnight?'**

I replied, **'O the Messenger of Allah! Our lives are in Allah's hands. If He wills to awaken us, He will.'** Hearing this, he turned away without answering me. As he left, he struck his blessed hand on his thigh and recited the following Noble Verse:

'But, man is ever more quarrelsome than anything.' (Qahf: 54)" (Bukhari)

Here, there is both a command and an insistence directed at the people of Truth.

It is hoped that the one who performs night worship, whose face becomes radiant, will eventually have their entire body illuminated.

•

The earth does not decay the luminous ones, nor does fire burn the luminous ones. Here we come and here we go. Let us illuminate our bodies so that we do not decay in the grave and the fire does not burn us. The goal is to become light.

The Messenger of Allah -peace be upon him- said in his Noble Saying:

"On the Day of Judgment, as they cross the bridge of Sirat, the fire of Hell will call out: 'Pass, O believer! Your light extinguishes my flames.'" (Jami' alSaghir)

This address is to the illuminated ones. What if such a person were to fall into Hell?

Being from the Community of The Messenger of Allah -peace be upon him- is not just a matter of words. It is necessary to do what he did, live as he lived, and love what he loved.

He is our most exemplary guide.

Though he was a prophet, he would worship at night until his blessed feet swelled. When our Mother, Exalted the Aisha -may Allah be pleased with her- asked, **"O the Messenger of Allah! Why do you do this when your past and future sins are forgiven?"**

"Should I not be a servant grateful to my Allah?" he declared. (Bukhari)

This is the most essential point.

The Light of Believers:

In the afterlife, believers will be granted light in proportion to their deeds, and their faces will shine like the moon in the darkness of night.

Allah the Almighty in His Noble Verse speaks of obedient believers and their light, saying:

"That day you will see the believing men and believing women, their light running before them and on their right." (Hadid: 12)

They will be told:

"Rejoice today, for you have gardens beneath which rivers flow, where you will dwell forever." (Hadid: 12)

"This is the great triumph!" (Hadid: 12)

Could there be a greater salvation than entering paradise?

Here we come, here we go. This light is gained in this world and transfers from the world to the hereafter.

Allah the Almighty says in the Qur'anic Verse:

"When Allah expands the heart of someone for Islam, they are upon a light from their Lord." (Zumar: 22)

The Messenger of Allah -peace be upon him- used to supplicate with the following prayer at the end of his night prayers:

"O Allah! Grant me light in my heart, light in my grave, light in front of me, light behind me, light above me, light below me, light in my ears, light in my eyes, light in my hair, light in my skin, light in my flesh, light in my blood, light in my bones, and light in my brain!

O Allah! Magnify my light, bestow upon me a light, and create for me a light!" (Tirmidhi)

•

The Messenger of Allah -peace be upon him- once approached a cemetery and said, **"Peace be upon you, O dwellers of the believing community!**

Inshallah (Allah willing), we will also join you. I would have loved to see our brothers."

They believed by seeing; they also believed without seeing.

When the noble companions asked, **"O the Messenger of Allah! Are we not your brothers?"** he replied, **"You are my companions. Our brothers are those who have not yet come."**

When asked, **"O the Messenger of Allah! How will you recognize your Community who have not yet come?"** he answered:

"If a man has a horse with a white forehead and white feet among a herd of completely black horses with no markings at all, would he not recognize his own horse? Of course, he would. Our brothers will come with their faces and limbs shining with the light of ablution (ritual purification). I will be waiting for them at the fountain." (Muslim)

The Darkened State of the Hypocrites:

After explaining the state of the believers on the Day of Judgment, Allah the Most High, also described the condition of the hypocrites:

"On that day, the male and female hypocrites will say to those who believed, 'Wait for us that we may acquire some of your light!'" (Hadid: 13)

While the believers attain their desires in the light, the hypocrites will remain in darkness.

"They will be told, 'Go back behind you and seek light!'" (Hadid: 13)

You loved inconstancy in the world and sought reasons to turn your back on faith. Now, if you can, return to the world and seek a light. Here, no one will look after you.

Though the believers always wished them well and constantly invited them to the Truth, striving to save them from misguidance, they mocked the believers' faith and prayers, making them objects of ridicule. Now, however, it is the believers' turn to mock.

"At length, a wall with a door will be set up between them, inside it will be Mercy and outside it will be torment." (Hadid: 13)

On the Day of Judgment, a wall is set up to separate the believers from the hypocrites. When the believers reach the wall, they enter through its door, which then closes, leaving the hypocrites in darkness and torment.

“The hypocrites will call out to the believers, ‘Were we not with you?’ They will reply, ‘Yes, but you deceived yourselves, you laid ambushes for us, you doubted, and false hopes deceived you until the Command of Allah came to pass.’” (Hadid: 14)

They never truly believed nor were they ever sincerely with the believers. They loathed the Light, chose darkness, and remained in misguidance.

“Today, no ransom will be accepted from you or from those who disbelieved. Your abode is the Fire. That is your companion, and what an evil destination it is.” (Hadid: 15)

Indeed, the punishment for disbelief and hypocrisy is eternal.

In other Verses of the Quran, it is said:

"To whom Allah has not given light, for him there is no light." (Nur: 40)

"On that day, some faces will be bright, others will be dark." (Al' Imran: 106)

The Outward and Inward Paradise:

The Brought Near servants, whose lives are intertwined with the Truth, experience everything spiritually and intimately, for within them resides the Truth.

The sage says; there is a lofty life and a base life. This condition extends into the afterlife. Those who live a lofty life will transition to a lofty existence, while those who live a base life will encounter a base existence.

The Brought Near inherit the inward aspect of the exalted paradise.

The Messenger of Allah -peace be upon him- stated in a Noble Saying:

"There is indeed a paradise in this world. Whoever finds it no longer yearns for the other. That paradise is the Gnosis."

This is the paradise of the heart. They entered this paradise while still in the world, and this state transitions to the afterlife in the same way.

While in the world, they did not strive for paradise. They worked for the Exalted the Allah and The Messenger of Allah.

In a Noble Saying:

“Whoever is for Allah, Allah will be for him,” it is stated.

They are His chosen servants, and He lets them live in the paradise of the heart on earth. He bestows upon them the most beautiful life, both inwardly and outwardly. It is because they chose the best that He gave them the best. Their choice was the Exalted the Allah, and Allah chose them as well. More precisely, He created them for Himself. He has loved, selected, and drawn them near to Him. To make them love Him, He has given them love. He absolutely does not want them to be occupied with anything else or to nurture any other desires. And indeed, that servant has no other desire but for Truth. No one knows the kind of life they live.

“This is Allah’s grace and bounty, which He bestows on whom He wills.” (Al-Jumu'ah: 4)

•

Other Allah fearing servants, however, inherit only the outward beauty of paradise. This is because, while they were in the world, they remained in the outward realm and could not transition to the inner world.

Due to their faith, worship, and obedience, the blessings granted to them are also infinite.

Now, we shall provide examples of those who remain in the outward paradise and those who have passed into the inward.

The Devout:

The devout servants who abstained from disbelief and other sins of the self in the world shall dwell in paradise amid gardens and orchards, by the flowing springs, in comfort and bliss.

The divine Verse states:

"The devout shall be amidst gardens and springs, receiving what their Lord has granted them, for they were indeed doers of good in the past world." (Adh-Dhariyat: 15-16)

These springs flow until the farthest corners of the gardens. No one there shall ever feel thirst, nor shall they ever be parched. Those who wish to drink do so purely for pleasure. Simply watching the flow of these springs grants a unique peace to the self.

In other divine Verses, it is said:

"There, they pass around a cup among each other, which neither causes idle talk nor sin." (Tur: 23)

They are offered the finest and most exquisite drinks. The cups presented are characterized by the pure nature of the water. Flowing rivers are filled with wine, ensuring they never fear depletion or emptiness.

"In it there is no intoxication, nor will they get drunk from it." (Saffat: 47)

Its taste and color are both beautiful. It is extraordinarily delicious and delightful. It does not cause headaches, impair the senses, or cloud the mind. It provides a sweet tranquility and prolonged joy.

"The righteous ones":

Allah the Almighty describes the gifts and blessings that will be granted to the believers known as "**The righteous ones**" in His Noble Verses:

"They will be given a sealed, pure drink. The seal will be of musk." (Al-Tatfif: 25-26)

Nothing is mixed with it, and it has no dregs. Allah the Almighty has made this drink so perfect for them that it ends up like musk. It's being sealed is to elevate the honor of those who drink it. Only they will be able to break these seals, which signifies special attention and care.

For in their earthly lives, they chose Allah the Almighty, showing affection only to Him. Because He knows this, He bestows this exclusive gift upon them.

Indeed, one must envy those who attain such a precious blessing.

Allah the Almighty states in the Noble Verse:

"Let the competitors compete for this, and let those who aspire, aspire to this." (Al-Tatfif: 26)

True aspiration should arise during one's time in this world. Envy his devotion to the Exalted the Allah and The Most Noble Messenger -peace be upon him- so that you may attain and be graced with this favor and beneficence.

One attribute of the pure drink mentioned in the Holy Noble Verse is:

"It's mixture is of Heavenly Spring." (Al-Tatfif: 27)

"Heavenly Spring" is the most exquisite, superior, and valuable of the beverages in heaven. It is called Heavenly Spring because it originates from the highest places in heaven.

When the pure drink is given to the **"The Righteous"**, a small amount of Heavenly Spring is mixed into it. It is offered as a supplement. This is considered a great blessing for them.

Drinking Heavenly Spring in its pure form is reserved for the **"The Brought Near"**.

Those brought near:

The finest and most precious wine of paradise is from Heavenly Spring, which the those brought near drink pure.

In the Noble Verse it is stated:

"This is a spring from which only those near to Allah drink." (Al-Tatfif: 28)

For they were pure, clean, and beautiful in the world. They were with the beautiful, and nurtured only His love in their hearts.

"They are those who direct their hearts solely towards Allah." (At-Tawba: 59)

"They are those who humbly submit to their Lord." (Hud: 23)

These are the chosen servants of Allạh the Almighty. They are the ones to whom sincerity has been poured into their hearts.

In a Sacred saying, it is said:

"Sincerity is one of my secrets. I place it in the hearts of those among my servants whom I love. Neither the angel can record it nor can the devil corrupt it."

Thus, by reason of that secret, they become aware of this mystery. None shall attain to their rank.

While in this world, they chose Allah the Almighty and turned solely to Him, desiring His companionship; now Allah the Almighty has chosen them and desires to be with them.

In another Sacred saying, it is stated:

"Verily, the righteous have an intense longing to meet me, and my longing to meet them is even stronger."

Can you imagine how much love Allah the Almighty has for them?

Those who have not achieved this spiritual nearness cannot hope to drink from that most splendid spring.

For in the world, they sought pleasure elsewhere. These, however, found delight solely in the Exalted the Allah.

The spring known as Heavenly Spring, mentioned in the 25th Verse of the Mutaffifin surah, surpasses even the **"pure wine, sealed"** spoken of therein.

Just as they turned sincerely to Allah the Almighty and The Messenger of Allah -peace be upon him-, Allah the Almighty bestows the most sincere upon them. This is a Divine gift to them.

"You chose me with a pure and clean heart, so I grant you the purest and the cleanest in return."

In another Verse of the Qur'an, it is revealed:

"Their Lord will give them a pure drink." (Insan: 21)

This drink, given directly by the Lord of all worlds, is utterly pure, with no additives whatsoever. It symbolizes the joy of union with the Divine Beauty.

And it is said to them:

"This is a reward for you, your efforts have been found worthy of recompense." (Insan: 22)

Those who toil do so with the capital given by Allah the Almighty. If He does not provide the capital, you cannot work, and if you do work, it will be through your ego.

If Allah the Almighty bestows His capital upon your heart, you can trade with Him using His gracious bounty, and you can engage in worship and devotion.

All goodness comes from Allah the Almighty; without His grant, it cannot be found.

Allah the Almighty has bestowed upon them such grace, allowing them to trade with Him. They engage in the finest trade, unparalleled in its value. Their currency is unmatched.

The Brought Near Ones are leaders who excel beyond all ranks in the divine presence.

As stated in the Noble Verses:

"They advance swiftly in the race of goodness and attain it. They are the foremost, the nearest to Allah, and in the gardens of bliss." (Waqi'ah: 10-11-12)

For they are with the Exalted the Allah in this world and the hereafter.

Heavenly Spring is their drink. They are quenched by Heavenly Spring and take great delight in it.

Just as Heavenly Spring is the highest of paradise springs, so are the Brought Near Ones the greatest among the dwellers of paradise.

In the spiritual paradise, Heavenly Spring is the joy of gnosis and the vision of His flawless beauty. The Brought Near Ones drink only from Heavenly Spring, meaning they are solely occupied with Allah the Almighty.

•

"To Allah belong the most beautiful names, so call upon Him by them."
(Al-A'raf: 180)

ASMA' AL-HUSNA

THE MOST BEAUTIFUL NAMES OF ALLAH

CHAPTER 25

**"Allah has ninety-nine names.
Whoever memorizes them will enter Paradise.
Indeed, Allah is one and loves those who reflect on His Oneness."**
(Bukhari - Muslim)

ASMA' AL-HUSNA

(THE MOST BEAUTIFUL NAMES OF ALLAH THE ALMİGHTY)

In the revered Noble Verse of the Holy Qur'an, it is stated:

"The most beautiful names belong to Allah. So call on Him by them." (A'raf: 180)

According to the narration from Abu Hurairah -may Allah be pleased with him-, The Messenger of Allah, -peace be upon him-, said in a Noble Saying:

"Allah has ninety-nine names. Whoever memorizes them will enter Jannah. Allah is single and loves what is single." (Bukhari-Muslim)

In a narration by Tirmidhi, The Messenger of Allah -peace be upon him- described the names of Allah the Most High as follows:

Allah: The personal name of The One whose existence is necessary, other than whom there is no deity. This name encompasses all attributes specific to divinity. Among His names, it is the greatest and the most blessed.

In another revered Noble Verse, it is stated:

"Have you ever known anyone else to bear the name of Allah?" (Maryam: 65)

The name Allah cannot be translated into other languages. In Persian, He is called "Hüdâ," in Turkish "Tanrı," and in English "God"; these terms are not the equivalent of the name Allah but rather match the term "Ilâh". The name Allah is not derived from any word nor borrowed from another language; from the beginning, it has been used as a unique name. Just as Allah the Almighty's very essence has existed before all names and attributes, so too does His name Allah.

This sacred name does not stem from the attribute of divinity; rather, the nature of divinity and worshipfulness is derived from it.

Allah the Almighty is not Allah because He is worshipped; He is worshipped because He is Allah. His divinity inherently makes Him worthy of worship and servitude.

A person may worship an idol, fire, the sun, or beloved things, and when worshipped, these things become deities. However, when abandoned, they lose their divine attributes. In contrast, whether people recognize Allah the Almighty as their true Lord or not, He is inherently the deity. Everyone owes worship and servitude to Him.

Ar-Rahman (The Most Merciful) The One who bestows countless blessings upon all His creation without distinction between believers and nonbelievers, the obedient and the disobedient, and The One who protects them.

This is another unique name of Allah the Almighty. However, it is a name of attribute, not essence, signifying **"The One with great mercy."**

Ar-Rahim (The Most Compassionate) The One who shows immense compassion, rewarding those who believe and perform righteous deeds, and those who utilize the given blessings wisely with even greater and eternal rewards in the hereafter.

Allah the Almighty's **"Rahman"** reflects His mercy without a beginning, and His **"Rahim"** refers to His mercy without end. Hence, through the initial mercy of Allah the Almighty as the Rahman, creatures grow from His provided blessings, and by His Mercy nature, they prosper from the ensuing mercy in the hereafter. He is the Ar-Rahman for both believers and nonbelievers, yet the Ar-Rahim for believers alone.

Al-Malik (The King) The One who, in His essence and attributes, is independent of all means; the sole owner of the dominion and the entirety of creation, the true sovereign, and the absolute ruler.

No matter how powerful a servant may be as a ruler, he is in need of the true Owner of dominion; his property and power are temporary.

Everything is subject to His control and power, under His authority. There is nothing that can limit His sovereignty.

Al-Quddus (The Most Holy) The One who is free from all deficiencies and imperfections, pure and immaculate.

He is beyond any attributes that emotions and thoughts can conceive. His perfection is also limitless, endowed with qualities of completeness far beyond human comprehension. He cannot be confined by any boundaries or concepts, accepts no partnership in His dominion, and shares His sovereignty with no one.

As-Salam (The Source of Peace) The One who is free from oppressing His creation, who brings them to safety from dangers, and who greets His fortunate servants with peace.

A believer who perfects his Islam and faith becomes a manifestation of the attribute of Salam; Muslims remain safe from his tongue and hands, and such a person attains the blessing of meeting the Truth with a sound heart.

Believers are under the protection and guardianship of their Lord, living in safety and peace.

As He is the source of all peace, He is also The One who will grant peace to those seeking it.

Al-Mu'min (The Giver of Security): The One who bestows faith, grants security, takes under His special protection those who seek refuge in Him, and brings them to peace.

He is the giver of safety and security from all dangers and disasters; everything is always in need of turning to Him for solace.

He affirms the faith of His faithful servants.

In this name, a person is described with one of Almighty Allah's sublime attributes, elevating them to the highest station of the Celestial Assembly (Melei âlâ).

Al-Muhaymin (The Protector): The One who oversees all creation, who observes, directs, and governs everything, who is witness to all, the ultimate protector, the absolute sovereign.

Al-Aziz (The Almighty): The unique and unbeatable victor, unrivaled in worth and honor, powerful, and perpetually supreme.

He punishes those who attack His sacred honor and those who seek to commit polytheism, He defeats and devastates them with His severe vengeance. He enforces His will over all things. The universe operates according to the laws He has established.

Victory and invincibility are only possible through Him.

Al-Jabbar (The Compeller): The One who mends all forms of brokenness, who is capable of making anything happen as He wills, whose being is supremely exalted.

No force or power can oppose Him; He executes His will as He pleases.

Al-Mutakabbir (The Supreme): The One unrivaled in grandeur and majesty, manifesting His greatness in all things and events.

He alone holds the attributes of greatness, sublimity, and majesty. No one other than Him can be called Mutakabbir, for arrogance and boasting are not qualities befitting creation.

Al-Khaliq (The Creator): The One who creates everything out of nothing with perfect order and precision, arranging and fulfilling all needs.

Allah the Almighty alone creates everything with perfect estimation and innovation.

Al-Bari (The Evolver): The One who creates each being in conformity and novelty, without precedent, out of nothing.

Al-Musawwir (The Fashioner): The One who meticulously ascribes form and distinctiveness to everything, organizing and fashioning in the most beautiful manner, reflecting the perfection of His beauty.

Al-Ghaffar (The All-Forgiving): The One who reveals beauty and goodness; repeatedly forgiving and pardoning His servants with boundless mercy, concealing their sins in this world; abundant in forgiveness, vast in compassion.

Al-Qahhar (The Subduer): The One who prevails and dominates as He wills, subduing all creation under His command and will.

He is The One who crushes the pride and arrogance of the tyrants and oppressors, rendering them powerless.

Al-Wahhab (The Bestower): The Giver of boundless gifts, ever bestowing His bounties from the unseen treasury without expecting anything in return.

He has no need of His servants that He should expect anything from them.

Ar-Razzaq (The Provider): The one who grants abundant sustenance to all creations.

There is both an outward and an inward sustenance. Outward sustenance includes food and drink, while inward sustenance is spiritual, bestowed by Allah the Almighty (the Most High) to whom He wills.

Al-Fattah (The Opener): The One who opens the doors of mercy for His servants and makes all difficulties ease away.

The keys to all blessings and opportunities are in His possession. Through His guidance and support, every problem is resolved. Just as He opens the gates of fortresses, He also opens the celestial gates of the heavens to His devout friends, allowing them to witness the manifestation of His beauty.

Al-Alim (The All-Knowing): The One who, with everlasting and eternal knowledge, knows everything big and small, hidden and apparent, past and future without limitation of time and space. Nothing is concealed from His boundless and infinite knowledge. His knowledge encompasses everything.

Al-Qabid (The Withholder): The one who contracts and constricts.

All constrictions happen by His will. He narrows some hearts by subjecting them to 'Divine Grasp', while He expands others by subjecting them to 'expansion'. Whenever He desires, He withdraws the blessings He has granted to His servant.

Al-Basit (The Expander): The One who opens and widens.

All forms of expansiveness occur by His will. He grants 'inshirah' (relief and openness) to the hearts of those He desires, encouraging them towards goodness, extending some people's lives, and abundantly providing sustenance to others.

Al-Khafid (The Abaser): The One who lowers and abases.

He humiliates the disbelievers due to their disbelief and rebellion, cursing them and distancing them from His mercy, casting them down to the lowest depths of degradation. He can reduce a person from a state of honor and glory to one of disgrace and ignominy in an instant.

Ar-Rafi (The Exalter): The One who raises and elevates.

Everything rises due to His raising, everything is exalted by His elevating.

He elevates the believers through faith and guidance, drawing His friends closer to Himself, honoring them with His attention and favor.

Al-Mu'izz (The Giver of Honor): The One who grants honor and makes one mighty.

Those who obey are exalted. The ones blessed with His grace become esteemed and dignified, embodying solemnity. It is He who bestows sovereignty upon whom He wills, thus making them noble.

Al-Mudhill (The Giver of Dishonor): The One who brings to disgrace, who humiliates and belittles.

Those who defy are humiliated. The ones He reduces to disgrace and diminishment lose their honor. It is He who withdraws sovereignty from whom He wills, subjecting them to humiliation.

As-Sami (The All-Hearing): The All Hearing. He hears all sounds simultaneously. His hearing of one sound does not prevent His hearing of another. He doesn't need sound, air, or ears to hear.

Those who partake in this sacred name always open their ears and hearts to hear the Truth.

Al-Basir (The All-Seeing): The All-seeing His vision knows no bounds. Seeing one thing does not prevent Him from seeing another. He doesn't need eyes, light, or distance to see.

Al-Hakam (The Judge): The Absolute Judge, who administers justice and decrees rightfully.

The sole ruler is He. None can alter His commands, and none can overturn His decrees. He is the most just of judges, the Judge of all judges. He discerns the good from the evil, the Truth from falsehood.

He, whose judgments are full of wisdom, performs every act with wisdom.

Al-Adl (Al-Muqsit (The Just): The supremely just, who governs with fairness, never exhibiting the slightest injustice, and never oppresses.

He alone is the just. The awe-inspiring balance and order of the universe are the manifestations of His justice.

He loves those who are just and orderly among the believers, restrains the transgressors, and punishes them.

Al-Latif (The Subtle): He who performs the most delicate tasks, who knows the intricacies of all matters, endlessly compassionate.

He brings blessings, beauties, and graces to His servants through subtle and unseen ways.

His grace is of such infinite delicacy that just as He makes the oyster a treasure of pearls, the bee a treasure of honey, and the Caterpillar's cocoon a treasure of silk, He also makes the human heart a treasure of Gnosis.

Al-Khabir (The All-Aware): The one who knows the inner reality of everything, aware of their hidden aspects.

Knowing the most hidden states is unique to Him. No apparent or hidden event, no major or minor occurrence, no piece of news can ever remain concealed from Him. He rewards those who do well and punishes those who do evil.

Al-Halim (The Forbearing): One endowed with great clemency, who does not hasten to punish the guilty.

Allah the Almighty is exceedingly patient and immensely merciful. Despite the many rebellions of His sinful servants and unbelievers, He leaves the door of repentance open, does not rush to punish, grants respite, and sustains them, even though He has the power to do otherwise.

Al-Azim (The Magnificent): The Magnificent and the Sublime.

His majesty cannot be comprehended by intellects, His grandeur eludes understanding; He is as great as His greatness, and everything bears witness to His magnificence.

Al-Ghafur (The Forgiving): The Abundantly Forgiving and the Exceedingly Pardoning.

The surpassing of His mercy over His wrath, His covering and forgiving of sins and faults, is the sole hope and the only refuge for sinners.

Ash-Shakur (The Appreciative): The One who generously rewards good deeds done for His pleasure, bestowing great ranks in return for small acts.

He is aware of all the thankfulness shown by His servants. He accepts the gratitude of the thankful and increases His favors, grace, and blessings upon them. Allah rewards even the smallest act of worship, even the tiniest deed, without letting any good go to waste, bestowing abundant rewards for all good actions.

Al-i (The Most High): The Exalted One.

True exaltation and majesty belong solely to Him, and His grandeur knows no bounds in any manner. There is no being equal to or greater than Him in loftiness and sovereignty. No height, power, or supremacy can be conceived of that He does not surpass. The cosmos bears witness to His exaltation. He elevates the pious and humbles the arrogant.

Al-Kabir (The Most Great): The Great One.

He is the singular grand, without parallel. The vastness of the universe signifies His greatness. Majesty is unique to Him. To Him, there is no difference between creating a speck and creating worlds. When He says **"Be!"** it instantly comes into existence, and when He says **"Be not!"** it vanishes at once.

Al-Hafiz (The Preserver): The Protector, the Keeper.

The true guardian is He, and everything continues its existence under His safeguard and protection.

He preserves the universe and all within it for a determined period, from all kinds of known and unknown, seen and unseen calamities and afflictions. He is free from errors or forgetfulness.

He records all human deeds and words, and brings them to account for what they have done.

Al-Muqit (The Sustainer): The Creator of material and spiritual provisions, the Sustainer, the Shelterer.

It is He who creates the nourishing sustenance that grants strength to the soul and body, providing both the material and spiritual sustenance for every creature.

He has established the means of livelihood for people, and has obligated everyone to seek lawful means for their sustenance.

Furthermore, He enlightens hearts with the radiance of divine manifestation, providing spiritual nourishment to the soul.

Al-Hasib (The Reckoner): The One who knows in precise detail all that each person has done throughout their lives, sufficient for His servant.

Allah the Almighty knows everything that can be computed as an outcome without needing any investigation or condition. He records the accounting of good and bad deeds and grants reward and punishment accordingly.

He suffices for all things. Whoever journeys for His sake, He shall suffice for them.

Al-Jalil (The Majestic): The One who possesses majesty and grandeur.

He is great in both essence and attributes. He holds greatness without restriction or comparison. He is the sovereign whose decree pervades everywhere, whose treasures are inexhaustible, and who holds no vizier. He is the All-knowing who never forgets, the All-powerful who never tires. His power is immense, His mercy and generosity vast, His forgiveness and compassion unlimited. He is adorned with all attributes of majesty.

Al-Karim (The Generous): The One who generously bestows upon His servants without demand, reason, or compensation, most munificent and exceedingly generous.

The absolute source of generosity is He; when He gives, He gives abundantly, bestowing without needing causes or requests. He does not consider to whom or how much He gives; He spreads the treasures of His mercy before them.

He is such a Generous One that He punishes whom He wills with His justice and forgives whom He wills with His generosity.

He never turns away those who come to His door, taking under His special protection those who seek refuge and sanctuary with Him.

Ar-Raqib (The Watchful): The One from whom nothing is hidden, the oVerseer of all beings, who holds all affairs under His supervision.

He is the sole observer. Without the slightest neglect or error, He sees and watches everything. There is no mistake in His determination, no error in His vigilance.

He rewards those who act with decorum, mindful of always being in His presence.

Al-Mujib (The Responsive): The One who answers the prayers of His servants, granting the wishes of those who supplicate to Him.

The only door of need is His door. All needs are presented to Him; He fulfills all desires and needs. He alone brings desires to fruition. As desires multiply, so do His beneficence and generosity. As needs increase, His gifts and favors increase.

He fulfills the need He wills, delays the need He wills, and leaves unanswered the need He wills.

Al-Wasi (The All-Encompassing): His mercy encompasses all things, and His blessings are abundant and vast.

There are no bounds or measures to His grace and kindness. He grants and bestows as He wills.

There can be no limits conceived about His attributes.

Al-Hakim (The Wise): The one whose commands and actions are filled with wisdom, who executes everything perfectly and in the best manner.

He is the sole possessor of wisdom, and the beauty of His wisdom is evident in creation. There is no deficiency or flaw in what He does.

All His commands and prohibitions are wise; none of His actions are without purpose or benefit.

Al-Wadud (The Loving): The one who loves His obedient servants deeply, who deserves to be loved the most.

Allah the Almighty greatly loves His devoted servants, draws them to Himself, and illuminates their hearts with the light of gnosis.

Allah the Almighty is the beloved of pure souls. The highest rank attainable for a servant is to love Him alone, to know Him, and to joyfully obey His commands.

There is no higher rank, either in this world or in the hereafter, than to be a friend to Him.

Al-Majid (The Glorious): The One whose generosity is boundless, whose glory is exalted.

Allah, whose essence is beautiful, attributes magnificent, rank lofty, blessings abundant, works sublime, benevolence and munificence widespread, forgiveness and mercy vast, and grace and favor limitless! What an honorable Lord He is!

Al-Baith: The One who resurrects after death.

Allah the Almighty will resurrect and bring forth all humans from their graves, from the first to the last, and gather them before Him, directing them to the place of assembly.

Ash-Shahid (The Witness): The One who sees and knows everything with precision, who is present and witnessing at every moment and every place.

Allah the Almighty's a witness to everything, both near and far, equally close to every atom. He knows the inner and outer aspects of events unknown to His servants unless He manifests them. He perceives every action and hears every word, and on the Day of Judgment, He will reveal to everyone their deeds.

Al-Truth: The One who truly exists, whose existence remains unaltered.

The essence of Allah the Almighty does not accept nonexistence nor any alteration. Only Allah is truly existent; everything else appears to exist through His creation.

He who ensures that people's rights are not violated and delivers justice to the rightful owners on the Day of Judgment is The One.

Al-Wakil (The Trustee): The One who takes care of the affairs of those who entrust them to Him, providing better than they could achieve.

He is the absolute authority who administers and manages the affairs of His servants, supplies their needs, suffices those who turn to Him for everything, preserves what is entrusted to Him, and guards the faith of believers.

Al-Qawi (The Strong): The One with complete power and immense strength.

His power encompasses all beings. There are no bounds to His might, it cannot be measured. He is capable of all things unconditionally; nothing is difficult or burdensome for Him. He is free from weariness, fatigue, and any flaw.

Al-Matin (The Firm): The One Who is exceedingly firm, unshakable, encountering no difficulty in any of His tasks.

His strength is intense, possessing supreme power. He needs no one's assistance, no one can defy His will, and no one can escape His might.

Just as no force can prevent the mercy He wishes to bestow upon His loved ones, there is no power that can deliver one from His wrath.

Al-Wali (The Protector): The Protector and Friend of the righteous servants.

Allah the Almighty is the close companion of His beloved and chosen servants, taking them under His special protection. He aids them, leading them to success and prosperity in good deeds. He saves them from darkness, bringing them into the light, and illuminates their hearts. Those who see them are reminded of Allah.

They recognize no friend but Allah. Because they have no fear or expectations from anyone but Him, they remain fearless when others are afraid, and they are untroubled when others are anxious.

The only being worthy of winning friendship is Allah.

Al-Hamid (The Praiseworthy): The one who is praised and extolled, deserving of all commendation and glorification.

He is the one to whom all praises, thanks, and glorifications are due, and He is the patron and benefactor to be reverenced and worshiped. For all the perfections that necessitate praise and glorification exist solely in Him.

The most beautiful praises befit Him alone; He deserves all compliments.

Al-Muhsi (The Reckoner): The one who encompasses everything, knowing the count of all things from atoms to planets.

Allah the Almighty's eternal knowledge spans from past to future, encompassing everything that has been and will be. He knows the measure and number of His creations; everything is bound by determined calculations and programs with Him.

Al-Mubdi (The Originator): The creator who originates everything from the very beginning, bringing forth existence from nothing.

In eternity, Allah was, and nothing existed besides Him. Later, in His wisdom, He willed to manifest His existence and perfection by creating the universe, and He created it in the form and order He desired. It is He who brings forth the first example of everything.

Al-Muid (The Restorer): The One who restores life after He has exterminated creatures.

Everything that comes to life by His power dies by His will and judgment. Then, by His power, it is resurrected. Allah is the one who recreates the dead and scattered beings just as they were in their initial creation.

Al-Muhyi (The Giver of Life): The One who bestows life upon the lifeless, the giver of life, the reviver.

He is The One who creates living beings from nothing, brings them into the realm of existence, and after their death, revives them.

Without His exalted will, no being would come to life.

Al-Mumit (The Creator of Death): The One who creates death, the taker of life.

Allah has appointed a fixed term for each creature. He actualizes the events of death through the chain of causes He has arranged.

He is the one who revives, and He is the one who causes death.

Al-Hayy (The Ever-Living): The One who lives with eternal and everlasting life, omnipotent in every sense.

True life belongs solely to Him. His life is a perfect one, knowing everything, able to do anything. He is The One who grants life to His creations.

Al-Qayyum (The Self-Subsisting): The One who dominates over everything, the sustainer of all existence.

Allah the Almighty is alive by His essence, while His creations live by His grant of life, through His power. He has endowed everything with reasons to stand firm until a specified time. Everything subsists by the Truth; He alone is Al-Hayy and Al-Qayyum.

Al-Wajid (The Perceiver): The One who finds what He desires whenever He wishes, whose wealth is never diminished.

There is nothing beyond His power or that will ever be beyond it; everything belongs to Him just as it is. He acts according to His will at any moment; nothing can hide itself from Him.

Al-Majid (The Noble): The One whose dignity is supreme, whose glory is exalted, whose generosity and benevolence are abundant.

He is the possessor of the highest honor. His favors and gifts to His servants are beyond expression. He steers them towards faith and righteous deeds, then praises them by acknowledging their good actions, granting them worldly happiness and eternal peace in the hereafter.

Al-Wahid (The One): The One who is unique. In His essence, attributes, actions, names, and judgments, there is none like Him and none comparable to Him.

Allah the Almighty is singular in every aspect. He resembles no being, and no being resembles Him. His existence has no beginning, nor does it have an end.

The signs of His oneness are clearly visible in the beings He has created.

As-Samad (The Eternal): The sole refuge for all needs, the singular support to seek comfort from.

He is the only source who meets and surpasses all needs. He alone is the one to turn to for the fulfillment of demands. It is He who creates healing in medicines, and remedy in treatment. He is in need of nothing and is free from all needs.

Al-Qadir (The Omnipotent): The omnipotent who does as He wishes, in any way He wishes.

His power is eternal and boundless, surpassing all imagination, encompassing everything. It is impossible not to see the signs of His omnipotence in the universe.

Al-Muqtadir (The Powerful): The sovereign who exercises His will over the mighty and powerful.

All strengths belong to Him; He creates as He pleases and bestows as much strength and power as He desires in what He creates. If He wills, He makes the weak strong, the feeble mighty, and the helpless powerful. Only He is Al-Qadir and Al-Muqtadir.

Al-Muqaddim (The Expediter): He who advances whom He wills, placing them ahead.

All acknowledgments are according to His decree; He advances those whom He wills in honor and rank. Whomever He brings closer to Himself, He elevates. He is the foremost of everything, and everything ultimately returns to Him.

Al-Muakhkhir (The Delayer): He who delays whom He wills, who places them behind.

If Allah the Almighty distances someone, he remains behind. There is no one to advance those whom He keeps behind.

Some matters He postpones to a specific time, some punishments He defers to the hereafter.

Al-Awwal (The First): Without beginning.

One cannot conceive a beginning for Him. For the existence of everything is from Him. His existence is by the necessity of His essence. He existed before creating time and space. As He was before creating them, so He remains after creating them.

Al-Akhir (The Last): Without end.

Just as His existence has no beginning, it has no end. The place reached and the destination to be arrived at both lead to Him; there is no beyond or ahead.

As the creator of everything, He is the first, and as the one who sustains and annihilates everything, He is the last.

From the first knowledge, He is the beginning; as the ultimate destination, He is the end.

Az-Zahir (The Manifest):

All existence is a work and proof of His being. From the smallest particle to the vast cosmos, everything came into being by His divine command, **"Be!"** and they all testify to His presence.

"For one who sees, it is evident; for the blind, what could be there?"

Al-Batin (The Hidden): The secrets of divinity are concealed in every particle of the universe and are aware of all.

All existence is the place where the light reflecting from the divine lights of Allah the Almighty manifests.

He is both manifest and hidden.

Al-Wali (The Protector): The One who manages and governs His kingdom and all happenings within it by Himself.

Allah the Almighty is such a supreme sovereign; He oversees all His creation's affairs, guiding everything according to His eternal decree.

He is The One who creates monarchs and governors.

Al-Mutaali (The Exalted): Transcendent above the attributes of created beings, sublime and exalted beyond any deficiency.

He is exceedingly exalted above all that seems conceivable for creation, with no end or limit to His grandeur.

As the number of those who seek increases, so does His generosity and benevolence; He gives according to His will and wisdom, never exhausting His treasures.

Al-Barr (The Beneficent): Exceedingly compassionate and kind to His servants, abundantly gracious and giving.

He is the source of all goodness. All acts of grace and bounty come from Him, surpassing all imagination and beyond reckoning.

He forgives the majority of transgressions, rewards a single good deed manifold, while the punishment for evil does not exceed its due. He always desires ease for His servants, not hardship.

At-Tawwab (The Acceptor of Repentance): The One who accepts the repentance of those who turn to Him, mercifully granting pardon.

Allah the Almighty always keeps the door of repentance open. He instills fears in the hearts of His sinful servants to turn them away from their sins, thus making the reasons for repentance easier and accepts the repentance of those who forsake sin.

Al-Muntaqim (The Avenger): The One who punishes the guilty with His divine justice, severe in giving punishment to whom He wills.

The vengeance of Allah the Almighty is exceedingly painful and severe. He does not immediately destroy the disbelievers, oppressors, and the sinful defiant ones for their rebellions; He grants them respite for a while, but the outcome of this grace is terrifying. This applies also to nations and societies that incline towards disbelief and rebellion.

Al-Afu (The Pardoner): The One who is abundantly forgiving, who pardons frequently.

With His boundless mercy, Allah the Almighty forgives those who genuinely regret their sins. He completely erases the traces of sins, orders the Noble Scribes to delete their records, and on the Day of Judgment, does not call His servants to account for these sins, so that they do not feel ashamed, and substitutes sins with good deeds.

Ar-Rauf (The Kind): The One who is exceedingly merciful and compassionate to His servants.

His mercy is vast, and He loves to forgive. He meets the forgivers with His forgiveness. He does not punish His servants immediately for their sins but gives them an opportunity to repent and turn back.

Malik-al-Mulk (The Master of Dominion): The sole owner of all dominion.

The possessions in the hands of His servants are His, and the servant himself is also His possession. He is both the owner and the sovereign of His dominion, exercising His will as He pleases. He has no equivalent, partner, or helper.

Dhul-Jalali wal-Ikram (Lord of Glory and Honor): The owner of all grandeur and every excellence and grace.

Magnificence, grandeur, sublimity, majesty... all virtues that are marks of greatness belong solely to Him. Every kind of praise and reverence befits only Him.

The countless, immeasurable blessings over creation are merely His generosity and His bounty. He is The One who grants existence to the void, life to the mortal beings.

Al-Muqsit (The Just): The One who arranges everything fittingly and executes justice without deviation.

He is the supreme possessor of justice. Having created the universe in balance and ensuring equity, disorder cannot be found. He protects all rights justly, takes the oppressed's rights from the oppressor, corrects injustices, and ensures justice is carried out.

Al-Jami (The Gatherer): The One who gathers whom He wills, when and where He wills.

Allah, Most High, has encapsulated all perfections and superiorities within His essence and attributes.

He has demonstrated His wisdom and artistry in the largest sphere of the cosmos as well as in the tiniest particle.

He has shown His grandeur by bringing together opposites like water and fire, pairs like man and woman, contrasts like night and day, and similitudes like snow and rain.

He will gather people on the Day of Judgment for accounting and punishment; then, he will assemble the good in paradise and the wicked in hell.

He is the one who gathers meanings wherever He pleases.

Al-Ghani (The Self-Sufficient): The Self-Sufficient, the one rich beyond need of anything.

The dominion is His, sovereignty belongs solely to Him, and He possesses endless wealth. He needs nothing in any way, while everyone is in need of Him, and He fulfills all needs.

He is the Creator, the one who knows the trouble, the one who prepares the remedy.

Al-Mughni (The Enricher): The One who gives sufficiently, who enriches those of His servants whom He wills through His grace.

He bestows wealth upon whom He wills, making them live a life of abundance. To whom He wills, He leaves in poverty throughout their life. He makes some wealthy after poverty, and some impoverished after wealth.

Al-Mani (The Preventer): The One who prevents something from happening, who protects those He loves from the harm of others.

A person's desires and wishes depend on certain reasons, and reasons depend on the judgment of Allah the Almighty. If He wills, He creates a reason and fulfills a wish; the matter is accomplished instantly. For some wishes, He does not permit, preventing the matter, and the reasons sought by the one asking become ineffective. Either the time for that matter has not yet come, or that matter is not decreed.

Ad-Darr (The Distresser): The Creator of that which causes harm and pain.

Both good and evil are tests for humanity. Allah the Almighty tests whom He wills with pain. He rewards His patient servants. There is none but Him to avert the harm intended for a servant.

An-Nafi (The Benefiter): The Creator of that which brings good and benefit.

All good is in His hands; He bestows well and benefit upon whom He wills. No one but Him can prevent the good intended for a servant.

An-Nur (The Light): The One who illuminates the worlds.

Light is the manifestation of Allah the Almighty's apparent divine name. Existence comes into being through the manifestation of this Light.

Allah the Almighty is the Light of the heavens and the earth.

Al-Hadi (The Guide): The Creator of guidance, who leads whom He wills to righteousness.

Allah the Almighty, out of His grace and favor, creates success in His servants for knowing His essence and finding the right path. Whoever He guides is indeed on the right path. And whoever He leaves in their misguidance, they cannot find the right path.

He supports His servants in accordance with their determination, enhances their guidance, increases their provisions, opens their paths, and shines light before them.

Al-Badi (The Incomparable): Creator of incomparable, astonishing, and wondrous things.

When He wills to create something, He needs neither contemplation nor planning, nor is He bound by time or space. He has created the universe and everything within it without any precedent. He is the Creator of perfection in all things.

Al-Baqi (The Everlasting): The One whose existence never changes, the Eternal.

The existence of Allah the Almighty is everlasting and infinite. He is free from ceasing to exist. Everything apart from Him is transient and bound to perish.

Al-Warith (The Inheritor): The One who remains after everything else has perished, the true Owner of all wealth.

He grants people the right to use His possessions for a limited time as He pleases. After their deaths, all belongings return to their true Owner, Allah the Almighty.

Ar-Rashid (The Guide to the Right Path): The One who flawlessly orchestrates everything according to His eternal decree.

Every action occurs by His will. He cannot err in His rule, nor can He falter in His wisdom. He guides humanity towards what is right, good, and beautiful. Every creature reaches the purpose of its creation through His guidance.

As-Sabur (The Patient): The Very Patient One, who does not hasten to take revenge on the rebellious, who postpones punishment for a certain period.

All patience of those who endure comes into being through His mercy and grace.

•

Some of the topics in this book have been mentioned before. However, as many people do not read the books, we wanted to distill these subjects and felt the need to publish this book to declare and announce that the real guide is Allah.

On the other hand, this book has been carefully prepared concisely to differentiate between true Sufis and authentic proponents of The Unity of Being from the false ones, and it has been presented for the benefit of Muslims.

•

MUNÂJÂT (Supplication)

My sin is very great, but not greater than the Exalted and Supreme Essence.

My true sin and rebellion are immense, yet not greater than your mercy.

You have always bestowed and granted favors, while this weak one continually rebels.

O my Sovereign Who is The One! Forgive me, I have no other refuge.

I have no good deeds, not even once did I truly remember.

O source of generosity! Not even once did I worship you in Truth.

While devotion is due to the Most Exalted and Glorious One, I did none.

Not even once did I walk the path of true submission.

What will become of me if not for your grace and generosity!

Eyes may sleep, but sleep does not come to the eyes of this humble one.

He weeps in desolate places with tears of regret.

Grant repentance to his many faults.

My misdeeds are countless, impossible to enumerate.

O Allah, the Most Merciful of the merciful!

Have mercy on this wretched, sinful servant.

Ya Sattar! Conceal all my sins and flaws.

Have mercy on those who turn towards you and read this book.

O Lord of all worlds! I beseech you through The Messenger of Allah, the Prophet of mercy,

Muhammad -peace be upon him-.

Forgive us, I rely on your grace and favor.

"THIS IS MY SUPPLICATION OF WORDS, THE SUPPLICATION OF STATE CANNOT BE EXPRESSED..."

About the Author:

Omer Ongut -may his secret be sanctified- 1927-2010

In the esteemed year of 1927, in the town of Yenipazar, which lies within today's Sandzak region of the former Yugoslavia, Ömer Öngüt,-may his secret be sanctified-, graced this world with his presence. His father was Muharrem Sir, and his mother, Çelebiye Hanım. He descended from the blessed lineage of the Prophet Muhammad, peace and blessings be upon him, being the grandchild of **Master Ahmed** of Medina -may his secret be sanctified- a noble ancestor hailing from the Prophet's lineage.

Master Ahmed -may his secret be sanctified- was a revered figure during the Ottoman era, counted among the most esteemed scholars and luminaries of Medina the Radiant. He was a man of miracles, a learned and virtuous individual held in high regard. By some means, the Ottoman government dispatched him temporarily to the Bosnian Province for two years. Upon his journey back, he passed away in the town of Yenipazar. Following this event, his family, including two children, chose not to return to Medina the Radiant but instead settled in Yenipazar.

The declarations of the Esteemed Ömer Öngüt -may his secret be sanctified- regarding his grandfathers and his noble lineage are as follows:

"His Eminence Master Ahmed Sir -may his secret be sanctified- was the father of my maternal grandfather. Stemming from the lineage of the Prophet

Muhammad -peace be upon him- His Eminence Master Ahmed Sir -may his secret be sanctified- was both the Master and the sovereign of Medina the Radiant. He was among the greatest scholars of the area.

In every land he visited, all the shops would close in honor of his presence. The people would gather to bid him farewell, and only after his departure would the shops reopen. Owing to his noble origin from the esteemed lineage of the Prophet Muhammad -peace be upon him- he won deep love and respect from everyone... While returning to Medina the Radiant, he fell ill in Yenipazar and passed away there. His burial in that location sparked immense satisfaction among the people. It is said that during the washing of his body, strangers came to perform the ablutions (ritual washing) and shroud him properly. Amidst these events, his two children remained in Yenipazar.

My aunt used to recount that his wife could hear the remembrance of Allah resonating from his heart during the night. He hailed from the noblest lineage of Arabs. We too are his descendants, our lineage traces back to him. However, divine providence bestows its gifts on whom it wills."

The father of the esteemed Ömer Öngüt -may his secret be sanctified- Muharrem Sir, was a revered figure in his hometown of Yenipazar. Known for his completeness, adherence to the divine commandments, and his generosity, he was a prominent merchant. The esteemed Ömer Öngüt, -may Allah sanctify his secret-, was only six years old when his father passed away.

Following the departure of his father to the realm beyond (the afterlife), the esteemed Ömer Öngüt -may his secret be sanctified- migrated to Turkey with his family around the age of 9 or 10 in the year 1936. "May Allah grant him rest in a light-filled abode; my father was well-Versed in the art of nurturing children, educating through his gaze alone. He was a disciplined and well-organized man. The orderliness he possessed seems to have ingrained itself in us, for we continue to reap its benefits even now. We are not familiar with my paternal grandfather. My mother mentioned that he was 'a saint endowed with miracles.'"

A Life Adorned with Guidance:

When the esteemed Ömer Öngüt, -may Allah sanctify his secret-, reached the age of 18-19, he embarked on his spiritual education. He pledged allegiance to Master Halil Fevzi -may his secret be sanctified- one of the disciples of the era's pole, Master Muhammad Es'ad Erbilî -may his secret be sanctified-. In serving this eminent personage, he attained perfection.

After the passing of Master Halil Fevzi -may his secret be sanctified- in the year 1950, he dedicated a full 60 years of his life to guiding and enlightening people until his own departure from this world

The esteemed Ömer Öngüt, -may Allah sanctify his secret-, was a great Sufi and a leading guide on the path of Truth and righteousness, a perfect spiritual mentor. His entire life was devoted to worship, guidance, struggle, and counsel, through which he disseminated his works. He fought and endured for the sake of Allah and the Prophet Muhammad.

In his conversations and writings, he elucidated Islam, faith, Allah and His Messenger, Sufism, and the Muhammadan Light.

The discourses he delivered were noted down in the 1970s, duplicated with mimeographs, and shared among the community. Subsequently, under his review and approval, these notes began to be published as books. This initiative culminated in a compendium that included interpretations of all Noble Verses of the Quran, known as “Kalplerin Anahtarı” "The Key to Hearts," comprising 41 volumes. This collection, embodying the essence of Quranic exegesis, was completed towards the end of his life.

Ismail Hakki Bursevi -may his secret be sanctified- in one of his revelations, profoundly stated:

"Cherish the love for the Khatam al-Awliya (Seal of the Saints), so that you may not even need intercession through it. For this love is such that it abolishes enmities. And this acknowledgment keeps Munkar and Nakir -the interrogating angels of the grave- in astonishment. This affiliation is such that even sovereigns envy it. And this knowledge is such that the minds of the wise are bewildered by it."

"And this is a sanctuary where the elite crawl on their faces to reach. And this dome over the tomb stands above the swiftly rotating celestial spheres. And the secret of this tomb is a grand secret that permeates all cities. And this is a book in which the Divine Scriptures are altogether encapsulated. And this is a pen whose tablet is the hearts of the knowledgeable."

"And this is a sanctuary where the elite crawl on their faces to reach. And this dome over the tomb stands above the swiftly rotating celestial spheres. And the secret of this tomb is a grand secret that permeates all cities. And this is a book in which the Divine Scriptures are altogether encapsulated. And this is a pen whose tablet is the hearts of the knowledgeable."

"And this is a uniquely distinct pattern, such that whoever is dyed with its color shall never fade eternally. And this is a form whose outcome no one can reach, and into whose circle of knowledge no individual can enter." ("Kitâb'ün-Netice"; Volume: 1, Page: 436)

He devoted himself to the cause of Allah, serving the path of Allah with no personal goals, aims, or benefits in mind. His life was a battle fought for the sake of Allah, striving to endear Allah and His Messenger to hearts, to unify in the love of Allah and His Messenger, to spread the Muhammadan Light, and to embed the reverence for Allah the Almighty and the Prophet Muhammad in the hearts of the faithful. He took Allah the Almighty and His Messenger as his examples, wholeheartedly submitting to the commands of the Almighty and the Practices of the Prophet Muhammad, -peace be upon him-. He was deeply attached to the Master of Both Worlds, Muhammad Mustafa, -peace be upon him-, with profound love and immense respect. He possessed a steadfast determination to follow in the footsteps of the Prophet. He exerted great effort in the revival of divine decrees and the esteemed Sunnah.

He delineated the radiant path to the Almighty Allah, emphasizing humility and righteousness, and taught this to others. His guide was the Quran and the Practices. He always spoke from the Noble Verses of the Quran and the Noble Saying.

Due to his contributions in knowledge and service on the path of Allah, he founded the "Hakikat Foundation" in 1988. He initiated soup kitchens in over twenty provinces across the country.

He began the "Foundation Talks" in Adapazarı in 1990, and at the end of his first talk at that time, he disclosed a secret wisdom:

"We, the humble seekers of divine grace, prayed, 'O Allah! Please make this place a branch of the Ravza-i Mutahhara (The Enlightened Garden). The grace is yours, the favor is yours."

This place is a sanctuary of brotherhood. Such a brotherhood where there is no goal, no purpose, no benefit, no rank, nothing at all, only divine contentment exists."

"In the path of Allah, there is only His pleasure."

A Life Passed in Faith, Struggle, and Service,

A Life Endured through Trials, Tests, and Tribulations:

Since the year 1950, this personage, known for enlightening people through guidance, was recognized by many. He never sought personal gain, fame, or reputation. Just as he answered every question with justice and Truth, he did not shy away from cautioning those who strayed from the path. Thus, he had as many admirers as detractors, facing enmity and slander.

In the path of Allah, against those who sought to divide religion and nation, he waged Struggle in the Path of Allah "without fearing the reproach of any critic."

"Be assured, my sole desire to remain in this world is for this Struggle in the path of Allah. It is this Struggle in the Path of Allah alone that sustains me. I am very inclined to depart; what purpose is there in living if not for this Struggle in the Path of Allah?."

His life was spent in Struggle in the Path of Allah, beset with various trials.

He always resided in a state of patience, gratitude, and trust in the Divine, humbly submitting to the Divine decree, wholly embracing His judgment. He expressed:

"My condition is one of utter tranquility and satisfaction. I am content, profoundly so, because it originates from Him. I have no complaints, no grievances whatsoever. It all comes from the Truth, for it emerges from the Beautiful. Everything bestowed by Him is magnificent. For this, I am thankful. What does this imply? Constant gratitude, continuous, unending gratitude. We are amidst trials, amidst tests, yet still, it's all gratitude, unending, infinite gratitude."

These trials are a legacy from the prophets, an integral part of the esteemed Sunnah.

He was so devoted to the Allah that he would say, "If I were to be given a thousand souls, a thousand beloveds, I would forsake them all, my thousand souls and my thousand beloveds."

In his final days at the hospital, the words he spoke one morning became his last counsel and testament: "Faith is a trust; those who betray their faith lose their belief. Proclaim this. Whether they heed or not."

He adopted the divine commandment, **"Be upright as you have been commanded" (Hud: 112),** as his principle and applied it throughout his life.

In his will, he advised, "Do not stray from the decrees of the Allah the Exalted and the Sunnah of the Messenger."

The Prophesied Seal of Saints:

Just as there is a Khatam al-Anbiya (Seal of the Prophets), there exists a Khatam al-Awliya (Seal of the Saints). For sainthood is the esoteric aspect of prophecy. The exoteric function of prophecy is to proclaim religious decrees and the Islamic law; its esoteric function, however, is to live out those proclamations personally and thus influence souls directly. While the exoteric aspect of prophecy, in terms of dissemination, has been completed, the role of the saints, as the manifestation of divine perfection on Earth, continues. Therefore, prophecy persists in the form of sainthood.

The Khatam al-Awliya (Seal of the Saints) signifies the final saint to arrive in the latter days. Allah the Exalted, has informed His chosen and beloved saints about the coming of the Khatam al-Awliya (Seal of the Saints) in the final era, and thus they knew.

All saints point to the same entity. Just as all Prophets, peace be upon them, informed their nations of a Prophet to come after them who is the Khatam al-Anbiya (Seal of the Prophets), the Noble Messenger similarly, many saints have foretold the arrival of a most esteemed individual, the Khatam al-Awliya (Seal of the Saints), in times to come.

In a Noble Saying reported by Nuaym bin Hammad from Ka'b -may Allah be pleased with him- The Messenger of Allah - peace and blessings be upon him - has said:

"One of the signs of the Mahdi's emergence is the appearance of the Flag Bearers, led by a limping man from the tribe of Kinde, coming from the west." (Suyuti, Kitabu'l-Arfi'l-Verdi fi Ahbari'l-Mehdi; Jarullah, no: 1494, p. 99. Vol. 7, Noble Saying no: 13)

"These five signs must be present in a person. If even one is absent, it is not valid. This is to prevent the emergence of false claimants. These five signs have illuminated the Truth and confirmed the matter."

In this Noble Saying, everything was made very clear for those who could see. The crucial part was to be able to see the individual mentioned in this Noble Saying. However, this was not granted to everyone. For the essence of all knowledge is hidden within the Noble Saying. As the Hakim al-Tirmidhi, may Allah sanctify his secret, states in his book "The Khatam al-Awliya (Seal of the Saints)":

"Just as the final prophet, Muhammad -peace be upon him-, was given the 'Seal of Prophet hood', and he is a proof of Allah the Exalted, over all prophets, so will the last of the saints be in the end times." (Pg. 436)

(For more information on this subject, see "The Khatam al-Awliya (Seal of the Saints)", "Words and Notes - 10", "The Essence of Sufism: Pearls of Reality and Gnosis", "Jewels of Allah - 1", "Jewels of Allah - 2", "Those Who Attain Happiness and Those Who Drift into Calamity", "The Secret of the Ultimate Rank")

The Perfect Exemplar:

Esteemed Ömer Öngüt, may Allah sanctify his secret, was the finest example in every aspect and moment of his life. He was a person of complete virtue, determination, and perseverance. He never had a moment wasted, never uttered idle words, and there were no gaps in his purpose. Every state and condition of his being was in adherence to divine commands and the prophetic tradition. Each moment was filled with divine awe. He was profoundly connected with his brothers and fellow humans through great love, humility, and tolerance.

At the same time, a great discipline prevailed around him. Each of his brethren felt and adhered to this discipline and divine awe. For:

"Beware of the insight of the perfect believer, for he looks with the light of Allah, the Almighty and Majestic." (Tirmidhi)

He was a complete guide, fully embodying the manifestations of this Noble Saying. Often, people would receive answers to their concerns without even having to voice them.

He would not speak unnecessarily; when he spoke, he chose the best of words, conveying much in few words. He spoke fluently, concisely, sincerely, and clearly, making it easy for everyone to understand, adapting his speech to the level of his audience with a unique style of conversation.

He showed deep tolerance and individual attention to everyone, young and old, valuing them, asking after them, listening to their troubles, resolving their issues, and guiding them in worldly and spiritual matters.

"I see everyone as valuable and myself as insignificant," he would say, never highlighting anyone's faults.

"I do not consider anyone lesser than myself to belittle, nor do I see anyone's faults greater than my own to criticize." He stated.

He always offered a smiling face, spreading kindness and compassion. Seeing him brought peace to one's heart, reminding one of the presence of Allah. He constantly mentioned "Allah..." and always spoke of Allah.

"The gaze upon the face of a scholar who acts according to his knowledge is akin to standing in a position of worship." (Munawi) He was a noble personage who had fully experienced the manifestations of this Noble Saying.

He ate little and slept little. While others slept, he was awake; while others laughed, he wept. He spent every moment in remembrance, contemplation, and gratitude. He would sleep for only 2-3 hours at night, dedicating the rest of his time to worship and obedience. He never omitted the Night prayer and Glorifying prayers except during travel or severe illness. He regularly performed the voluntary Ishraq, Duha, and Awwabin prayers and recommended them to others. He loved reading and listening to the Quran.

He was very cautious about lawful and unlawful matters.

"Our greatest ruin comes from our sustenance. If our sustenance were lawful, and our marriages were complete, things would change... Whatever we lose, we lose through our throats. Unless we place a filter at our throat, trust that wisdom will not emerge."

He would not eat meat of uncertain slaughter or suspicious foods and advised his brethren particularly on this matter.

Humility and Integrity:

His greatest attributes were humility and integrity. A significant portion of his discourses revolved around humility. He possessed immense humility and modesty, stemming from his closeness to Allah the Exalted. For closeness to the Owner of the kingdom, the Majestic Creator, is possible only by acknowledging one's insignificance, poverty, incapacity, and nothingness, a grace bestowed upon the friends of Allah.

He declared that he never spoke of experiences he had not lived.

"Our path is based on annihilation and nothingness. Throughout my life, I have slept on the floor until the doctors insisted otherwise. Therefore, our path is one of humility and nothingness, not of existence or ego!"

During the years they resided in Düzce, they had personally hosted guests in their home for many years. One day, to visitors who came, they imparted the following wisdom:

"Please, take the seats up high, though sitting down low is indeed better. However, when I sit up high and see someone else sitting down low, I feel shame and sorrow.

The virtue of sitting down low is as follows; in Düzce, in the guest room by the door, there's a pouffe. I always sat on that pouffe. Why? Lord made me fond of that spot. Men, women, children came, and everyone would sit up high. Yet, Lord, in His Majesty and Glory, favored this arrangement and one day revealed to me the secret of that place: 'Had I known, I would have sat upon my knees,' I said upon seeing how much Lord cherished it.

There are two places where Lord's approval is manifestly clear; we used to go to İzmir in the past, hold our talks, and then return. But during these talks, we wouldn't even eat, just drink tea and head back. One day, we went to Bornova early. Arriving early, we thought: 'Let's not be a burden to our host. Are we not just throats to be satisfied?' We bought cheese, tomatoes, and bread, withdrew to a corner and ate. When we reached our destination, two rooms were packed full. Knowing of our arrival, they said: 'Come, let's have a meal.' 'We have already eaten,' we replied. Lord was so pleased with this.

From this, it is understood that we must train our natures to not be a burden on humanity and to always place ourselves below and lesser than everyone else."

They would say that the path is the path of Allah and The Messenger of Allah, paying utmost attention to the path and its principles, and desiring their brethren to be raised in the same way.

"The path is Allah's path. When we say the path of Allah, let me describe its essence to you.

Allah the Exalted, states in His Noble Verse:

'Be upright as you are commanded!' (Hud: 112) This is Islam, this is the balance. Actions beyond this are incorrect."

"Our way is not one of existence, ego, rank, position, or benefit; such things have no place on this path."

In every state and circumstance, they were embodiments of sincerity, integrity, and humility, always advocating for these virtues. They never valued miracles, on the contrary, they proclaimed the necessity of moving from being to non-being, from non-being to nothingness, from nothingness to annihilation, and to become extinct.

"We always say, never wish to be one of those with miracles. Because many have been robbed in this valley. The miracle on this path is integrity.", "Proceed with sincerity, loyalty, and humility, walk upright within the divine commands."

Discipline, Order, and Elegance:

They conducted all their affairs with utmost order, never wasting a moment. Prayer times, moments for remembrance of Allah, Tasbih (glorification of Allah), and Tahleel (declaring the oneness of Allah), times for rest, and the hours set aside for welcoming guests and visitors were all precisely scheduled.

In all actions and deeds, in worship and obedience, they served as an exemplary figure.

They would use requests instead of commands.

"This path is the path of the heart, where one is refined through state, not words. If words are necessary, they come as requests, not commands. For ours is a path of elegance and humility. In the way of Allah, commandment comes only in the form of a request. What command cannot achieve, a request can," they would say.

They were exceedingly generous and benevolent.

They always preferred simplicity in everything, disliking decoration and luxury. "Simplicity is the finest form of elegance, a lean towards humility, whereas adornment can lead to arrogance," "A person should be clean both inside and out, in their actions and words," they would insist.

They loved cleanliness and elegance. They took great care of their clothing and personal hygiene. They would comb their beards, use pleasant scents. They were very orderly, dressed beautifully. They believed that a Muslim must serve as a role model. "No one has the right to present the clean and pure religion of Islam as anything but," they would declare.

Thus, they placed great importance on dress and appearance, stating that a Muslim must pay great attention to these, and even more so if a Muslim wears a beard.

They themselves were an unmatched example in this regard.

The Hope of the Community of Muhammad:

They were deeply concerned with the problems of Muslims. They closely followed the public sentiment, praying for events not to harm our country or the Islamic world. They were saddened by the strife that arose and the oppression by the unbelievers.

"If you pay attention, the only hope of Muslims under occupation is Turkey. They attach their hearts most to this place. Their hopes and hearts are in this homeland."

"The homeland preserves faith. Because without a homeland, faith cannot be gained. This homeland is beautiful, but we citizens do not realize it," they would say.

They wished for Islam and Muslims to be strong, were pleased with advancements in military weapons and equipment, and desired the country to be superior and powerful in every aspect.

"O you who believe! Do not take Jews and Christians as allies. They are allies of one another. And whoever among you takes them as allies, then indeed, he is [one] of them." (Al-Maeda: 51)

They would often remind of this Verse, stating that Jewish and Christian nations could not be friends, hence they would not include us in the EU.

In 2004, missionary activities exploiting the "Interfaith Dialogue" deceit of FETO peaked, with church houses opening everywhere. Esteemed Ömer Öngüt - may Allah sanctify his secret - responded with a counter-attack, producing brochures inviting Christians to Guidance and True Salvation. Hundreds of thousands were distributed across Turkey. They were printed in almost every language including English, French, German, Russian, Italian, Spanish, and Dutch, and distributed to churches and the public in all European countries and even the Vatican, causing great discomfort among the unbelievers.

Three Vital Responsibilities:

Esteemed Ömer Öngüt -may his secret be sanctified- stated:

"Allah the Exalted and Most Holy, must have sent this humble, needy, and flawed servant in this era for three main purposes:

Firstly, to struggle against the separatists.

Groups aiming to fragment our religion and homeland have appointed religious leaders among themselves, trying to sway Muslims towards their cause. Many books have been written on this topic. (See www.Hakikat.com.tr)

Secondly, to expose the true nature of the scholars of the end times.

While relentlessly battling these idolized highway robbers operating in the darkness of rebellion and oppression, on the other hand, we strive to reveal the inner faces of the end times' scholars and convey the Truth to Muslims confused by their contradictory religious verdicts, with few but definitive words, aiming to eliminate disputes. The religious verdict on organ transplantation and wills was one such instance. We proved with the Noble Verse and Noble Sayings that it is absolutely not permissible.

Thirdly, to eliminate the disputes and conflicts regarding the concept of The Unity of Being.

We have provided solutions to debates about The Unity of Being that have been misunderstood for centuries.

Muhyiddin Ibn Arabi -may his secret be sanctified- said, 'Everything is Him.' Imam Rabbani -may his secret be sanctified- said, 'Everything is from Him.'

This matter, seeming contradictory, has occupied Muslims to this day.

Allah the Exalted, has granted this humble servant a solution that satisfies hearts.

Both statements are true. We reconcile the declarations of both in one sentence, saying: 'Everything was created by Allah, and everything exists through His Being.'

Therefore; 'It is both Him and from Him.'

Invitation to Divine Consensus:

Their blessed life was dedicated to inviting to Allah the Exalted, and The Messenger of Allah, -peace be upon him-; to a 'Divine Consensus.'

"We invite to the 'DIVINE CONSENSUS.' We endeavor to instill in those who come the love of Allah and His Messenger -peace be upon him- and His commands, purifying them from all forms of division and uniting them solely in Allah and His Messenger -peace be upon him-, striving to establish true brotherhood among them."

"Our primary aim is the spread of the Muhammadan Light, uniting our Muslim brothers in Allah and His Messenger.

Let us truly unite in Allah and His Messenger so we can struggle against internal and external enemies."

Their will regarding the foundation they established is as follows:

"'The Hakikat Foundation' is the name of this foundation. Beware, do not attribute it to our path and fall into division. Beware, let not another name for division emerge among you.

Our goal is 'ISLAM,' not names.

Our desire is for Allah and His Messenger, not any of the separatists." ("Invitation to Divine Consensus," p. 132)

To those who ask, "What is the name of your group?" they would respond: "Praise be to Allah, Lord of the worlds. Our religion is Islam, our book is the Holy Quran, and The Messenger of Allah is Muhammad, -peace be upon him-." ("Invitation to Divine Consensus," p. 130)

Their purpose and goal were to endear Allah and His Messenger to others, unite Muslims in Allah and His Messenger, spread the Muhammadan Light, and strive to free and purify hearts from anything other than the Truth. In this endeavor, they asked for nothing from anyone, fighting with their life and wealth.

"Our goal is His pleasure, to save the Community of Muhammad, to spread the light. We have no other aim."

Faith and Homeland:

Esteemed Ömer Öngüt -may his secret be sanctified- said, "We have two goals: faith and homeland," and ordered the statement, "A homeland without faith, and faith without a homeland, cannot be preserved," to be placed in the logo of the Hakikat Magazine, which he founded.

"Disbelief is a single nation. Let's not give them a chance. Their goal is to eradicate faith and plunder our homeland. We should not trust those who belong to the people of disbelief and those who honor them. Because a homeland without faith, and faith without a homeland, cannot be defended. If one goes, the other will also go." ("The True Face of Traitors," p. 13)

Therefore, they fought against those who caused division in religion and homeland, and tried to awaken Muslims by publishing works about them.

"The external enemy has a front, the internal enemy does not." They fought against these enemies of religion and homeland, saying, "They are more dangerous than external enemies." They tried to extinguish the corruption and the fires of sedition they ignited, for the salvation of people's eternal lives, to save their faith.

"Our entire goal is to save faith.

I love my homeland, my flag, very much. I am also against those who are enemies of my religion and my homeland. We are waging this Struggle in the Path of Allah to protect and defend both our religion and our homeland. We state that the state comes from alliance, and statelessness from division. Because without a state, you cannot live your religion.

Let's be united in our religion and our state. If we lose the state due to disunity while enemies surround us on all sides, and if we fall under the rule of disbelievers, what will our situation be? May Allah protect us," they said.

Esteemed Ömer Öngüt - may Allah sanctify his secret - had been alerting the public about the treacherous nature of FETÖ (a terrorist organization), its betrayal of the homeland, and its ties to American espionage, both in our magazines (the first article was published in March 1994 in Hakikat Magazine with the title "Fethullah Gülen Announces the Religion of Narcissism!") and through books published about them ("The True Face of Narcissists Who Tolerate Disbelief", First edition: 1999) 30 years before their betrayal became evident.

Because of this struggle, all these divisive groups harbored great enmity towards him. They tried to slander and defame him, and some took him to court. FETÖ, as it conspired against all its opponents, also tried to trap this noble person. They wanted to include his name in a campaign started by the Taraf newspaper in 2009. Esteemed Ömer Öngüt - may Allah sanctify his secret -'s book "The Treacherous Plot" was published because of this slander campaign. These slanders marked the beginning of the end for this treacherous group.

They explained this situation in their book titled "The Treacherous Plot" as follows:

"Thus, these dividers wish to silence us.

We have forsaken comfort and rest, ornamentation, and luxury. We dedicated our lives to the safety of the Islamic faith. Unlike these dividers, we did not gather money or establish banks. We did not discard the decrees of the Islamic religion behind us. We did not attempt to change the decrees of the Islamic religion to gather people and win supporters. I seek refuge in Allah. On the contrary, we reminded [people] of the Noble Verses of Allah, the Almighty. But they did not listen. ...

However, all these oppressors, these dividers, did these things. They prioritized gathering followers over the Islamic faith. They worshipped money. When they could find no place to keep the money they gathered, they established banks. They tried to replace the Islamic religion with their own concocted religions. ...

Our fight damaged the interests and the contrived religions of many frauds. They tried everything they could, resorting to all kinds of slander. They tried to discredit us in the eyes of the public. They tried every way to prevent our works from being read." ("The Treacherous Plot," pp. 90-91)

Esteemed Ömer Öngüt - may Allah sanctify his secret - spent years warning and guiding against such dividers of religion, stating, and "These are internal enemies. The internal enemy does harm that the external enemy cannot do."

The July 15 coup attempt clearly demonstrated to our nation both how great an enemy FETÖ and similar other dividers are, and how the internal enemy can inflict damage that the external enemy cannot.

•

They would predict upcoming events and wars, and while praying for Allah the Exalted, to grant victory, they also advised preparation.

"O Allah! Forgive the Community of Muhammad! Preserve our homeland! Grant victory to our army!" they would pray.

They endeavored to make known the value and significance of this homeland, this state, and announced that this ship will not sink:

"Allah the Exalted, will not let this ship sink. The reason for this is that I saw The Messenger of Allah, -peace be upon him-, dressed as a Turk twice. I understood that Allah the Exalted, has a gaze, a grace upon Turkey. Out of respect for Him, Allah the Exalted, will not let this ship sink. No matter how much they wanted to sink it, this ship will not sink; it will float again. The Allah the Almighty will protect and preserve this homeland. ... Therefore, our prayers are always for others, for the faith and safety of the Community of Muhammad."

"O Lord! Halilullah (Abraham -peace upon him-) prayed for Mecca,
O Lord! The Messenger of Allah prayed for Medina,
O Lord! This poor one prays for this state, do not bring decline to this state!"

The Struggle against Dividers Who Idolize Their Soul and Betray Our Religion and Homeland:

(See "Words and Notes-10", pp. 492-501)

"Who are we struggling against?

With misleading religious leaders worse than the Antichrist, with the most malevolent people under the sky, the scholars of the end times.

Whether these misleading religious leaders or the scholars of the end times, all appeared in the guise of Truth, as leaders and saviors of Islam. Pure and innocent Muslims joined them in large numbers and became affiliated with them. However, these Antichrists, who appeared in the guise of Truth, revealed their true identities upon seeing these masses. Once they saw a crowd around them, each declared their own religion. To sustain the religion they established, they deemed lawful the decrees Islam has forbidden. In this way, they tried to maintain their religion and led masses of Muslims astray into their fabricated religions while also plundering and shearing their worldly possessions. Indeed, even the Antichrist could not achieve this."

Esteemed Ömer Öngüt - may Allah sanctify his secret -'s first treatise published to warn and guide Muslims was in 1985.

They continued this warning and guidance through articles published in the Hakikat Monthly Islamic Magazine, which began publication in 1993, and through books they authored. From the Seal of the Saints, all of humanity receives

He had no tolerance for those who wanted to deviate Islam from its essence. He first warned those who fostered division in religion and homeland and sought personal glory among Muslims, then exposed them, wrote books about them, and published articles in the Hakikat Magazine numerous times. Works like "The True Face of Narcissists Who Tolerate Disbelief," "The Fake Caliph, The Fake Hero Cemalettin Kaplan and His Son's True Face," "The True Face of Suleymancılar," "A Response to the Mullahs of Mahmut Sir of the Welfare Religion," "The True Face of End Times Scholars," and similar works were published.

They called this struggle the "Struggle in the Path of Allah of saving faith."

"For me to be able to struggle against misleading religious leaders without faith, fake Masters, fake Mahdis, fake Jesuses, fake Dabbat al-Ard, these fraudsters and hypocrites, Allah the Exalted, has bestowed this knowledge today. These thieves of faith have both led the nation astray from faith and divided and shattered our religion and homeland for the sake of fame, benefit, leadership, and guidance.

Not an enemy of religion and homeland, not a priest, not even the Antichrist could do what these Allahless religious leaders and these infidels have done to our religion and our homeland in terms of great destruction and severe blows," they stated.

The Struggle against Pocket strugglers:

"Our path differs from others at this Noble Verse:

'Follow those who ask no reward of you, and they are [rightly] guided.' (Yasin: 21)

This Noble Verse is a barrier. Whoever collects money is declared to be not on the right path by this Noble Verse."

"When money and personal gain enter the cause of Allah, that path cannot be the path of Allah."

"Their holy struggle is to destroy and distort the Islamic religion. They are pocket strugglers. They have opened holy struggle against pockets."

"They portray their paths of misguidance as the true path and then use the Islamic religion for personal gain, position, and fame. They practice pocket struggle to plunder the people."

"They think about how to plunder the people, how to fill their pockets. Because they have no interest in the Islamic religion at all."

They asked for nothing from anyone, expected nothing from anyone, and never took back what they gave. They never begged, never used Islam for worldly gain.

They provided for their own livelihood through their manual labor and income. Despite having the opportunity to expand the shoe manufacturing and trade business he started at the age of 16, he dedicated himself to knowledge and guidance, liquidated his workshop, and worked alone in a small shop for years. Despite having so many admirers and visitors, he never burdened anyone. Even for the books he gifted, he would pay the foundation the selling price.

Some Wills:

"Choose the path of piety when you work. Piety directs to the Truth, other paths lead to the people.

•

Let there be few students, but let them be sincere. Let us stand hungry, not stretching our hands out. Do not let ornamentation and luxury enter our hearts.

•

The good gives, does not take. The bad works for self-interest, and that does us no good.

•

Do not ask from anyone, do not refuse what is given. But do not accept from other organizations.

•

Do not assign duties to those who are in the life of this world and the path of wastefulness. Choose those who live with sincerity. For tomorrow, they may prove you indebted. Choose the sincere, even if the work they do is little.

•

Beware of those who are harsh, contrary, and pursue personal and egoistic interests. For they are divisive and may cause division in the future."

Today is Today, Tomorrow is known by Him:

Esteemed Ömer Öngüt -may Allah sanctify his secret- often reminded of the 58th Noble Verse of Surah Isra:

"We will not spare any town before the Day of Judgment; either we will destroy it or punish it with a severe punishment." (Isra: 58)

They would proclaim that the days mentioned in the Noble Verse are approaching, the world is boiling from within, dreadful wars and calamities will occur, and the appearance of Exalted the Mahdi and Jesus, -peace be upon him-, is near. They advised to be prepared for all sorts of events after their time.

In one of their statements, they said:

"Today is today, and the Creator knows what will happen tomorrow. A wise person should always turn towards Allah...

When Allah the Exalted, pulls this pillar out, this nation will fall into great ruin, which will spread throughout the Islamic world. For a while, the Islamic world will be in great turmoil.

At the moment when mischief is most widespread, Allah the Exalted, will send exalted the Mahdi to open a path, to raise the flag, and will grant him permission. With the permission granted to him and spiritual support, he will proceed to the intended point and fulfill his duty.

Then, He will also withdraw the authority in his hands. When He intends to grant authority to the Antichrist, he will weaken considerably against his power. The reason is that Exalted the Mahdi will venture far, and he will begin his conquest. Chaos will reign.

When Exalted the Mahdi becomes very weak, to save his followers and triumph Islam, Allah the Exalted, will send exalted the Jesus, -peace be upon him-, as the third. The Antichrist and the Jews will be cleansed in that manner. The Islamic world will be liberated from the infidels and the tyranny of the Jews.

But it will not stop there. Seeing this situation, China will move, saying it wants to invade the world emptied by wars until that time. They will march like tanks, but Allah the Exalted, will destroy them in one night. Their destruction will not come through war, but through prayer. And thus, the world will be emptied."

The Death of a Scholar is Like the Death of the World:

Esteemed Ömer Öngüt - may Allah sanctify his secret - departed from this world, filled with endless hardships and trials, to the afterlife, filled with inconceivable rewards and blessings, on 16 Rajab 1431, Monday, 28 June 2010, during the time of the Morning Prayer.

Due to kidney disease, he spent most of his last two years in hospitals, and finally, he surrendered his noble soul in a hospital in Bursa. On Tuesday, 29 June, he was buried in his sacred tomb and transitioned to his true homeland.

He never valued worldly life, always loved and spoke of the afterlife, and declared the need to prepare for it.

"Yesterday was winter, today is spring. Today you are on top, tomorrow you are below, today your eyes are open, tomorrow they will be closed."

"The young will grow, the elders will leave, and thus the cycle of the world will end."

He chose Allah the Exalted, as his friend. He was with Him in this world and the hereafter.

"A friend takes you to the grave. But be with such a friend that you are together in eternal life," he said.

During his illness and at his death, he burdened no one, preferring humility, silence, tranquility, and simplicity over pomp and show. "My shroud, my plank, everything is ready. Let me not be a burden to anyone," he said and made all preparations himself. The lover reached the Beloved.

"My heart flows towards the hereafter, but He does as He wills."

"How beautiful is death! It is the most beautiful means of bringing a creature to its Creator."

"Death is very sweet for us. You may run from it, but we rush towards it."

"Have confidence, life begins after death. Death is a release."

"I will go to my Allah as a guest."

"I love death, I love it, and I want to die. But I cannot say, 'Take me.' Trust in my words, I want to die, even say; when they take me, do not grieve, I am going to the Divine presence, to the Divine feast, be at ease!" he said.

His heart was always there. His desire and goal were Him.

Halil Fevzi - May Allah Sanctify His Secret - (1867-1950):

Esteemed Ömer Öngüt's -may his secret be sanctified- Master, Halil Fevzi -may Allah sanctify his secret-, was born in the district of Karnabat in Bulgaria in the Hijri year 1283 (Gregorian 1867). During the conflict known as the "93 War," or the Russo-Turkish War of 1877, they migrated to Turkey, where his father, Hüseyin Ağa, was killed by Bulgarian bandits on the way. In 1877, the family was settled in the village of Muhacir taşköprü in Düzce.

Halil Fevzi -may his secret be sanctified- completed his studies at the Fatih madrasas in Istanbul and became a teacher. His spiritual journey began in 1924 with a visit to the then Gavs-ı Azam, Master Muhammad Esad Erbili -may his secret be sanctified-, at his mansion in Erenköy, Istanbul. He was hosted there for about forty-five days. He was deeply moved and soon after this short period, he was authorized to teach the followers of the Path and appointed as the caliph for guidance in worship by Esad Sir -may his secret be sanctified-.

Master Halil Fevzi - may Allah sanctify his secret - was a person of great perfection and sanctity, with a high level of spiritual influence. Allah the Exalted, had taken his speech and granted him influence. This was the will of the Lord.

Muhammad Esad Erbili -may his secret be sanctified- (1847-1931):

Among the rare ones, Master Muhammad Esad Erbili -may his secret be sanctified-, was born in the town of Erbil, attached to the Mosul province of Iraq, in the Hijri year 1264 (Gregorian 1847). He was a Seyyid from both his father's and mother's side. He was tall, stout, dark-skinned, radiant, smiling, sweet-spoken, dignified, and majestic.

At around the age of twenty-three, he became affiliated with the Master and pole of his time, Taha al-Hariri -may his secret be sanctified-. After serving him for five years, he completed his spiritual journey, received his khilafah (authorization), and was also certified in the Qadiriyya Path.

During the reign of Sultan Abdulhamid II, he was at one point appointed to the council of Masters. Later, in 1914, Sultan Mehmed Reshad appointed him as "Reis-ul Meşayıh" (Head of Masters). He worked towards the reform of tekkes (Sufi lodges) and the appointment of qualified individuals to Masterdoms.

Close to his passing, he said:

"In the early years of my affiliation, a feeling came to my heart: 'O Lord! Let me come to your divine presence naked. If I have any deeds worthy of acceptance, let me donate them to your sinful servants.' Now, I am filled with the same feelings."

Esteemed Ömer Öngüt -may his secret be sanctified- expressed their following in their footsteps as follows:

"They have left behind a pure path. No hand, no intervention has touched it. It continues in the same state. It proceeds with annihilation, not with existence. In this regard, our principle is the path of our Masters. We are on this path, we show this path to those who want to walk on the path of Truth, and we leave this path."

•

Having received lessons as an Uwaysi from Master Esad Erbili -may his secret be sanctified-, and being entrusted with the spiritual legacy of Master Halil Fevzi -may his secret be sanctified-, Esteemed Ömer Öngüt -may his secret be sanctified- stated in one part of their will:

"To us, the path has ended. Wait for Exalted the Mahdi. Be of that intention, and die with that intention. Do not be deceived by false guides and disciples that will emerge. Know well that you will have no master in the hereafter. Those who step off the path are not of us."

In their will conversations, they also stated:

"We leave you with books supported and sealed with the word of Allah the Exalted, and the Noble Sayings of The Messenger of Allah, -peace be upon him-. Hold on to them."

•

"If Allah the Exalted, grants and bestows kindness, we would not bypass even those who greet us with love. We entrust our loved ones to Allah the Exalted, and leave those who do not love us to Allah the Exalted."

•

Mueyyiduddin Mahmud al-Jindi -may his secret be sanctified- in the last lines of his work titled "Sharh al-Fusus by Master Mueyyiduddin al-Jindi"; after sending blessings and peace upon the Khatam al-Anbiya (Seal of the Prophets) and Messengers, -peace be upon him-, also sends blessings and peace to the inner heir of the Khatam al-Awliya (Seal of the Saints), saying:

"May Allah's prayers be upon the Seal of the Messengers and Prophets, and upon the most perfect heir of his Seal ship, the Seal of the Muhammadan saints!" ("Book of Sharh al-Fusus by Master Mueyyiduddin al-Jindi"; Shahid Ali Pasha, no.: 1240, fol. 439b-440a)

CONTENT

Made in the USA
Las Vegas, NV
20 May 2025

b7e5e321-97cc-4cab-80d7-bda3f8dfe2c2R01